Dr.STONE

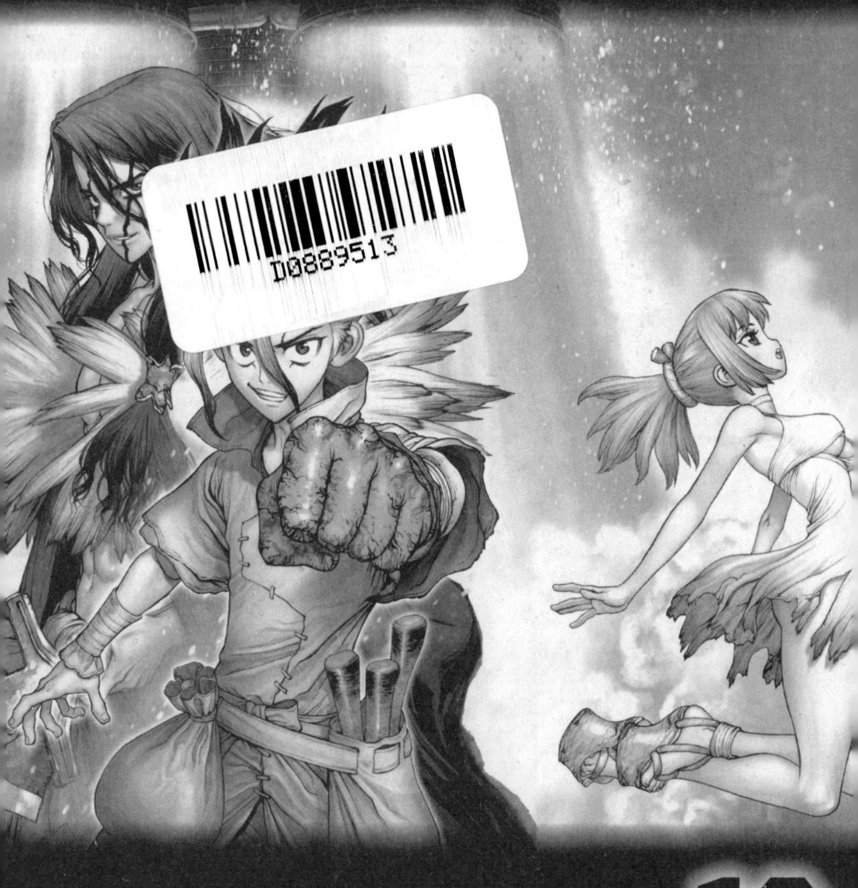

16

STORY **RIICHIRO INAGAKI**
ART **BOICHI**

MEDUSA VS. SCIENCE

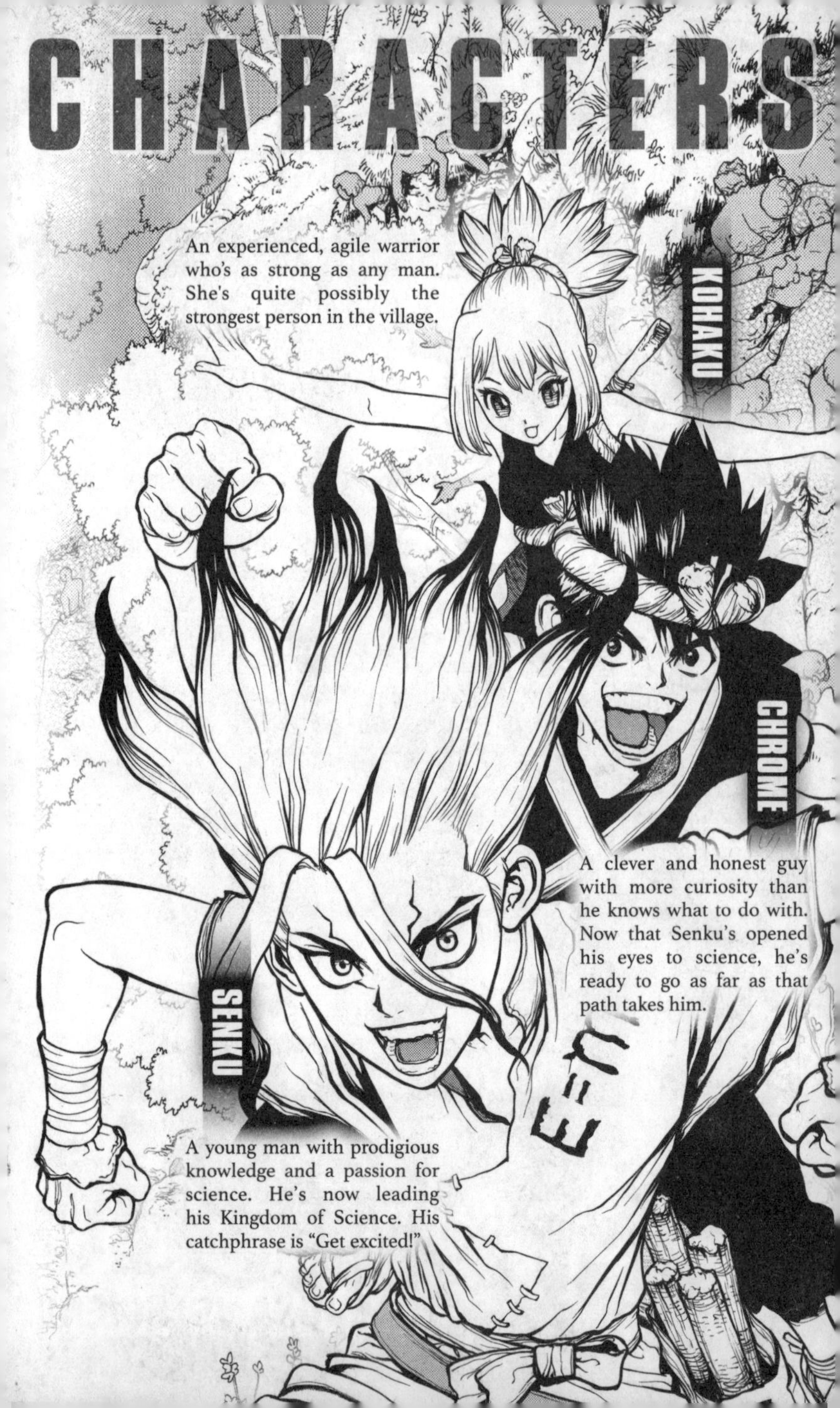
CHARACTERS
KOHAKU
An experienced, agile warrior who's as strong as any man. She's quite possibly the strongest person in the village.
CHROME
A clever and honest guy with more curiosity than he knows what to do with. Now that Senku's opened his eyes to science, he's ready to go as far as that path takes him.
SENKU
A young man with prodigious knowledge and a passion for science. He's now leading his Kingdom of Science. His catchphrase is "Get excited!"

Dr.STONE

STORY

Every human on earth is turned to stone by a mysterious phenomenon, including high school student Taiju. Nearly 3,700 years later, Taiju awakens and finds his friend Senku, who revived a bit earlier. Together, they vow to restore civilization, but Tsukasa, once considered the strongest high schooler alive, nearly kills Senku in order to put a stop to his scientific plans.

After being secretly revived by his friends, Senku arrives at Ishigami Village. But when word of Senku's survival gets back to Tsukasa, the war between the two forces begins! Eventually, the two factions make peace, but the traitorous Hyoga skewers Tsukasa. Senku cryogenically freezes Tsukasa's body.

Senku and friends arrive at the so-called "Treasure Island," where they create a drone to steal the petrification device in their final battle against the Petrification Kingdom. However, Minister Ibara's underhanded tactics have them on the ropes! With the island enveloped by the petrifying light and his friends turned to stone, what can Senku possibly do?!

KIRISAME

AMARYLLIS

GEN ASAGIRI

IBARA

OARASHI

MOZ

SOYUZ

CONTENTS

16

MEDUSA VS. SCIENCE

Z=134: Commander Face-Off

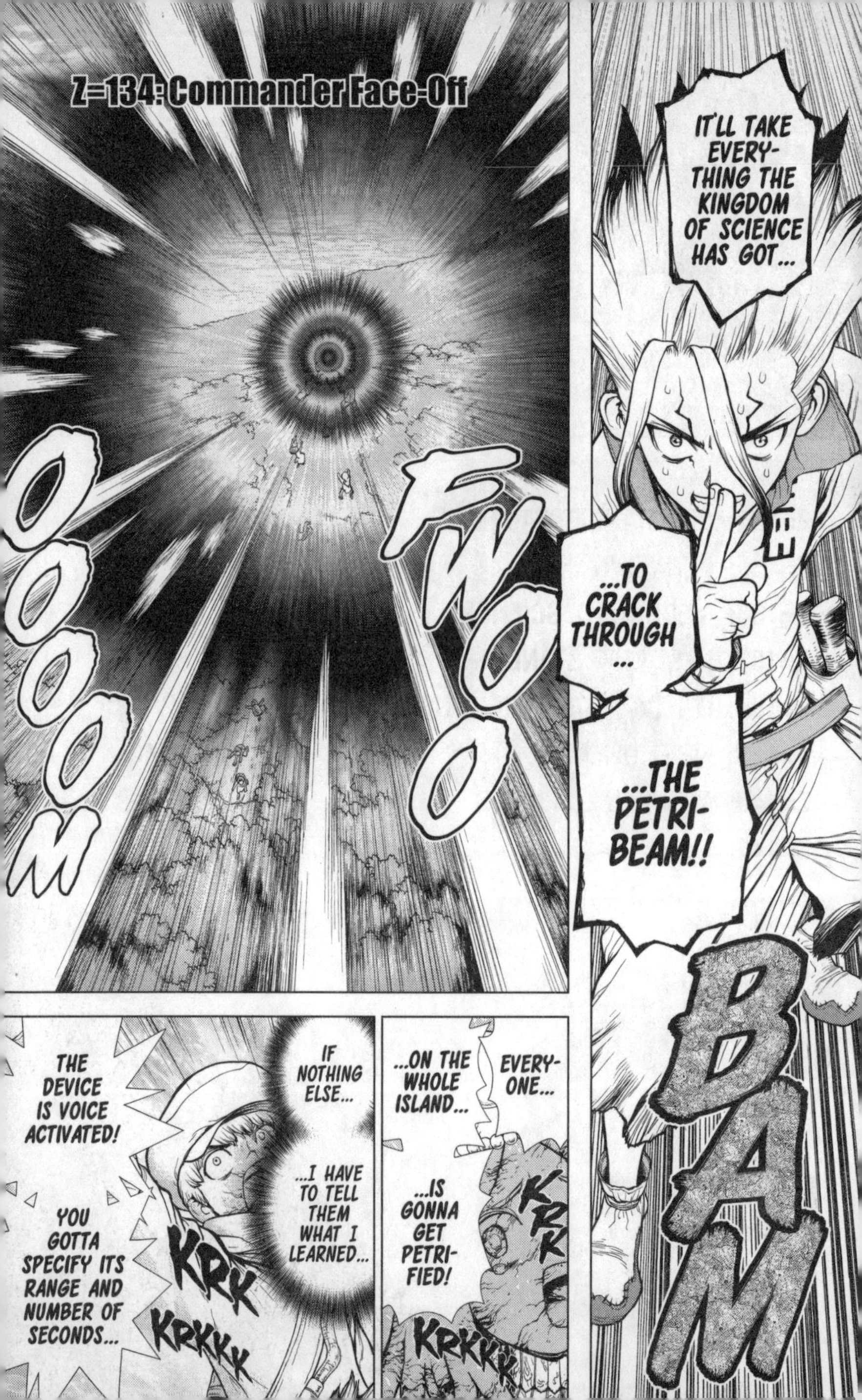
IT'LL TAKE EVERY-THING THE KINGDOM OF SCIENCE HAS GOT...
...TO CRACK THROUGH ...
...THE PETRI-BEAM!!
BAM
FWOOO
OOOOOM
EVERY-ONE...
...ON THE WHOLE ISLAND...
...IS GONNA GET PETRI-FIED!
KRK
KRKKK
IF NOTHING ELSE...
...I HAVE TO TELL THEM WHAT I LEARNED...
THE DEVICE IS VOICE ACTIVATED!
YOU GOTTA SPECIFY ITS RANGE AND NUMBER OF SECONDS...
KRK
KRKKK

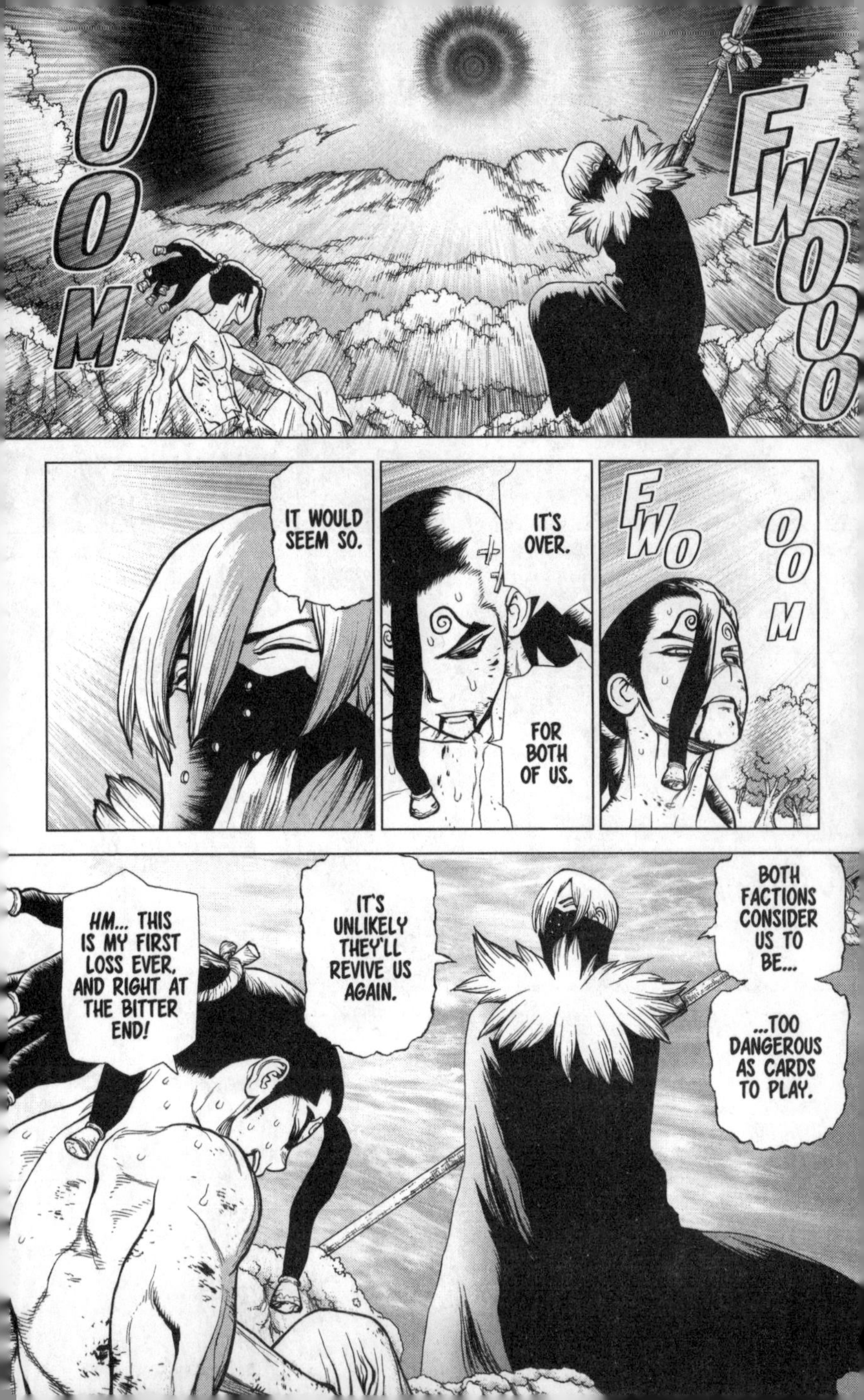
FWOOOO
OOM
FWO
OOM
IT'S OVER.
FOR BOTH OF US.
IT WOULD SEEM SO.
BOTH FACTIONS CONSIDER US TO BE...
...TOO DANGEROUS AS CARDS TO PLAY.
IT'S UNLIKELY THEY'LL REVIVE US AGAIN.
HM... THIS IS MY FIRST LOSS EVER, AND RIGHT AT THE BITTER END!

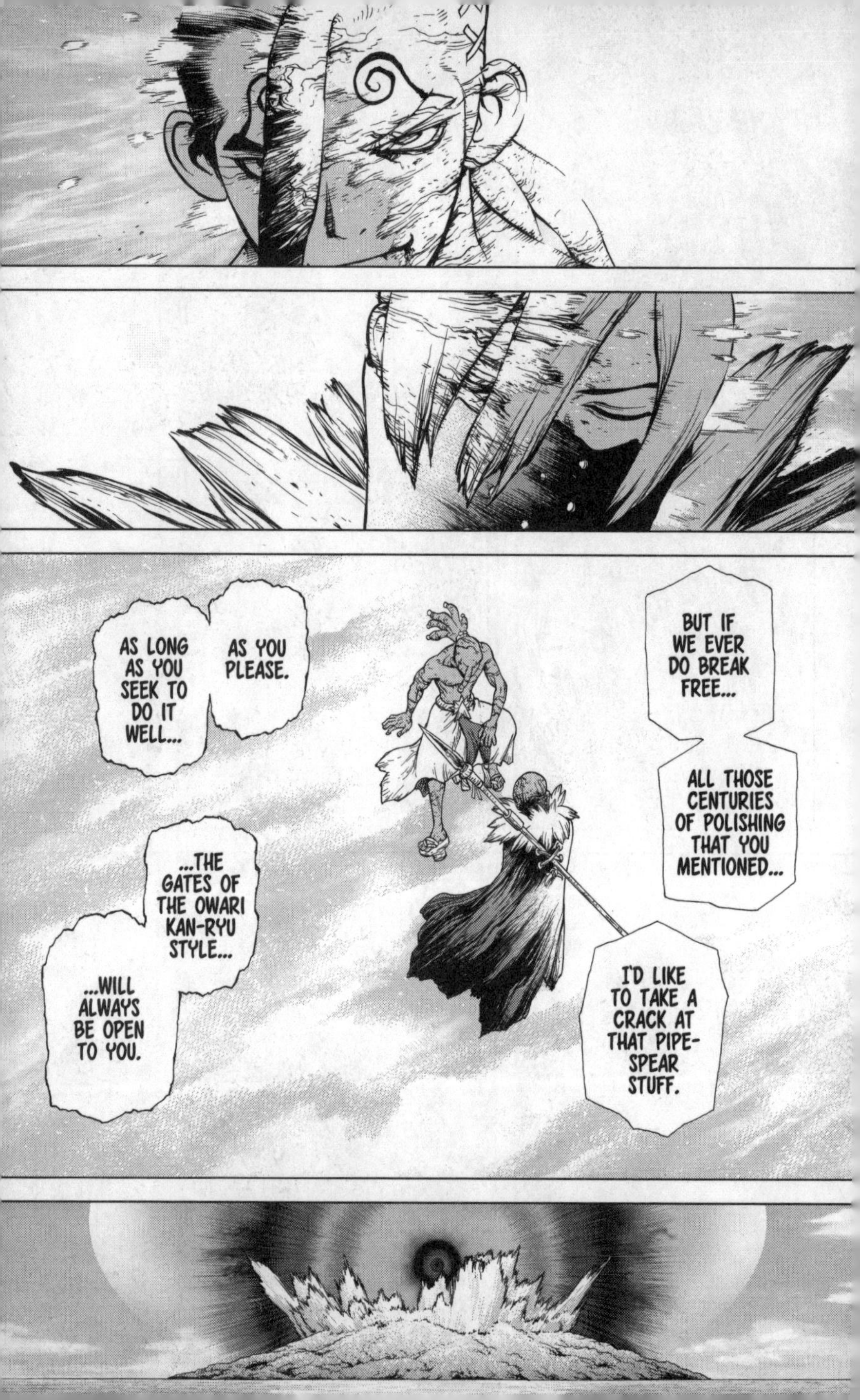
BUT IF WE EVER DO BREAK FREE...
ALL THOSE CENTURIES OF POLISHING THAT YOU MENTIONED...
I'D LIKE TO TAKE A CRACK AT THAT PIPE-SPEAR STUFF.
AS LONG AS YOU SEEK TO DO IT WELL...
AS YOU PLEASE.
...THE GATES OF THE OWARI KAN-RYU STYLE...
...WILL ALWAYS BE OPEN TO YOU.

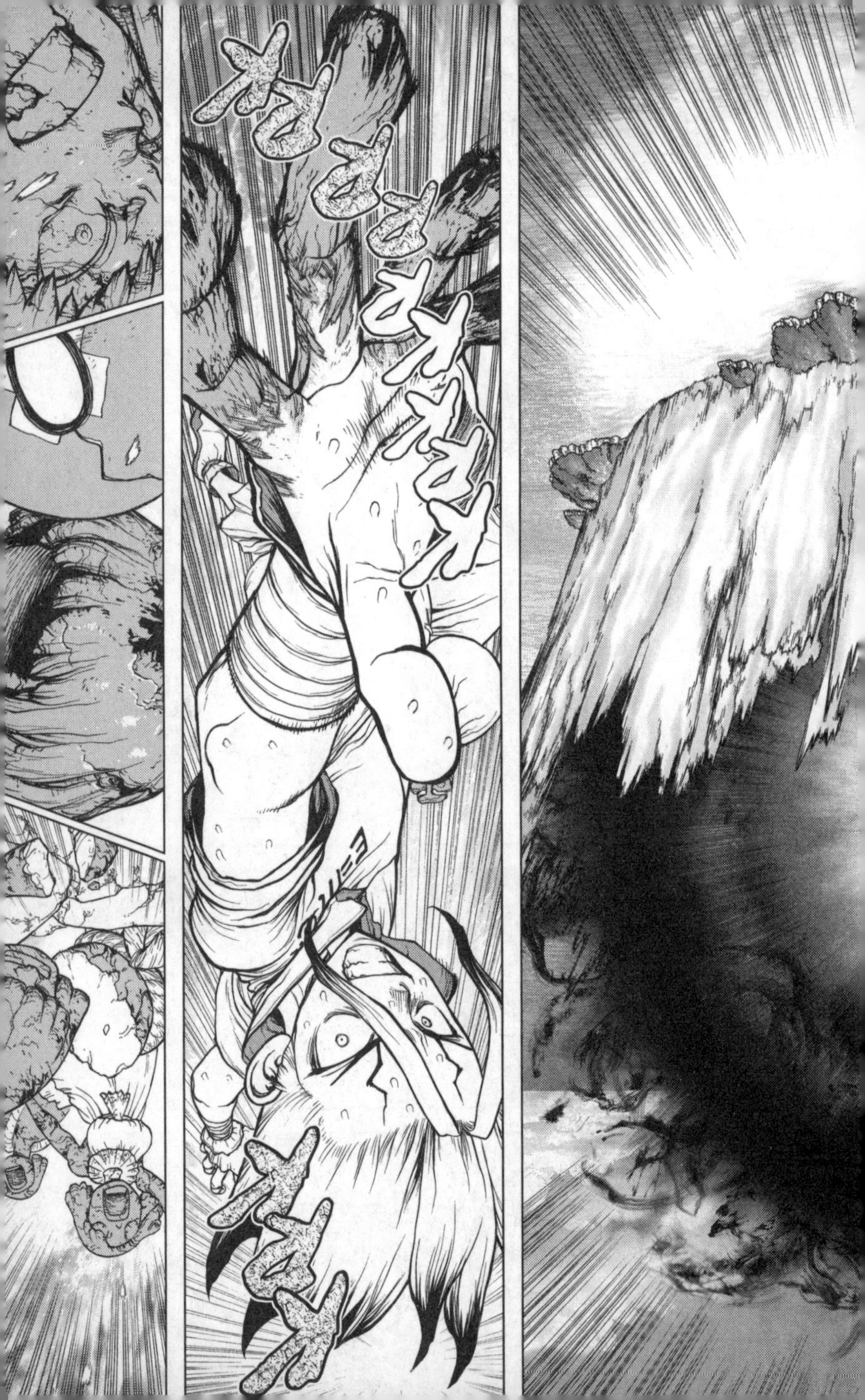

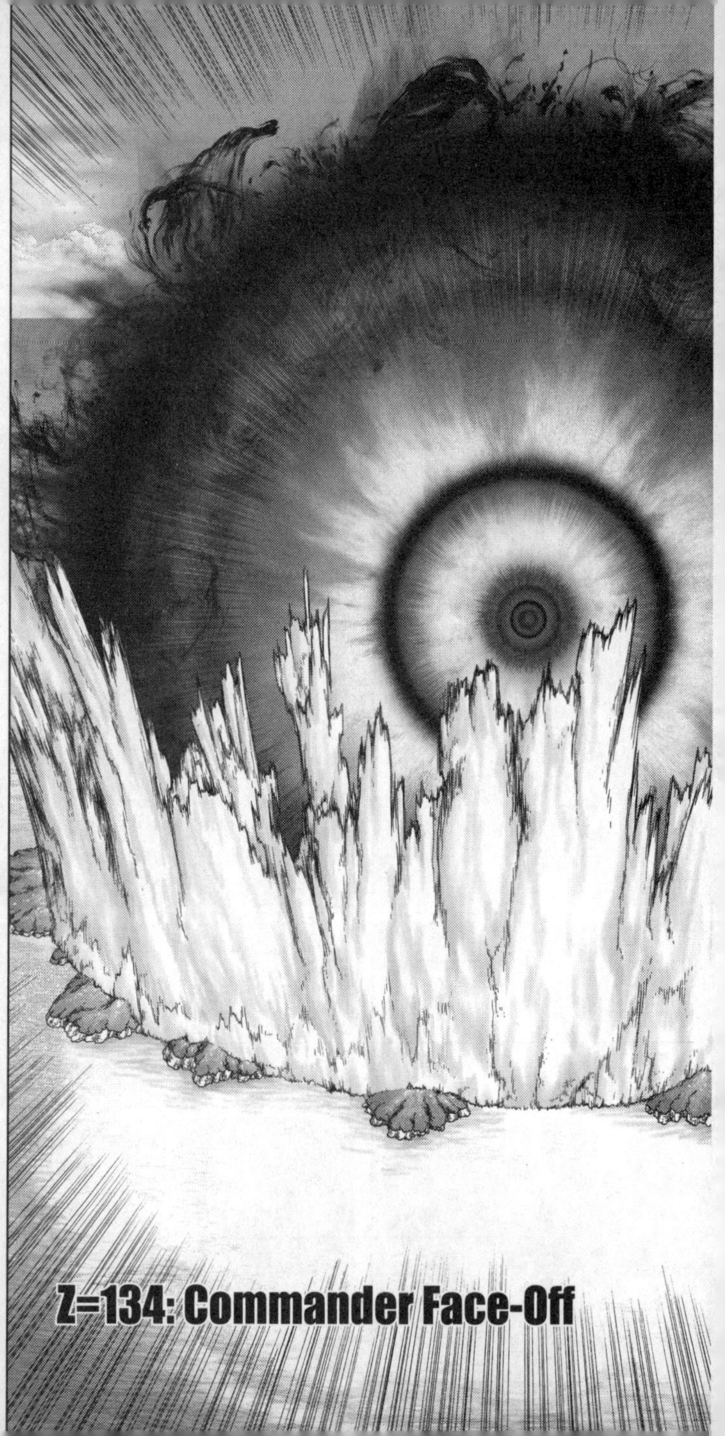
Z=134: Commander Face-Off
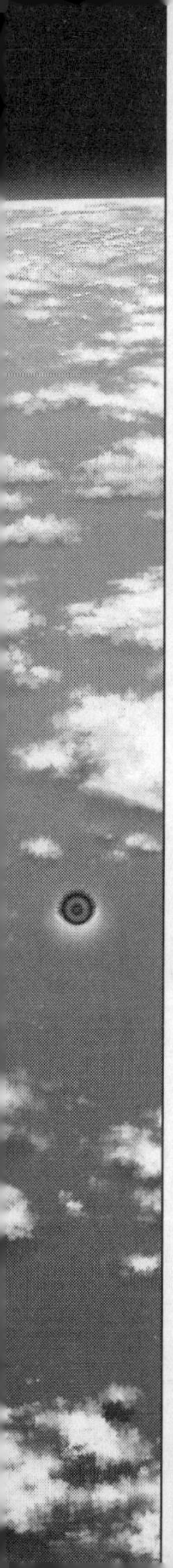

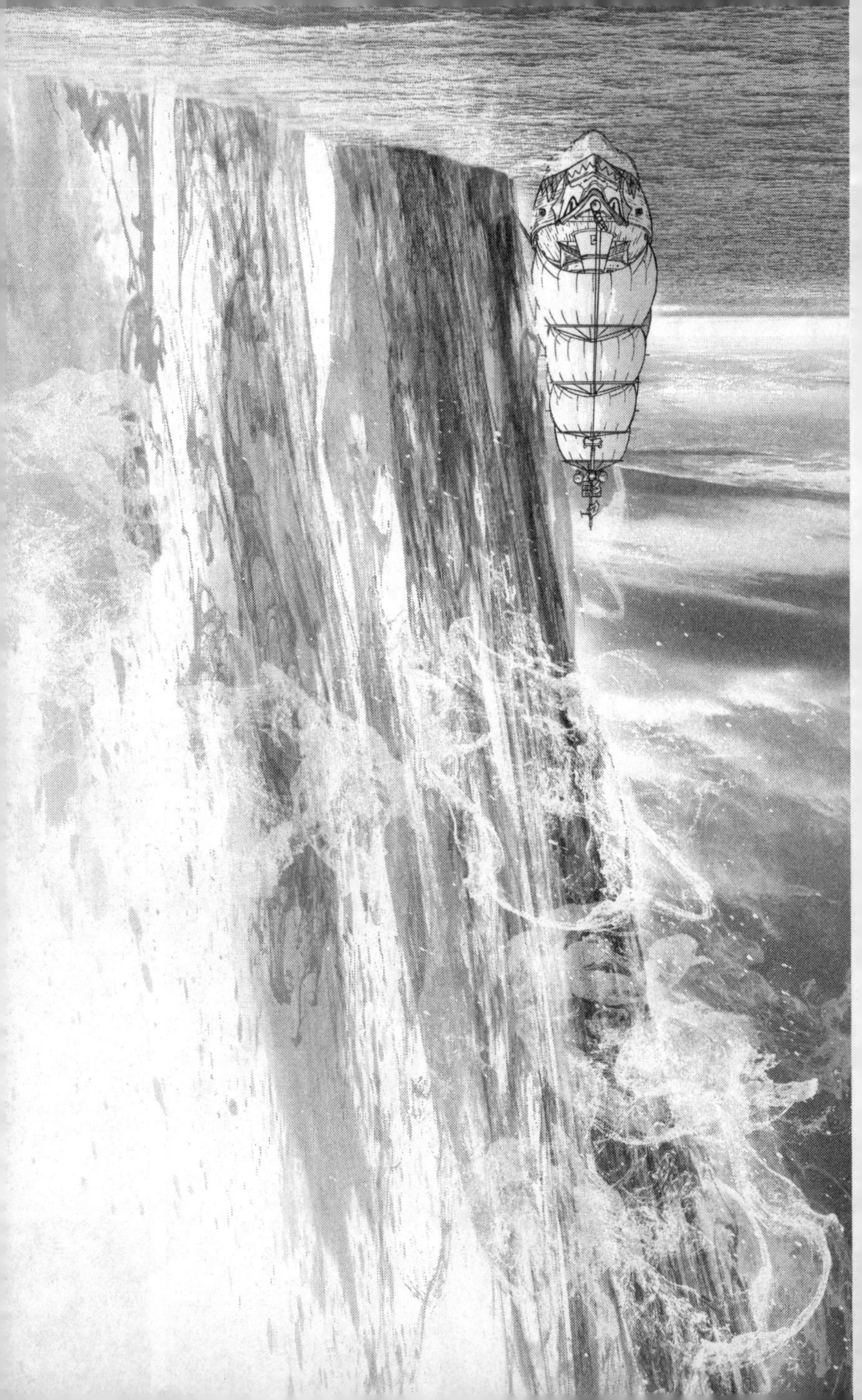

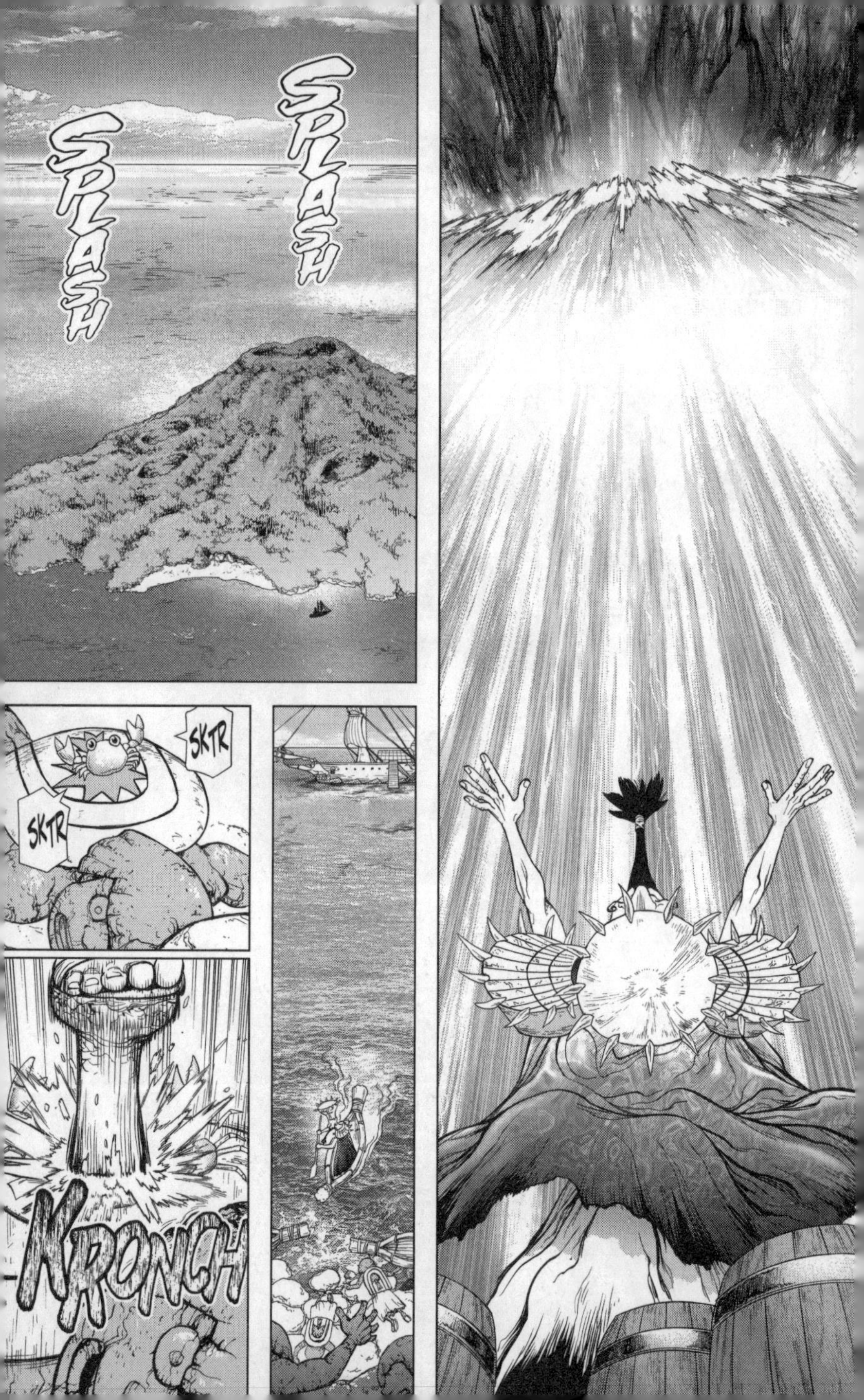
SPLASH
SPLASH
SKTR
SKTR
KRONCH

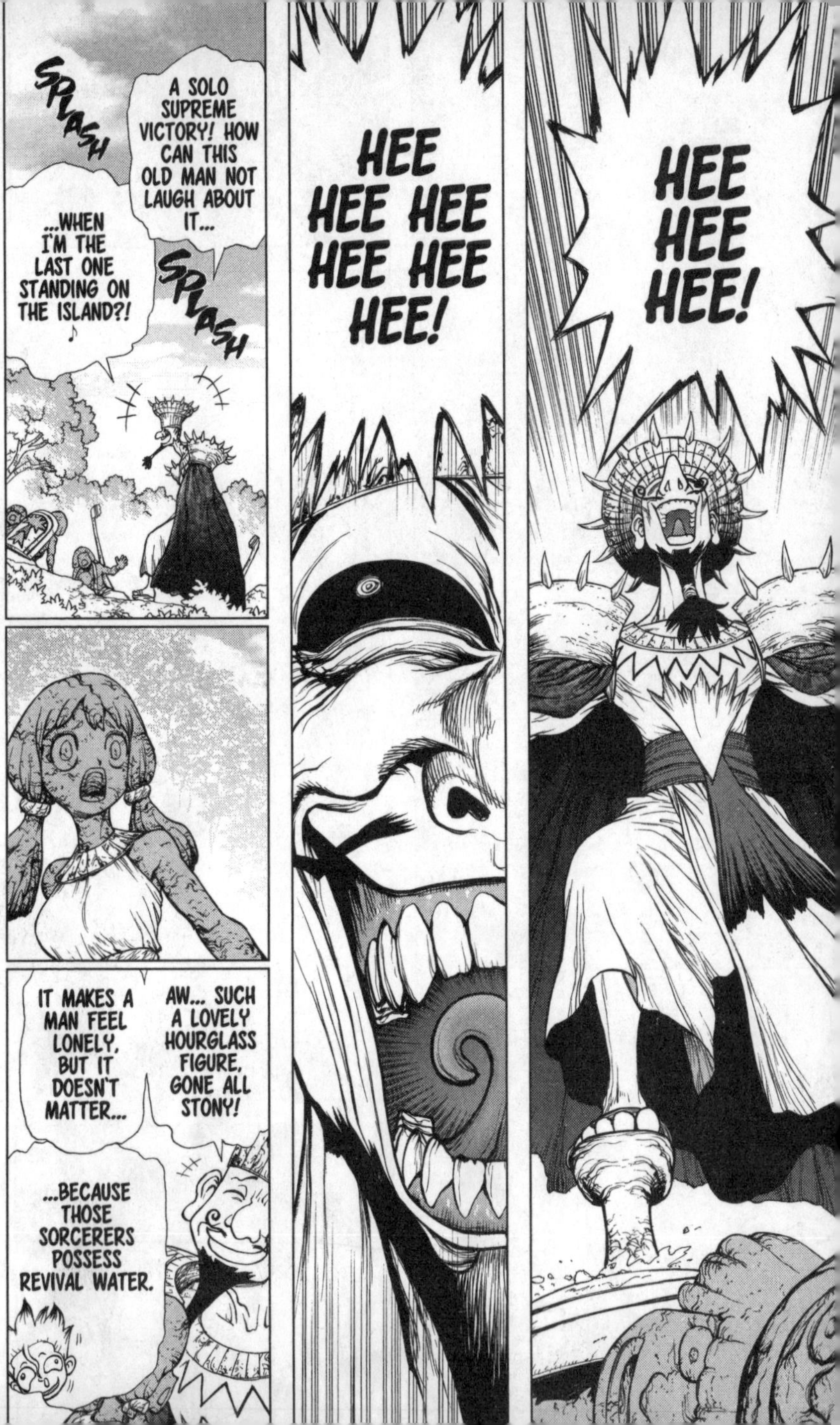
HEE HEE HEE!
HEE HEE HEE HEE HEE HEE!
A SOLO SUPREME VICTORY! HOW CAN THIS OLD MAN NOT LAUGH ABOUT IT...
...WHEN I'M THE LAST ONE STANDING ON THE ISLAND?! ♪
SPLASH
SPLASH
AW... SUCH A LOVELY HOURGLASS FIGURE, GONE ALL STONY!
IT MAKES A MAN FEEL LONELY, BUT IT DOESN'T MATTER...
...BECAUSE THOSE SORCERERS POSSESS REVIVAL WATER.

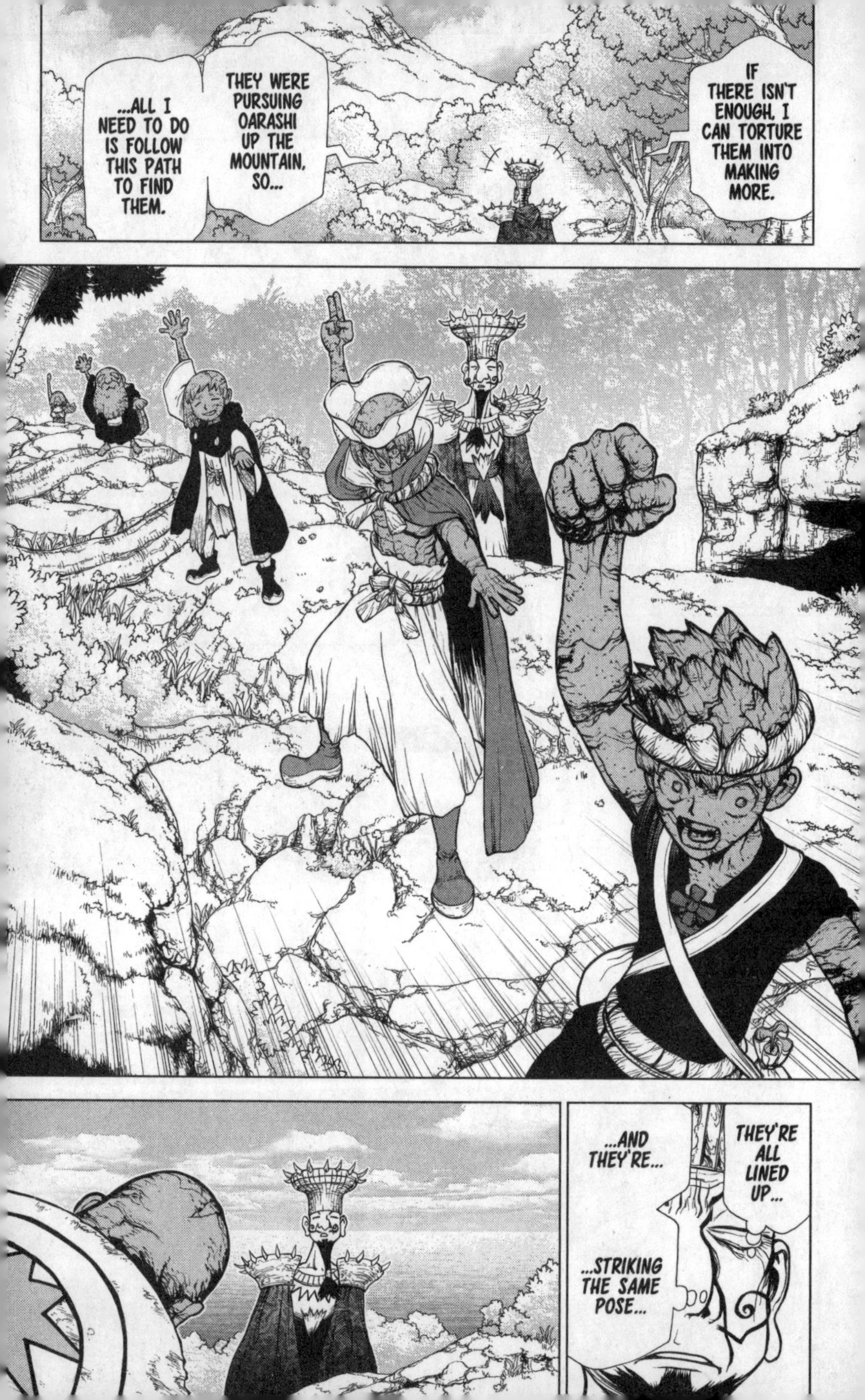
IF THERE ISN'T ENOUGH, I CAN TORTURE THEM INTO MAKING MORE.
THEY WERE PURSUING OARASHI UP THE MOUNTAIN, SO...
...ALL I NEED TO DO IS FOLLOW THIS PATH TO FIND THEM.
THEY'RE ALL LINED UP...
...AND THEY'RE...
...STRIKING THE SAME POSE...

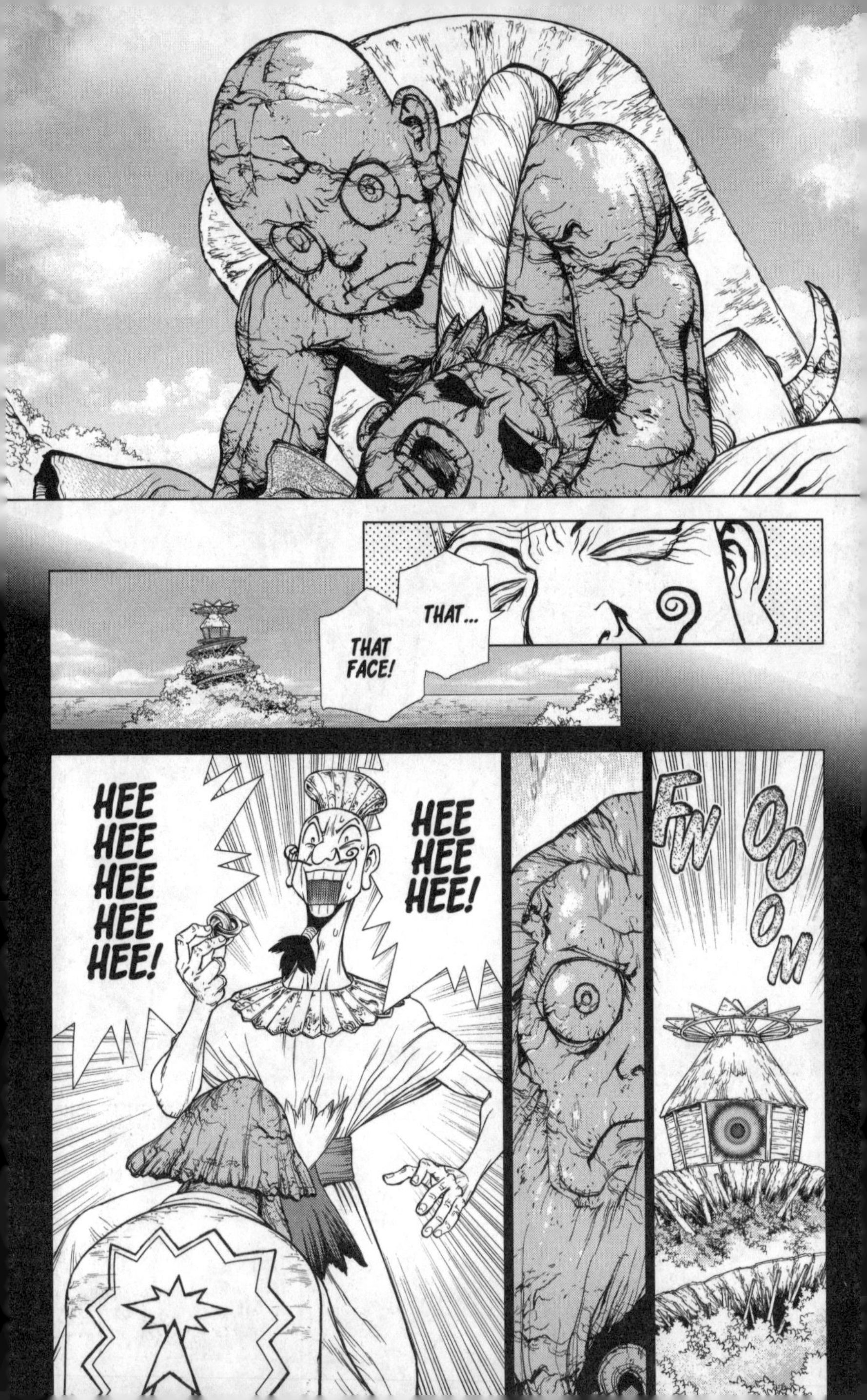
THAT...
THAT FACE!
FWOOOM
HEE HEE HEE!
HEE HEE HEE HEE HEE!

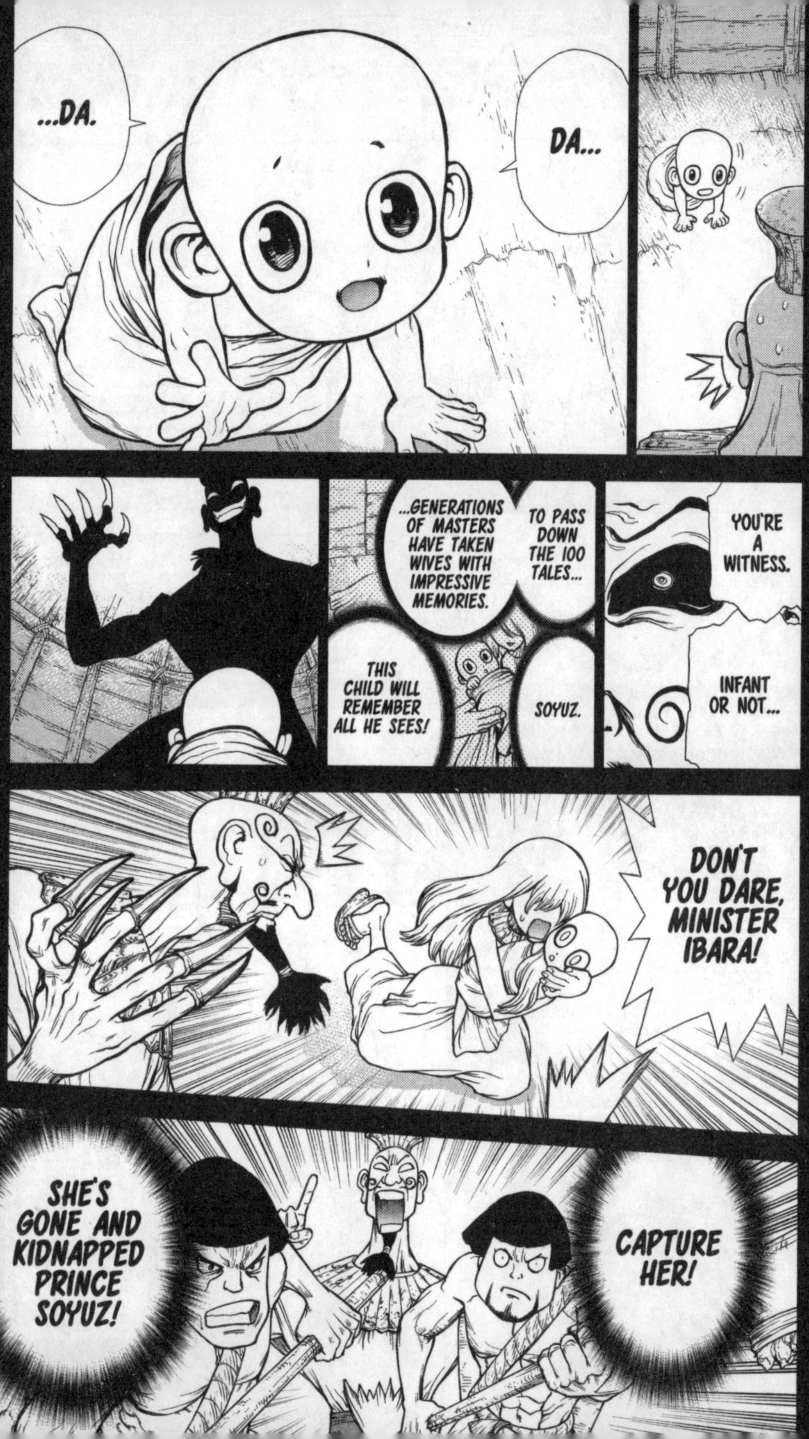
DA...
...DA.
YOU'RE A WITNESS.
INFANT OR NOT...
TO PASS DOWN THE 100 TALES...
...GENERATIONS OF MASTERS HAVE TAKEN WIVES WITH IMPRESSIVE MEMORIES.
SOYUZ.
THIS CHILD WILL REMEMBER ALL HE SEES!
DON'T YOU DARE, MINISTER IBARA!
CAPTURE HER!
SHE'S GONE AND KIDNAPPED PRINCE SOYUZ!

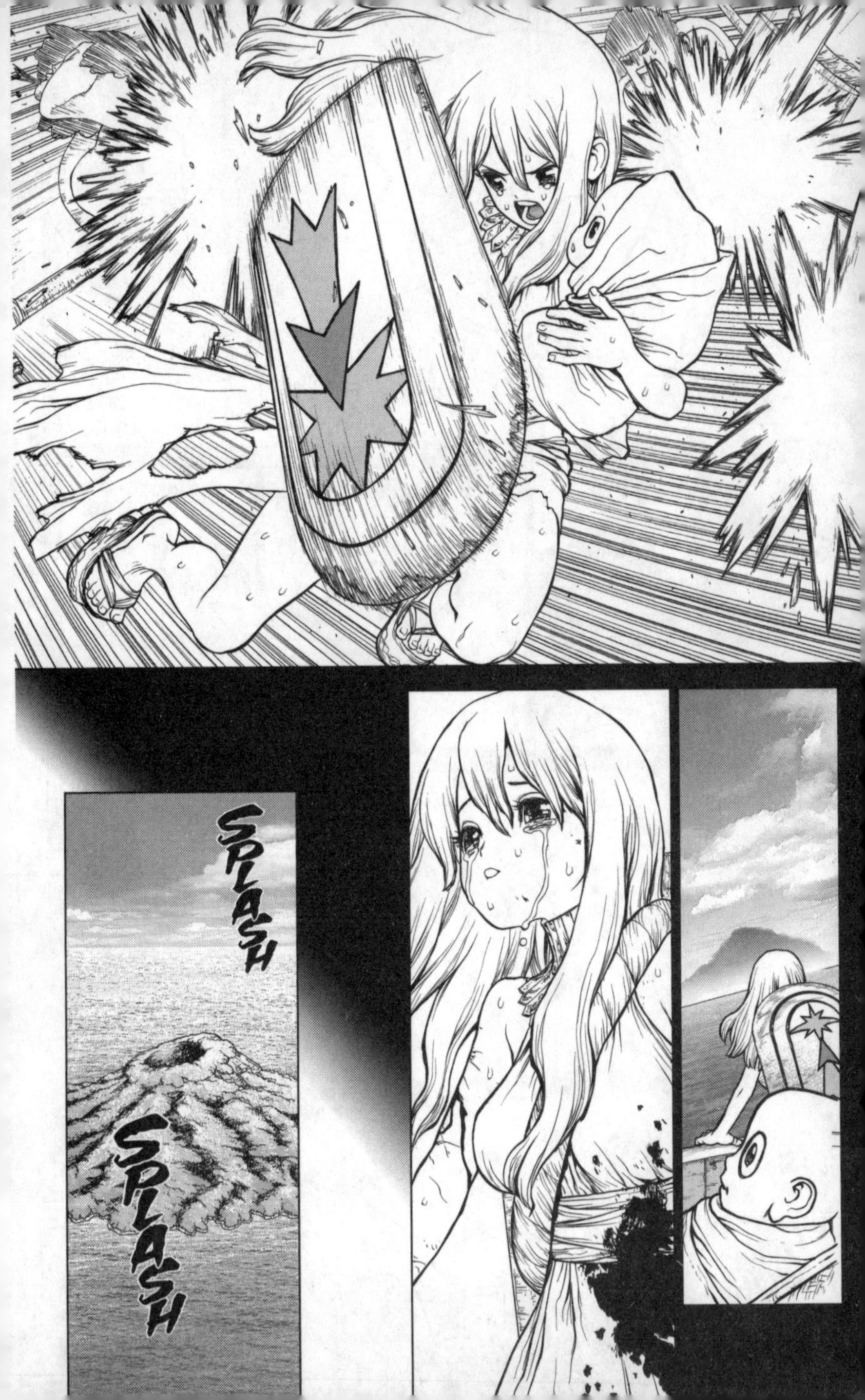
SPLASH
SPLASH

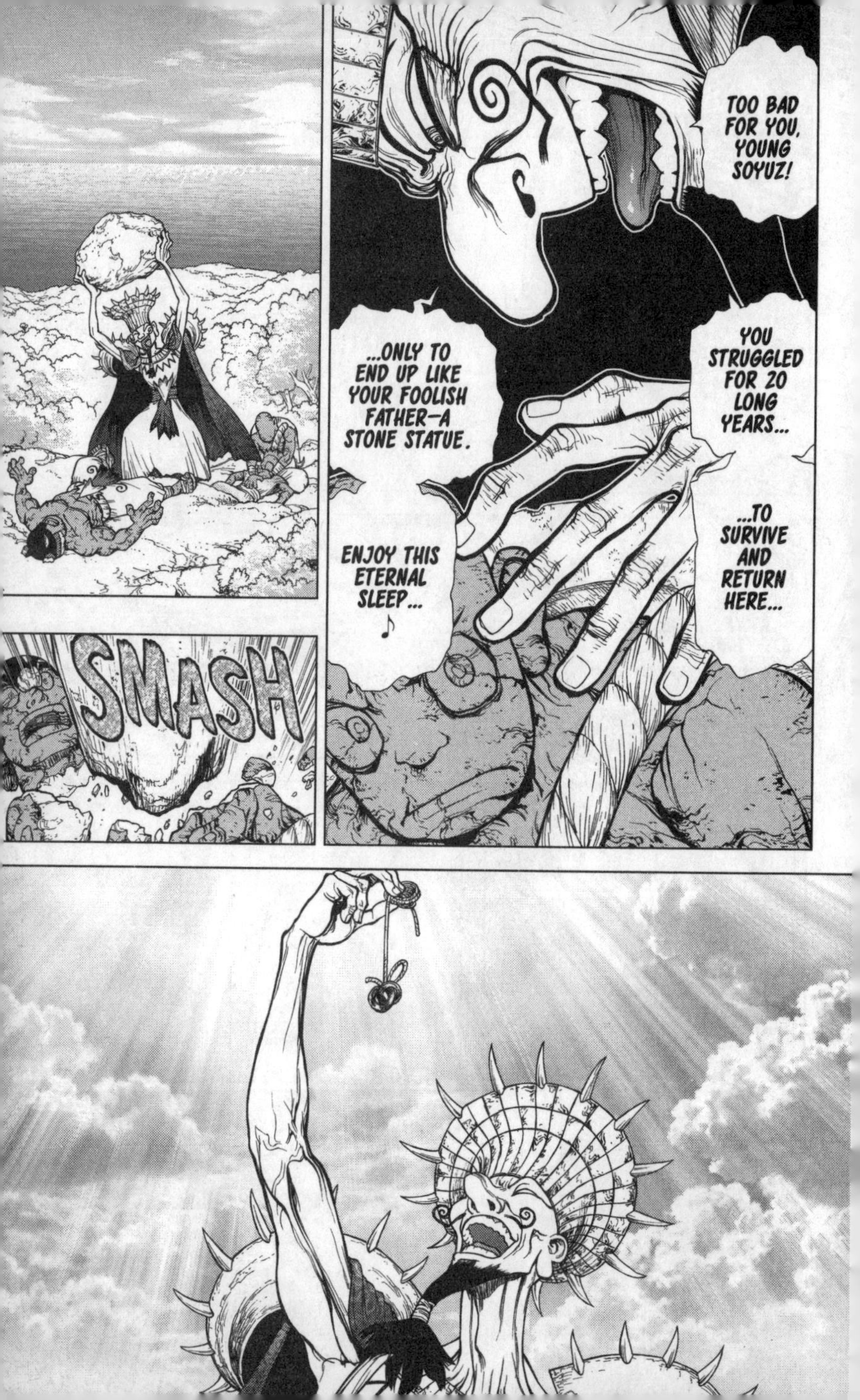
TOO BAD FOR YOU, YOUNG SOYUZ!
YOU STRUGGLED FOR 20 LONG YEARS...
...TO SURVIVE AND RETURN HERE...
...ONLY TO END UP LIKE YOUR FOOLISH FATHER—A STONE STATUE.
ENJOY THIS ETERNAL SLEEP... ♪
SMASH

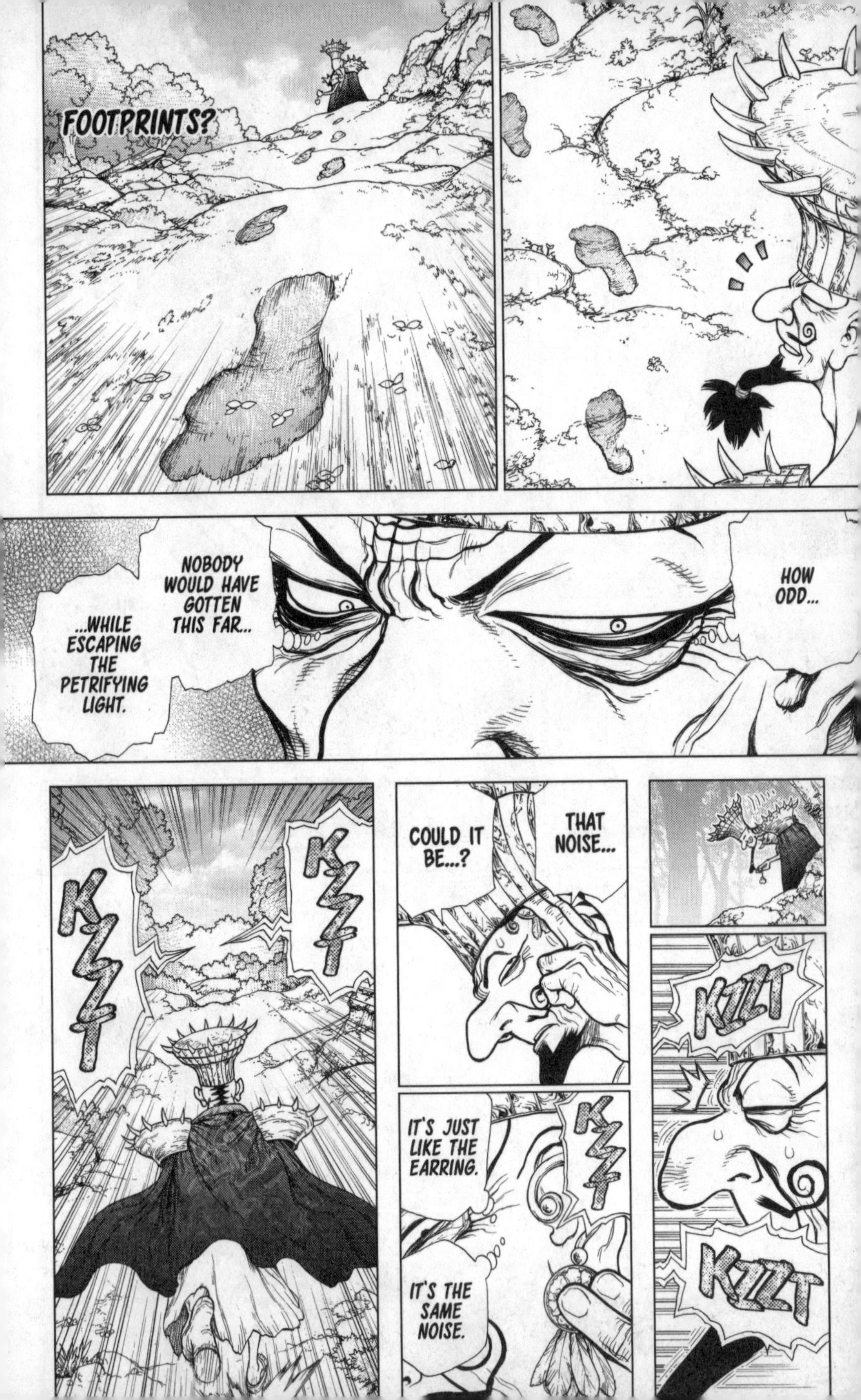
FOOTPRINTS?
HOW ODD...
NOBODY WOULD HAVE GOTTEN THIS FAR...
...WHILE ESCAPING THE PETRIFYING LIGHT.
KZZT
KZZT
THAT NOISE...
COULD IT BE...?
IT'S JUST LIKE THE EARRING.
KZZT
IT'S THE SAME NOISE.
KZZT
KZZT

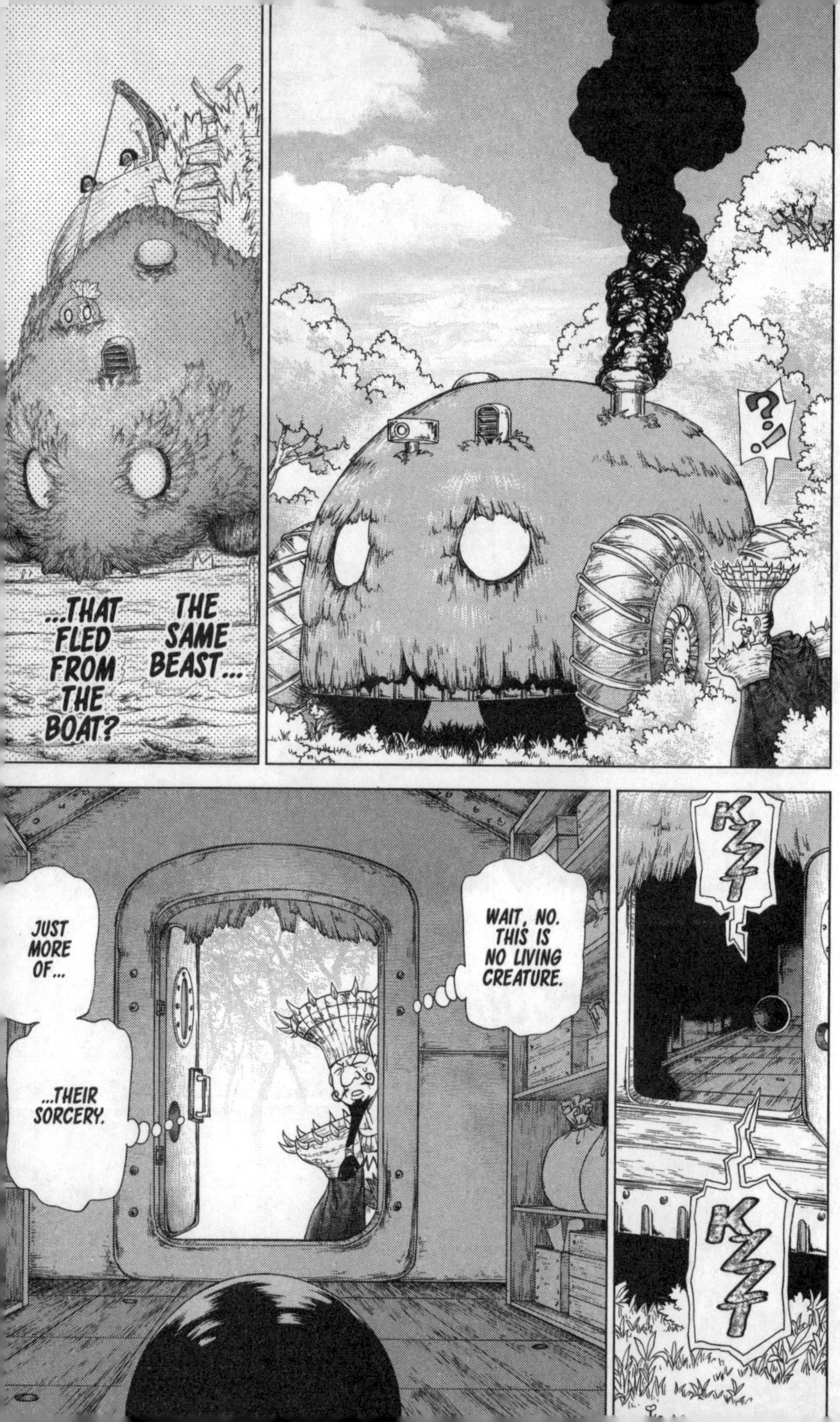
?!
THE SAME BEAST...
...THAT FLED FROM THE BOAT?
KZZT
KZZT
WAIT, NO. THIS IS NO LIVING CREATURE.
JUST MORE OF...
...THEIR SORCERY.

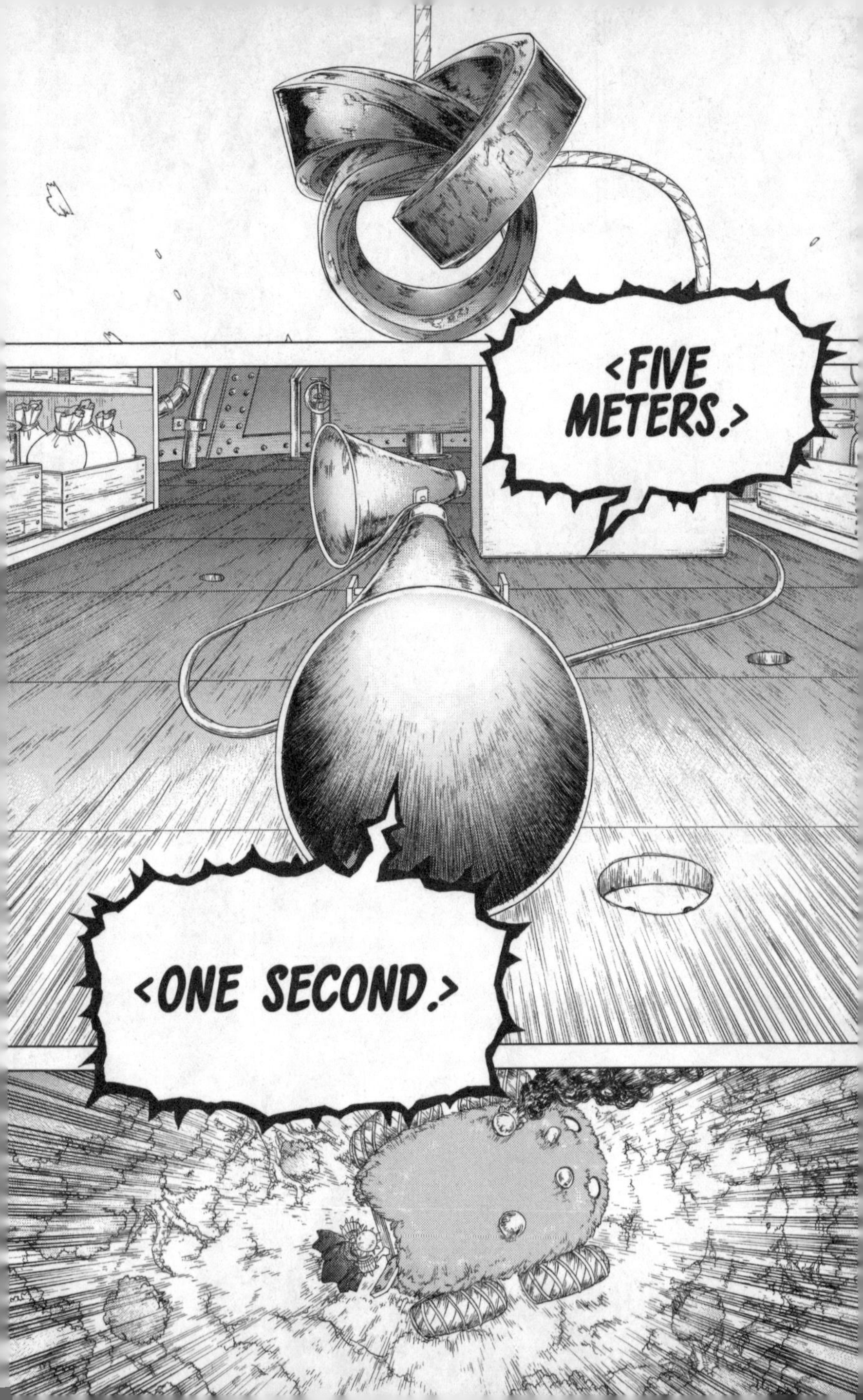
<FIVE METERS.>
<ONE SECOND.>

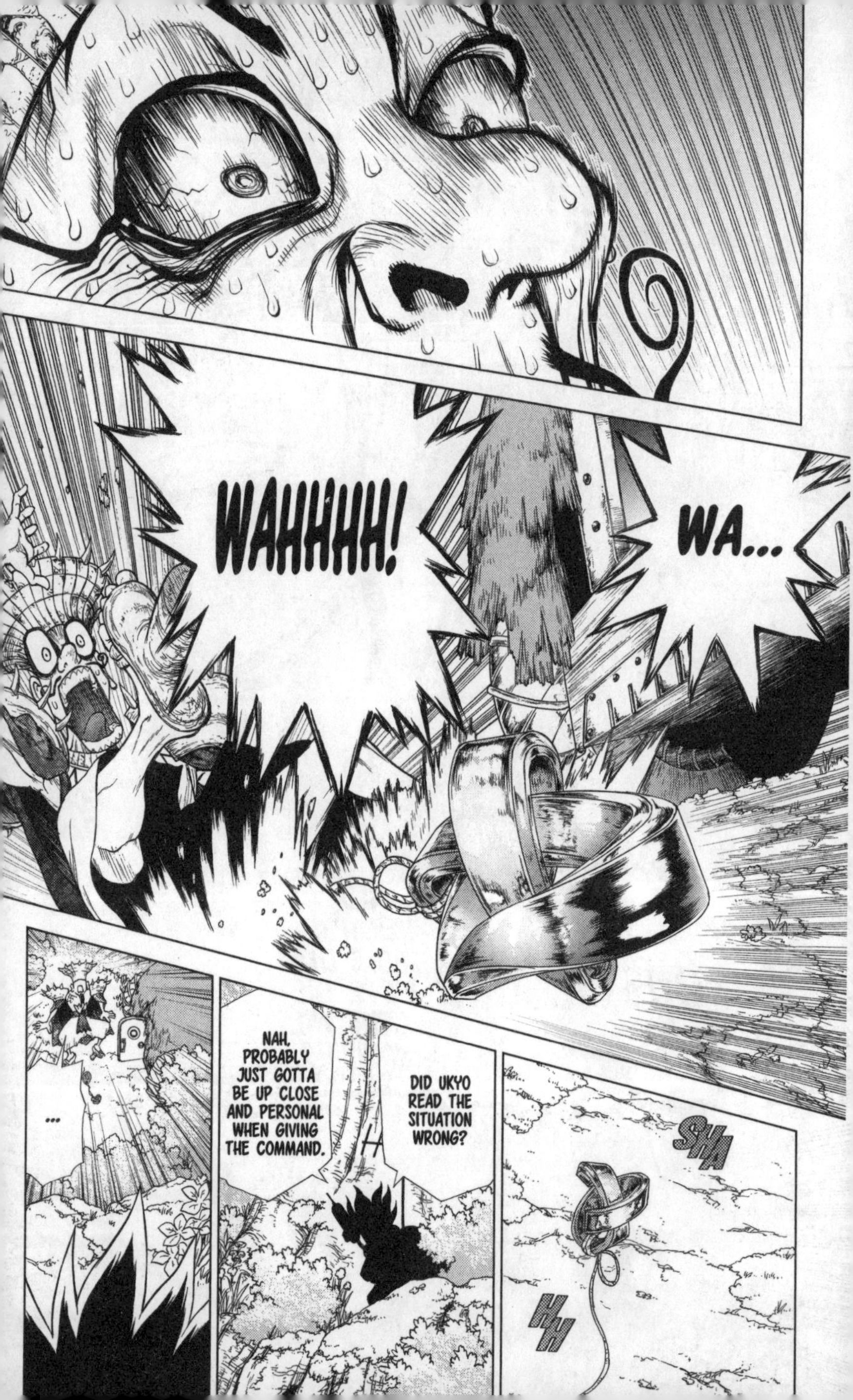
WA...
WAHHHH!
SHA
HH
DID UKYO READ THE SITUATION WRONG?
NAH, PROBABLY JUST GOTTA BE UP CLOSE AND PERSONAL WHEN GIVING THE COMMAND.
...

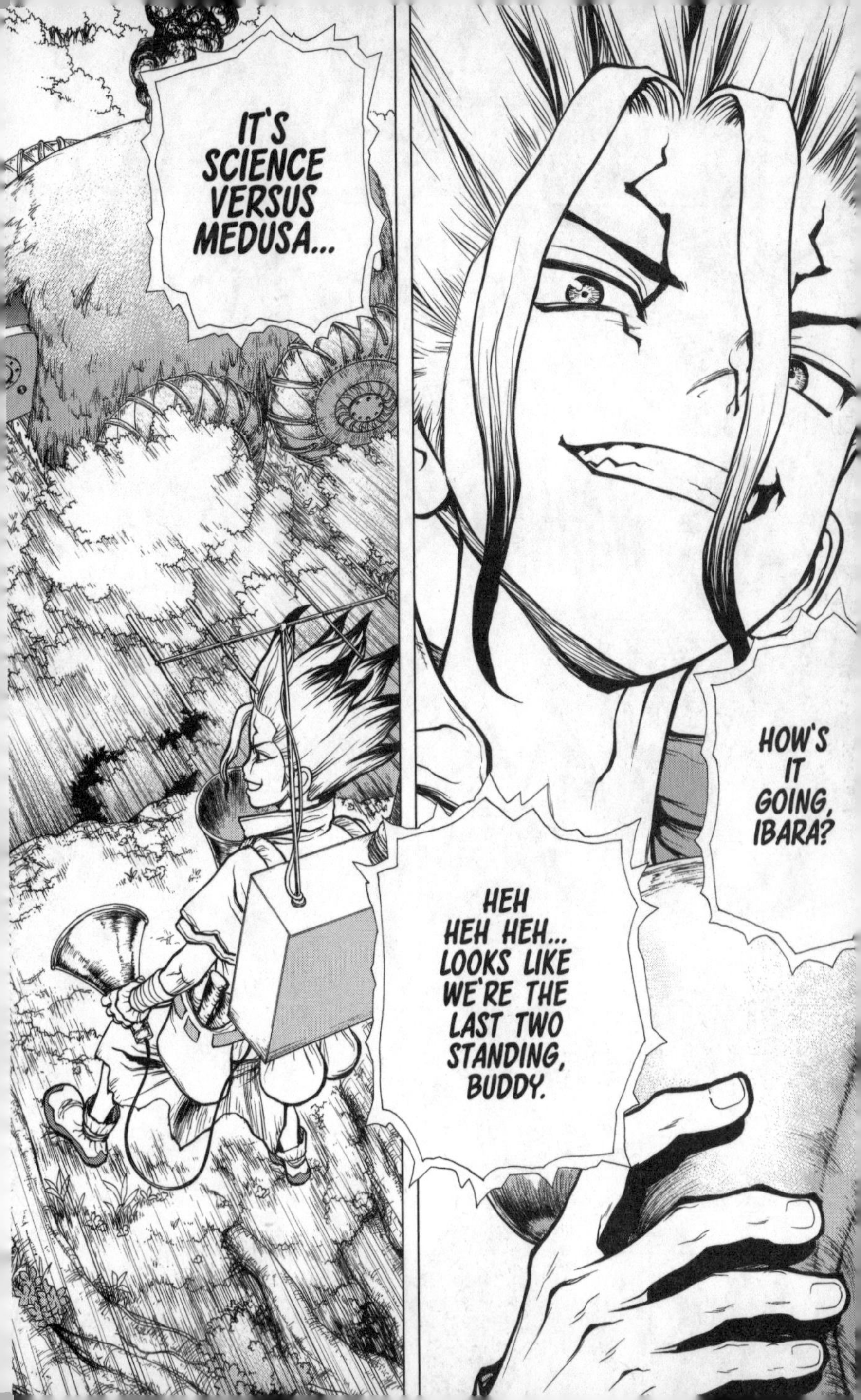
HOW'S IT GOING, IBARA?
HEH HEH HEH... LOOKS LIKE WE'RE THE LAST TWO STANDING, BUDDY.
IT'S SCIENCE VERSUS MEDUSA...

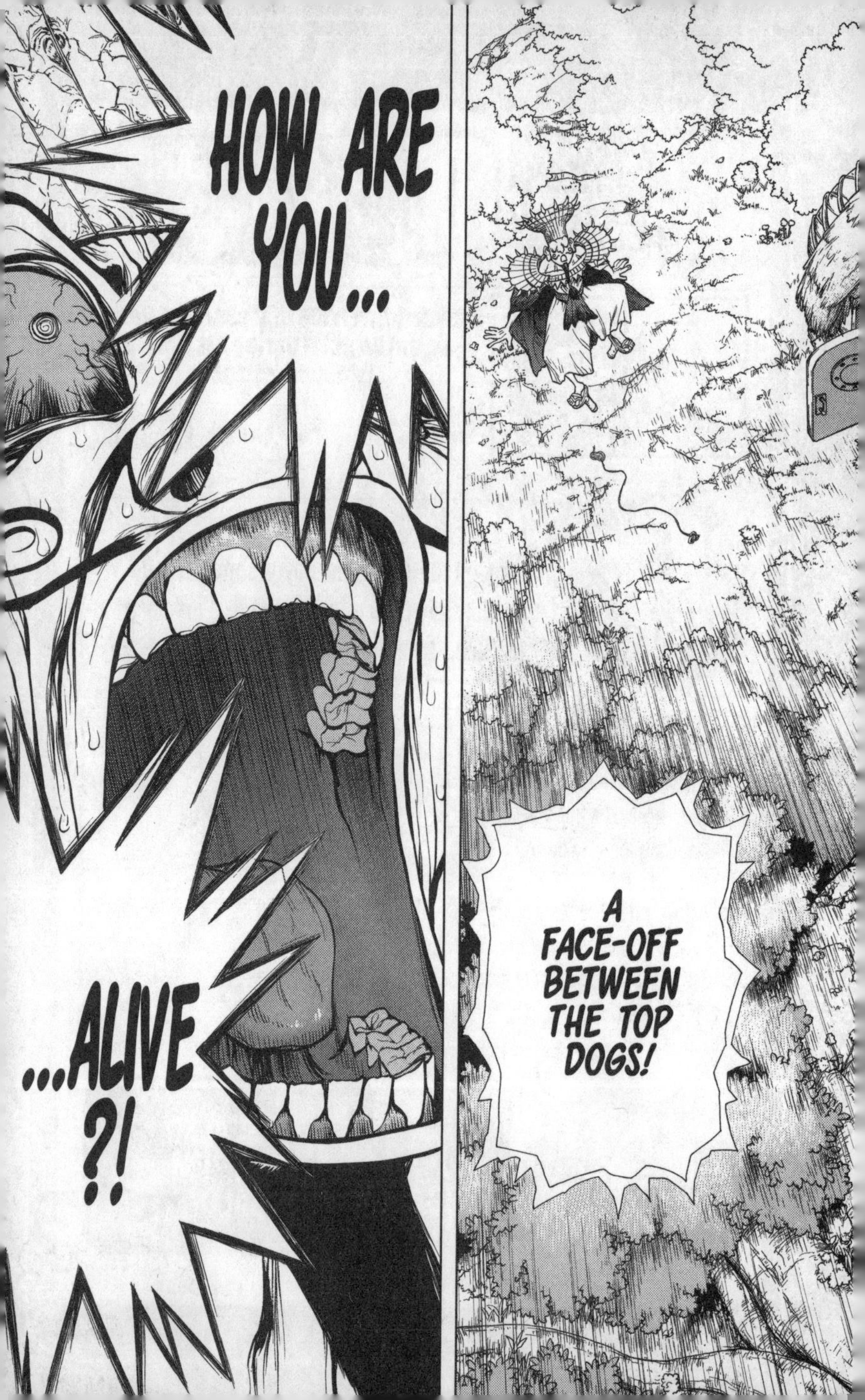
A FACE-OFF BETWEEN THE TOP DOGS!
HOW ARE YOU...
...ALIVE ?!

MECHA SENKU Q&A

SEARCH

Question Corner

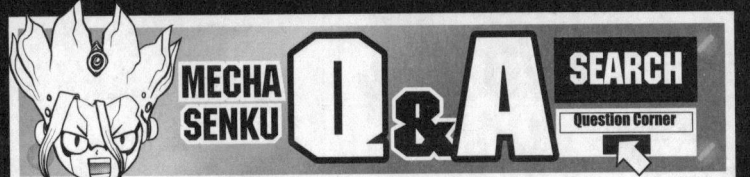

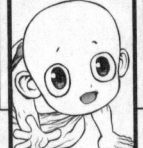

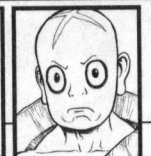

Soyuz didn't have that scar as a baby, so did he get it during his time in Ishigami Village?

Pop of Hokkaido **SEARCH**

In accordance with the folklore passed down through the 100 Tales, Soyuz's mother was desperately determined to reach Japan after escaping from the island.

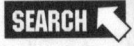

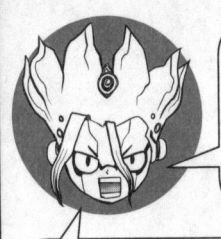

Fortunately, she was able to deliver baby Soyuz to the mainland safely, but he received a nasty wound on his head along the way during a storm.

That wound is the reason why Soyuz has headaches whenever he tries to recall detailed memories about the island!

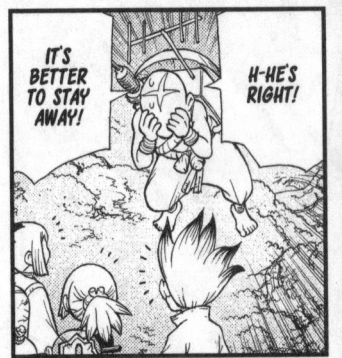

H-HE'S RIGHT!
IT'S BETTER TO STAY AWAY!

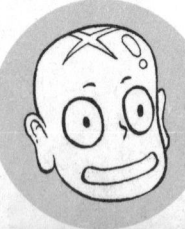

PROBABLY!

IT'S ALSO WHY I'M BALD!

Z=135: Counting

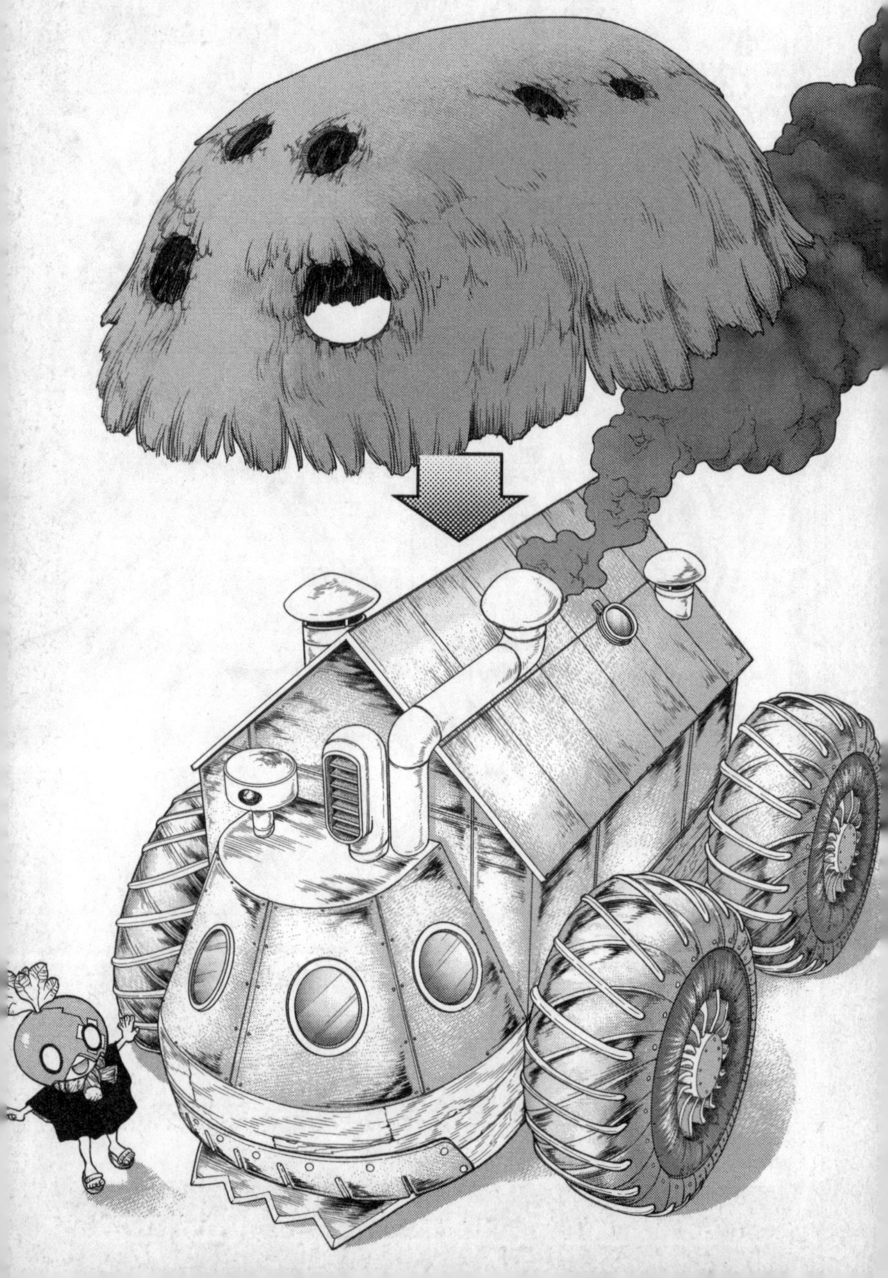

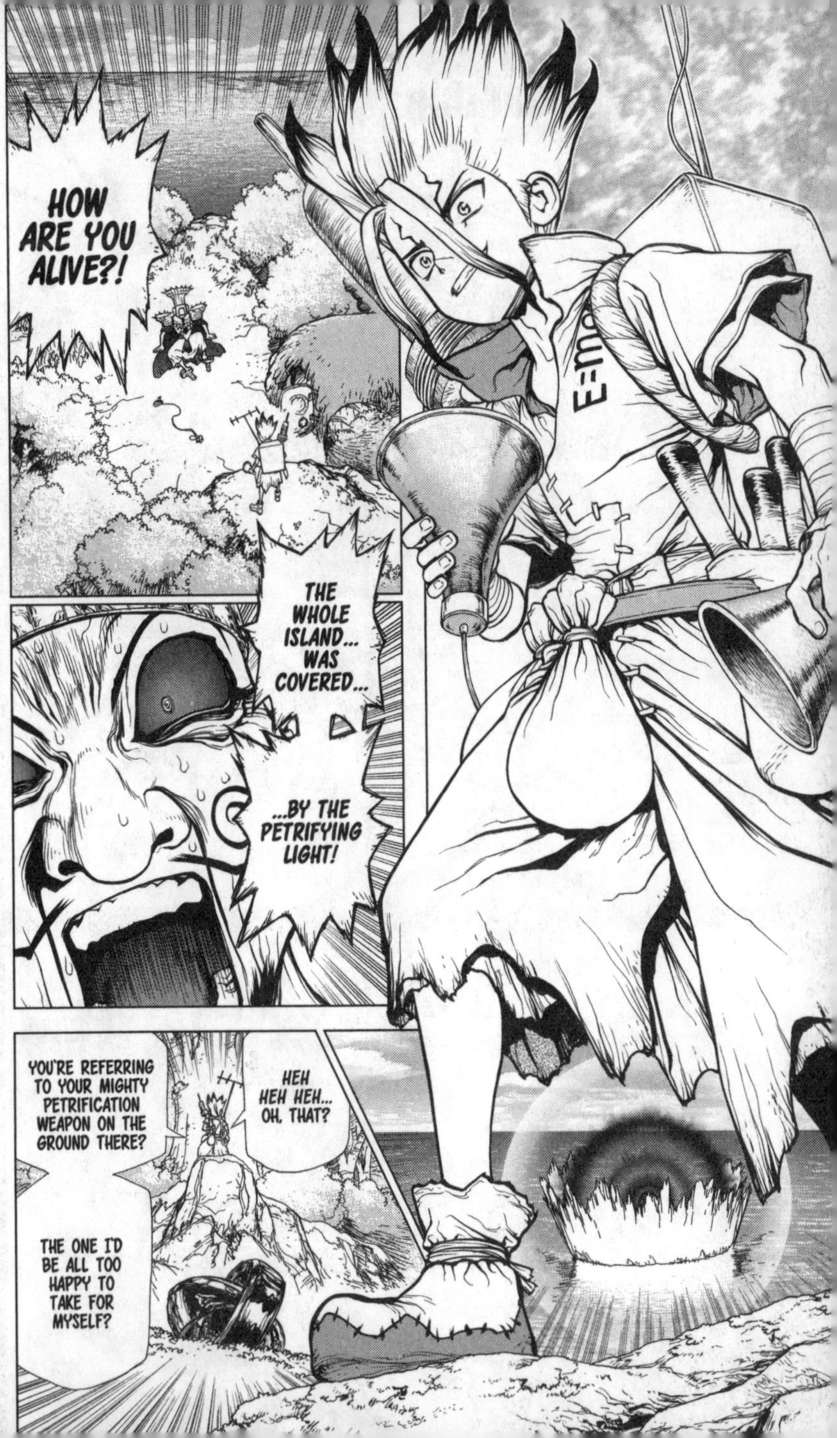
HOW ARE YOU ALIVE?!
THE WHOLE ISLAND... WAS COVERED...
...BY THE PETRIFYING LIGHT!
HEH HEH HEH... OH, THAT?
YOU'RE REFERRING TO YOUR MIGHTY PETRIFICATION WEAPON ON THE GROUND THERE?
THE ONE I'D BE ALL TOO HAPPY TO TAKE FOR MYSELF?

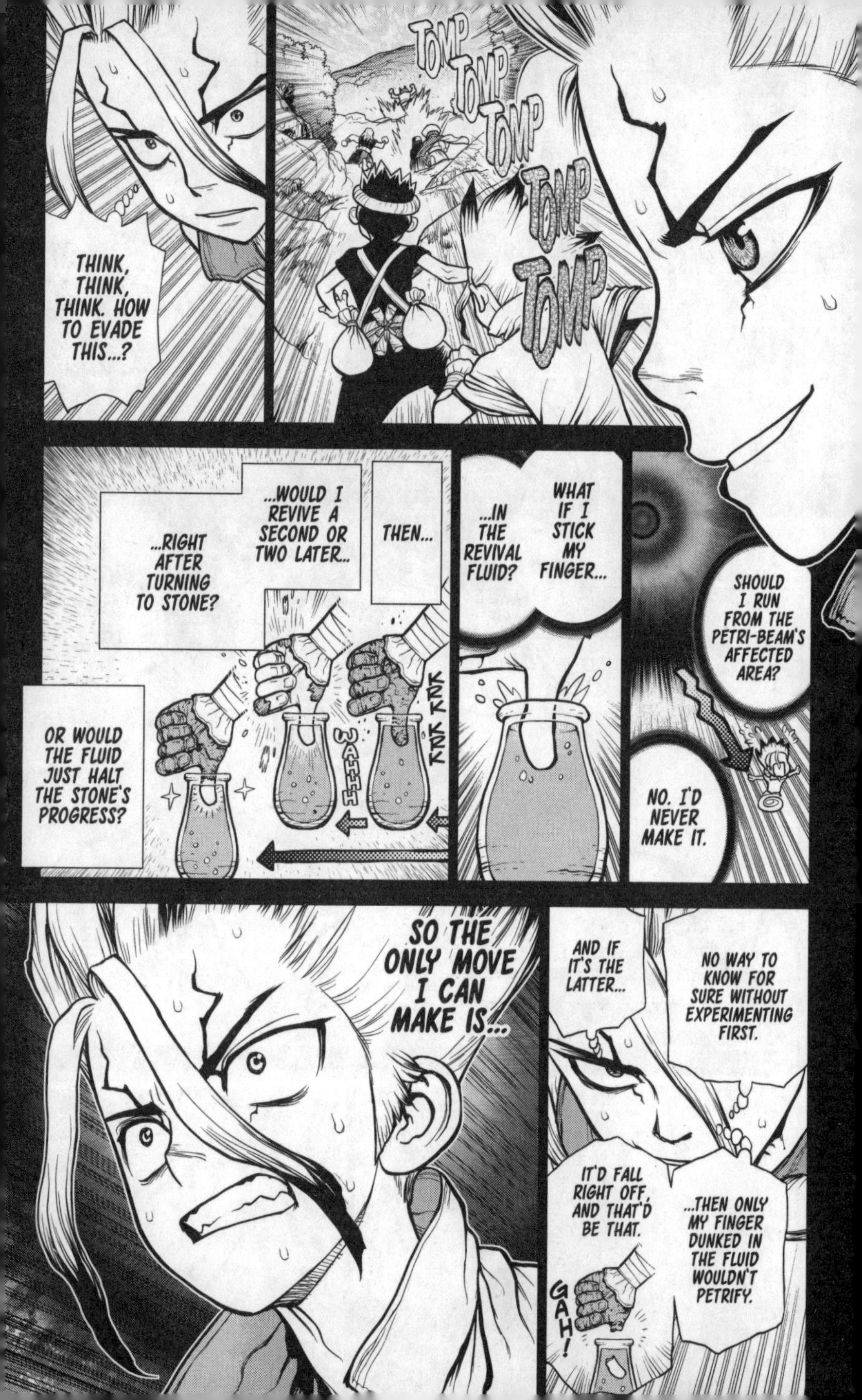
TOMP TOMP TOMP TOMP TOMP
THINK, THINK, THINK. HOW TO EVADE THIS...?
SHOULD I RUN FROM THE PETRI-BEAM'S AFFECTED AREA?
NO. I'D NEVER MAKE IT.
WHAT IF I STICK MY FINGER...
...IN THE REVIVAL FLUID?
THEN...
...WOULD I REVIVE A SECOND OR TWO LATER...
...RIGHT AFTER TURNING TO STONE?
KRK KRK
WAHHH
OR WOULD THE FLUID JUST HALT THE STONE'S PROGRESS?
NO WAY TO KNOW FOR SURE WITHOUT EXPERIMENTING FIRST.
AND IF IT'S THE LATTER...
...THEN ONLY MY FINGER DUNKED IN THE FLUID WOULDN'T PETRIFY.
IT'D FALL RIGHT OFF, AND THAT'D BE THAT.
GAH!
SO THE ONLY MOVE I CAN MAKE IS...

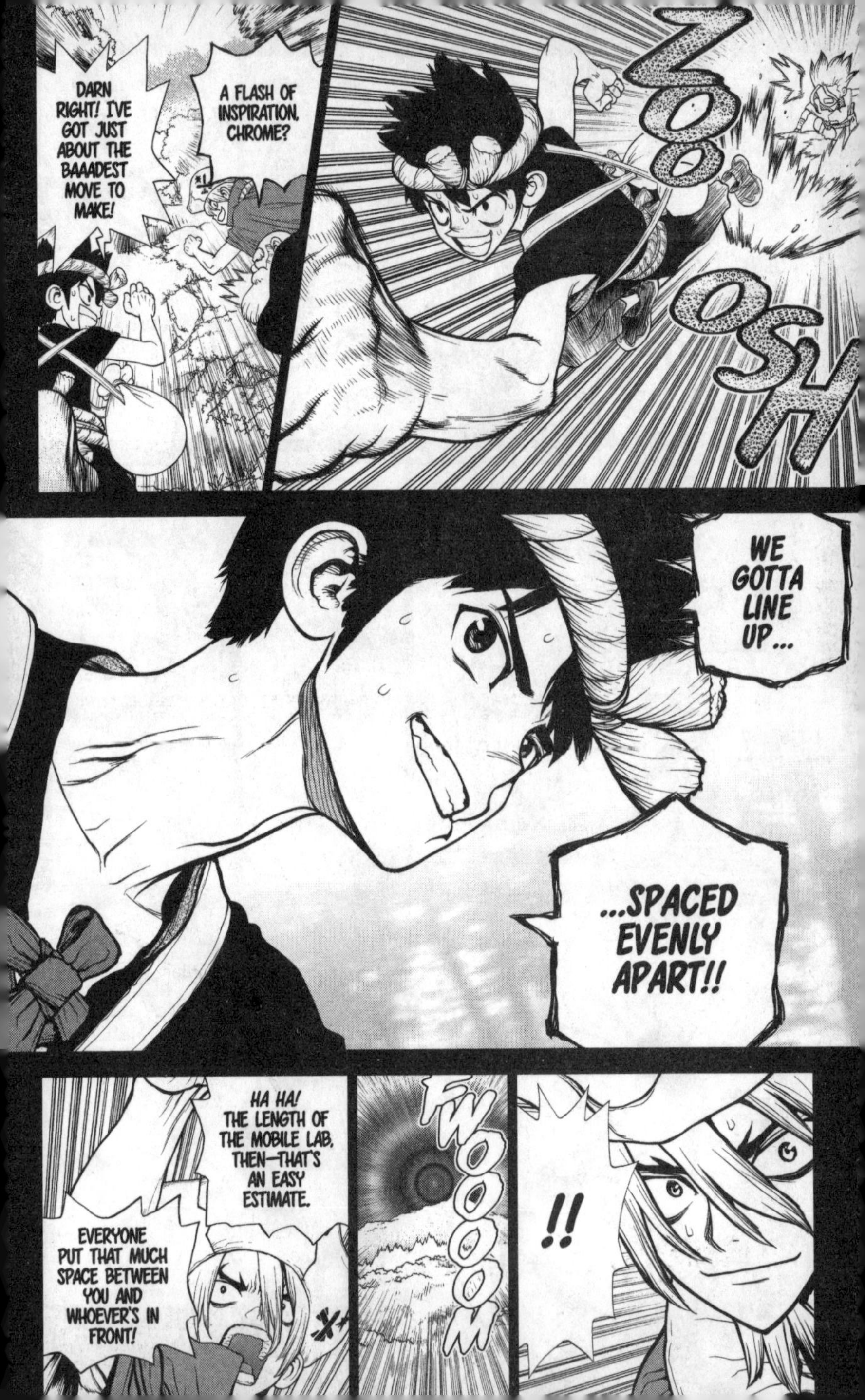
ZOOOSH
A FLASH OF INSPIRATION, CHROME?
DARN RIGHT! I'VE GOT JUST ABOUT THE BAAADEST MOVE TO MAKE!
WE GOTTA LINE UP...
...SPACED EVENLY APART!!
!!
FWOOOOOM
HA HA! THE LENGTH OF THE MOBILE LAB, THEN—THAT'S AN EASY ESTIMATE.
EVERYONE PUT THAT MUCH SPACE BETWEEN YOU AND WHOEVER'S IN FRONT!

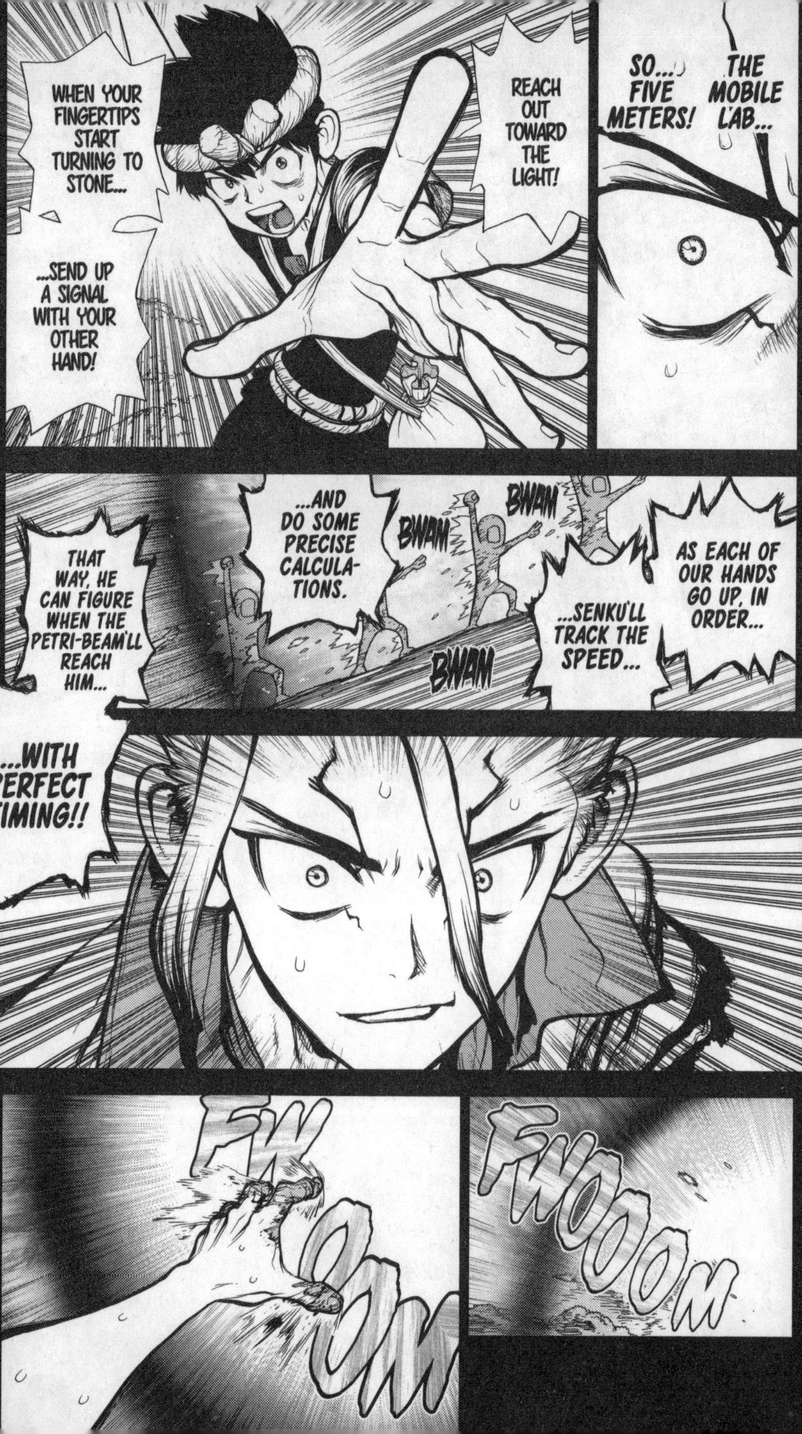
SO... FIVE METERS!
THE MOBILE LAB...
REACH OUT TOWARD THE LIGHT!
WHEN YOUR FINGERTIPS START TURNING TO STONE...
...SEND UP A SIGNAL WITH YOUR OTHER HAND!
AS EACH OF OUR HANDS GO UP, IN ORDER...
BWAM
...SENKU'LL TRACK THE SPEED...
BWAM
BWAM
...AND DO SOME PRECISE CALCULATIONS.
THAT WAY, HE CAN FIGURE WHEN THE PETRI-BEAM'LL REACH HIM...
...WITH PERFECT TIMING!!
FWOOOOM
FWOOM

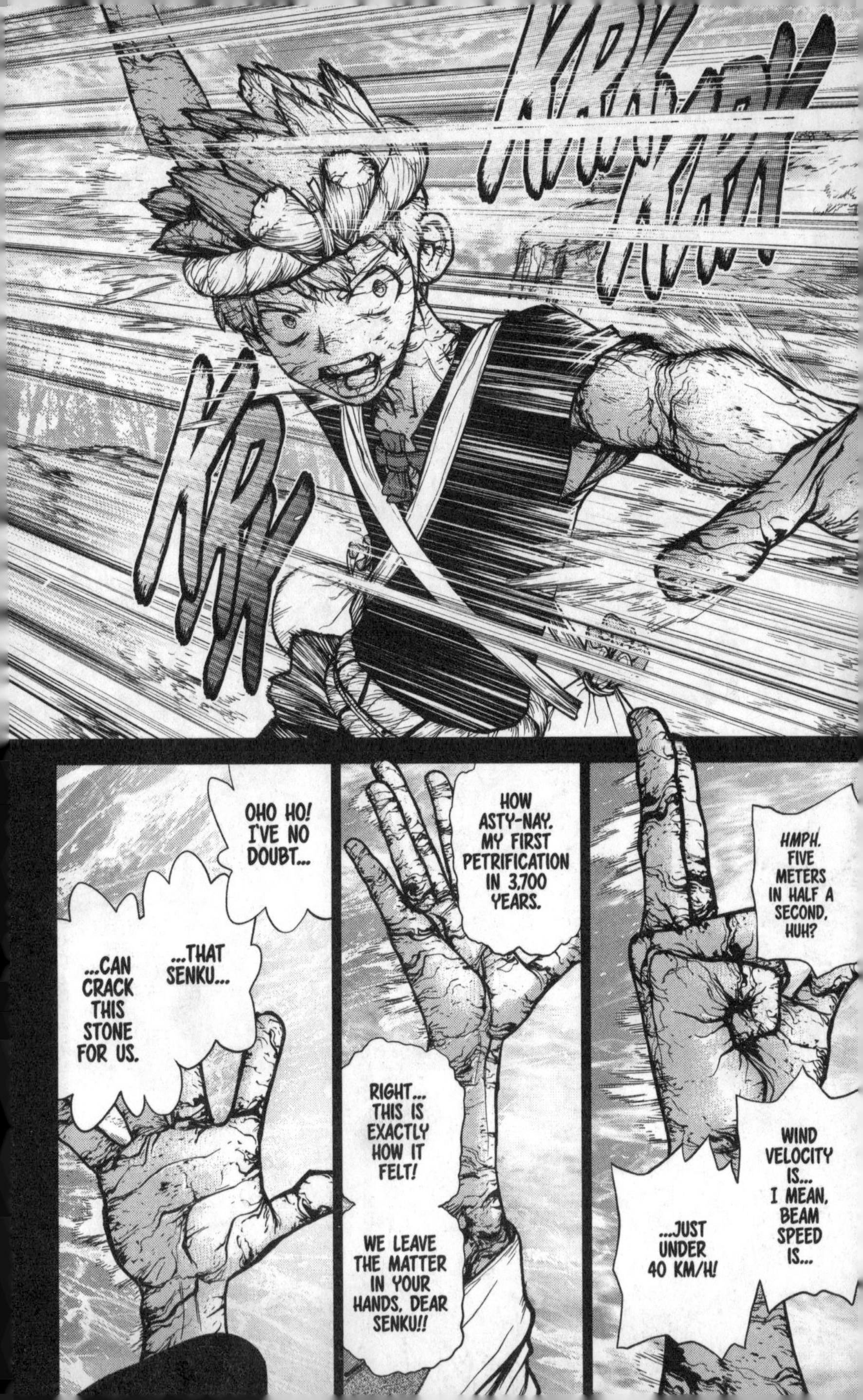
HMPH. FIVE METERS IN HALF A SECOND, HUH?
WIND VELOCITY IS... I MEAN, BEAM SPEED IS...
...JUST UNDER 40 KM/H!
HOW ASTY-NAY. MY FIRST PETRIFICATION IN 3,700 YEARS.
RIGHT... THIS IS EXACTLY HOW IT FELT!
WE LEAVE THE MATTER IN YOUR HANDS, DEAR SENKU!!
OHO HO! I'VE NO DOUBT...
...THAT SENKU...
...CAN CRACK THIS STONE FOR US.

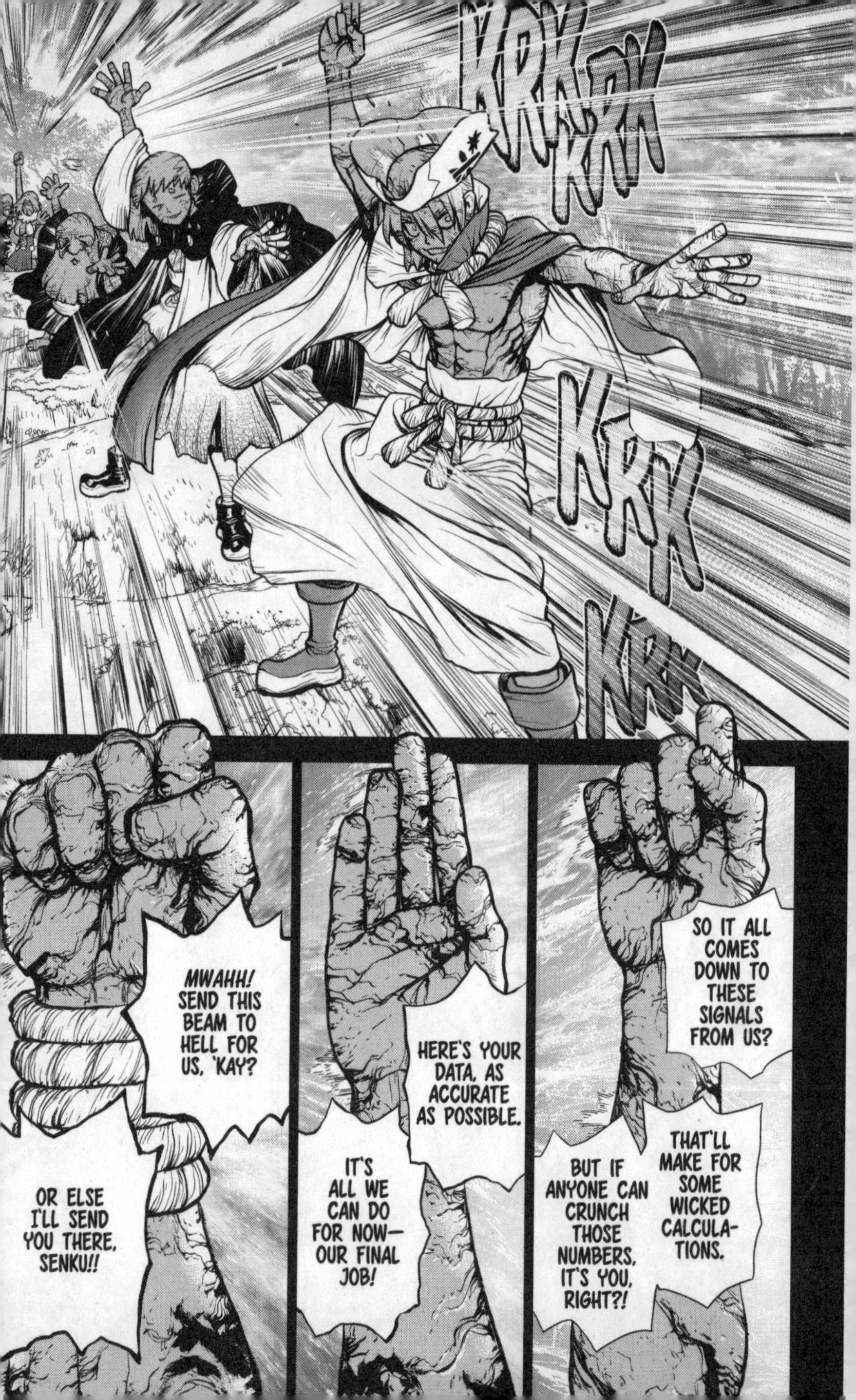
KRK KRK
KRK
KRK
SO IT ALL COMES DOWN TO THESE SIGNALS FROM US?
THAT'LL MAKE FOR SOME WICKED CALCULA-TIONS.
BUT IF ANYONE CAN CRUNCH THOSE NUMBERS, IT'S YOU, RIGHT?!
HERE'S YOUR DATA, AS ACCURATE AS POSSIBLE.
IT'S ALL WE CAN DO FOR NOW—OUR FINAL JOB!
MWAHH! SEND THIS BEAM TO HELL FOR US, 'KAY?
OR ELSE I'LL SEND YOU THERE, SENKU!!

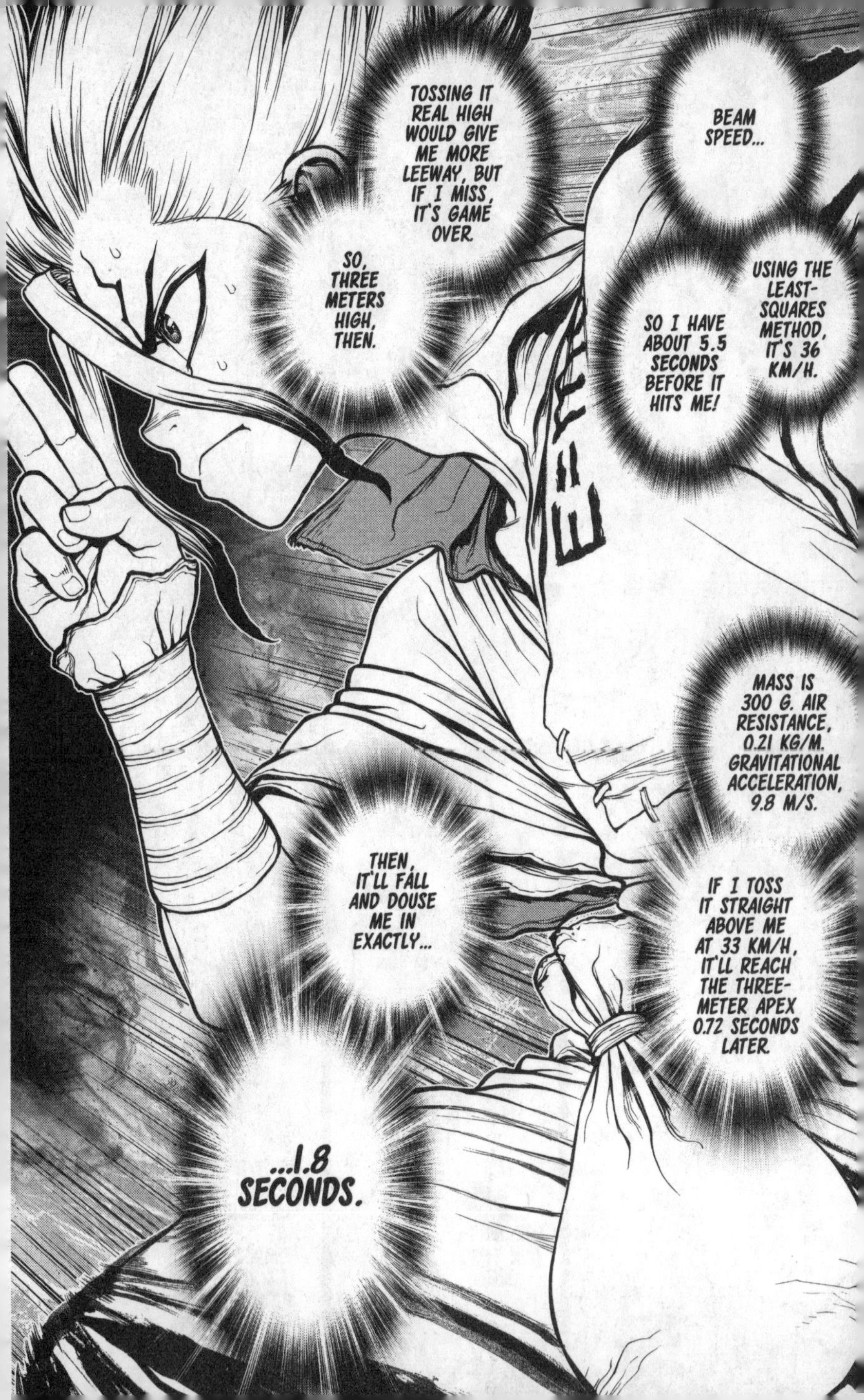
BEAM SPEED...
USING THE LEAST-SQUARES METHOD, IT'S 36 KM/H.
SO I HAVE ABOUT 5.5 SECONDS BEFORE IT HITS ME!
TOSSING IT REAL HIGH WOULD GIVE ME MORE LEEWAY, BUT IF I MISS, IT'S GAME OVER.
SO, THREE METERS HIGH, THEN.
MASS IS 300 G. AIR RESISTANCE, 0.21 KG/M. GRAVITATIONAL ACCELERATION, 9.8 M/S.
IF I TOSS IT STRAIGHT ABOVE ME AT 33 KM/H, IT'LL REACH THE THREE-METER APEX 0.72 SECONDS LATER.
THEN, IT'LL FALL AND DOUSE ME IN EXACTLY...
...1.8 SECONDS.

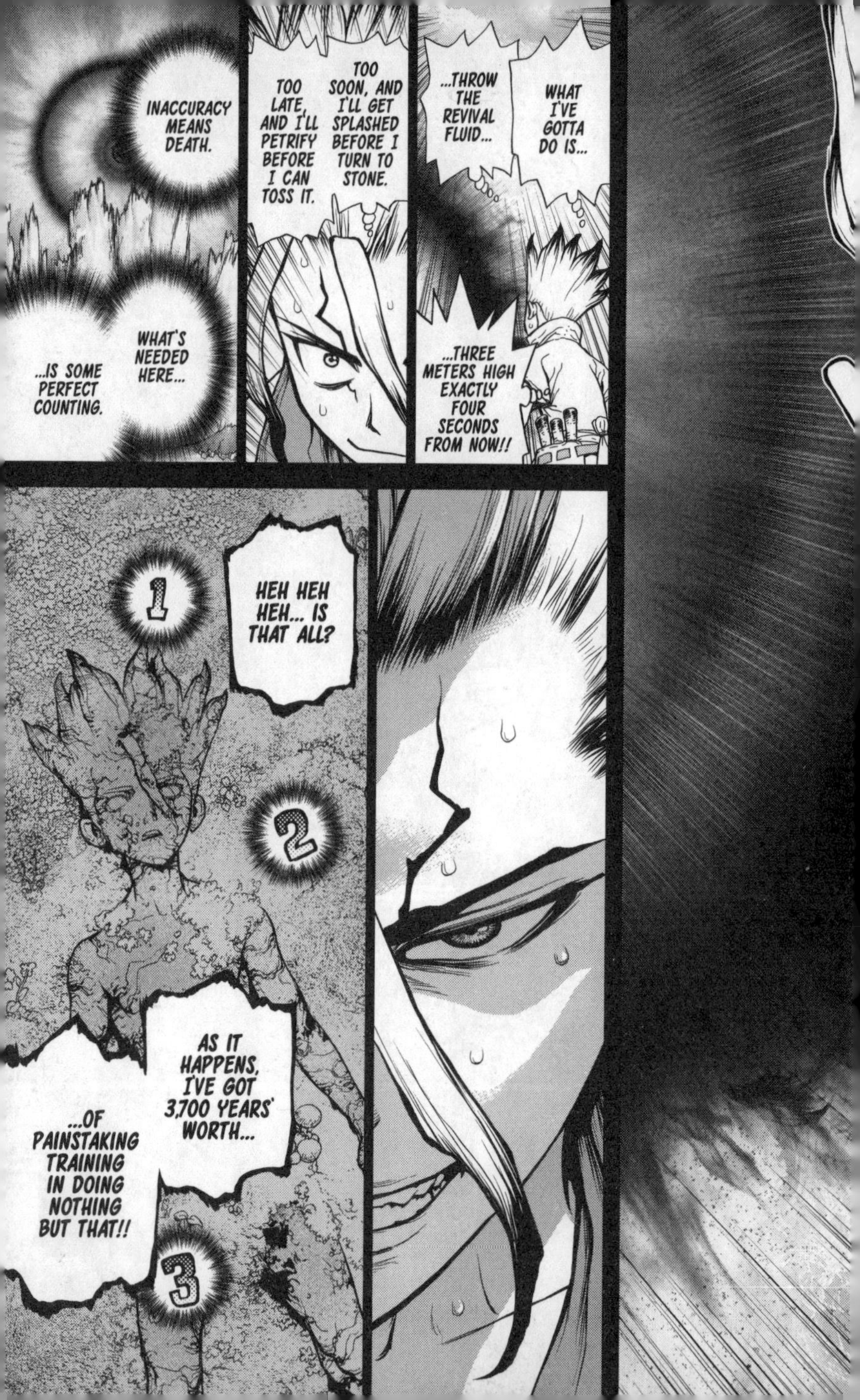
WHAT I'VE GOTTA DO IS...
...THROW THE REVIVAL FLUID...
...THREE METERS HIGH EXACTLY FOUR SECONDS FROM NOW!!
TOO SOON, AND I'LL GET SPLASHED BEFORE I TURN TO STONE.
TOO LATE, AND I'LL PETRIFY BEFORE I CAN TOSS IT.
INACCURACY MEANS DEATH.
WHAT'S NEEDED HERE...
...IS SOME PERFECT COUNTING.
1
HEH HEH HEH... IS THAT ALL?
2
AS IT HAPPENS, I'VE GOT 3,700 YEARS' WORTH...
...OF PAINSTAKING TRAINING IN DOING NOTHING BUT THAT!!
3

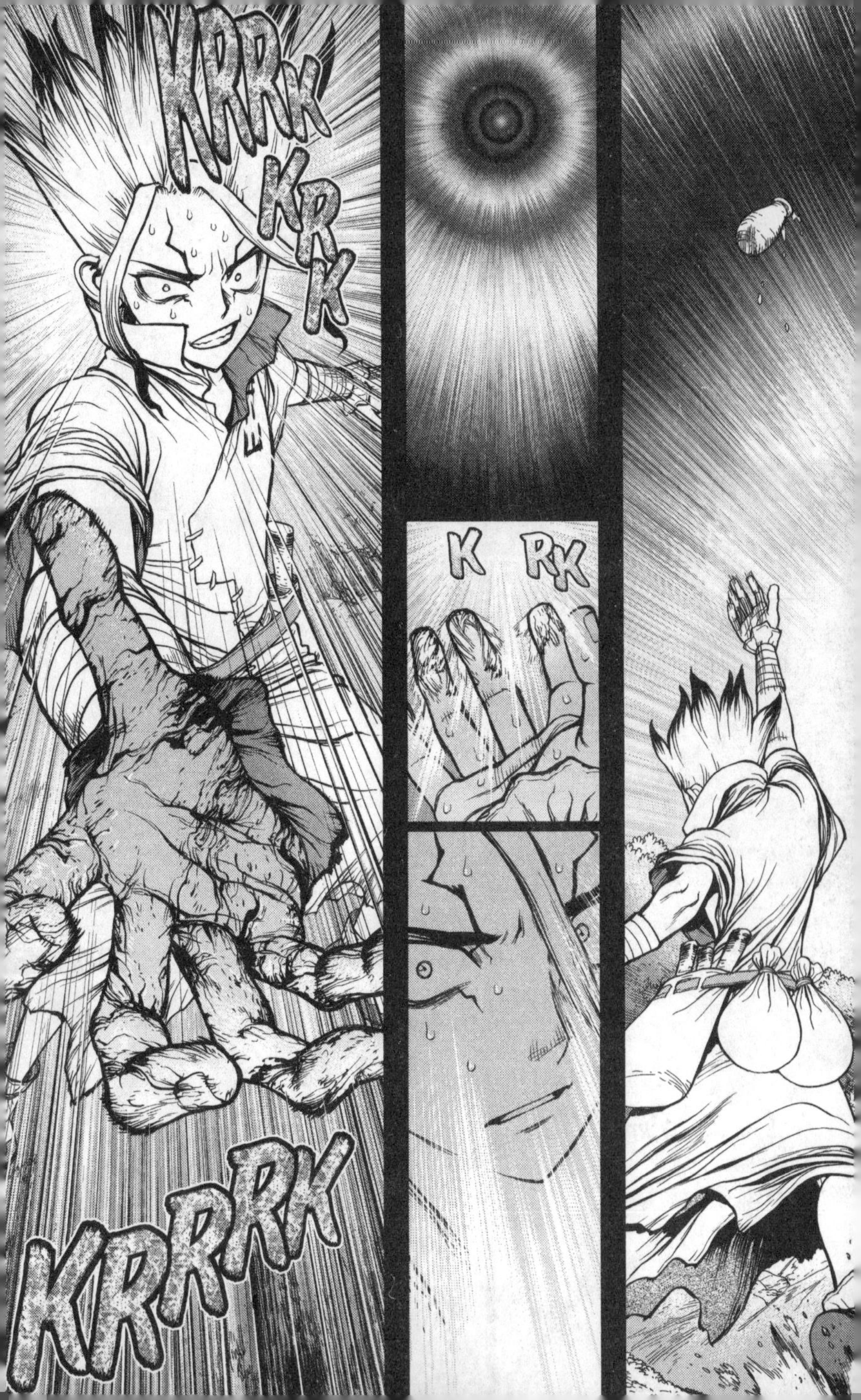
K RK
KRRK KRK
KRRRK

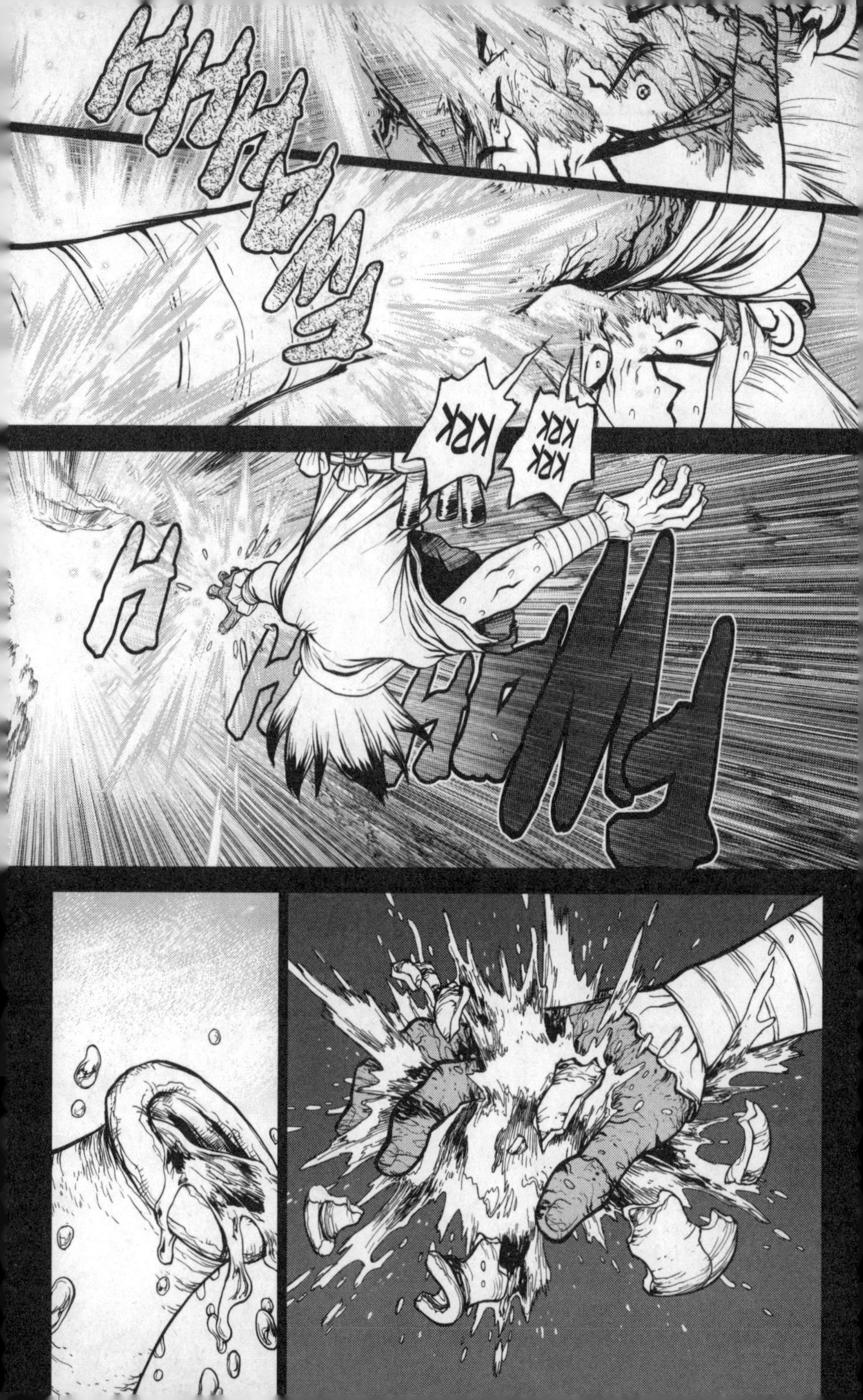
KRK KRK
KRK

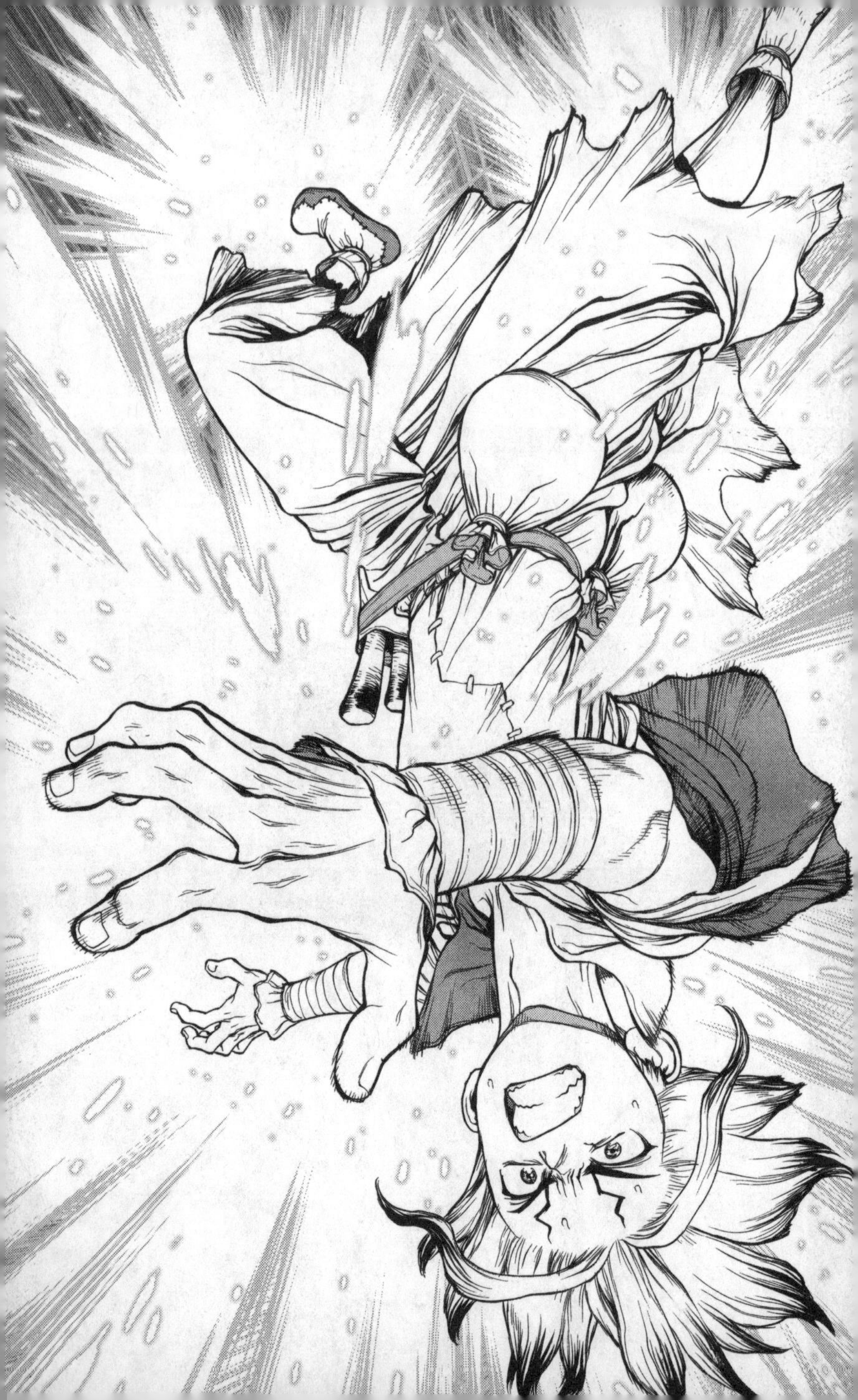

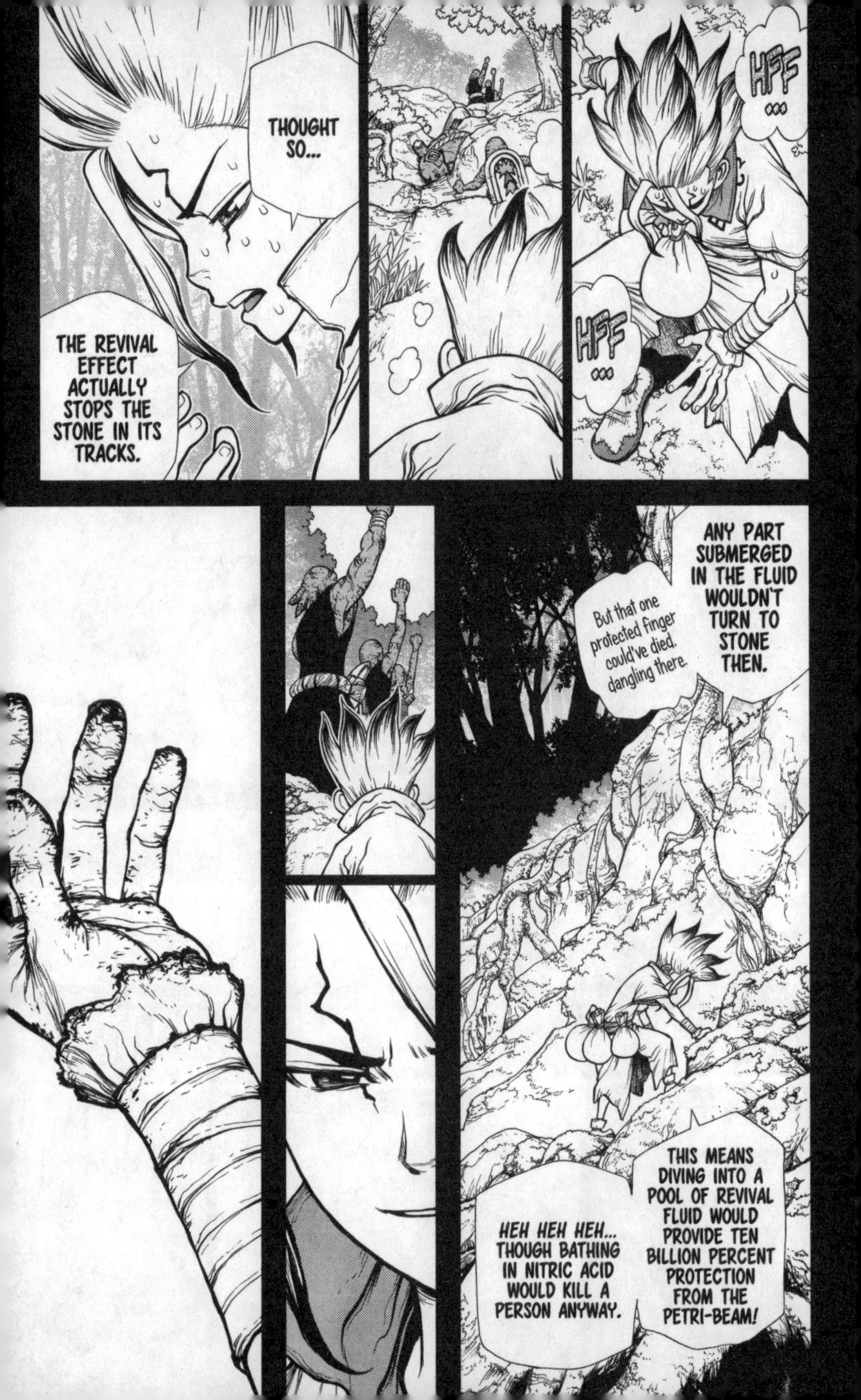
HFF...
HFF...
THOUGHT SO...
THE REVIVAL EFFECT ACTUALLY STOPS THE STONE IN ITS TRACKS.
ANY PART SUBMERGED IN THE FLUID WOULDN'T TURN TO STONE THEN.
But that one protected finger could've died, dangling there.
THIS MEANS DIVING INTO A POOL OF REVIVAL FLUID WOULD PROVIDE TEN BILLION PERCENT PROTECTION FROM THE PETRI-BEAM!
HEH HEH HEH... THOUGH BATHING IN NITRIC ACID WOULD KILL A PERSON ANYWAY.

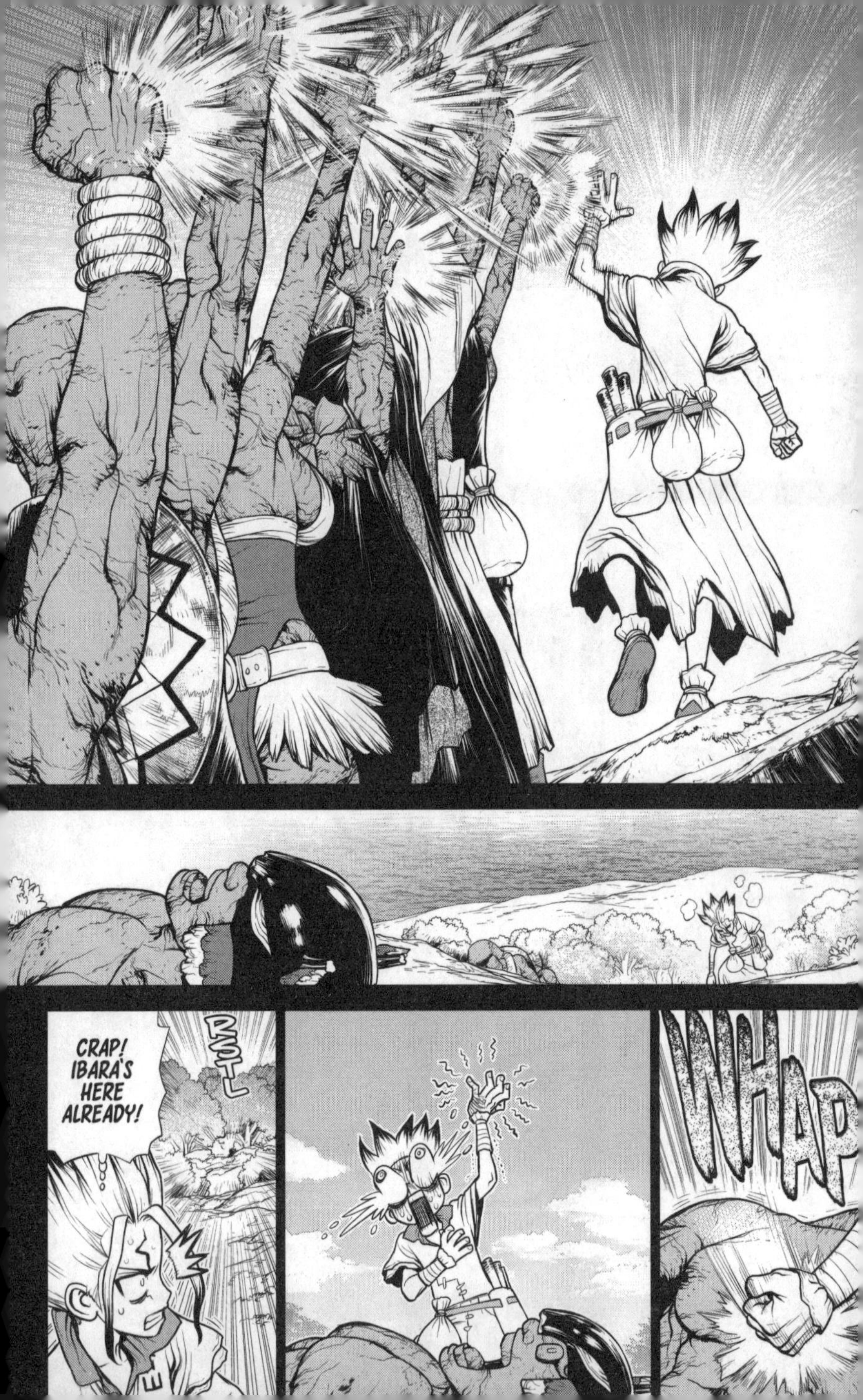
WHAP
RSTL
CRAP! IBARA'S HERE ALREADY!

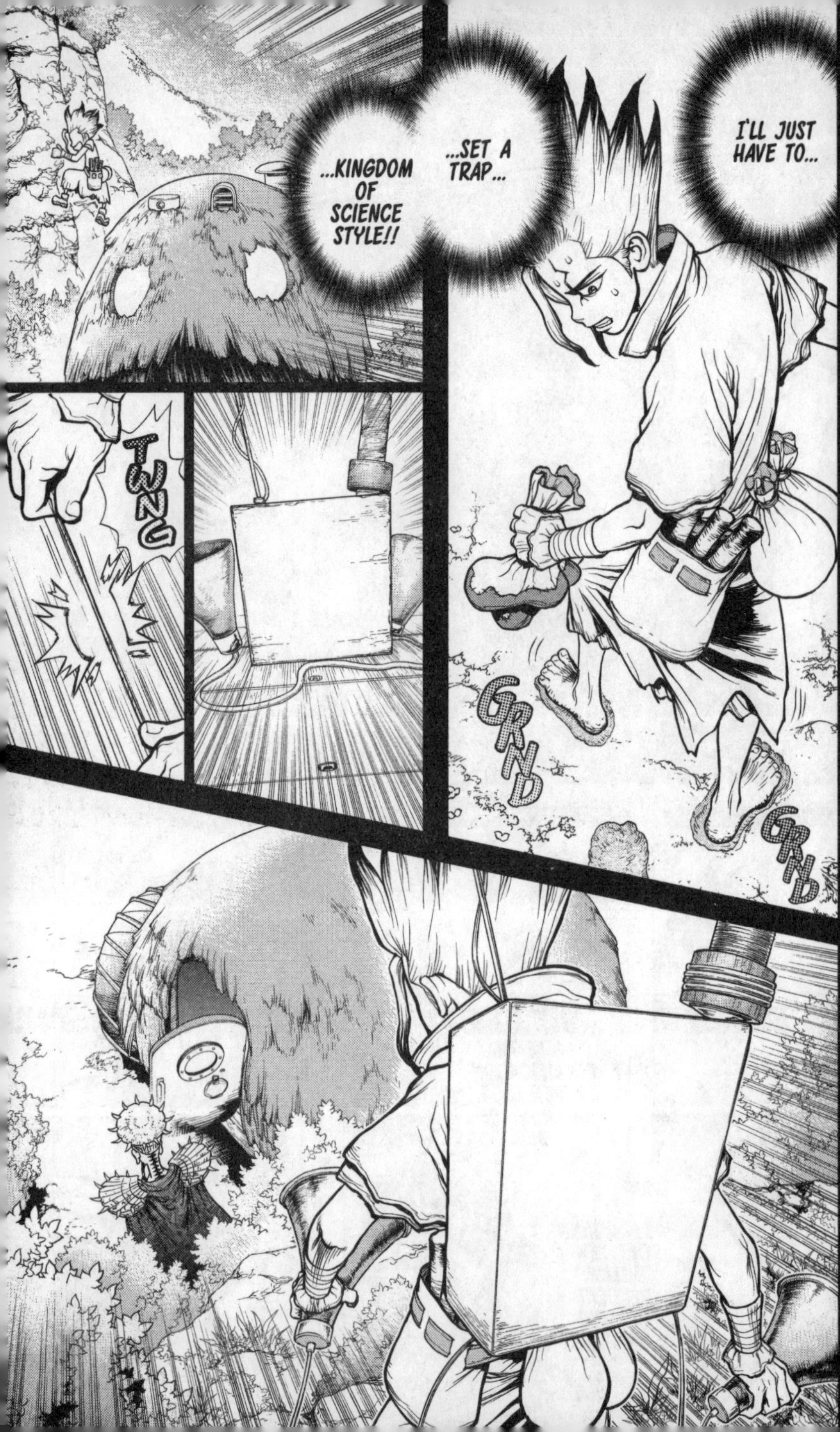
I'LL JUST HAVE TO...
...SET A TRAP...
...KINGDOM OF SCIENCE STYLE!!
GRND
GRND
TWNG

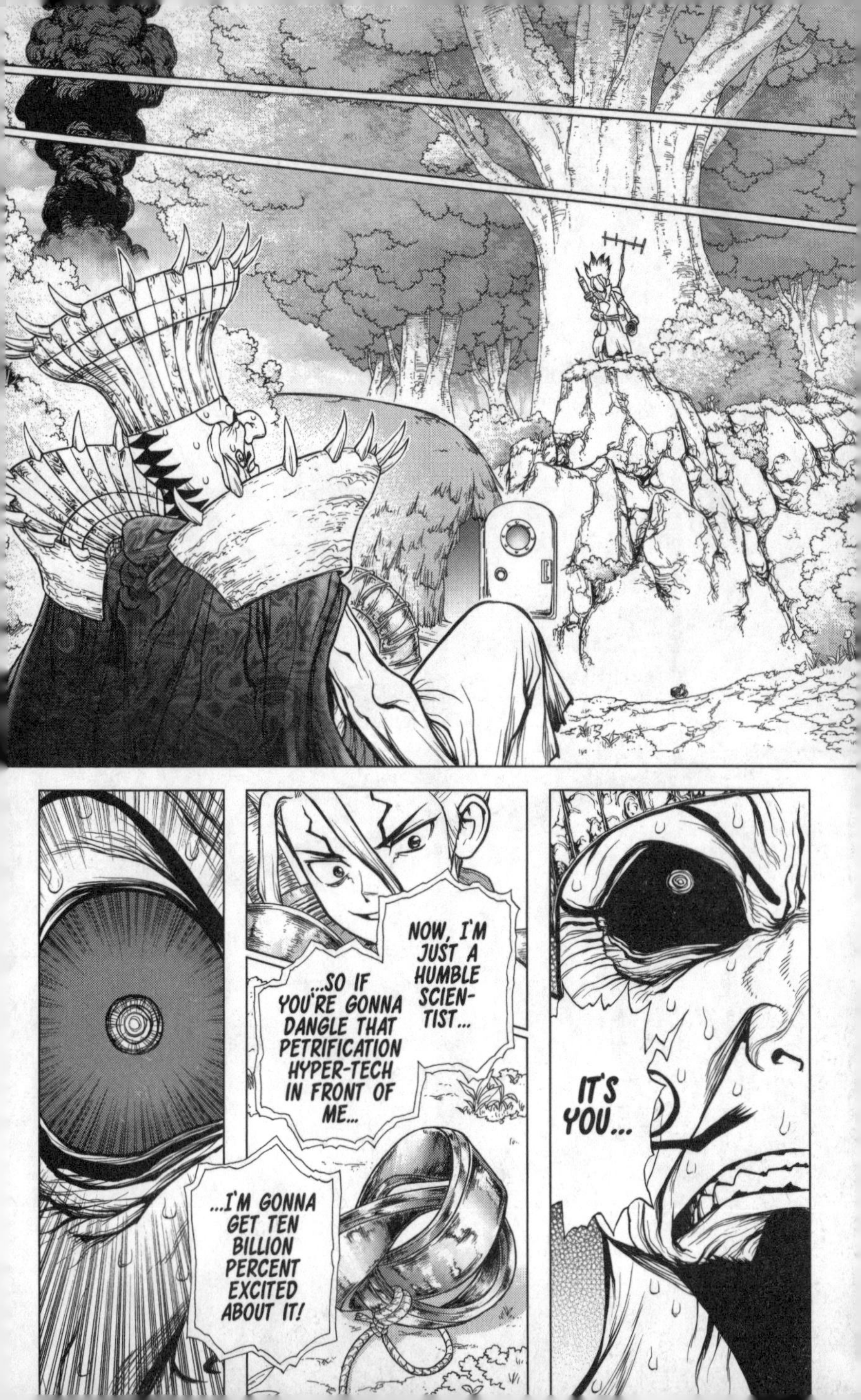
IT'S YOU...
NOW, I'M JUST A HUMBLE SCIEN-TIST...
...SO IF YOU'RE GONNA DANGLE THAT PETRIFICATION HYPER-TECH IN FRONT OF ME...
...I'M GONNA GET TEN BILLION PERCENT EXCITED ABOUT IT!

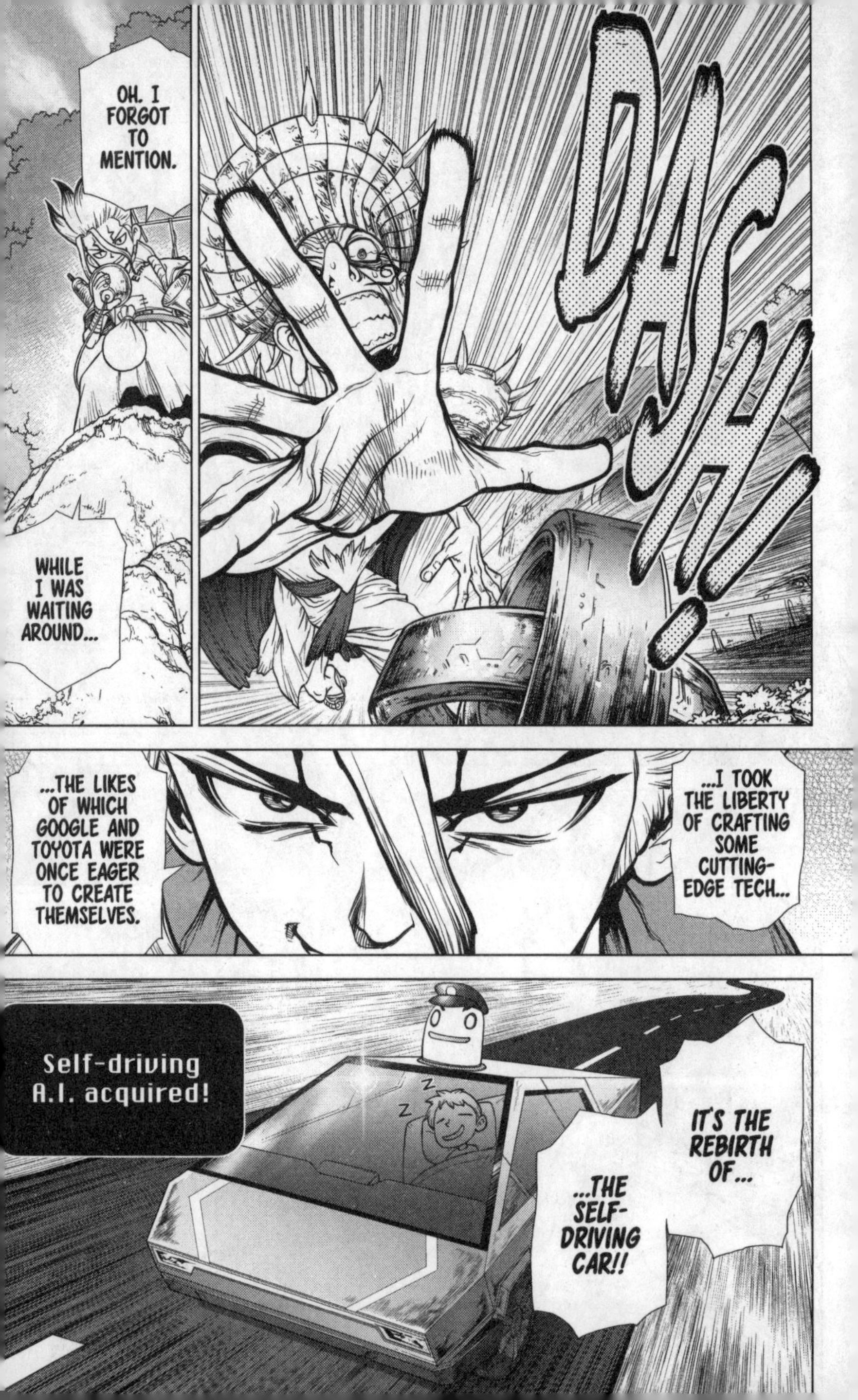
DASH!!
OH. I FORGOT TO MENTION.
WHILE I WAS WAITING AROUND...
...I TOOK THE LIBERTY OF CRAFTING SOME CUTTING-EDGE TECH...
...THE LIKES OF WHICH GOOGLE AND TOYOTA WERE ONCE EAGER TO CREATE THEMSELVES.
IT'S THE REBIRTH OF...
...THE SELF-DRIVING CAR!!
Self-driving A.I. acquired!

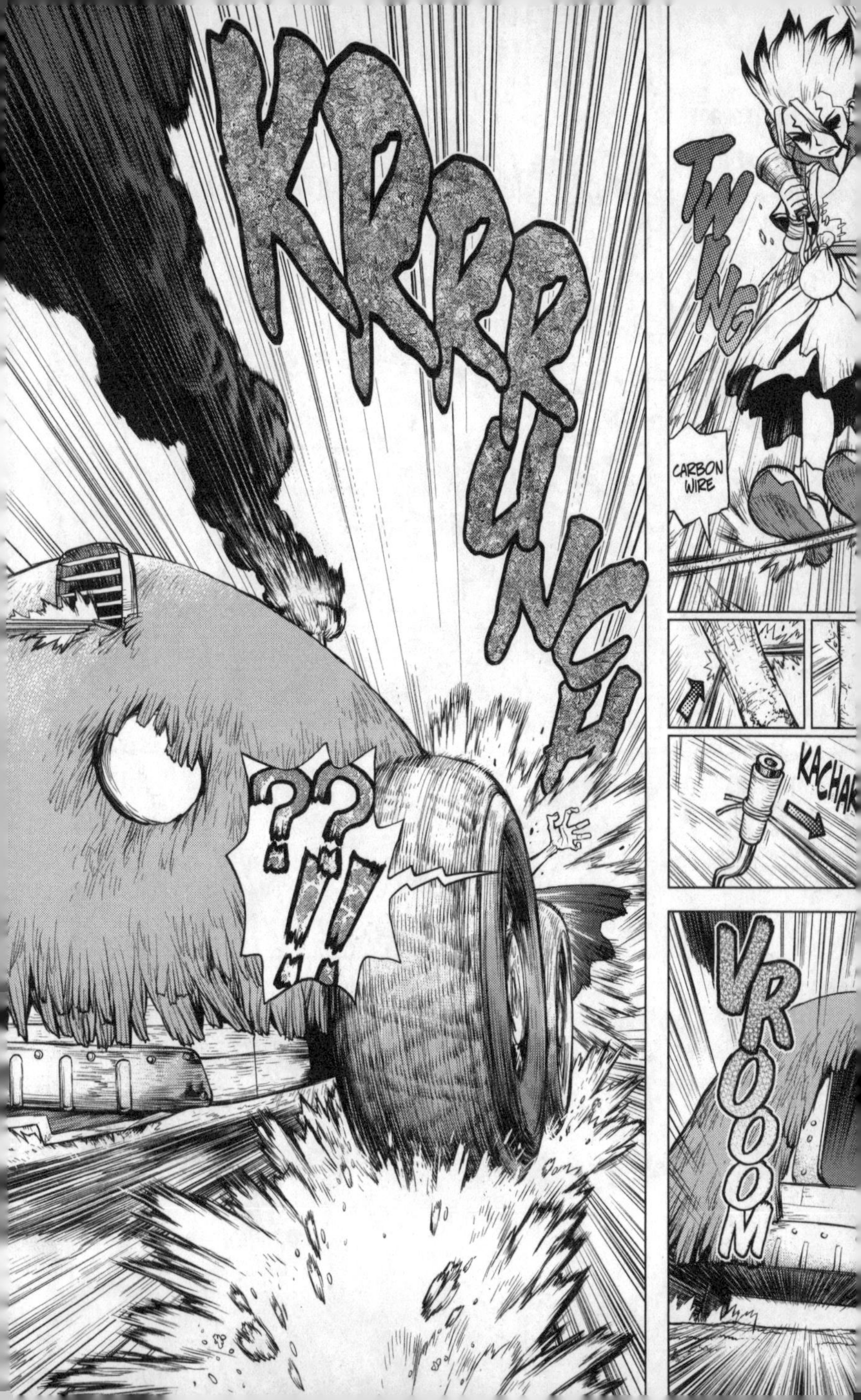
TWANG
CARBON WIRE
KACHAK
VROOOM
KRRRUNCH
??!!

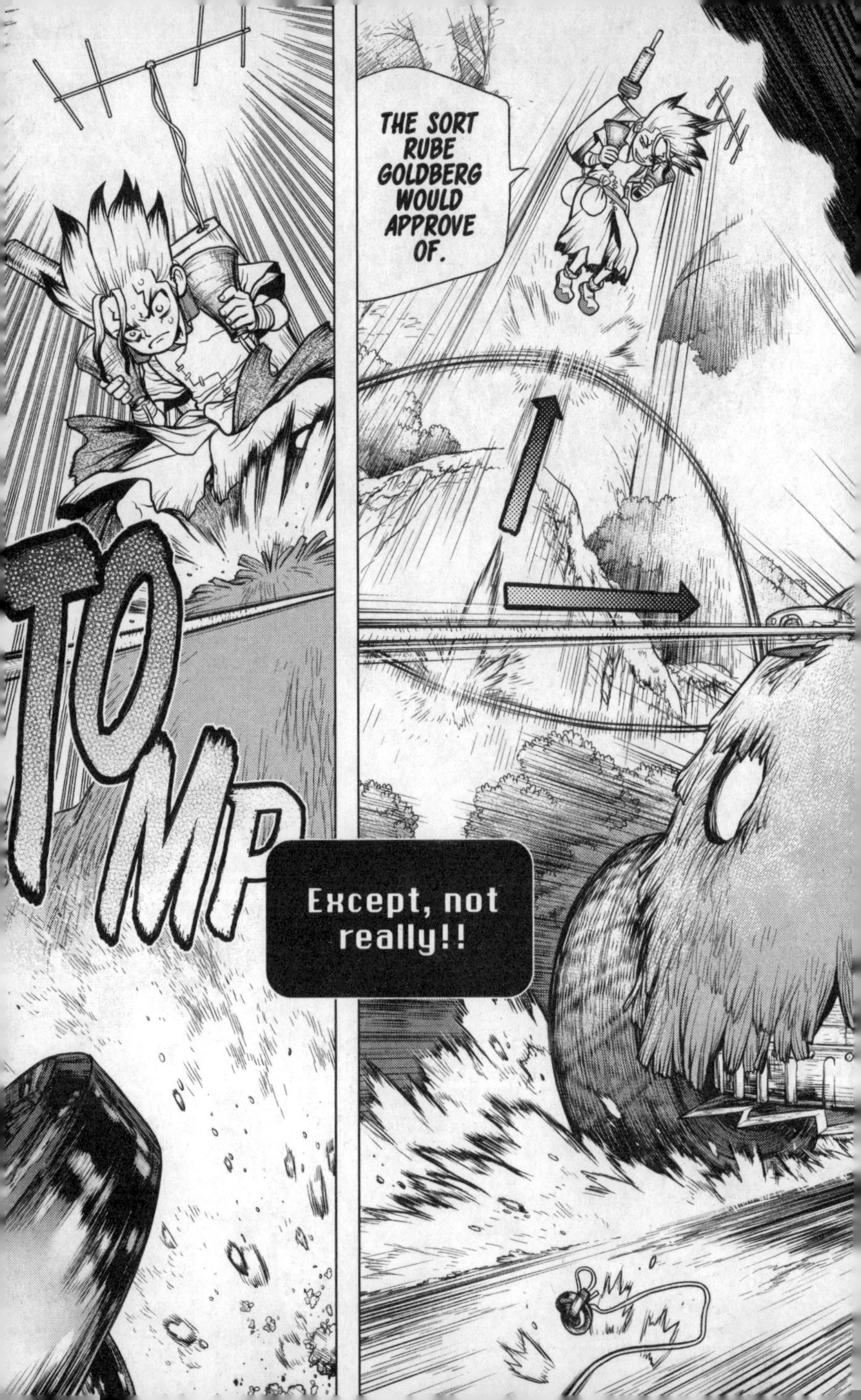
THE SORT RUBE GOLDBERG WOULD APPROVE OF.
Except, not really!!
TOMP

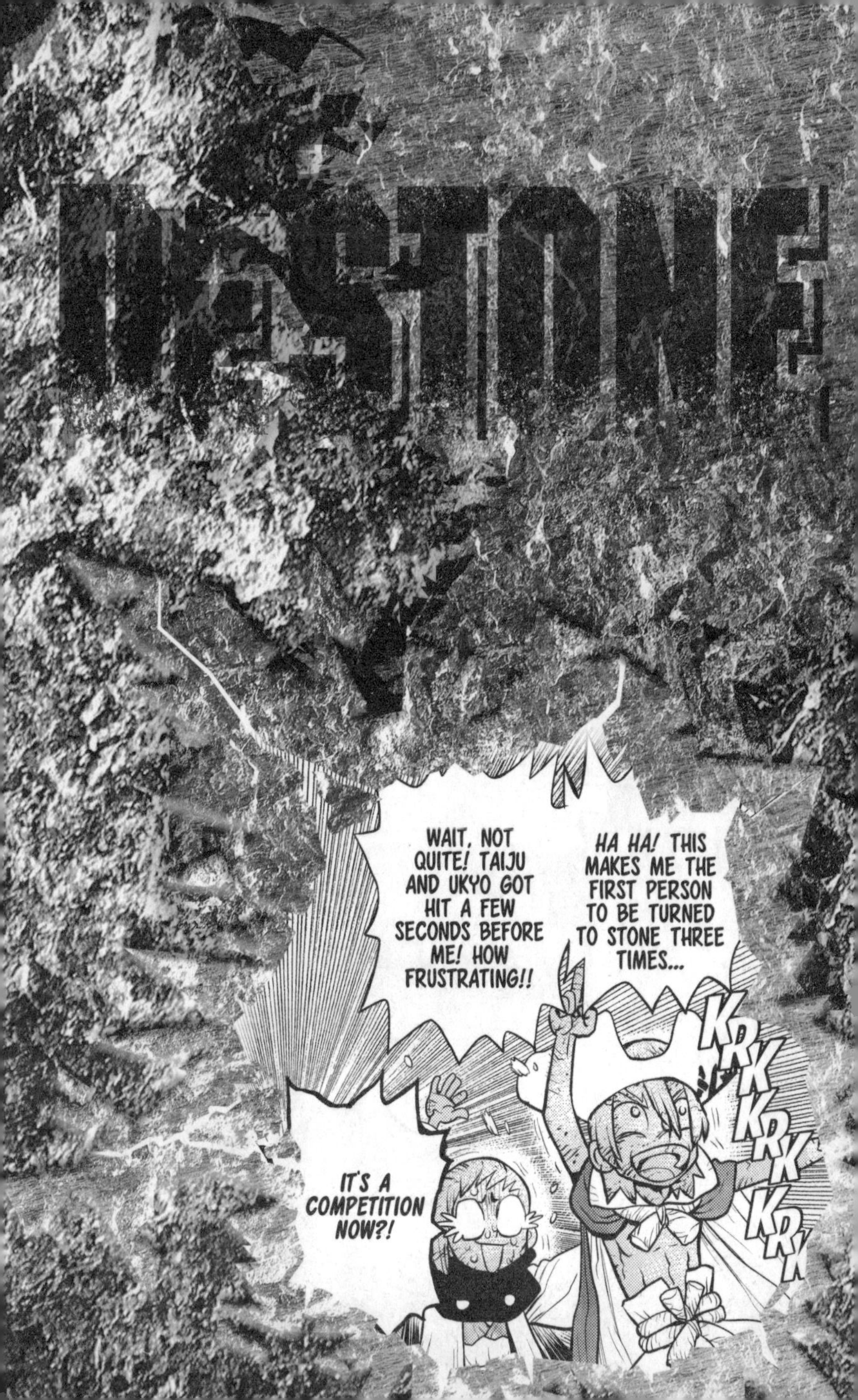
Dr.STONE
HA HA! THIS MAKES ME THE FIRST PERSON TO BE TURNED TO STONE THREE TIMES...
WAIT, NOT QUITE! TAIJU AND UKYO GOT HIT A FEW SECONDS BEFORE ME! HOW FRUSTRATING!!
KRK KRK KRK KRK
IT'S A COMPETITION NOW?!

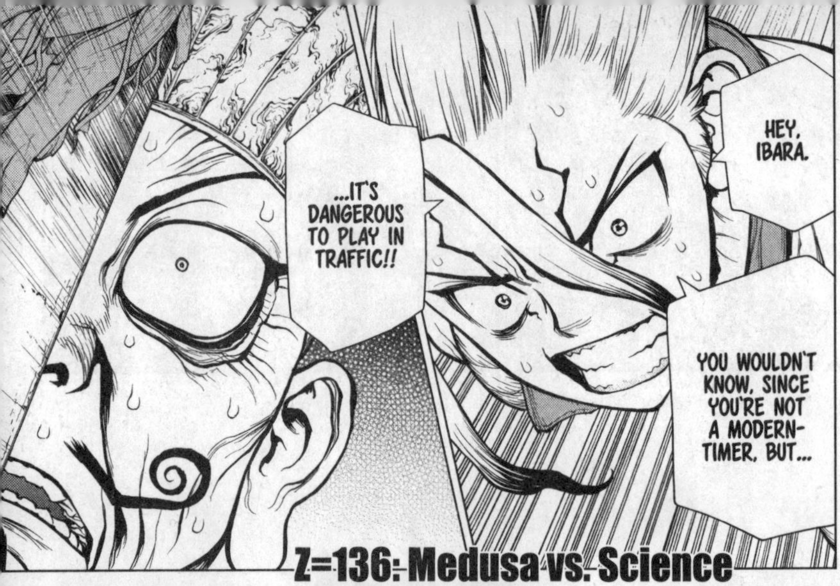
HEY, IBARA.
YOU WOULDN'T KNOW, SINCE YOU'RE NOT A MODERN-TIMER, BUT...
...IT'S DANGEROUS TO PLAY IN TRAFFIC!!

Z=136: Medusa vs. Science

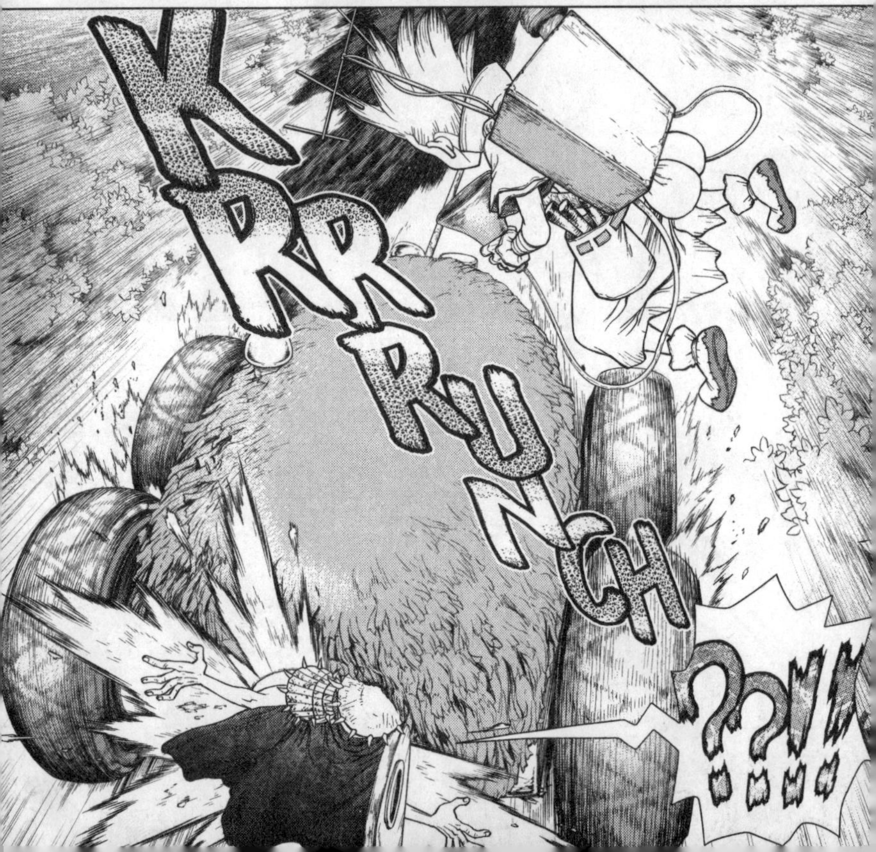
KRRRUNCH
??!!

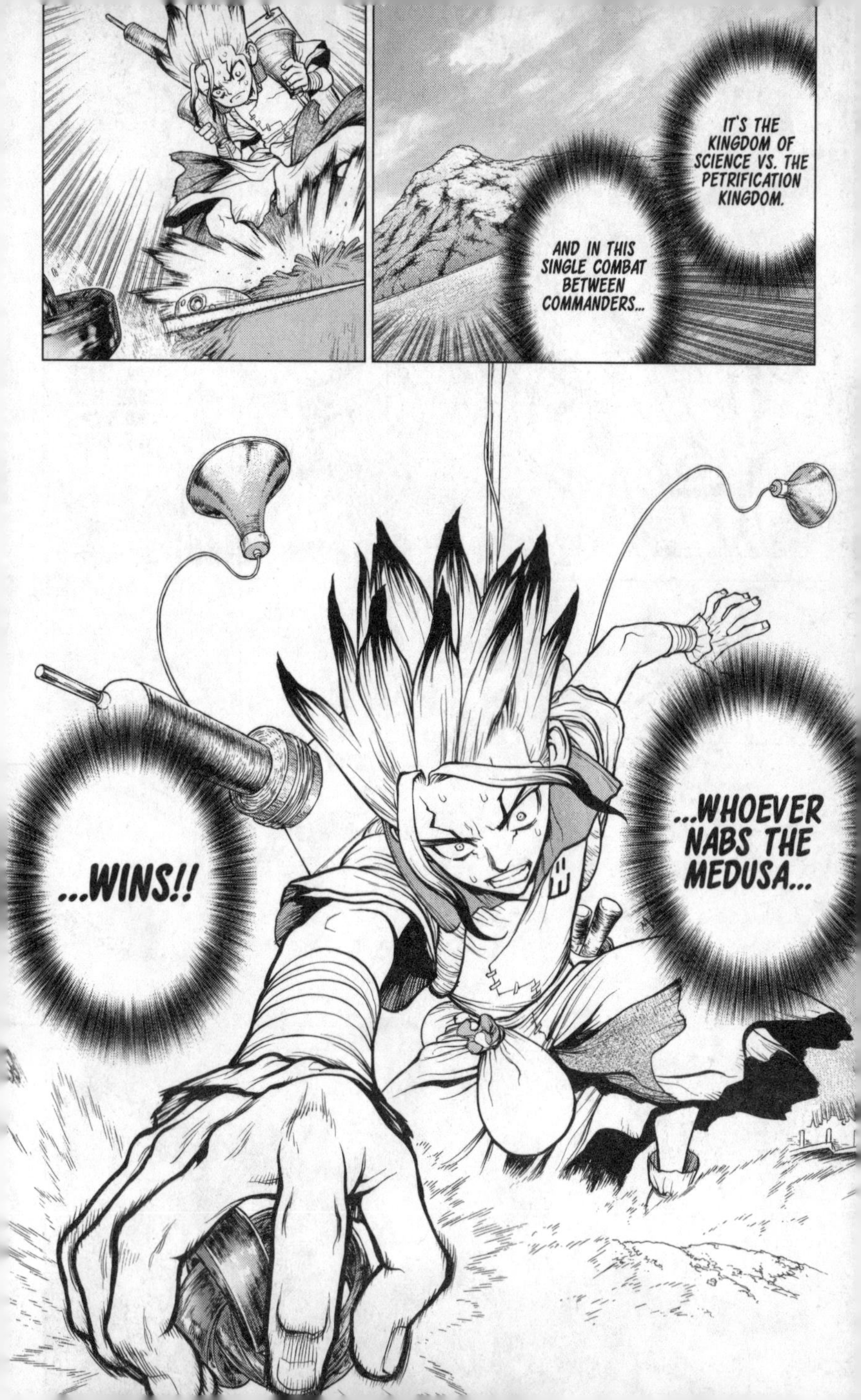
IT'S THE KINGDOM OF SCIENCE VS. THE PETRIFICATION KINGDOM.
AND IN THIS SINGLE COMBAT BETWEEN COMMANDERS...
...WHOEVER NABS THE MEDUSA...
...WINS!!

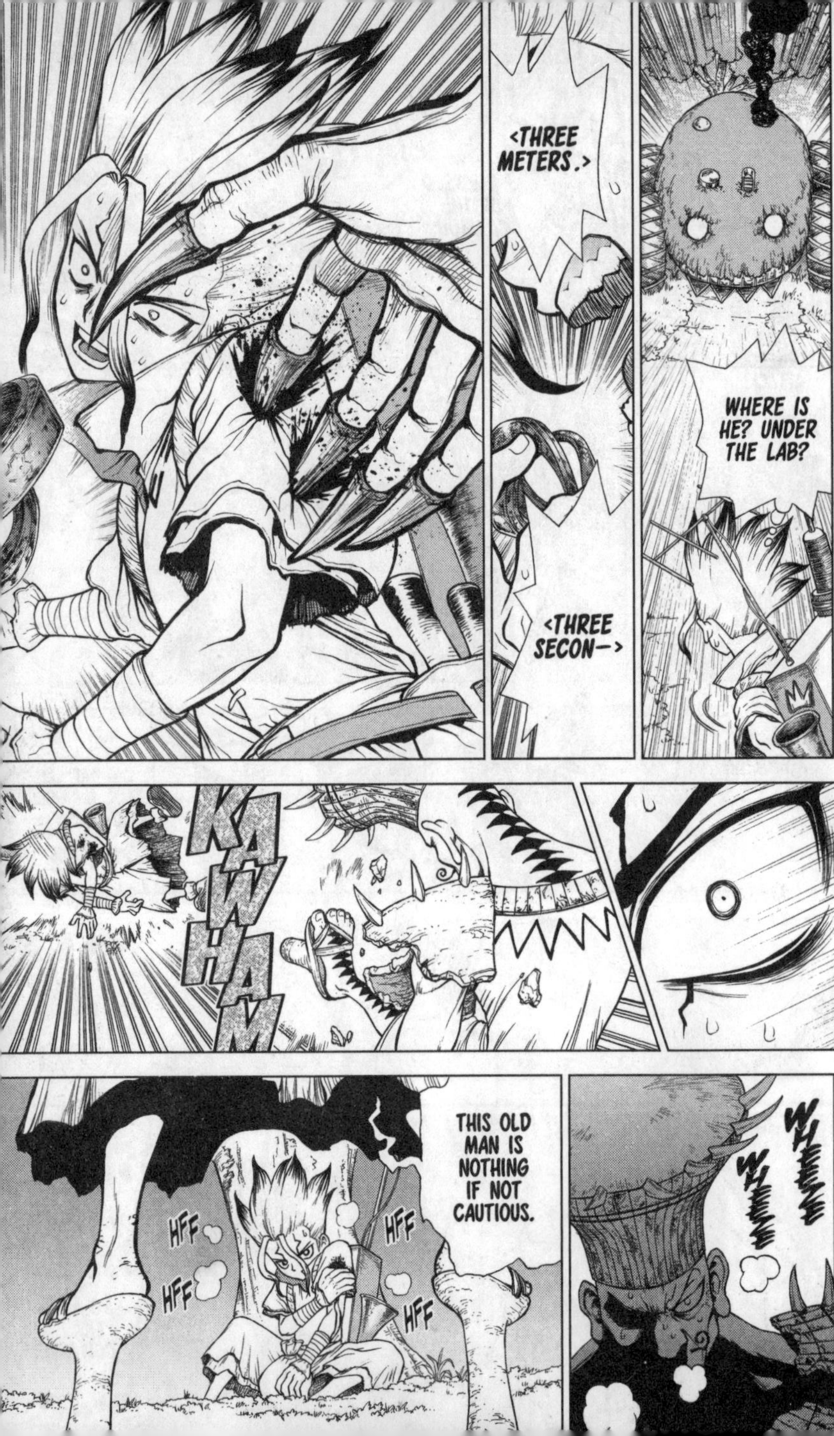
WHERE IS HE? UNDER THE LAB?
<THREE METERS.>
<THREE SECON—>
KAWHAM
WHEEZE
WHEEZE
THIS OLD MAN IS NOTHING IF NOT CAUTIOUS.
HFF
HFF
HFF
HFF

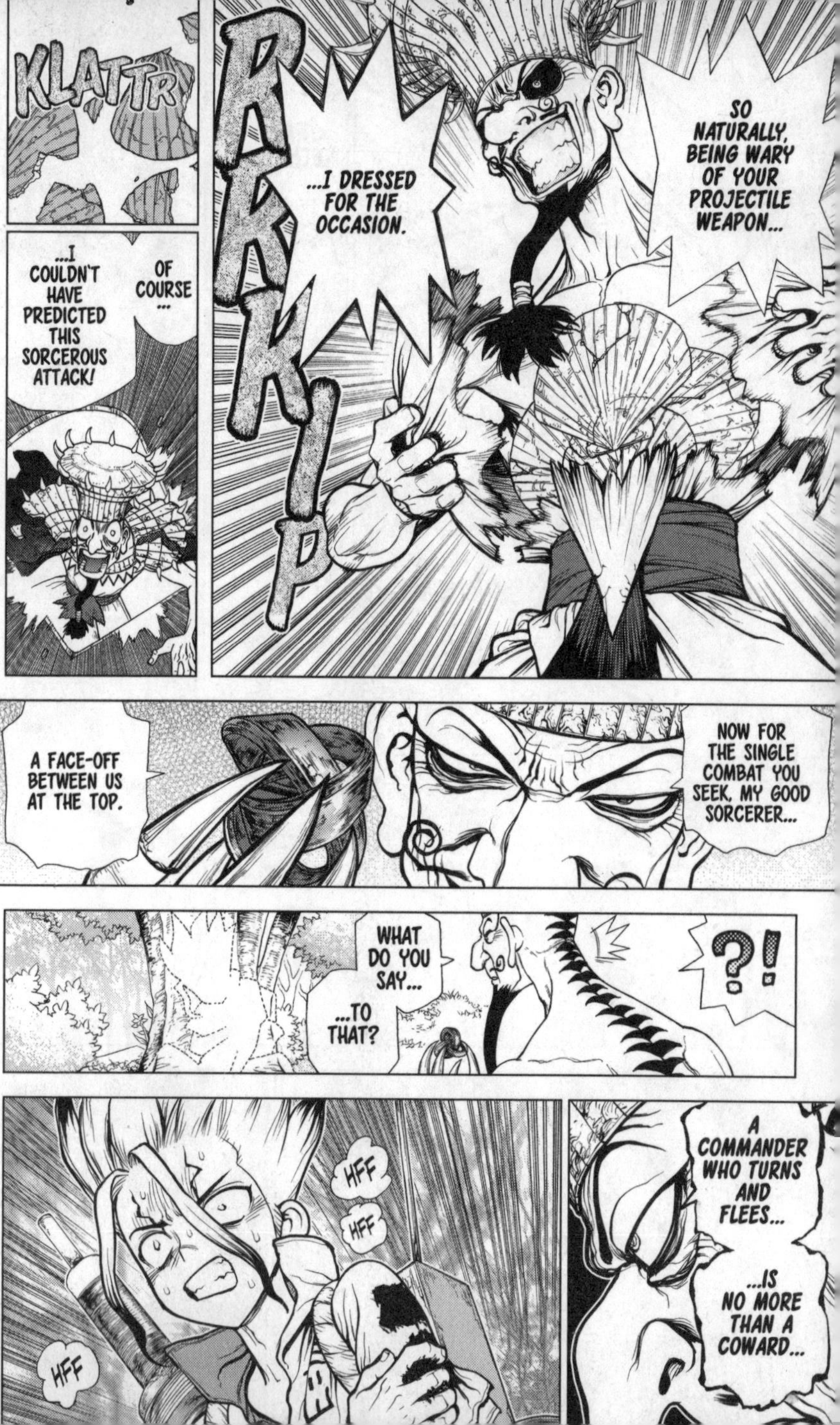
SO NATURALLY, BEING WARY OF YOUR PROJECTILE WEAPON...
...I DRESSED FOR THE OCCASION.
RRRIP
KLATTR
OF COURSE...
...I COULDN'T HAVE PREDICTED THIS SORCEROUS ATTACK!
NOW FOR THE SINGLE COMBAT YOU SEEK, MY GOOD SORCERER...
A FACE-OFF BETWEEN US AT THE TOP.
?!
WHAT DO YOU SAY...
...TO THAT?
A COMMANDER WHO TURNS AND FLEES...
...IS NO MORE THAN A COWARD...
HFF
HFF
HFF

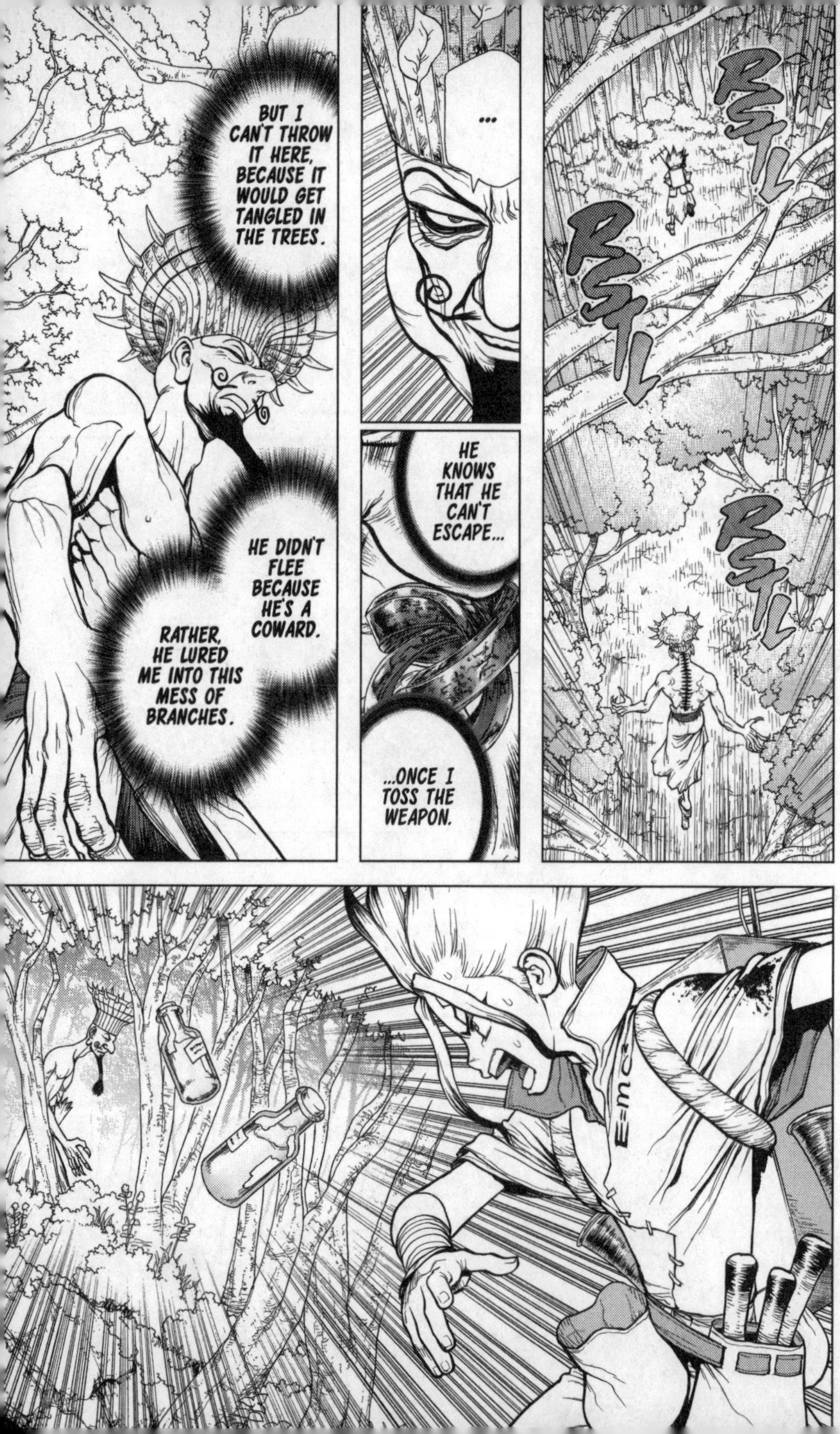
RSTL
RSTL
RSTL
RSTL
...
HE KNOWS THAT HE CAN'T ESCAPE...
...ONCE I TOSS THE WEAPON.
BUT I CAN'T THROW IT HERE, BECAUSE IT WOULD GET TANGLED IN THE TREES.
HE DIDN'T FLEE BECAUSE HE'S A COWARD.
RATHER, HE LURED ME INTO THIS MESS OF BRANCHES.
E=mc2

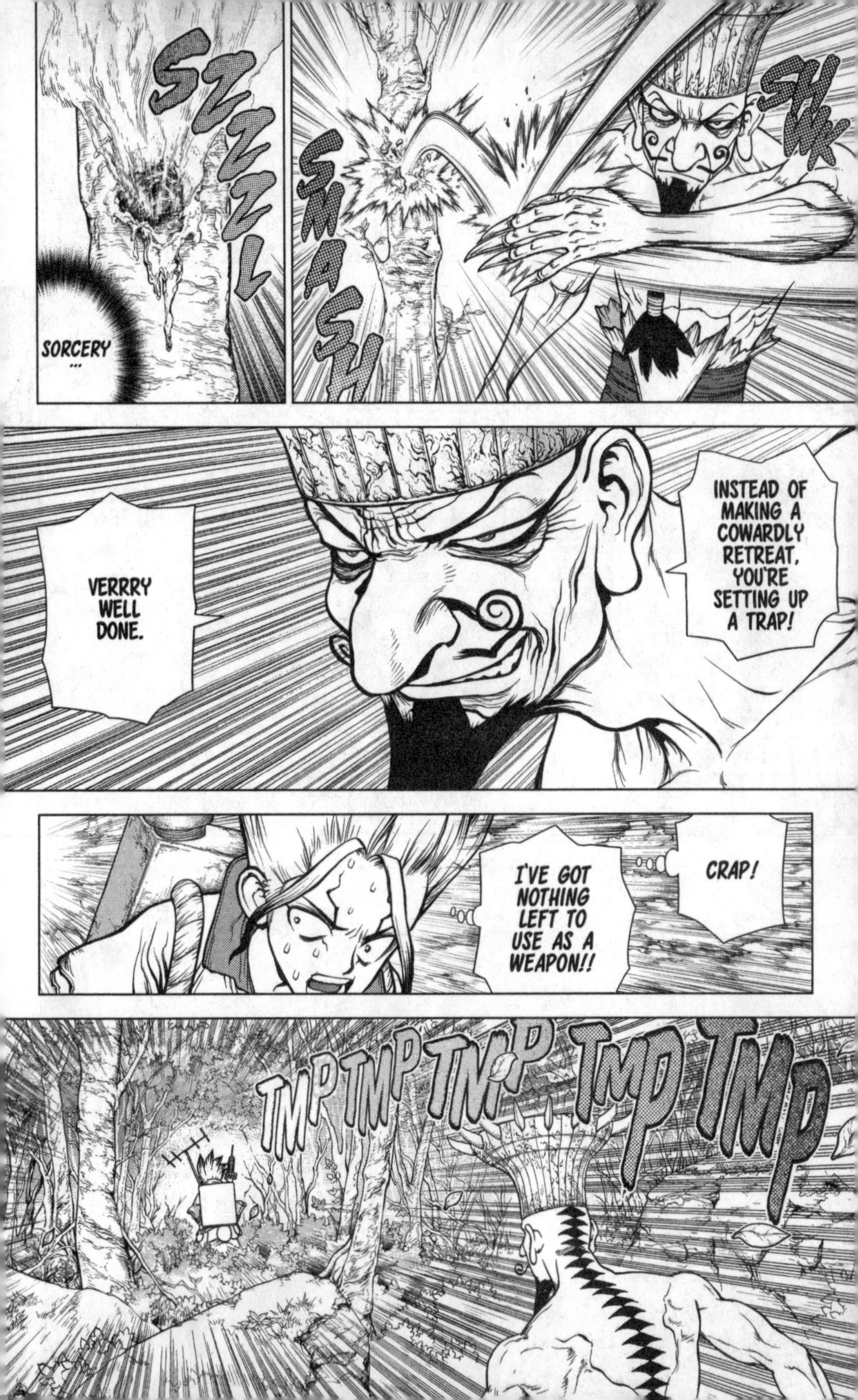
SHUK
SMASH
SIZZZLL
SORCERY ...
INSTEAD OF MAKING A COWARDLY RETREAT, YOU'RE SETTING UP A TRAP!
VERRRY WELL DONE.
CRAP!
I'VE GOT NOTHING LEFT TO USE AS A WEAPON!!
TMP TMP TMP TMP TMP

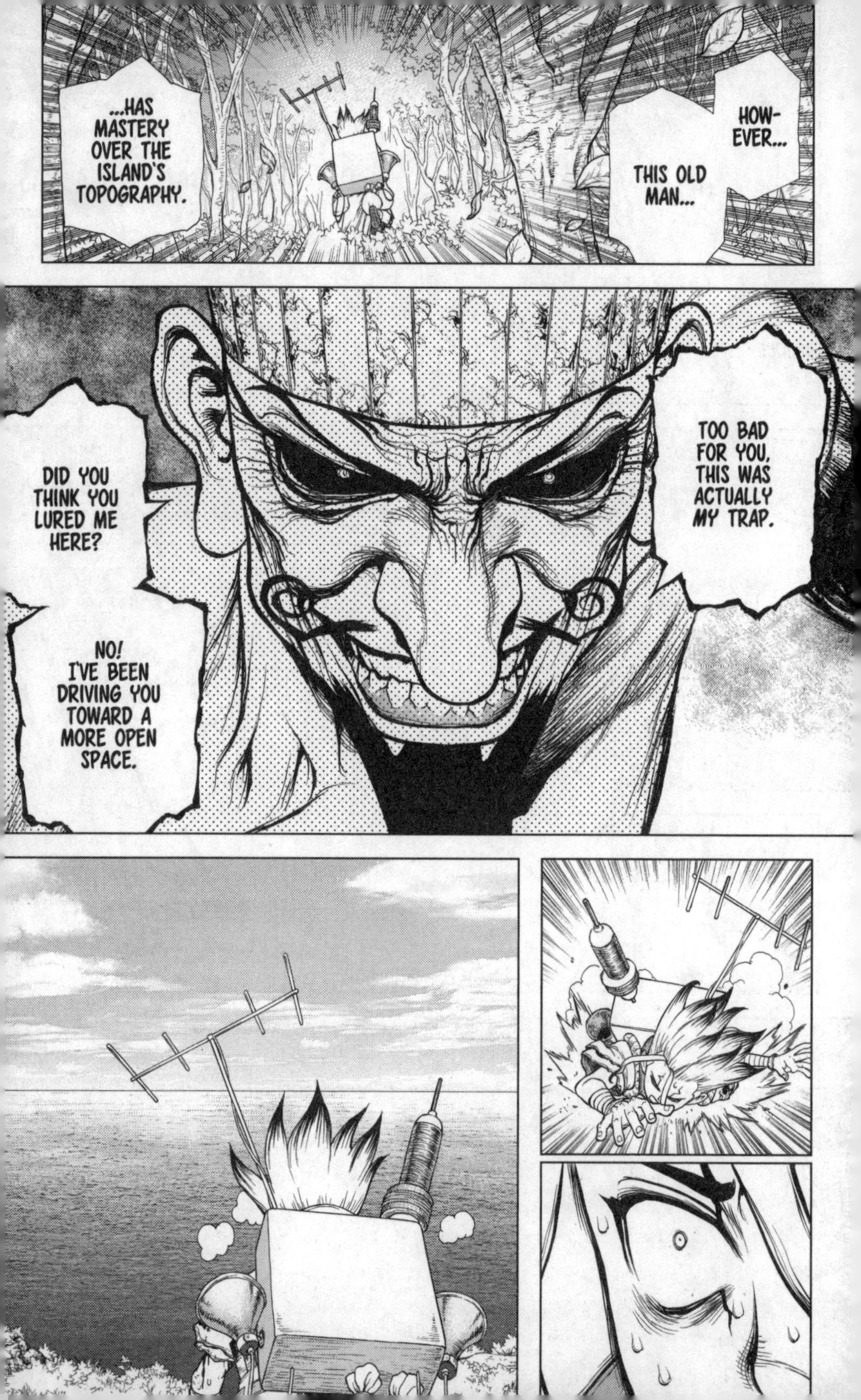
HOW-EVER...
THIS OLD MAN...
...HAS MASTERY OVER THE ISLAND'S TOPOGRAPHY.
TOO BAD FOR YOU, THIS WAS ACTUALLY MY TRAP.
DID YOU THINK YOU LURED ME HERE?
NO! I'VE BEEN DRIVING YOU TOWARD A MORE OPEN SPACE.

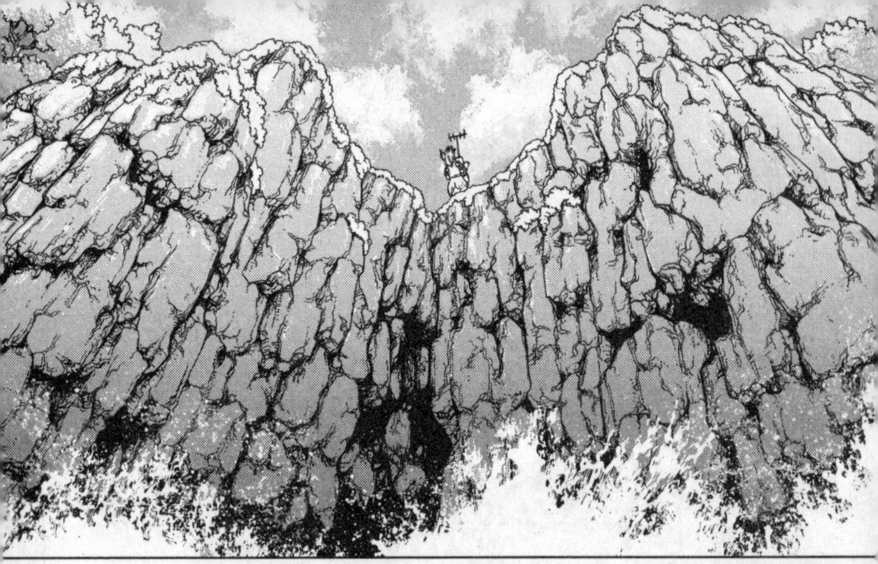
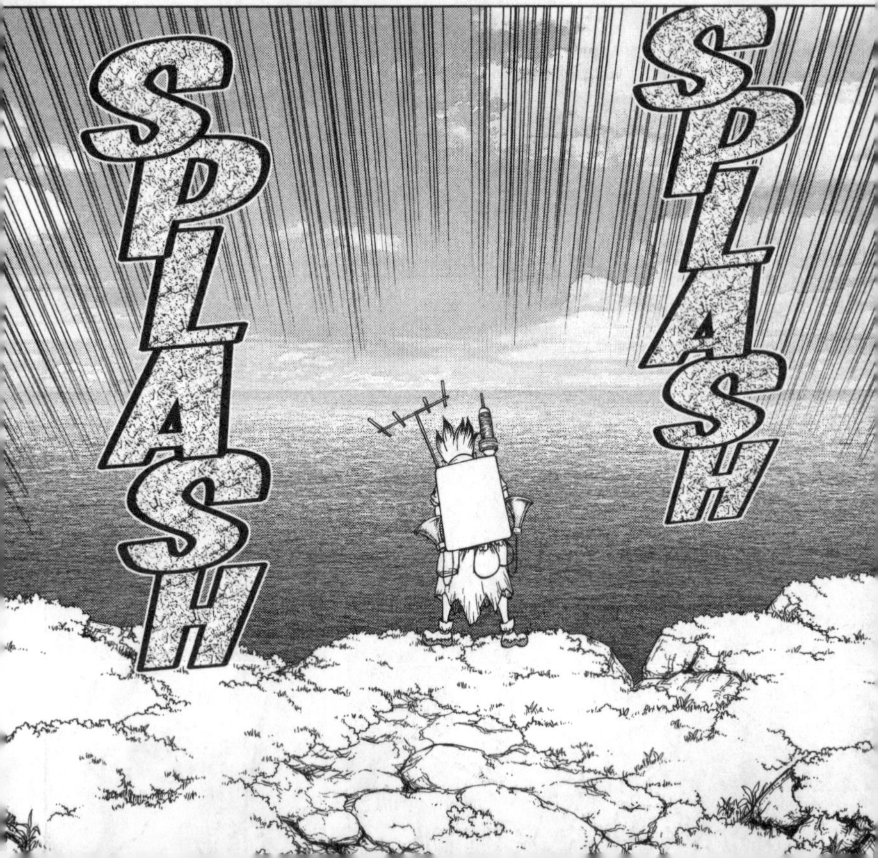
SPLASH
SPLASH

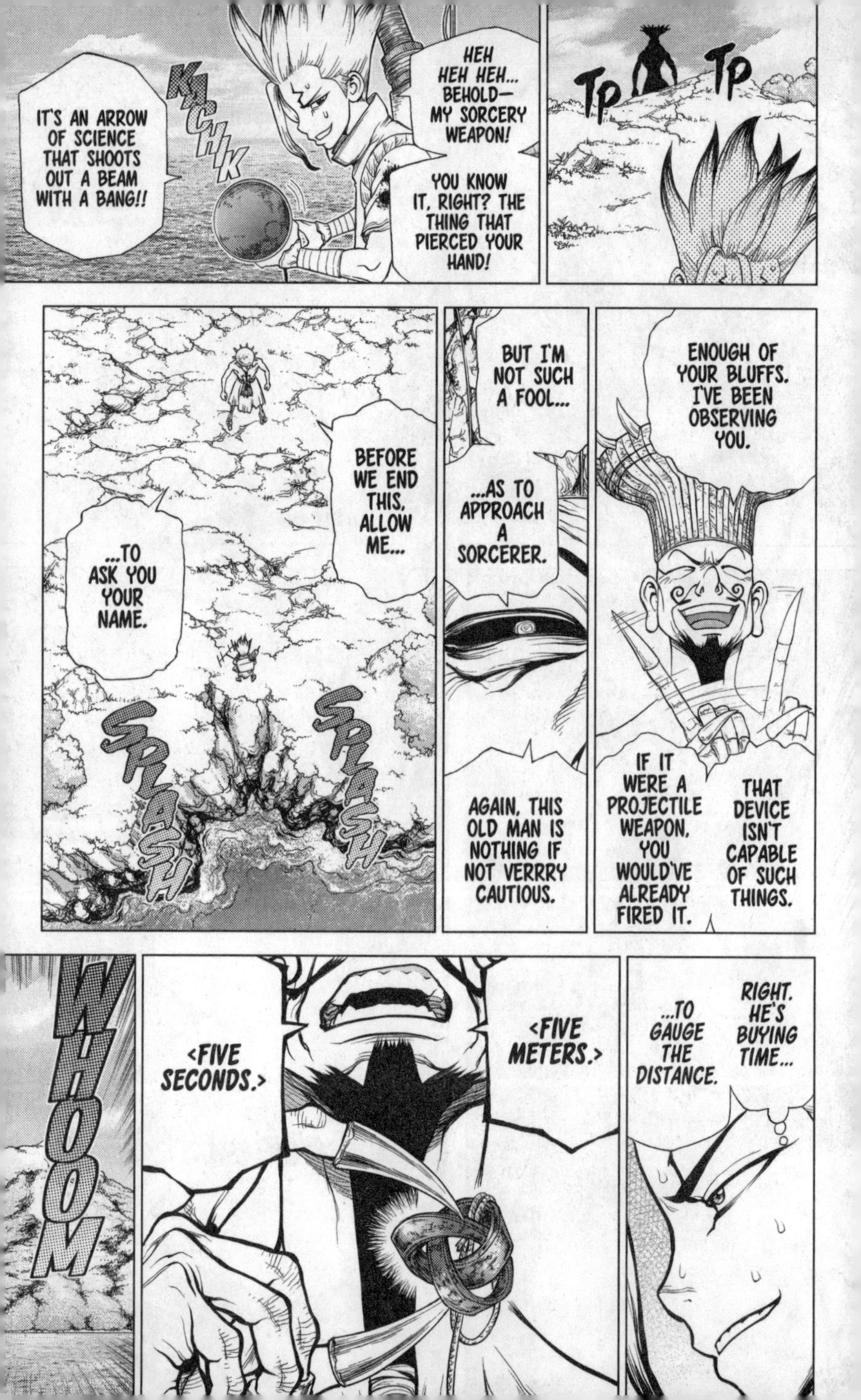
Tp Tp
HEH HEH HEH... BEHOLD— MY SORCERY WEAPON!
YOU KNOW IT, RIGHT? THE THING THAT PIERCED YOUR HAND!
KCHIK
IT'S AN ARROW OF SCIENCE THAT SHOOTS OUT A BEAM WITH A BANG!!
ENOUGH OF YOUR BLUFFS. I'VE BEEN OBSERVING YOU.
IF IT WERE A PROJECTILE WEAPON, YOU WOULD'VE ALREADY FIRED IT.
THAT DEVICE ISN'T CAPABLE OF SUCH THINGS.
BUT I'M NOT SUCH A FOOL...
...AS TO APPROACH A SORCERER.
AGAIN, THIS OLD MAN IS NOTHING IF NOT VERRRY CAUTIOUS.
BEFORE WE END THIS, ALLOW ME...
...TO ASK YOU YOUR NAME.
SPLASH
SPLASH
RIGHT. HE'S BUYING TIME...
...TO GAUGE THE DISTANCE.
<FIVE METERS.>
<FIVE SECONDS.>
WHOOM

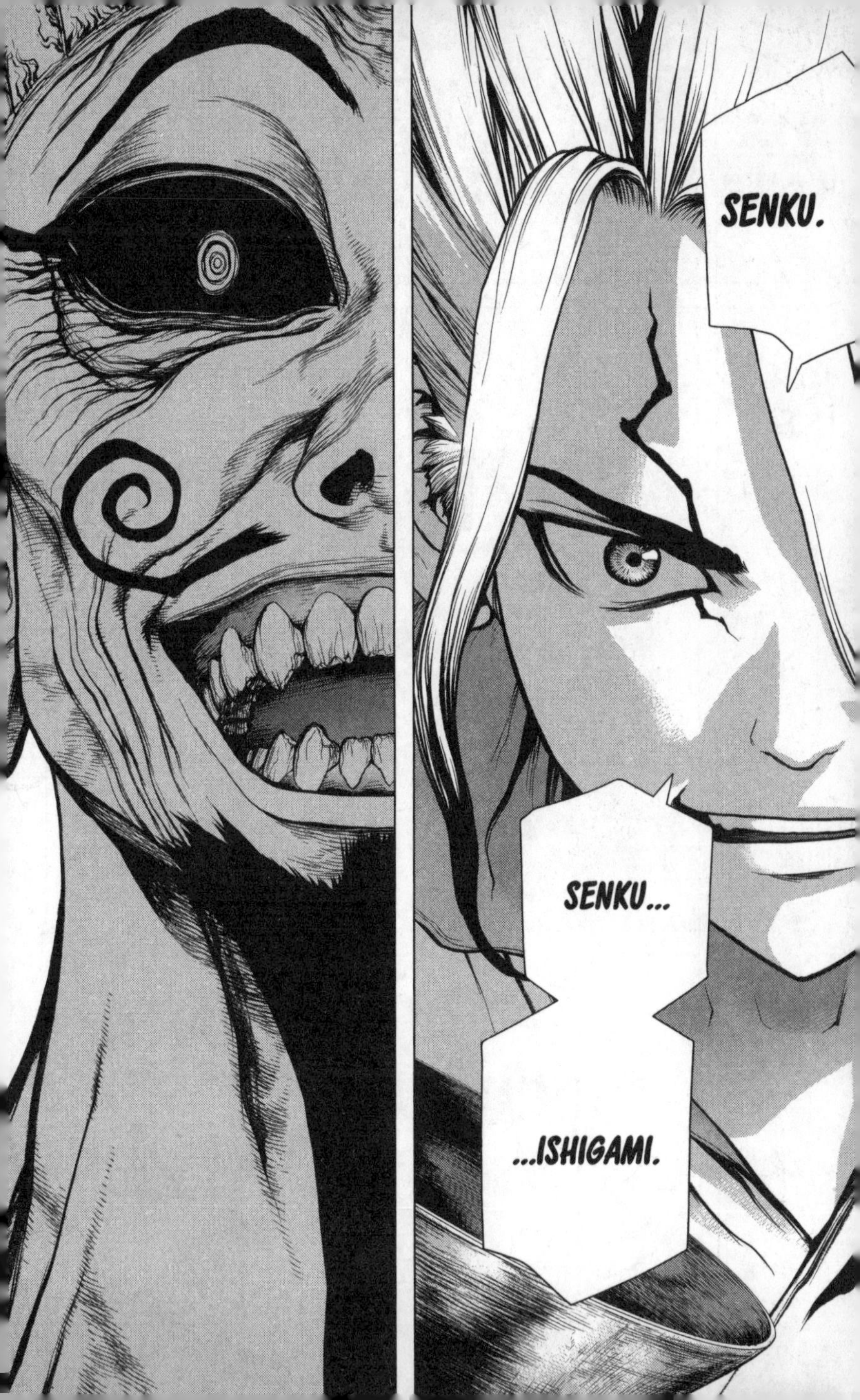
SENKU.
SENKU...
...ISHIGAMI.

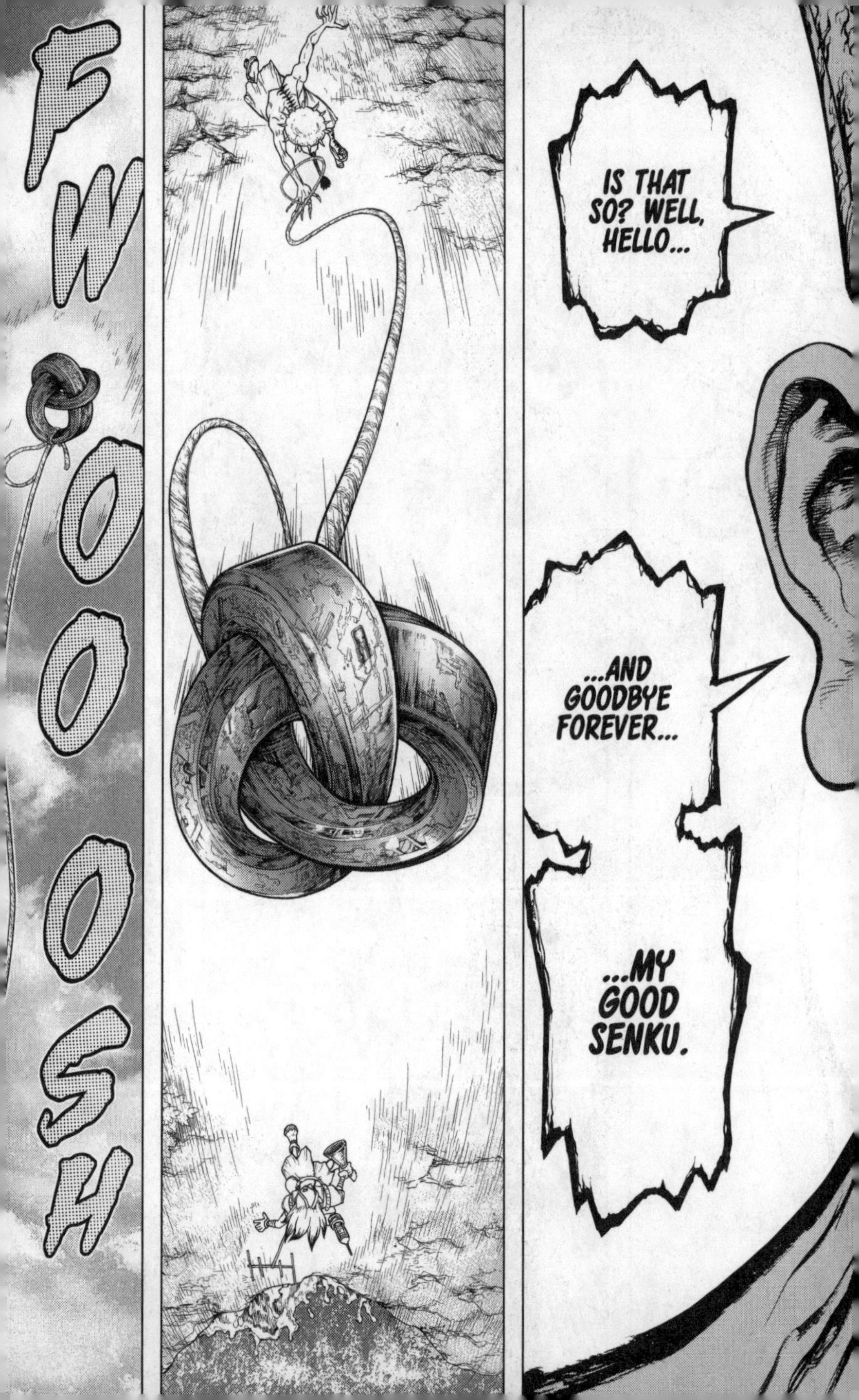
IS THAT SO? WELL, HELLO...
...AND GOODBYE FOREVER...
...MY GOOD SENKU.
FWOOOSH

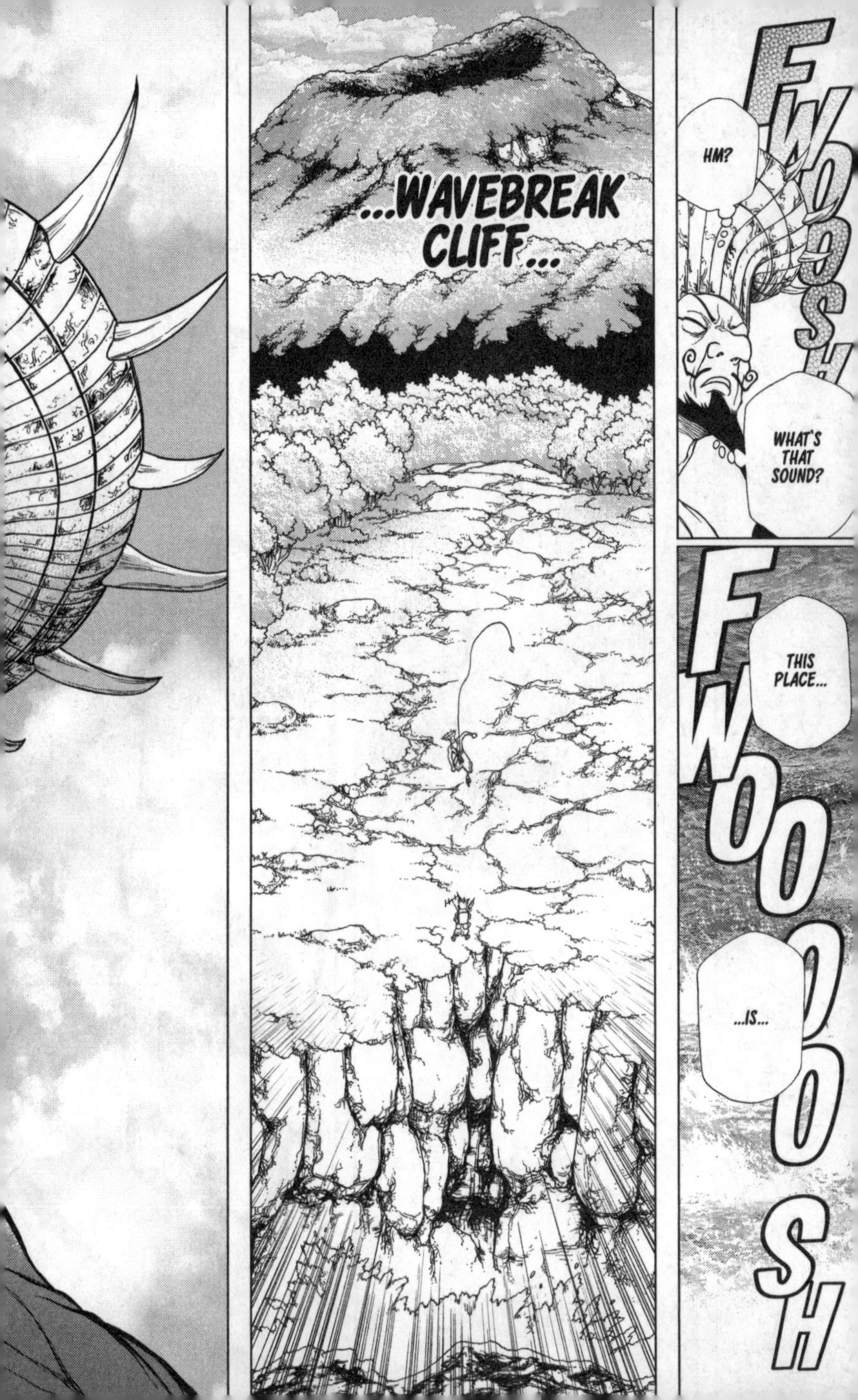
FWOOSH
HM?
WHAT'S THAT SOUND?
FWOOOOOSH
THIS PLACE...
...IS...
...WAVEBREAK CLIFF...

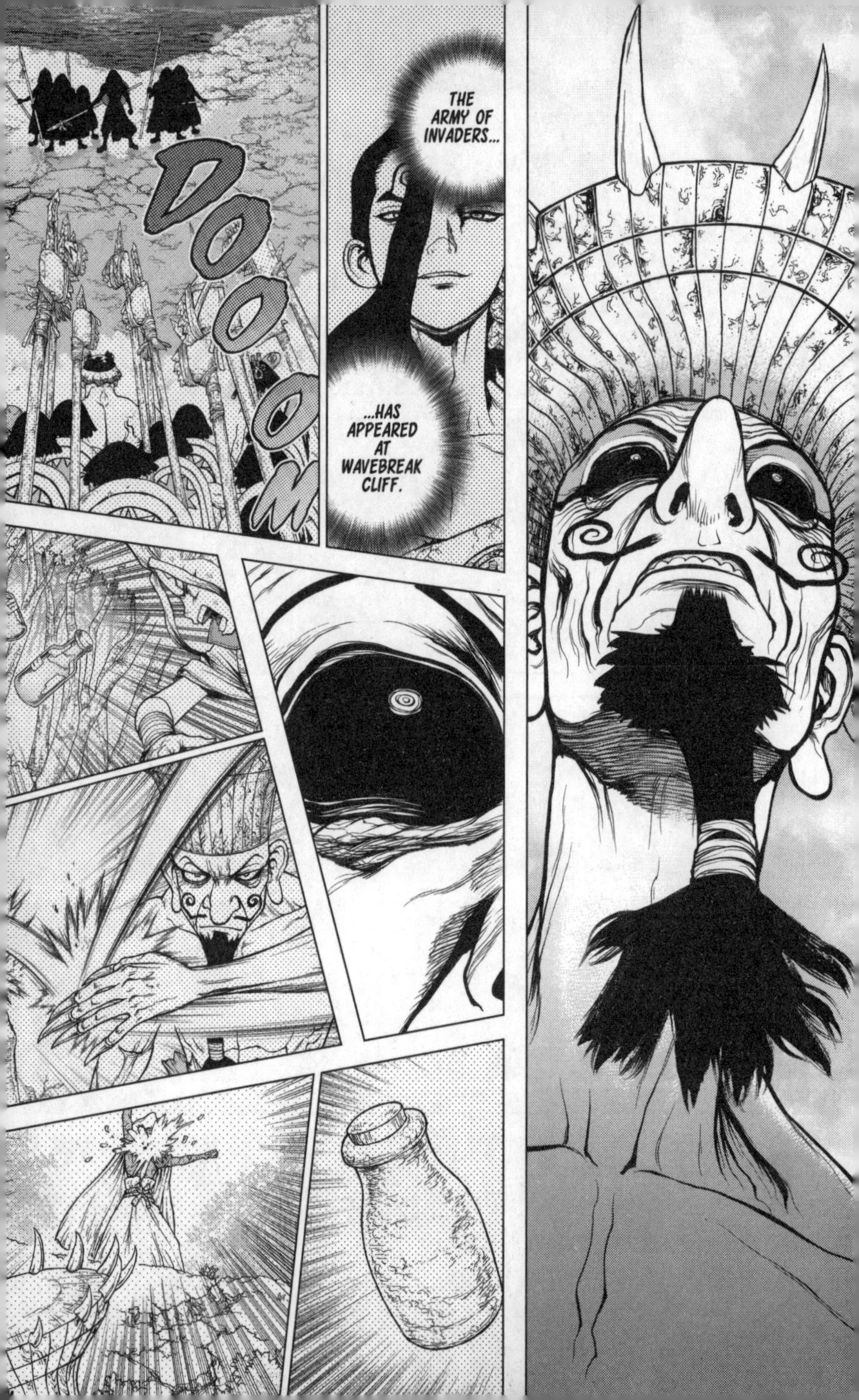
THE ARMY OF INVADERS...
...HAS APPEARED AT WAVEBREAK CLIFF.
DOOOOM

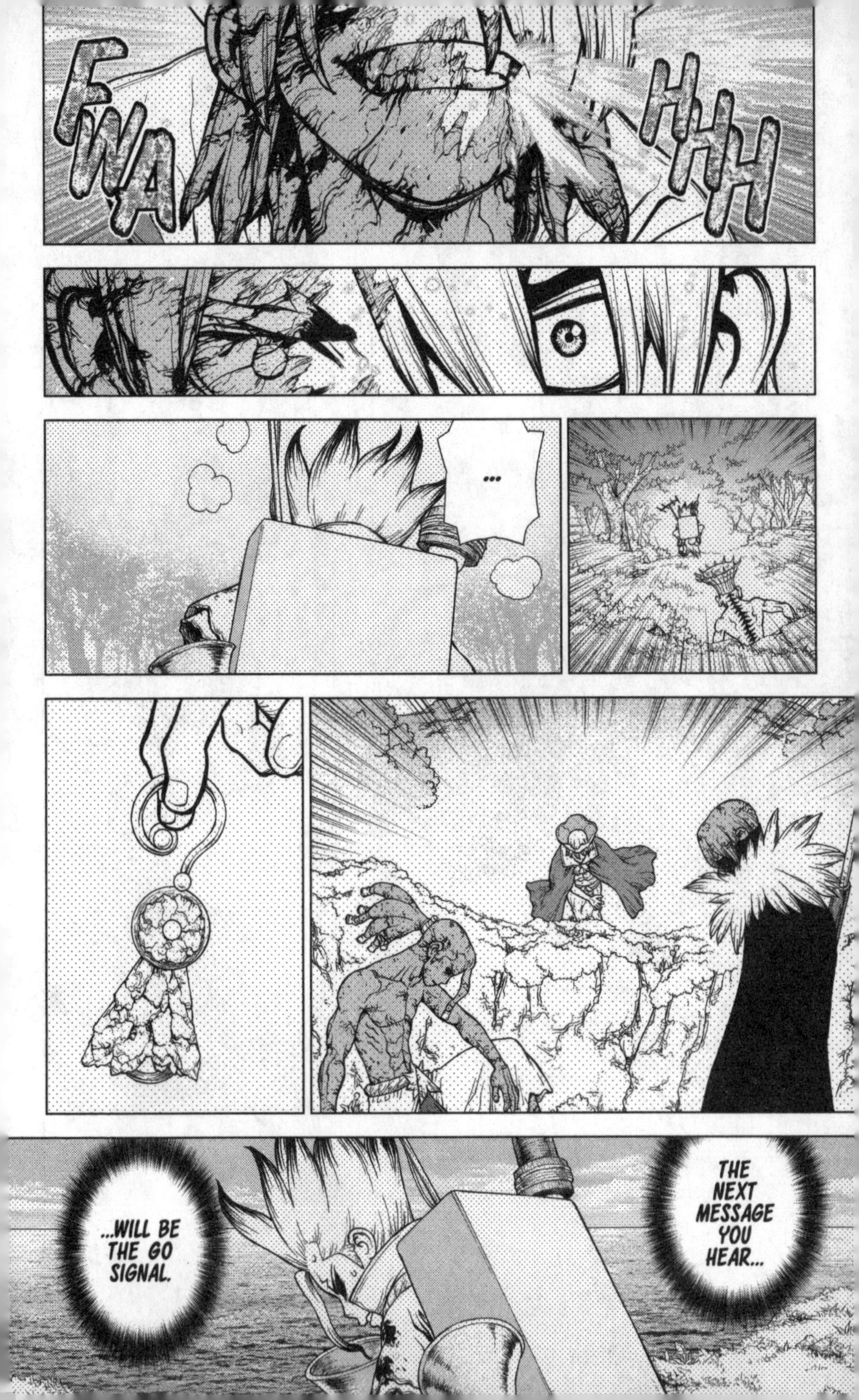
FWAHHH
...
THE NEXT MESSAGE YOU HEAR...
...WILL BE THE GO SIGNAL.

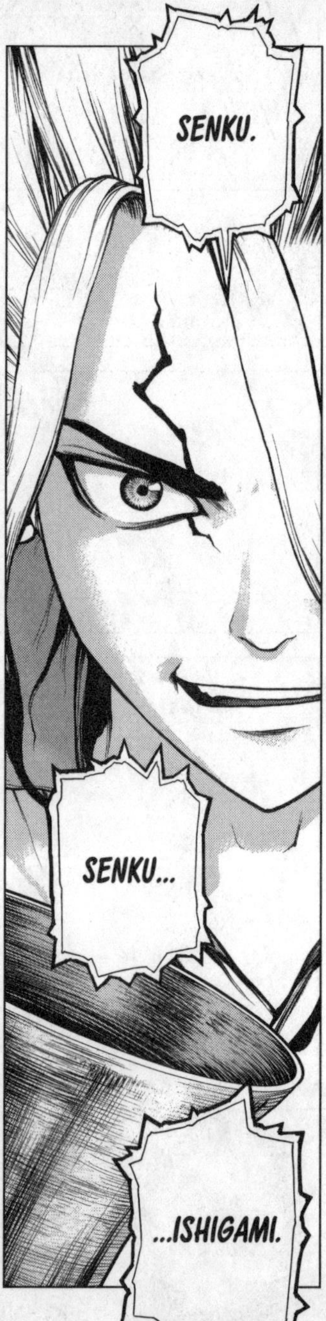
SENKU.
SENKU...
...ISHIGAMI.

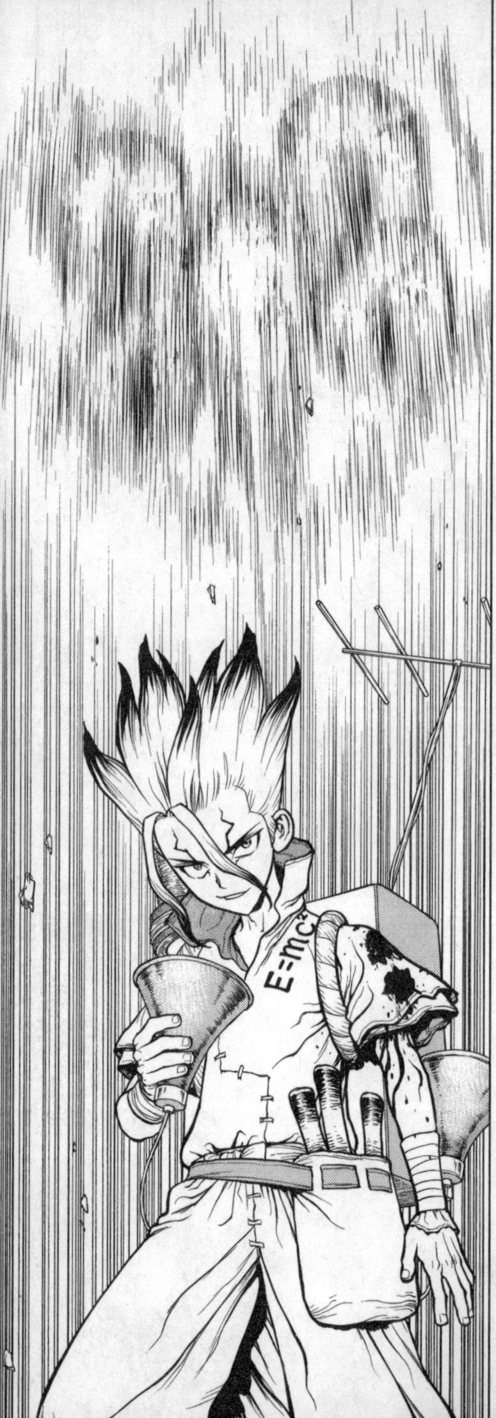
$E=mc^2$

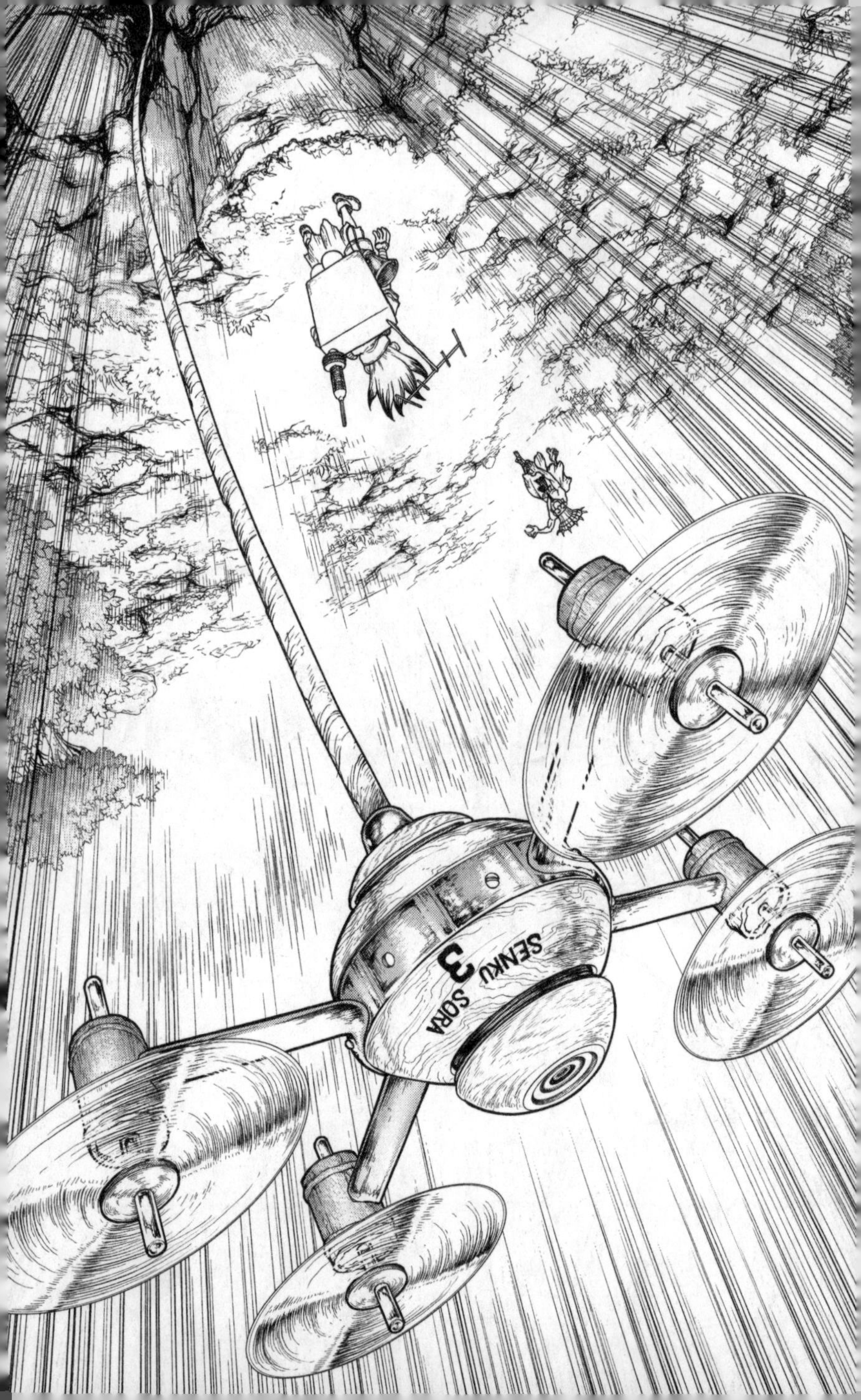
SENKU 3 SORA

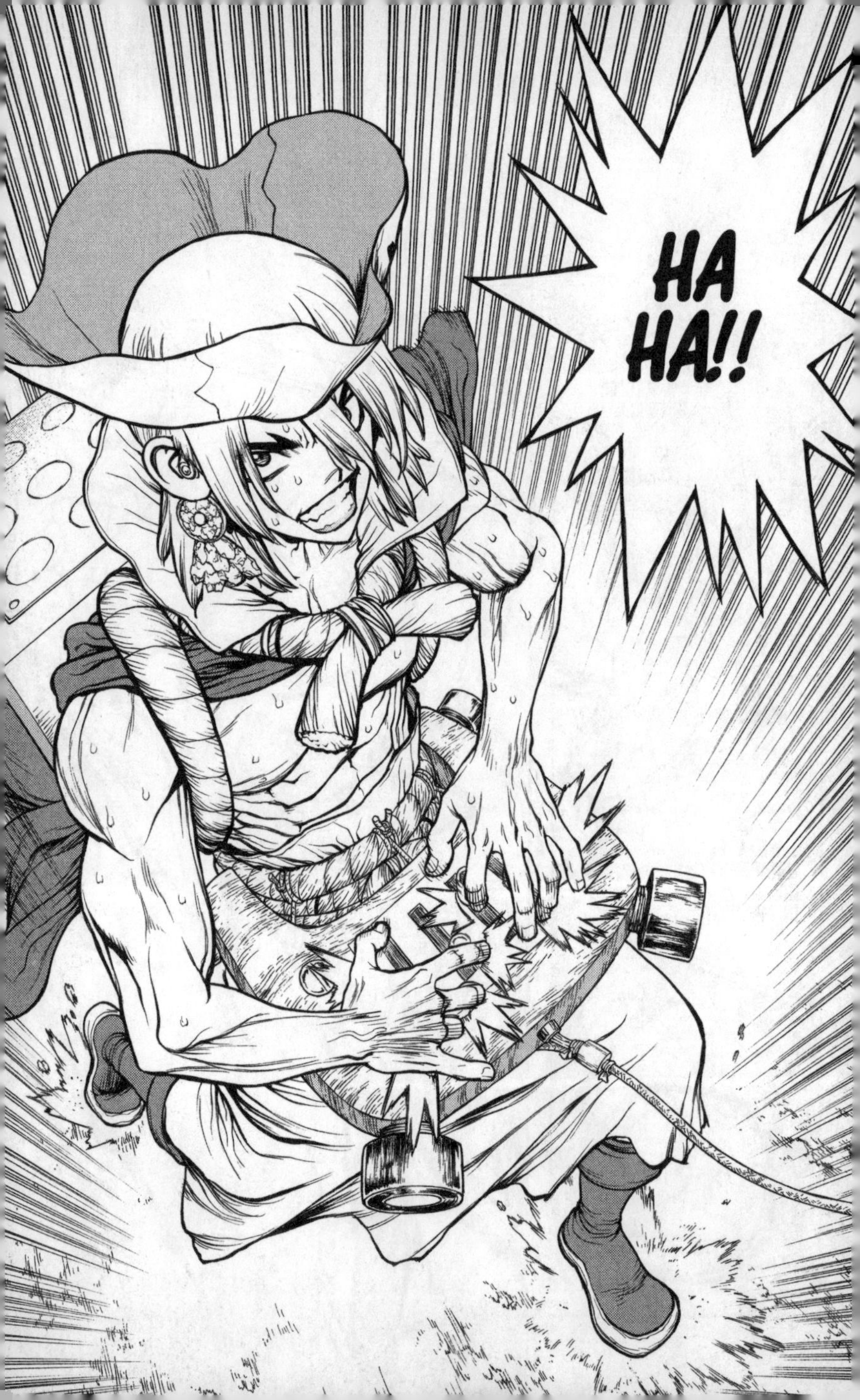
HA HA!!

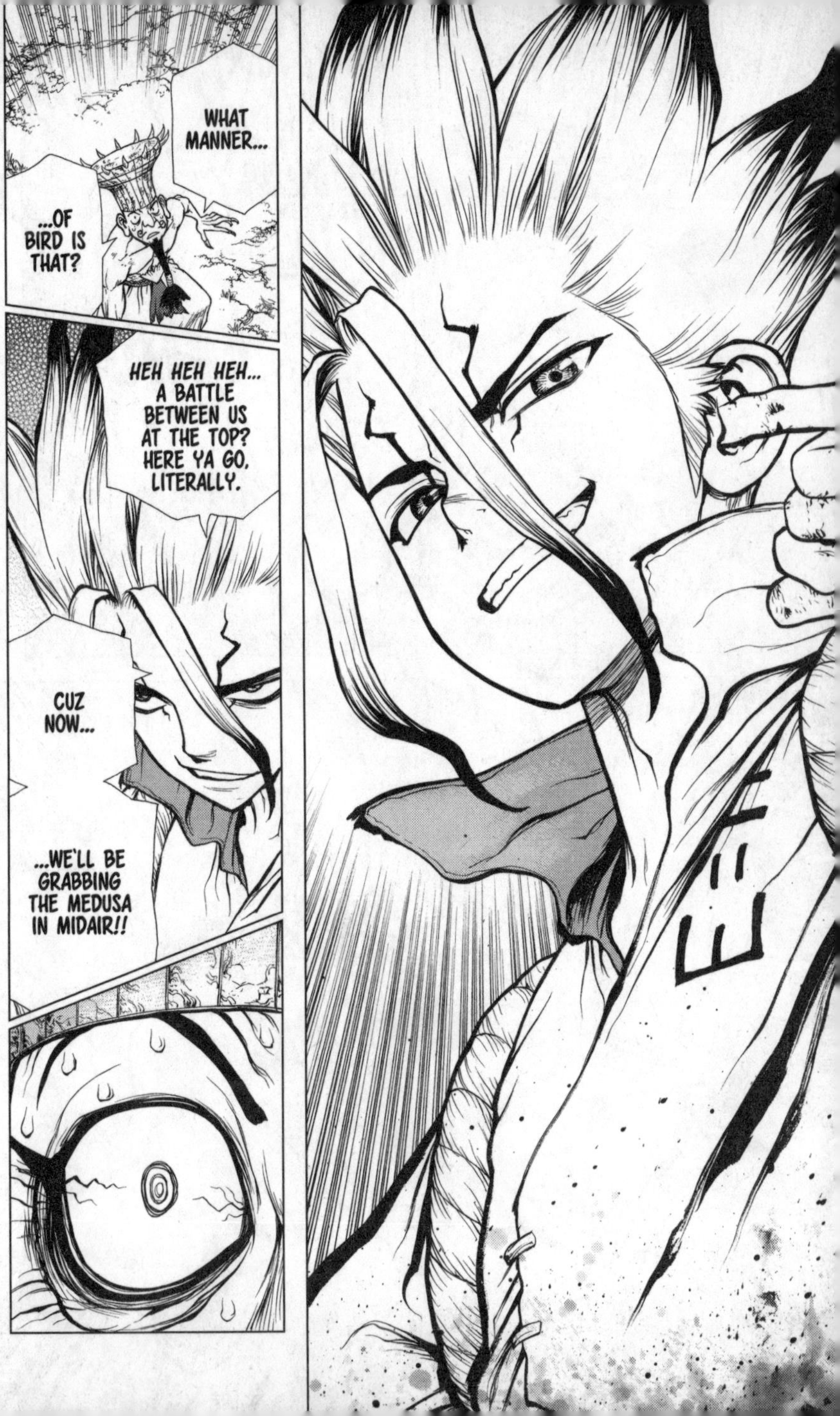
WHAT MANNER...
...OF BIRD IS THAT?
HEH HEH HEH... A BATTLE BETWEEN US AT THE TOP? HERE YA GO. LITERALLY.
CUZ NOW...
...WE'LL BE GRABBING THE MEDUSA IN MIDAIR!!

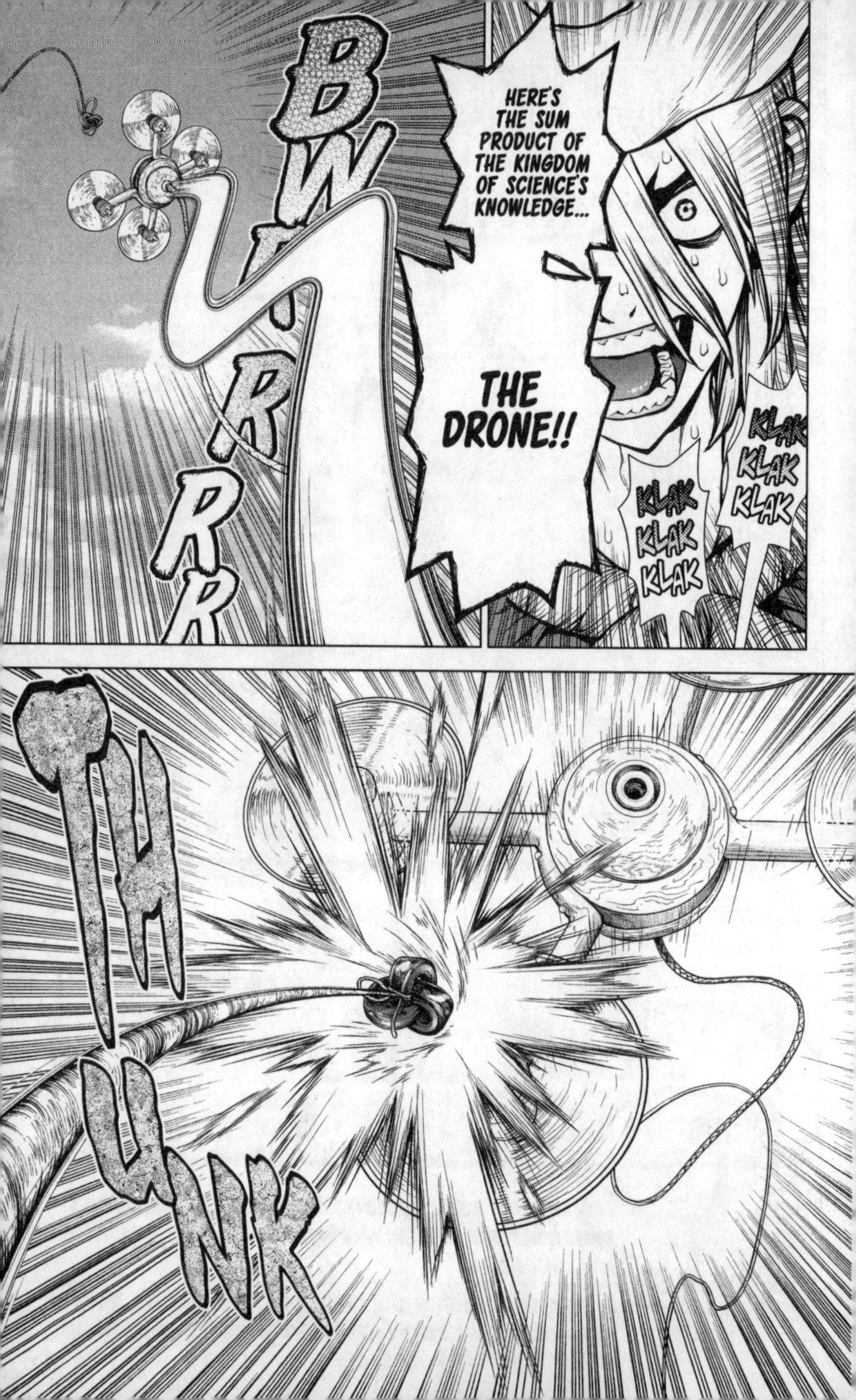
HERE'S THE SUM PRODUCT OF THE KINGDOM OF SCIENCE'S KNOWLEDGE...
THE DRONE!!
KLAK KLAK KLAK
KLAK KLAK KLAK
BWRRR
THUNK

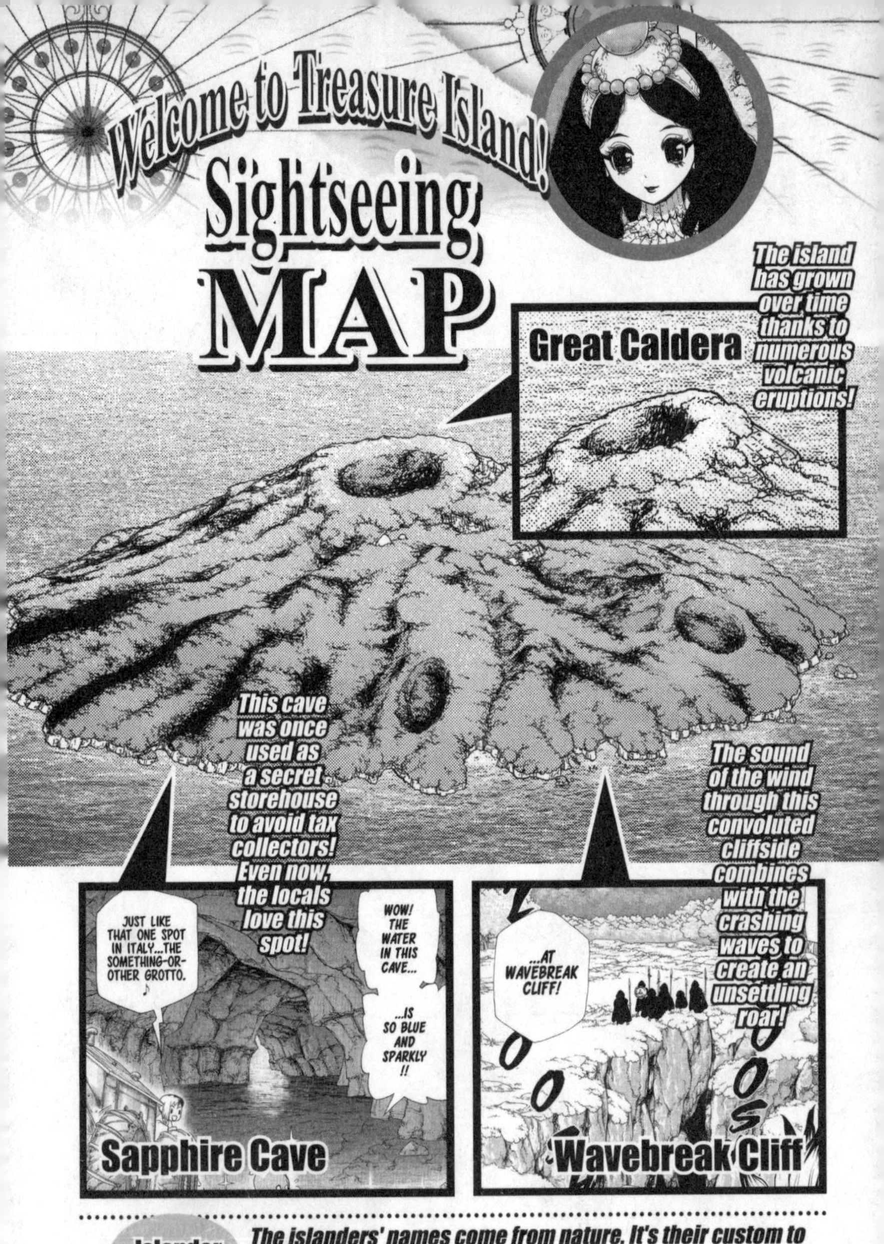
Welcome to Treasure Island!
Sightseeing MAP
Great Caldera
The island has grown over time thanks to numerous volcanic eruptions!
The sound of the wind through this convoluted cliffside combines with the crashing waves to create an unsettling roar!
...AT WAVEBREAK CLIFF!
OOOOS
Wavebreak Cliff
This cave was once used as a secret storehouse to avoid tax collectors! Even now, the locals love this spot!
WOW! THE WATER IN THIS CAVE...
...IS SO BLUE AND SPARKLY !!
JUST LIKE THAT ONE SPOT IN ITALY...THE SOMETHING-OR-OTHER GROTTO. ♪
Sapphire Cave

Islander Trivia — *The islanders' names come from nature. It's their custom to name newborns after the very first thing the baby sees at the moment of birth.*

Islander Culture Trivia — *Islanders accessorize with shells, pearls and the like. Since pearls are scarce, there's a widespread practice of polishing white stones to look like pearls.*

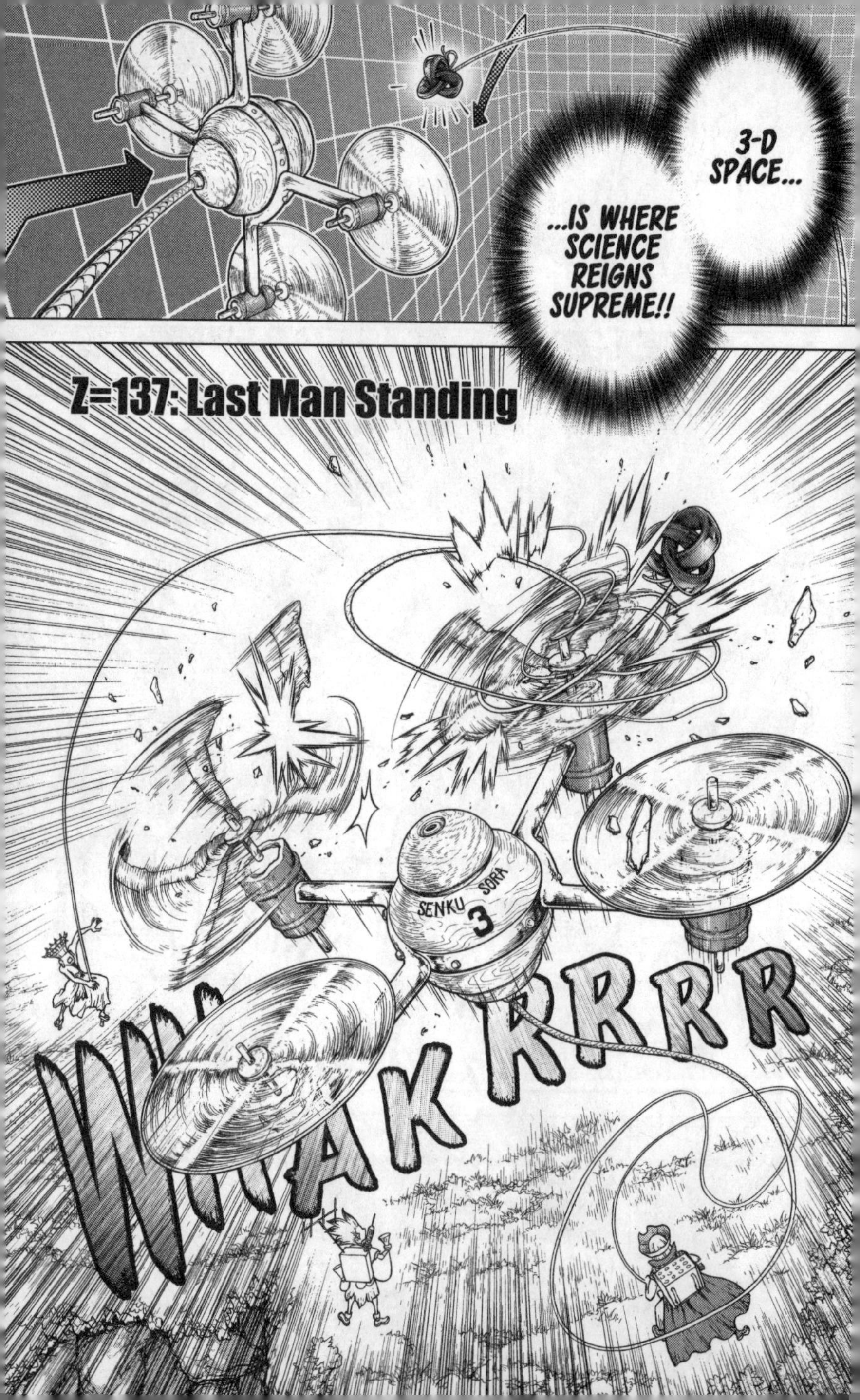
3-D SPACE...
...IS WHERE SCIENCE REIGNS SUPREME!!
Z=137: Last Man Standing
SENKU
SORA
3
WHAK RRRR

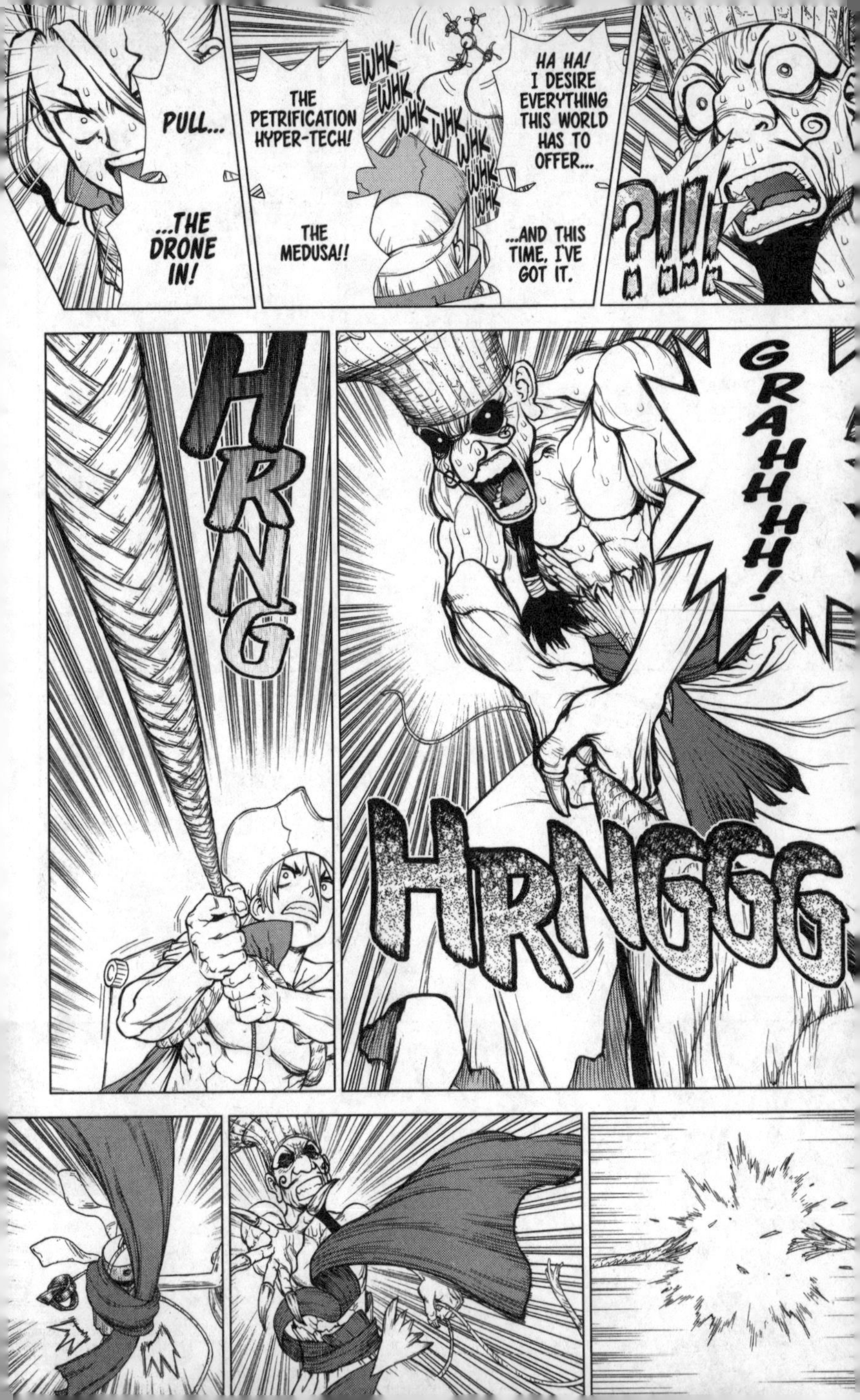
?!!!
HA HA! I DESIRE EVERYTHING THIS WORLD HAS TO OFFER...
...AND THIS TIME, I'VE GOT IT.
THE PETRIFICATION HYPER-TECH!
THE MEDUSA!!
WHK WHK WHK WHK WHK WHK WHK WHK
PULL...
...THE DRONE IN!
GRAHHHH!
HRNGGG
HRNG

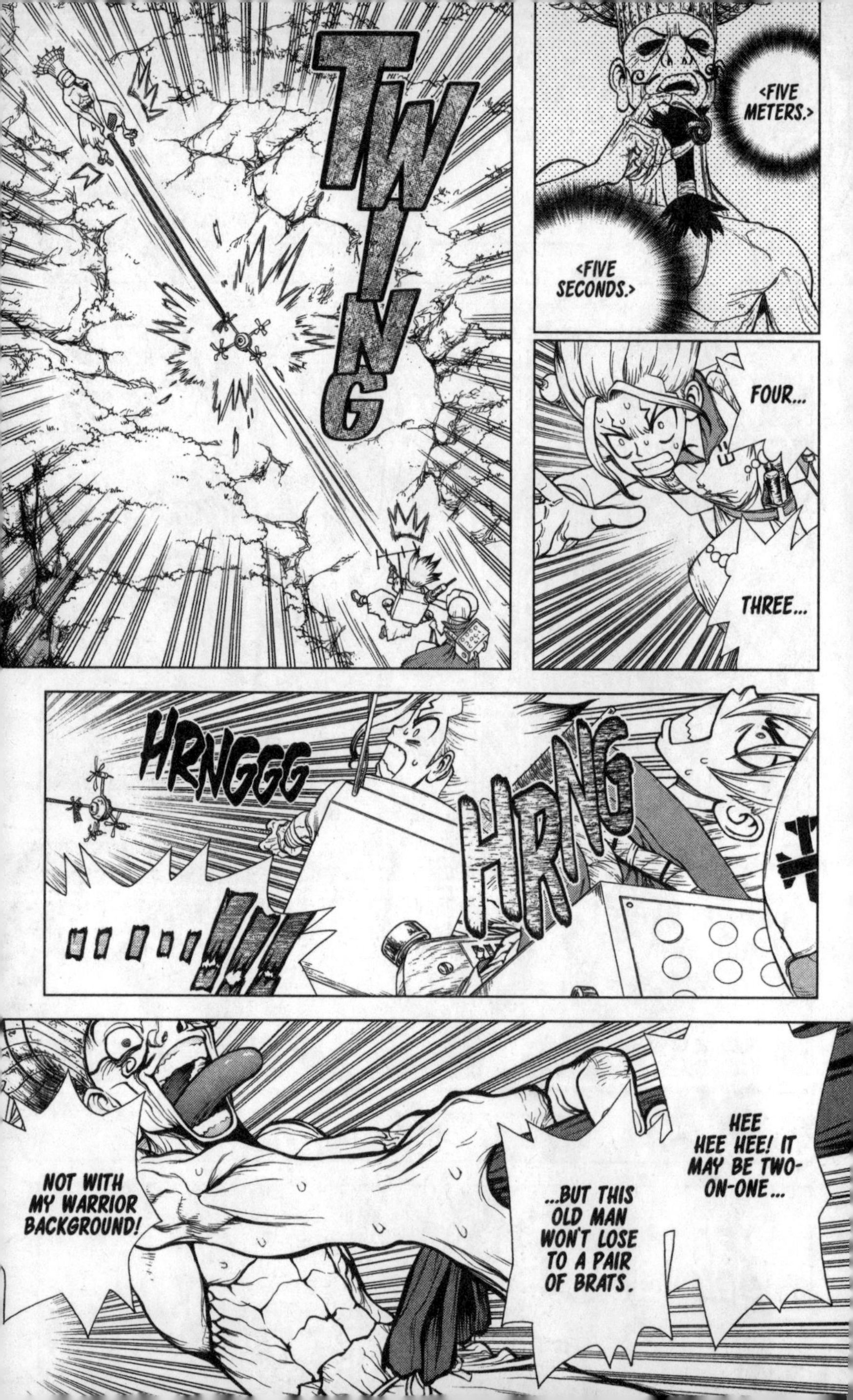

<FIVE METERS.>
<FIVE SECONDS.>
FOUR...
THREE...
TWING
HRNG
HRNGGG
......!!
HEE HEE HEE! IT MAY BE TWO-ON-ONE...
...BUT THIS OLD MAN WON'T LOSE TO A PAIR OF BRATS.
NOT WITH MY WARRIOR BACKGROUND!

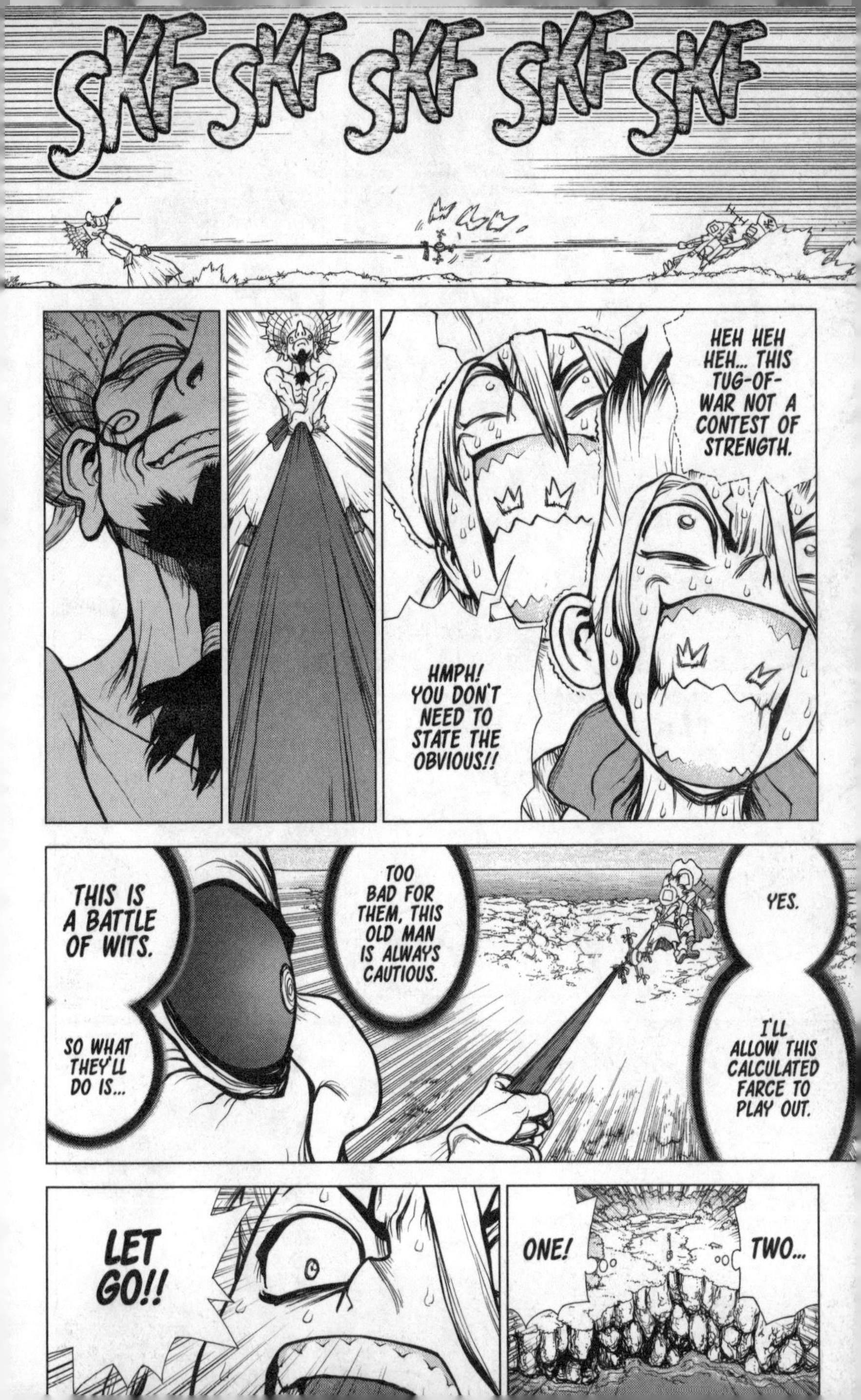
SKF SKF SKF SKF SKF
HEH HEH HEH... THIS TUG-OF-WAR NOT A CONTEST OF STRENGTH.
HMPH! YOU DON'T NEED TO STATE THE OBVIOUS!!
YES.
I'LL ALLOW THIS CALCULATED FARCE TO PLAY OUT.
TOO BAD FOR THEM, THIS OLD MAN IS ALWAYS CAUTIOUS.
THIS IS A BATTLE OF WITS.
SO WHAT THEY'LL DO IS...
ONE!
TWO...
LET GO!!

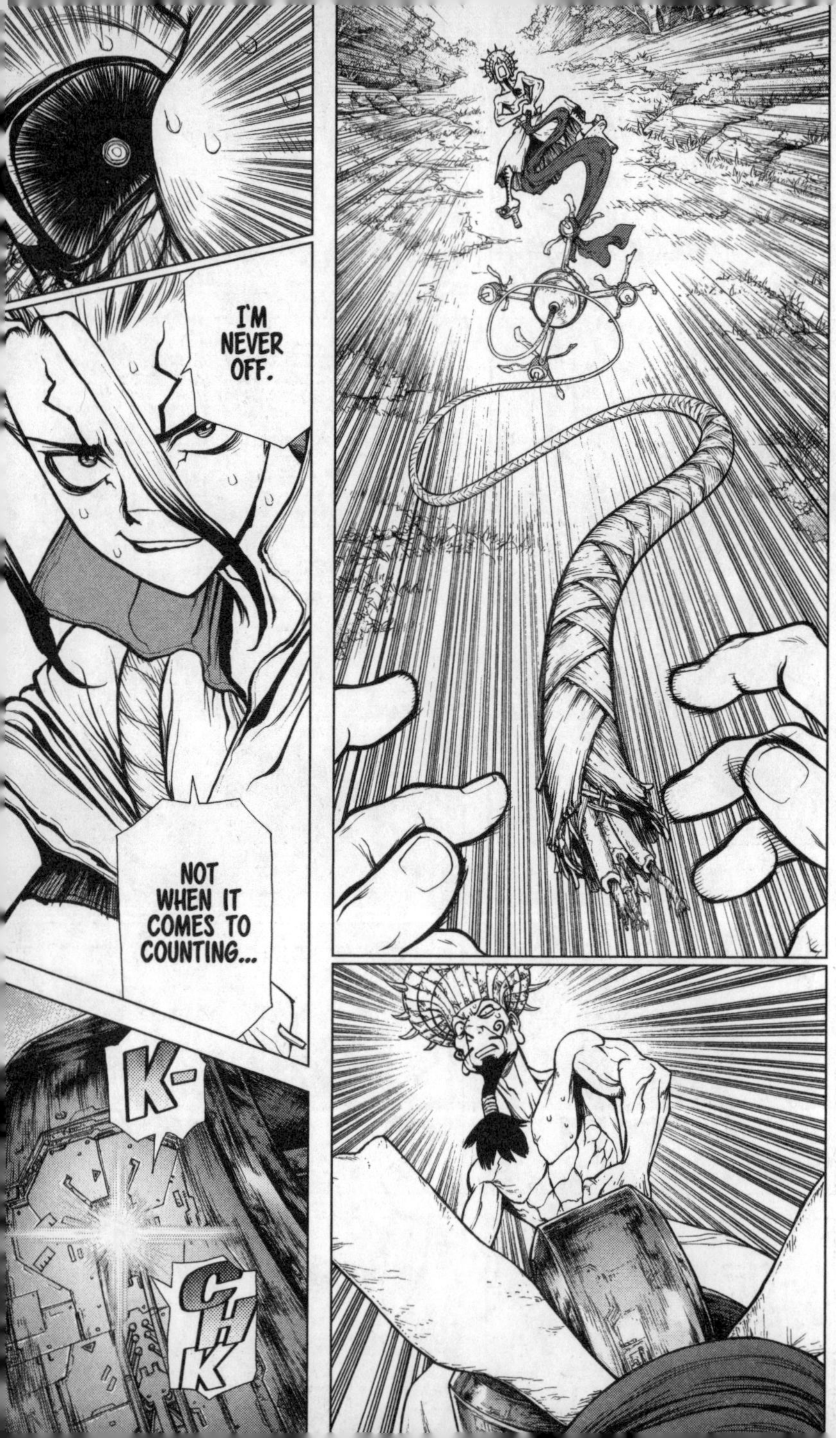
I'M NEVER OFF.
NOT WHEN IT COMES TO COUNTING...
K-
CHK

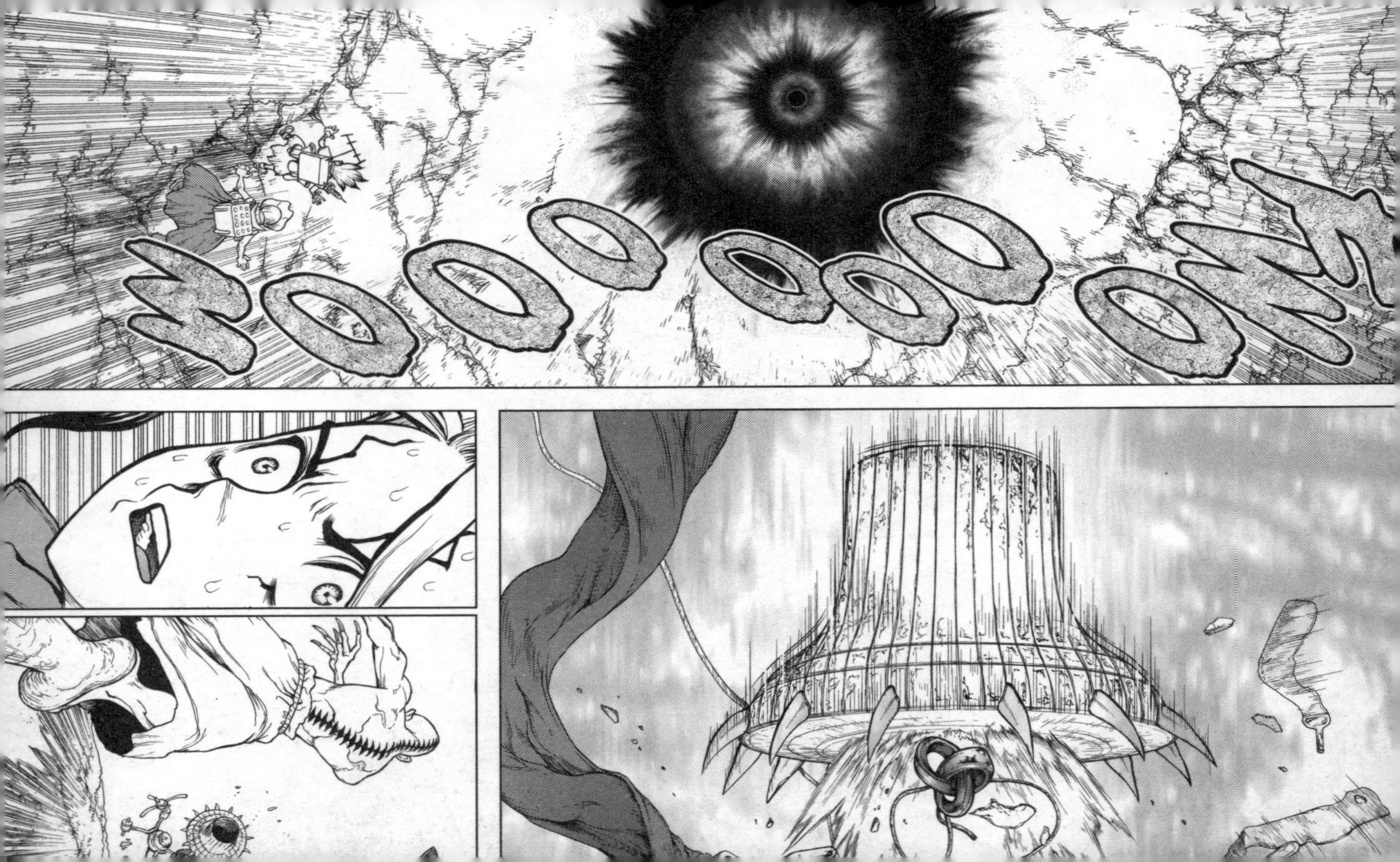
WOOOOOOOM

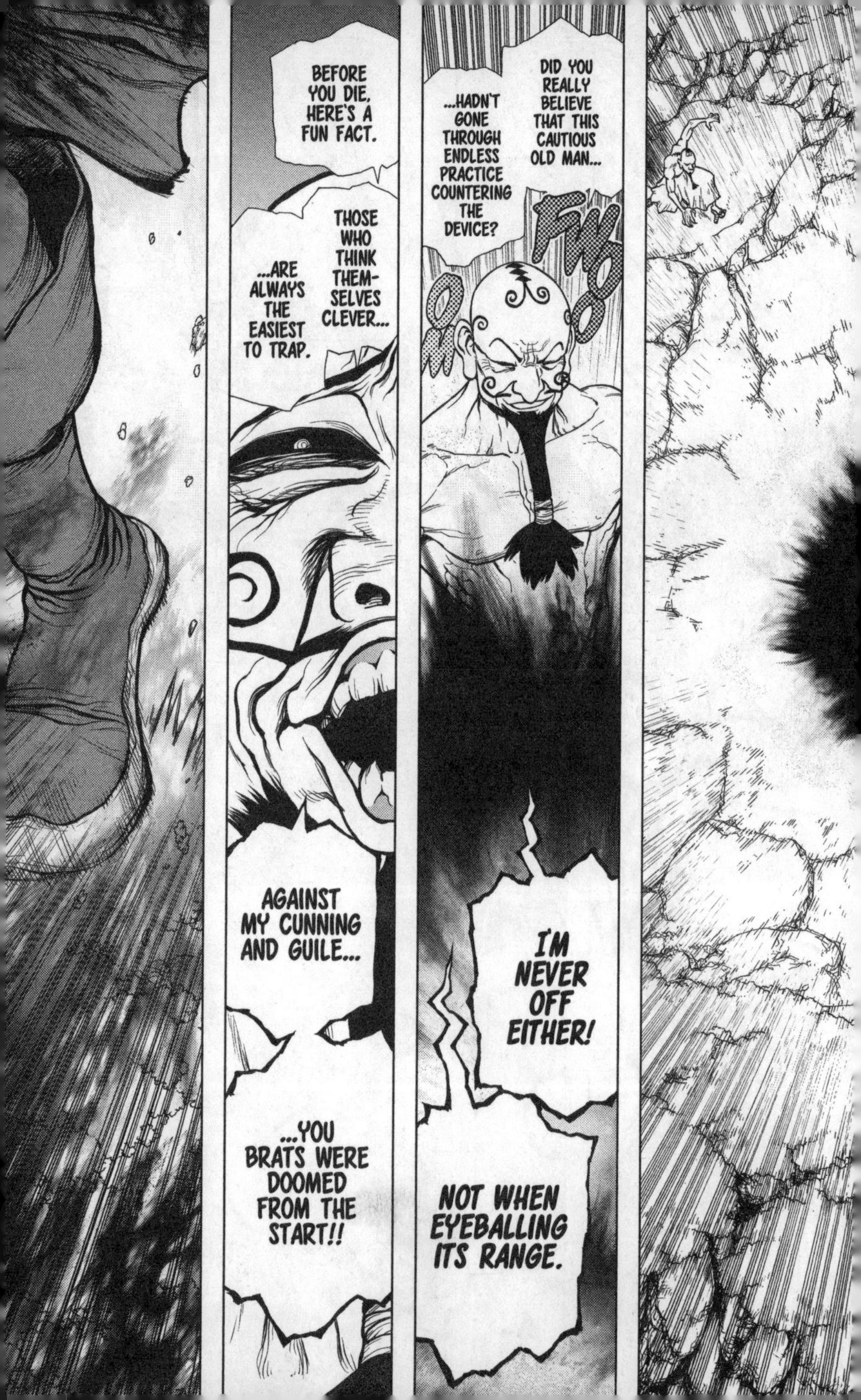
DID YOU REALLY BELIEVE THAT THIS CAUTIOUS OLD MAN...
...HADN'T GONE THROUGH ENDLESS PRACTICE COUNTERING THE DEVICE?
FWOOOM
I'M NEVER OFF EITHER!
NOT WHEN EYEBALLING ITS RANGE.
BEFORE YOU DIE, HERE'S A FUN FACT.
THOSE WHO THINK THEM-SELVES CLEVER...
...ARE ALWAYS THE EASIEST TO TRAP.
AGAINST MY CUNNING AND GUILE...
...YOU BRATS WERE DOOMED FROM THE START!!

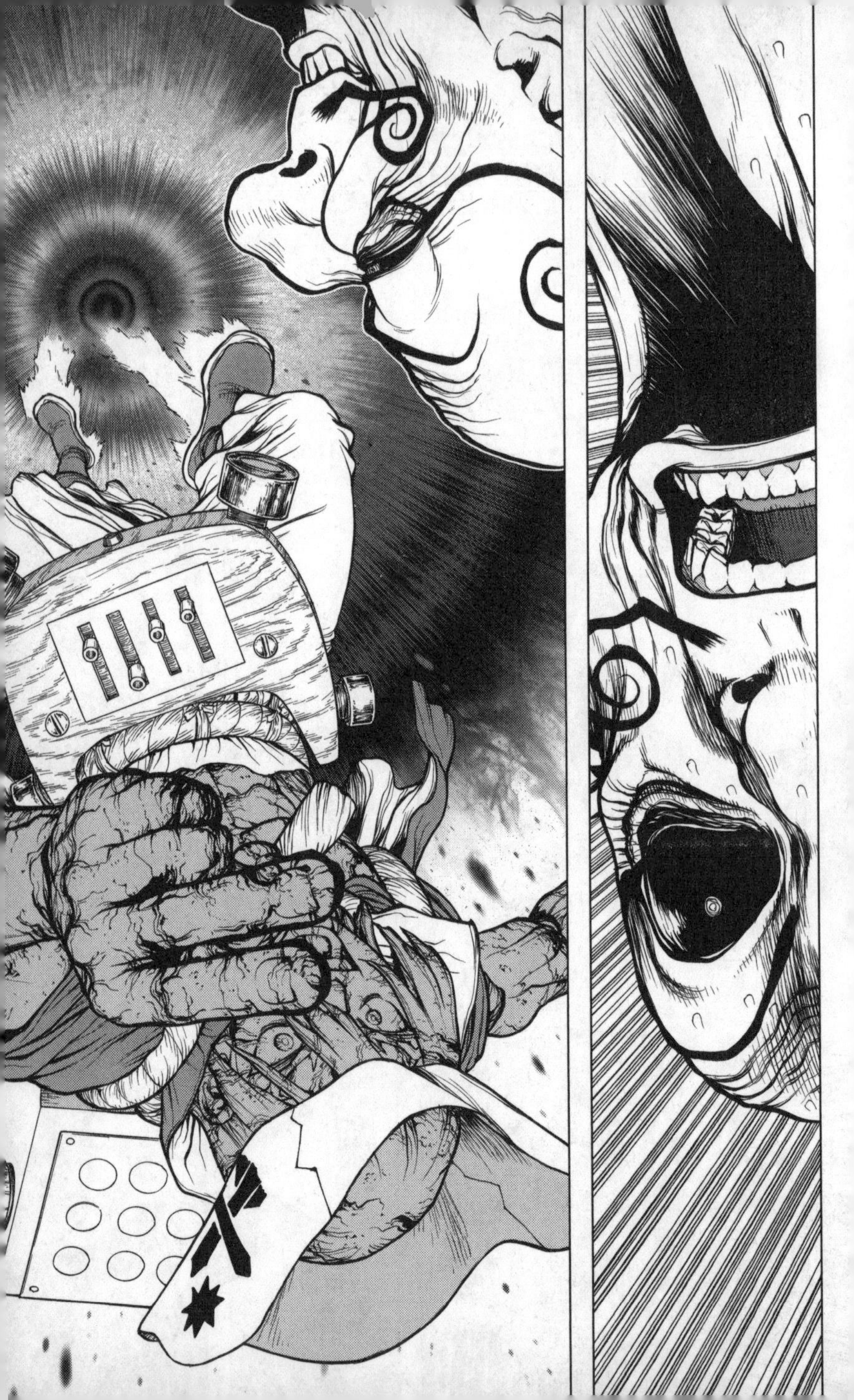

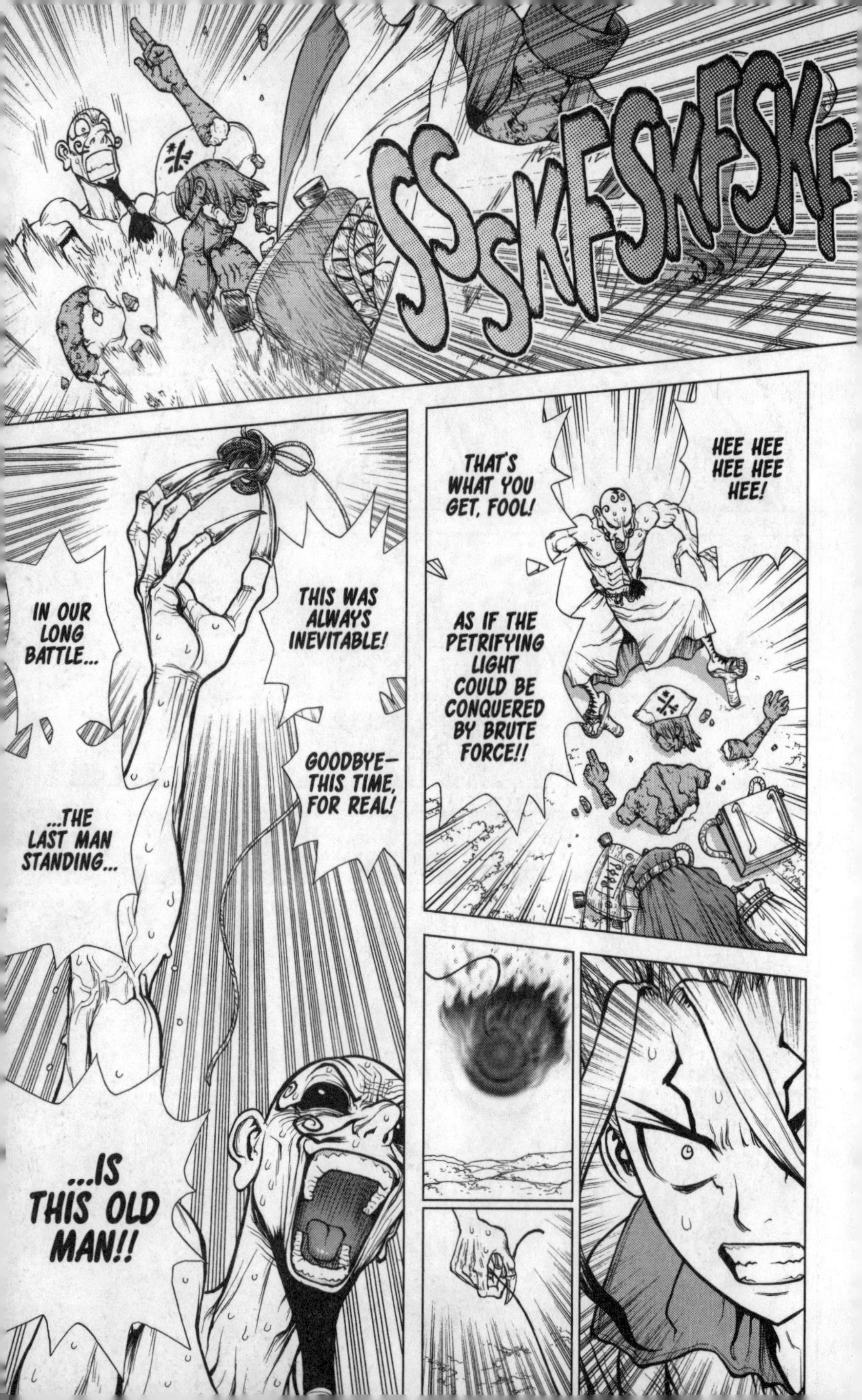
SSSKFSKFSKF
HEE HEE HEE HEE HEE!
THAT'S WHAT YOU GET, FOOL!
AS IF THE PETRIFYING LIGHT COULD BE CONQUERED BY BRUTE FORCE!!
THIS WAS ALWAYS INEVITABLE!
IN OUR LONG BATTLE...
GOODBYE—THIS TIME, FOR REAL!
...THE LAST MAN STANDING...
...IS THIS OLD MAN!!

HUH...?
THAT'S...THE ONE THAT EMITS NOISE.
HE ATTACHED IT...
YOU'RE TOTALLY RIGHT, IBARA.
GUYS WHO THINK THEY'RE CLEVER ARE THE EASIEST TO TRAP.

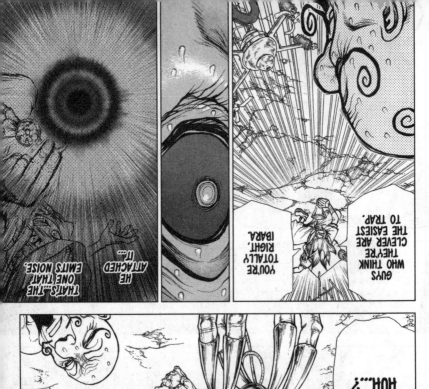

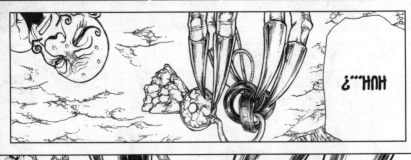

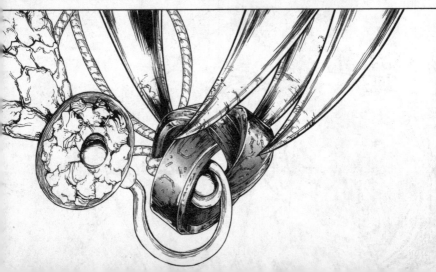

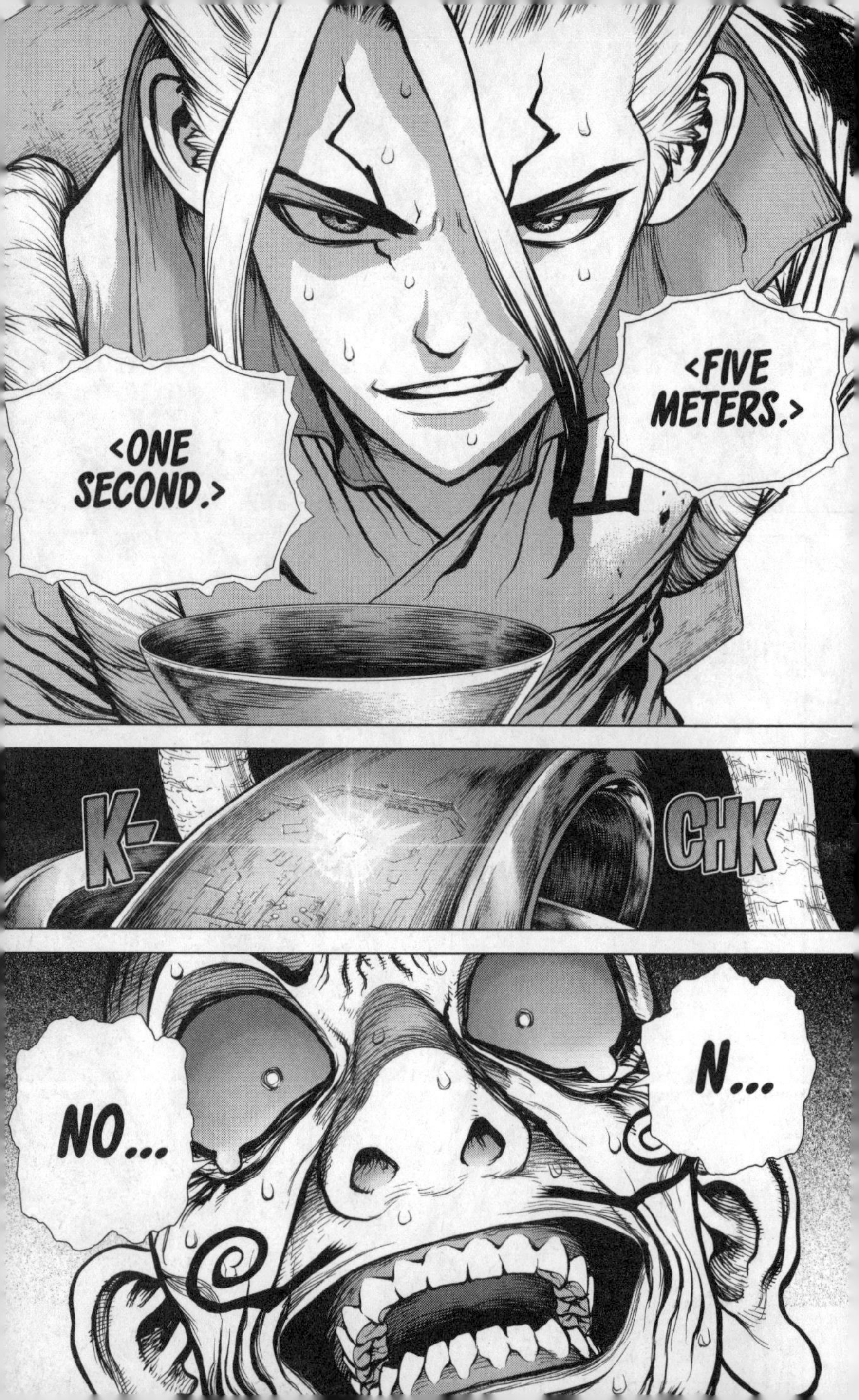
<FIVE METERS.>
<ONE SECOND.>
K-
CHK
N...
NO...

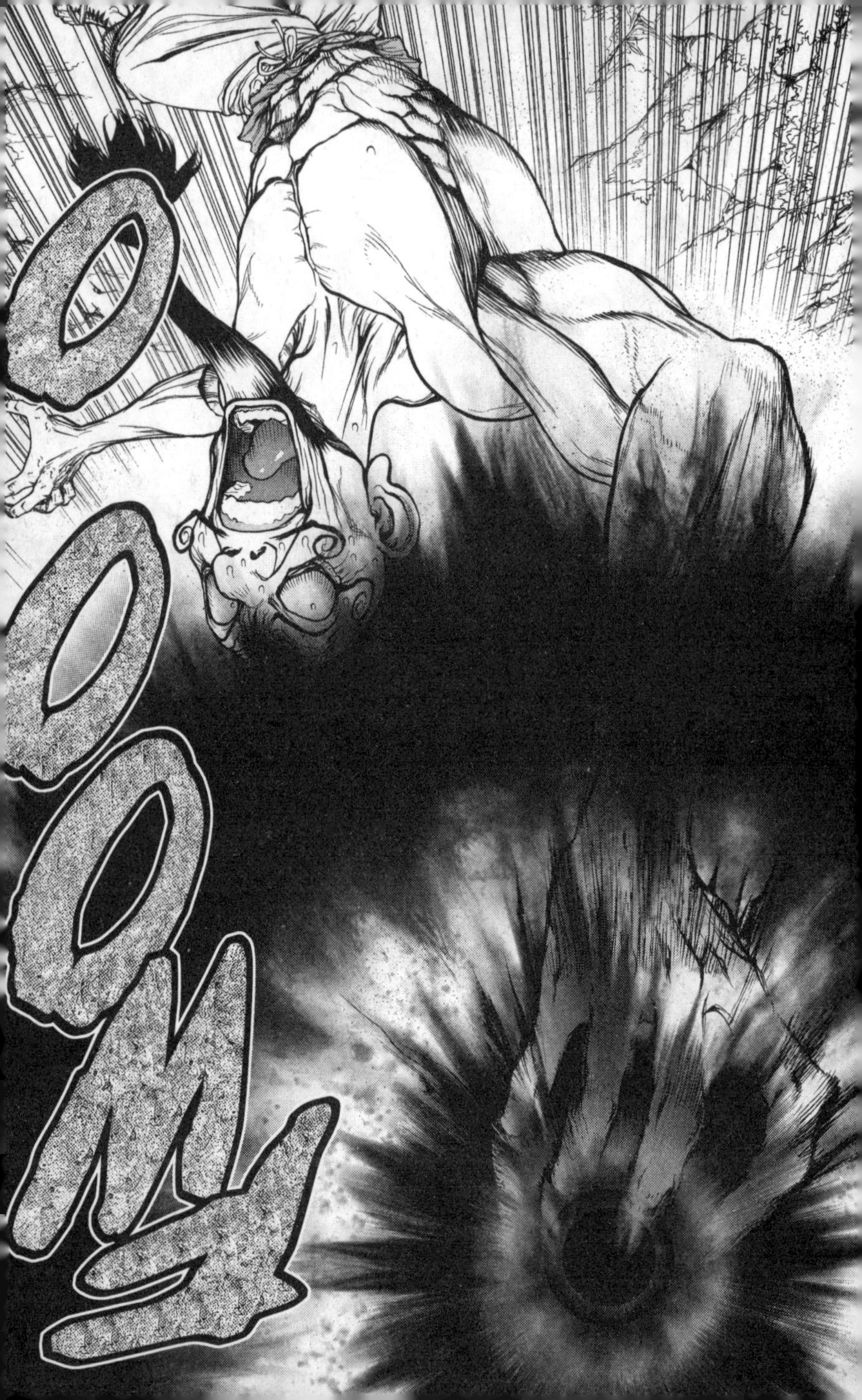

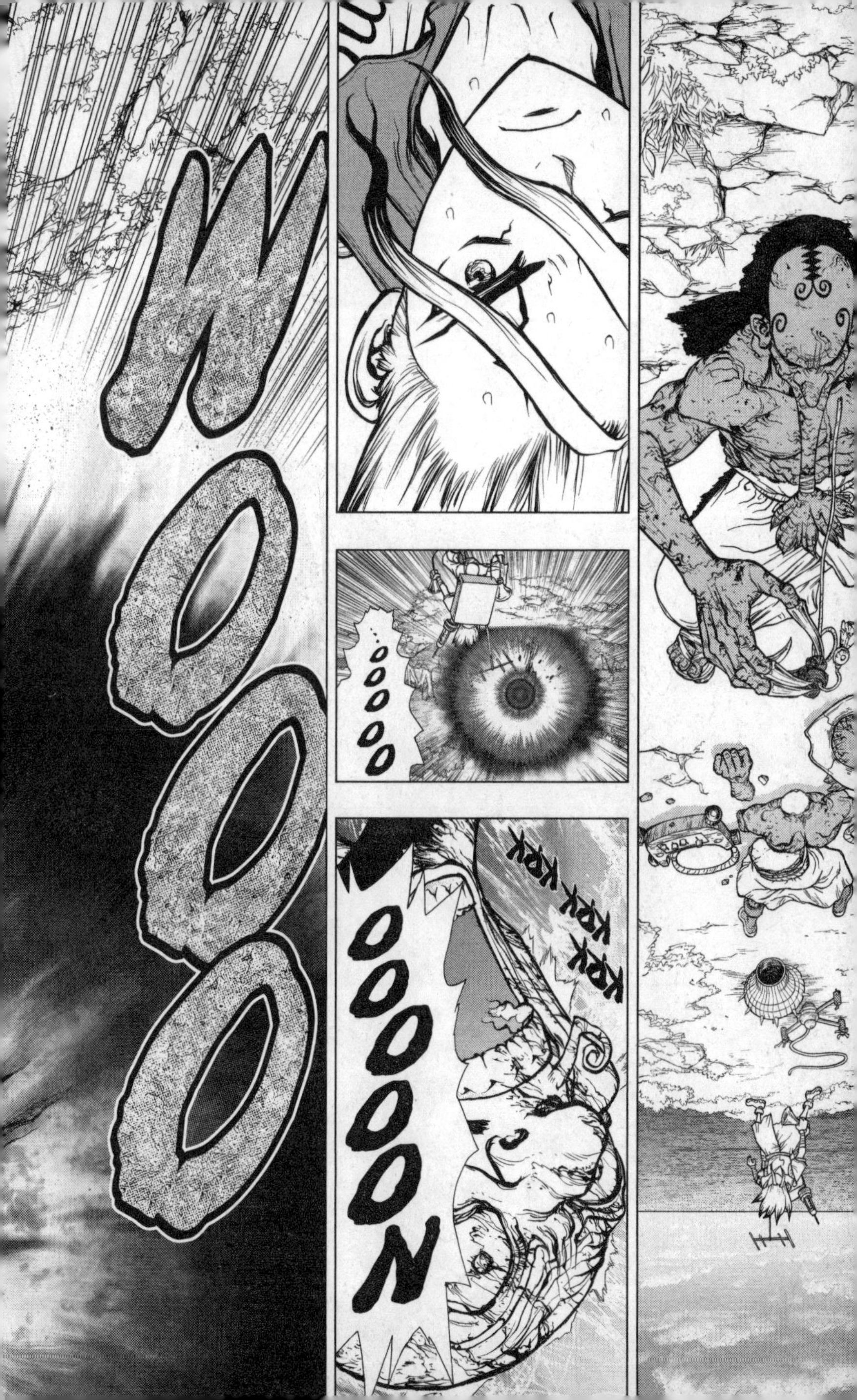
...OOOOOO
KRAK KRAK KRAK KRAK
OOOOOON
WOOOO

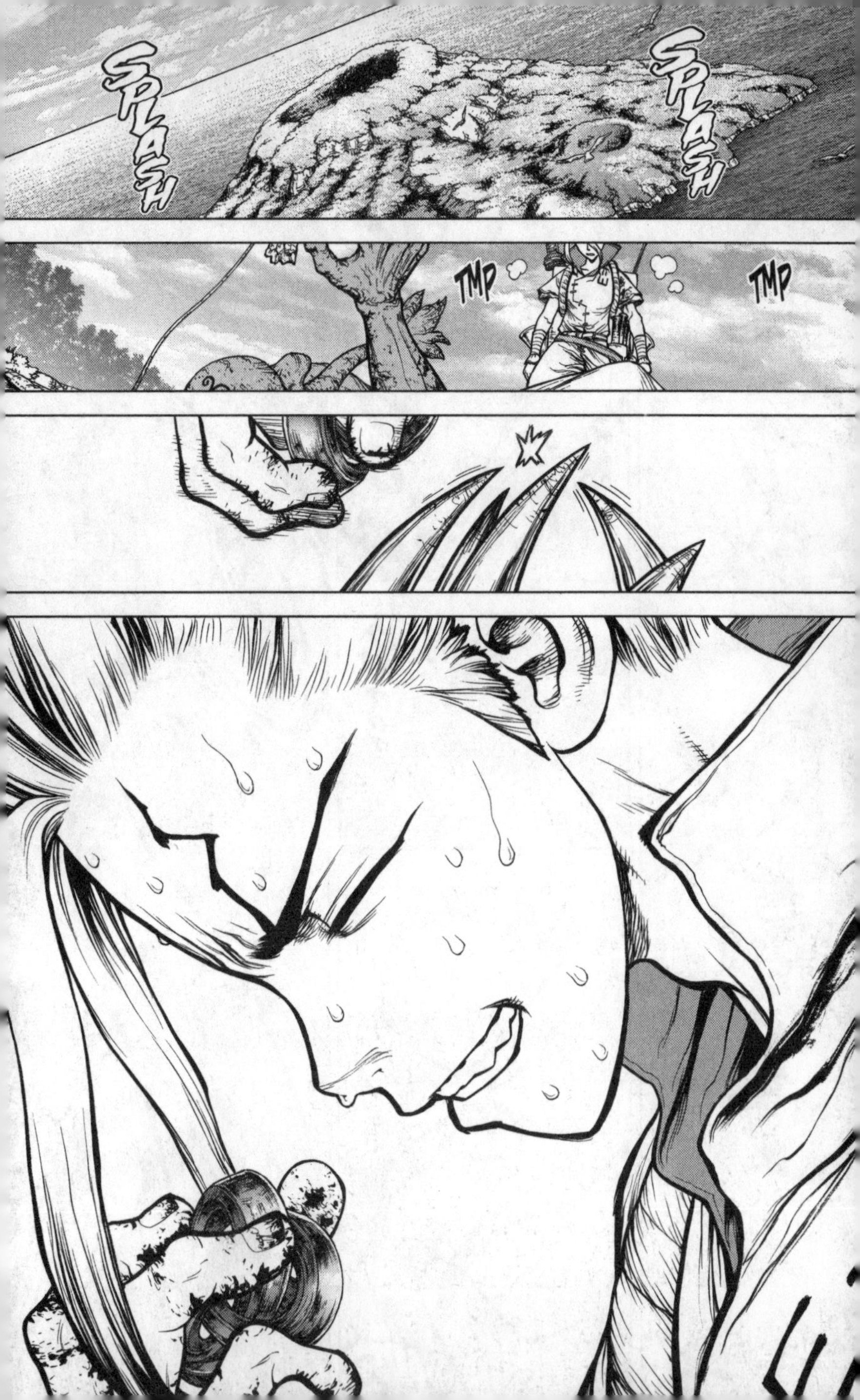
SPLASH
SPLASH
TMP
TMP

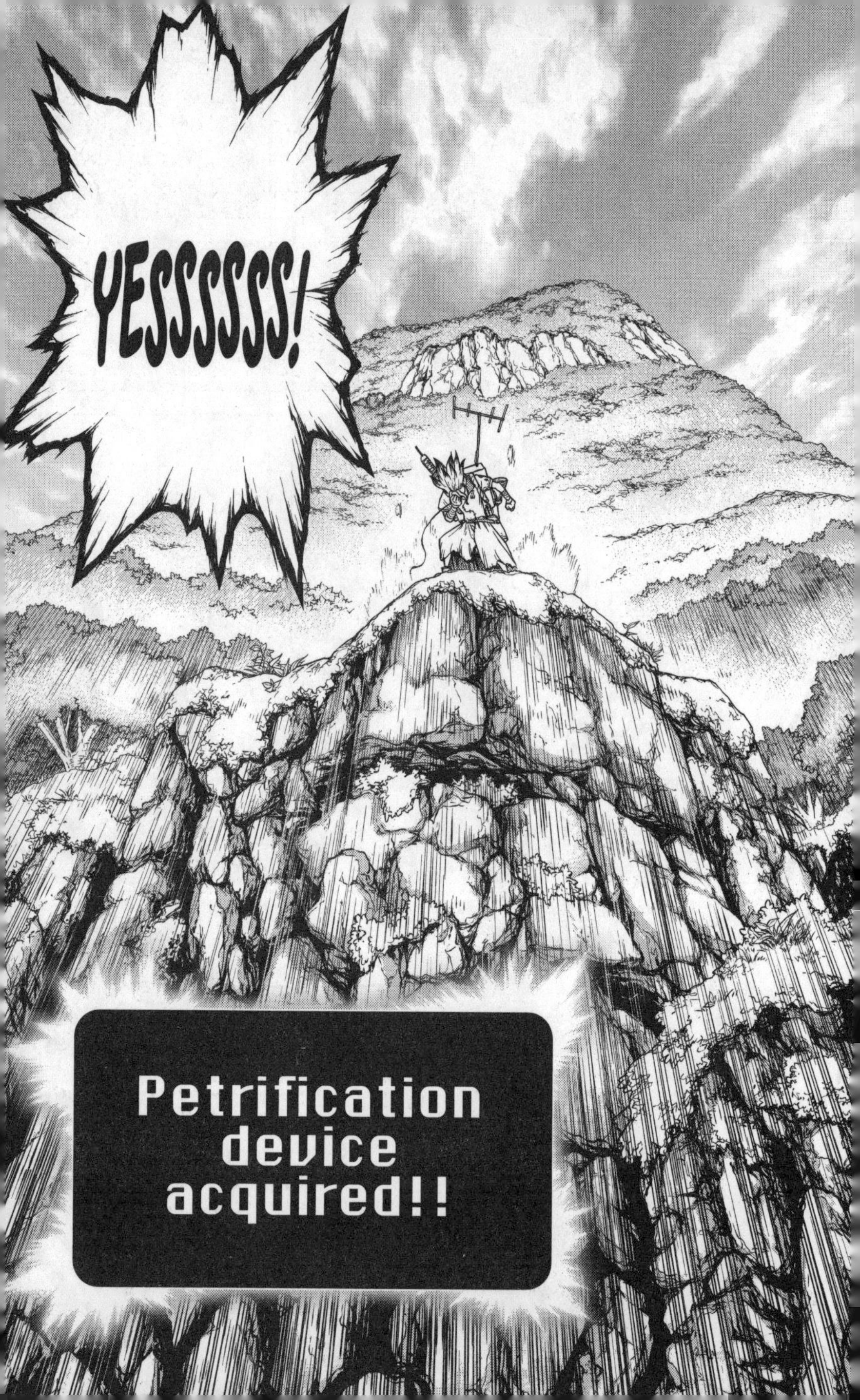
YESSSSSS!
Petrification device acquired!!

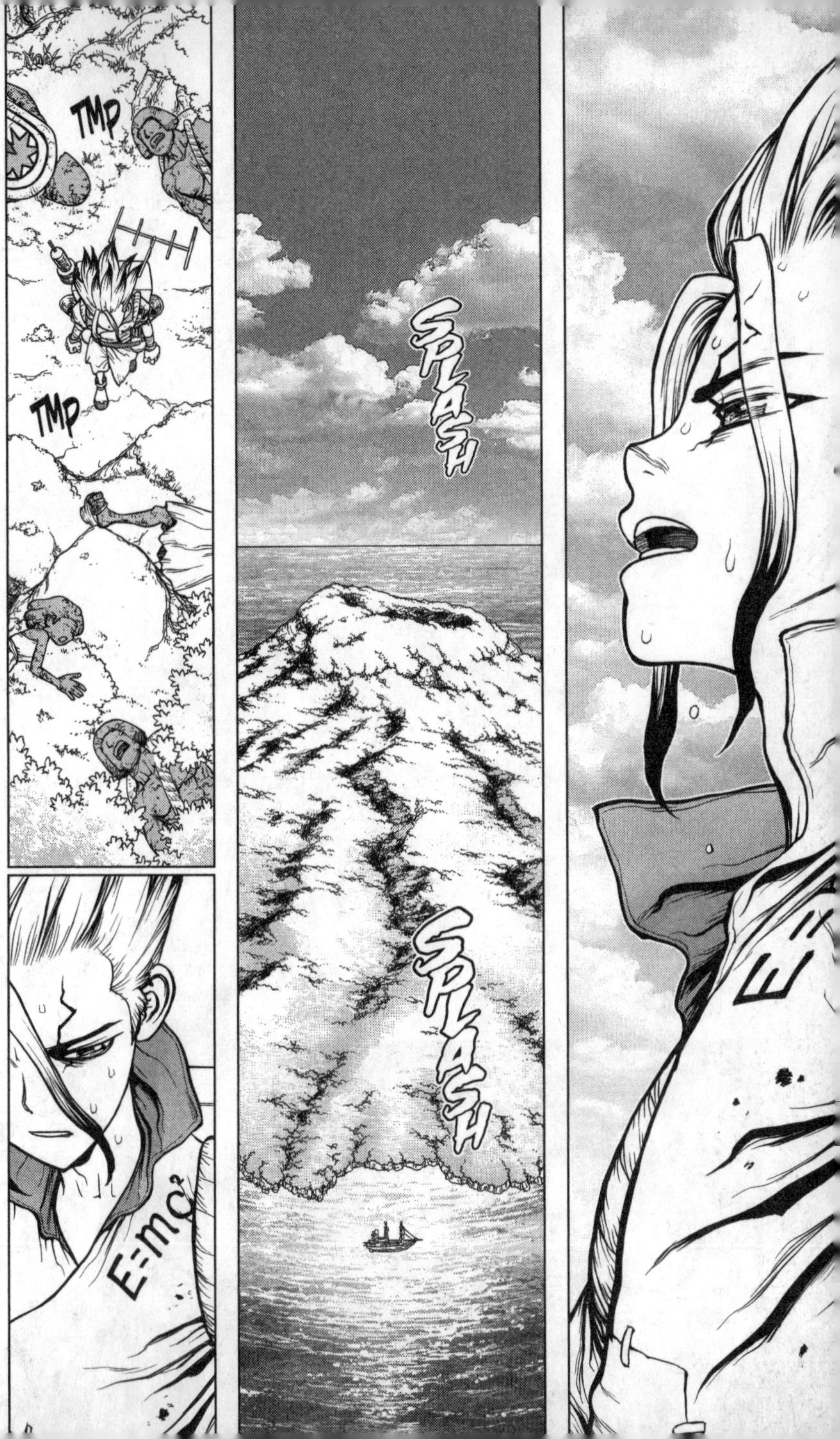
SPLASH
SPLASH
TMP
TMP
E=mc²

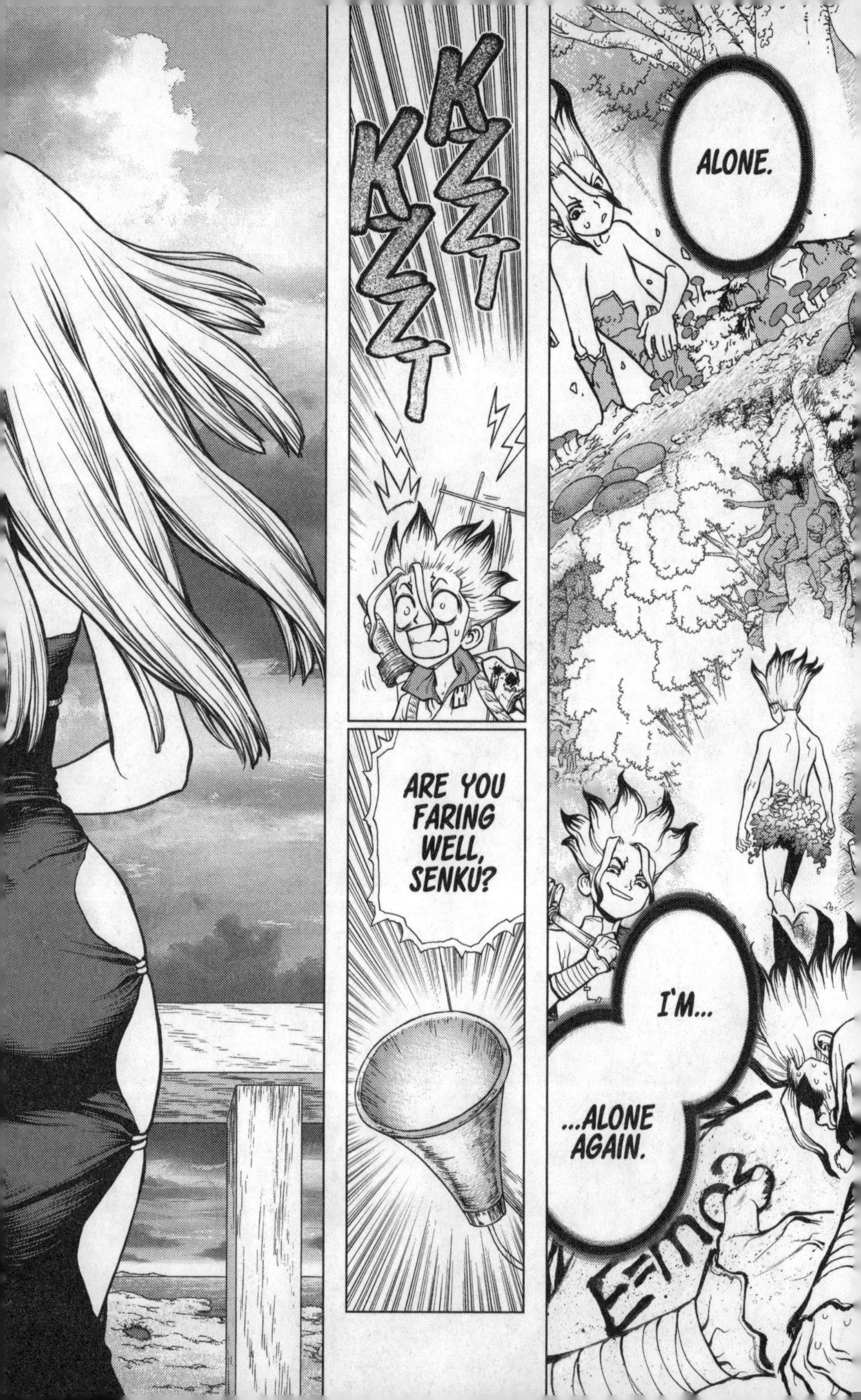
ALONE.
I'M...
...ALONE AGAIN.
E=mc2
KZZT
KZZT
ARE YOU FARING WELL, SENKU?

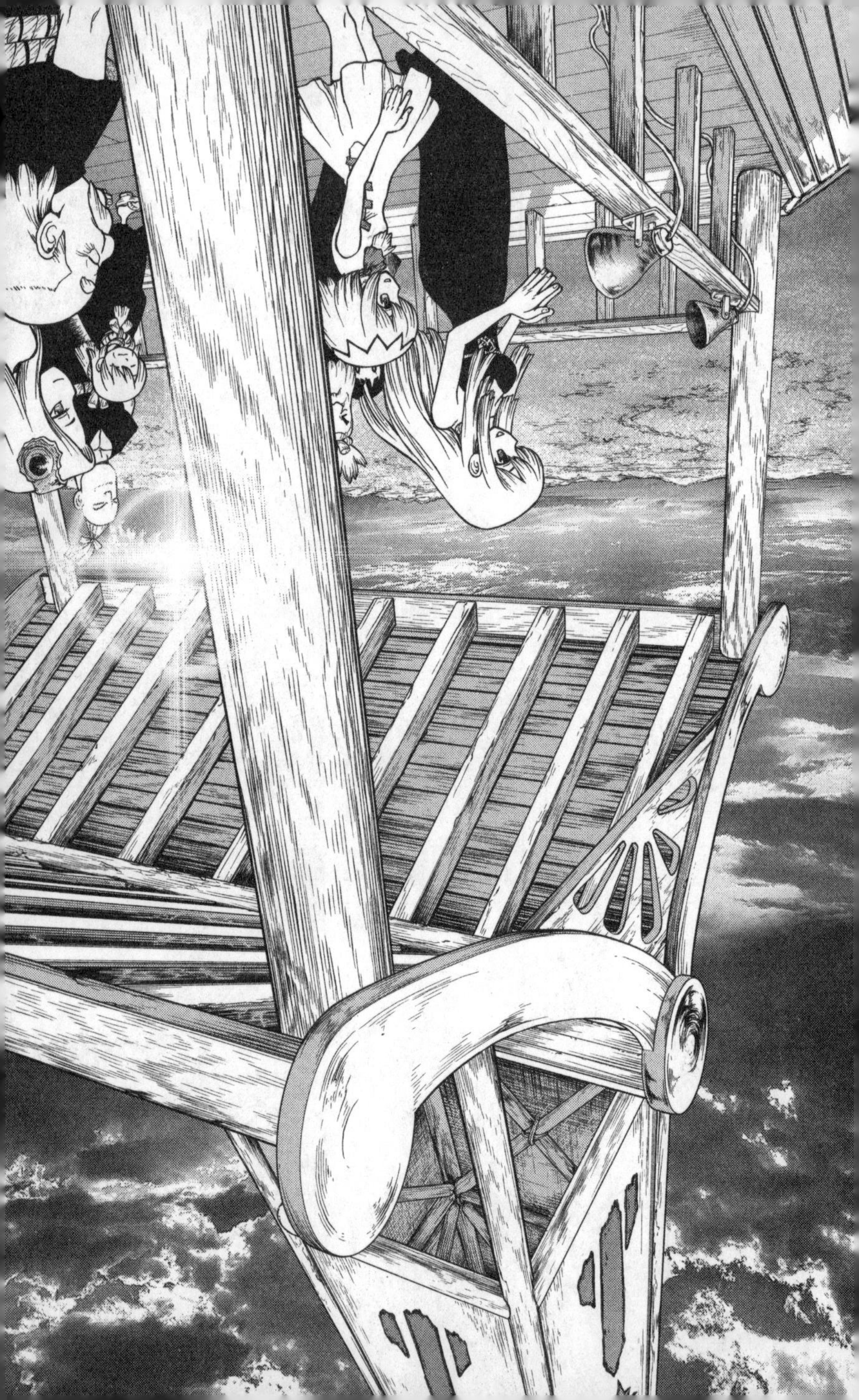

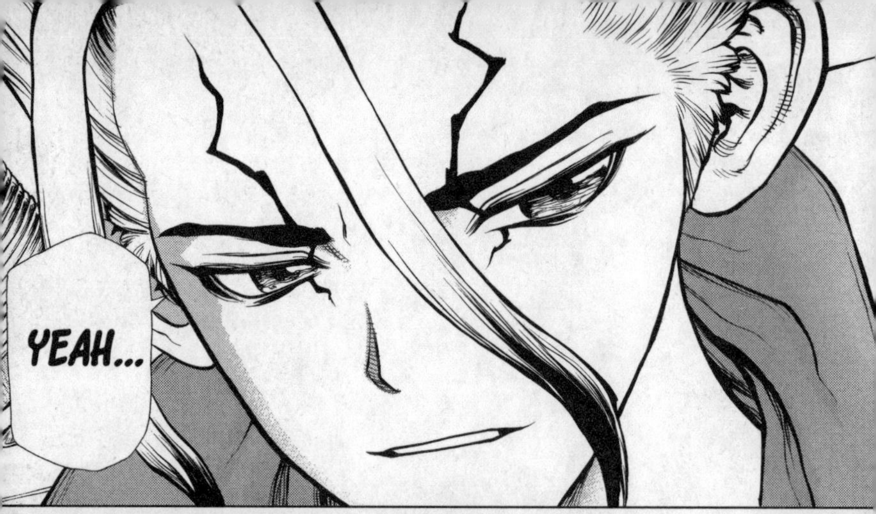
YEAH...
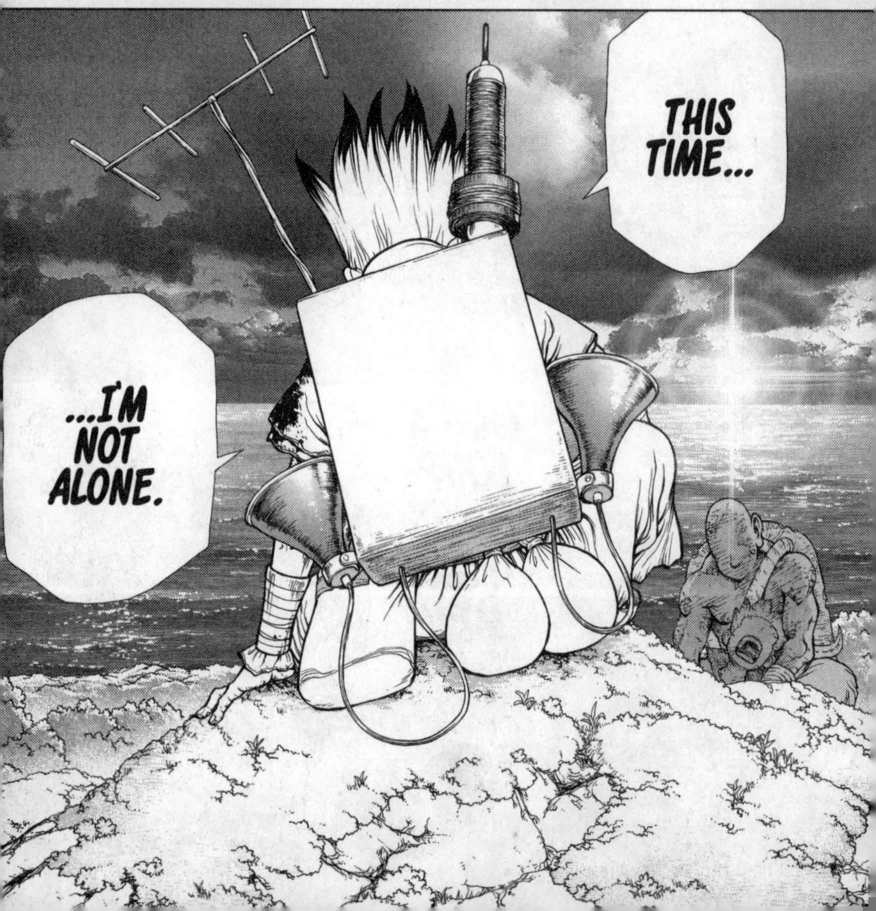
THIS TIME...
...I'M NOT ALONE.

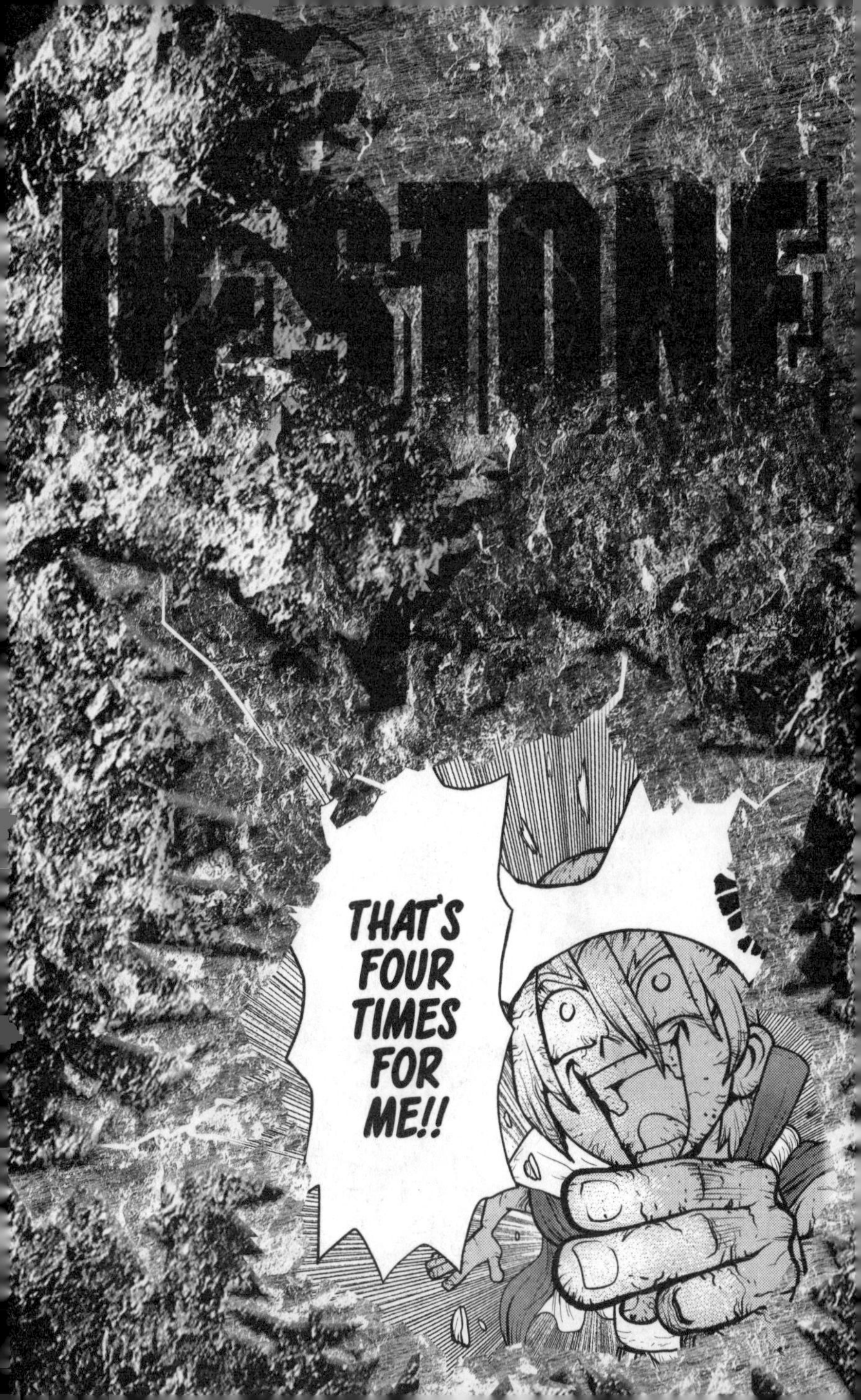
DR.STONE
THAT'S FOUR TIMES FOR ME!!

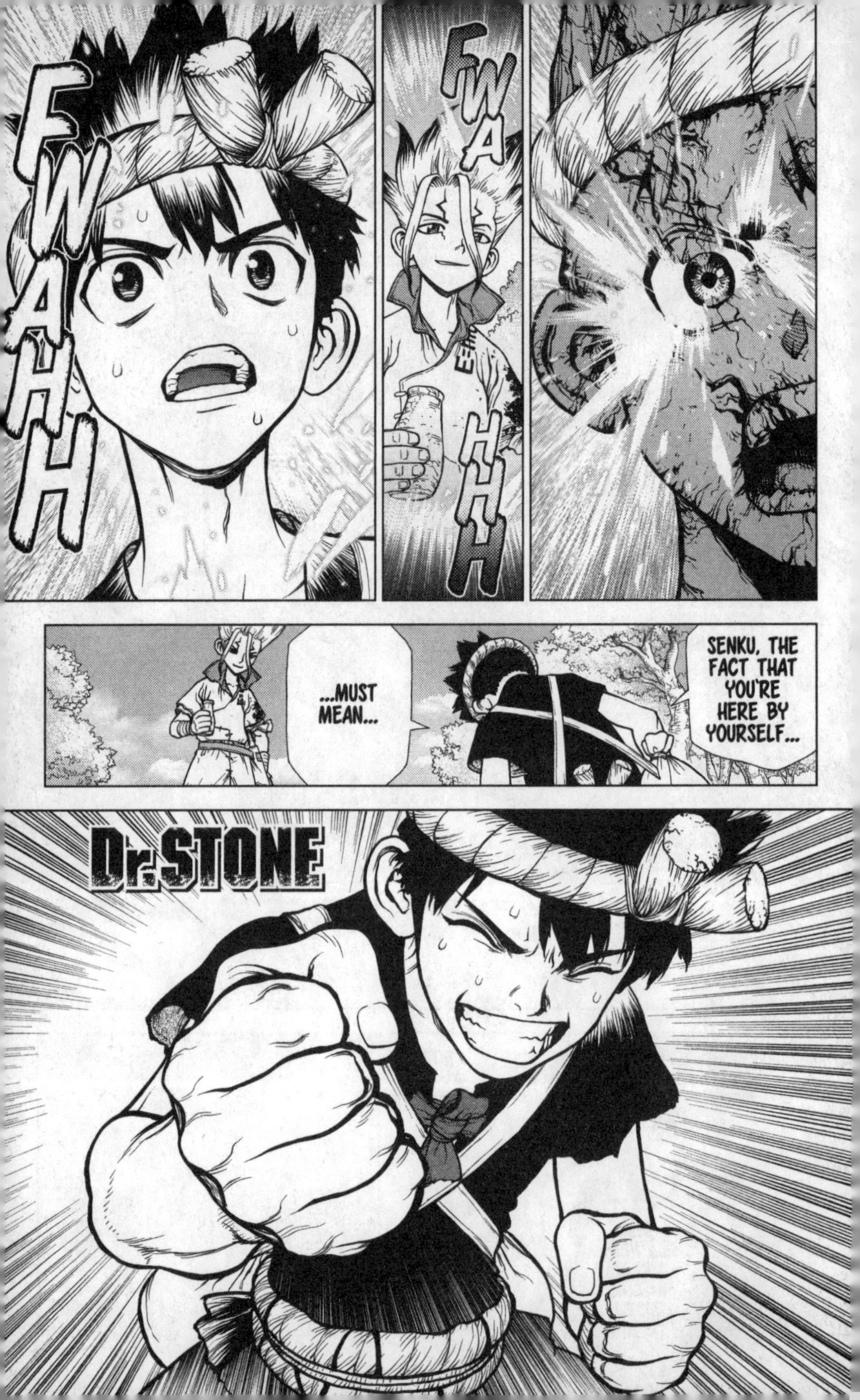
FWAHHH
FWAHH
SENKU, THE FACT THAT YOU'RE HERE BY YOURSELF...
...MUST MEAN...
Dr.STONE

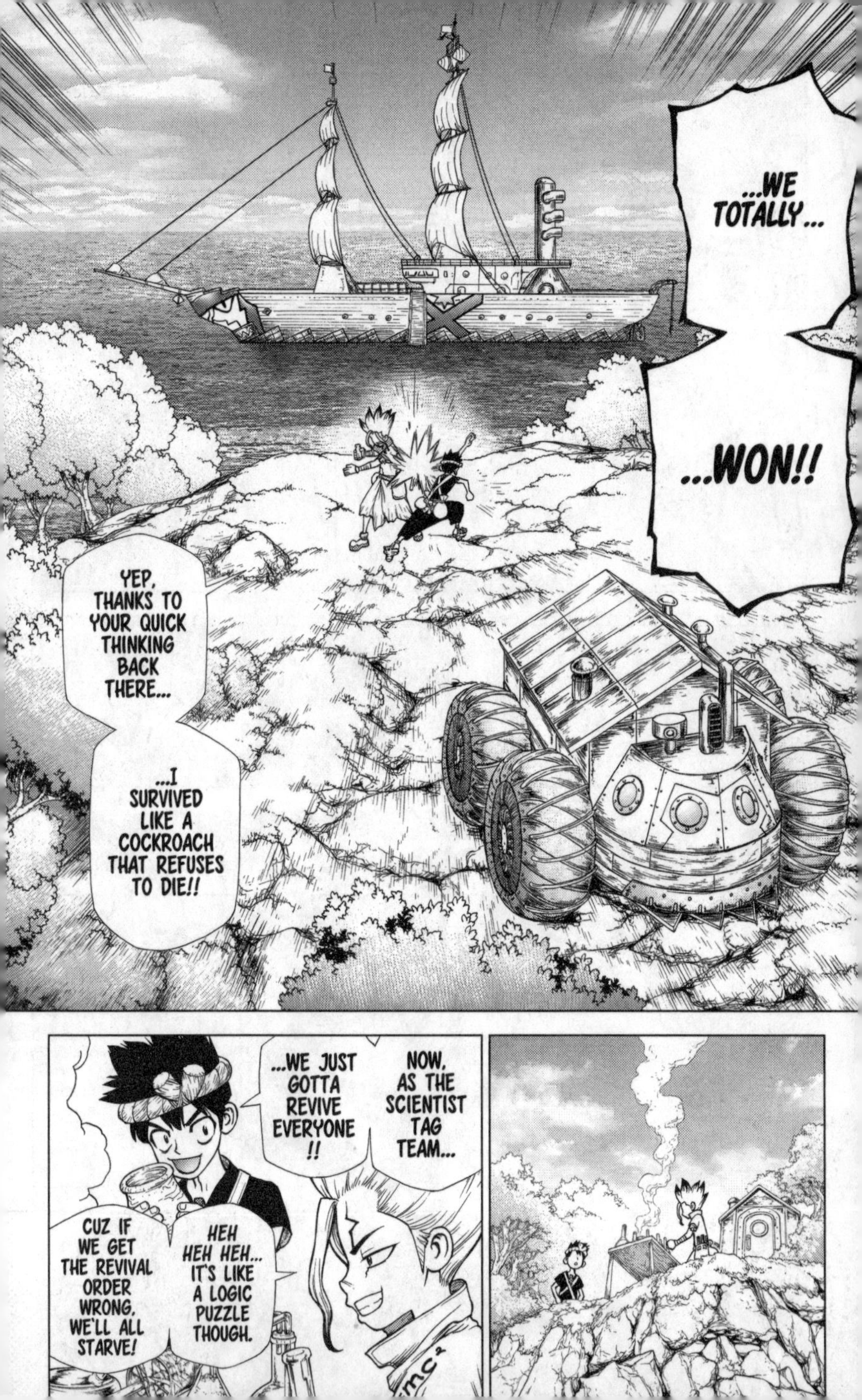
...WE TOTALLY...
...WON!!
YEP, THANKS TO YOUR QUICK THINKING BACK THERE...
...I SURVIVED LIKE A COCKROACH THAT REFUSES TO DIE!!
NOW, AS THE SCIENTIST TAG TEAM...
...WE JUST GOTTA REVIVE EVERYONE!!
HEH HEH HEH... IT'S LIKE A LOGIC PUZZLE THOUGH.
CUZ IF WE GET THE REVIVAL ORDER WRONG, WE'LL ALL STARVE!

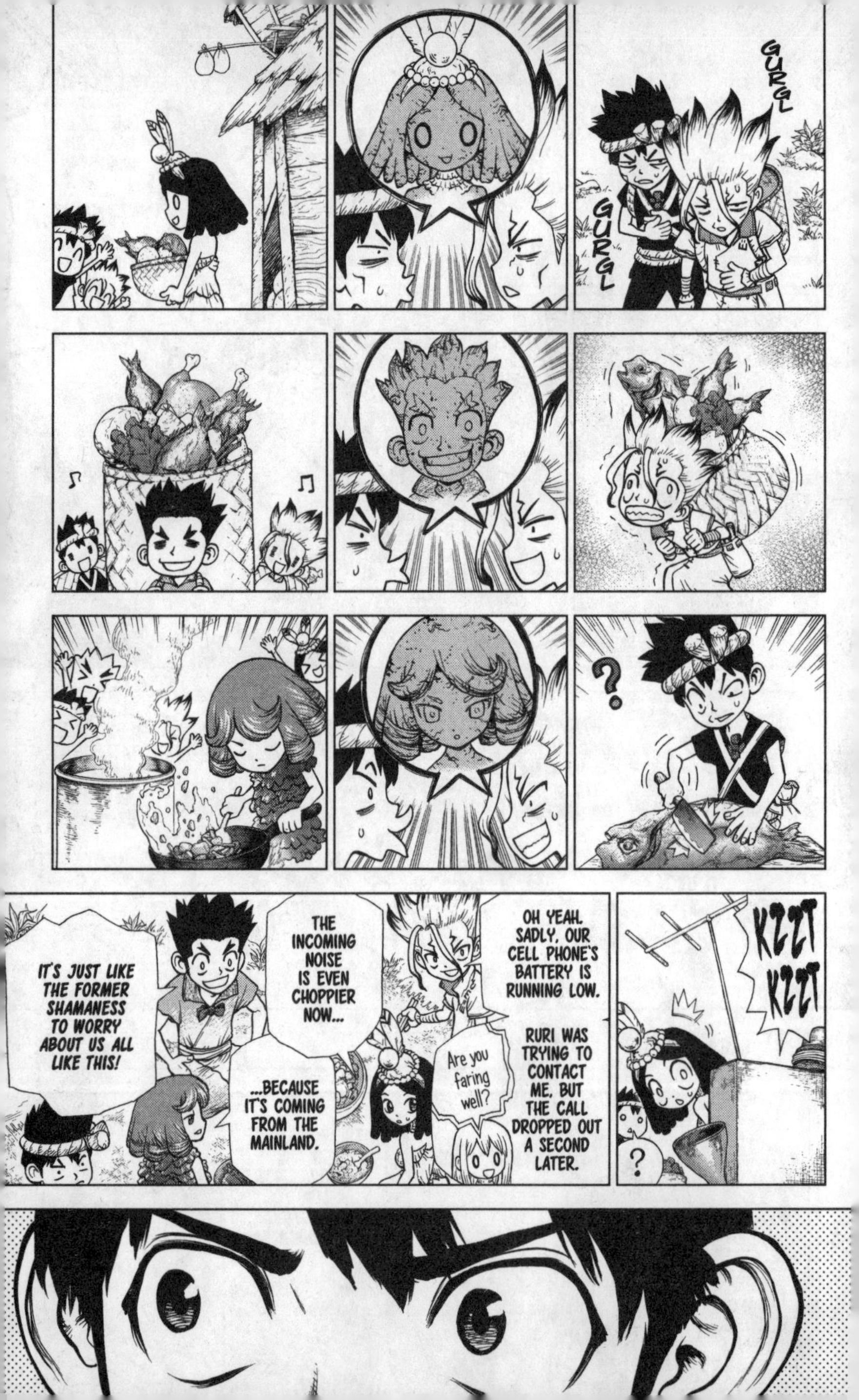
GURGL
GURGL
KZZT
KZZT
?
OH YEAH. SADLY, OUR CELL PHONE'S BATTERY IS RUNNING LOW.
RURI WAS TRYING TO CONTACT ME, BUT THE CALL DROPPED OUT A SECOND LATER.
Are you faring well?
THE INCOMING NOISE IS EVEN CHOPPIER NOW...
...BECAUSE IT'S COMING FROM THE MAINLAND.
IT'S JUST LIKE THE FORMER SHAMANESS TO WORRY ABOUT US ALL LIKE THIS!

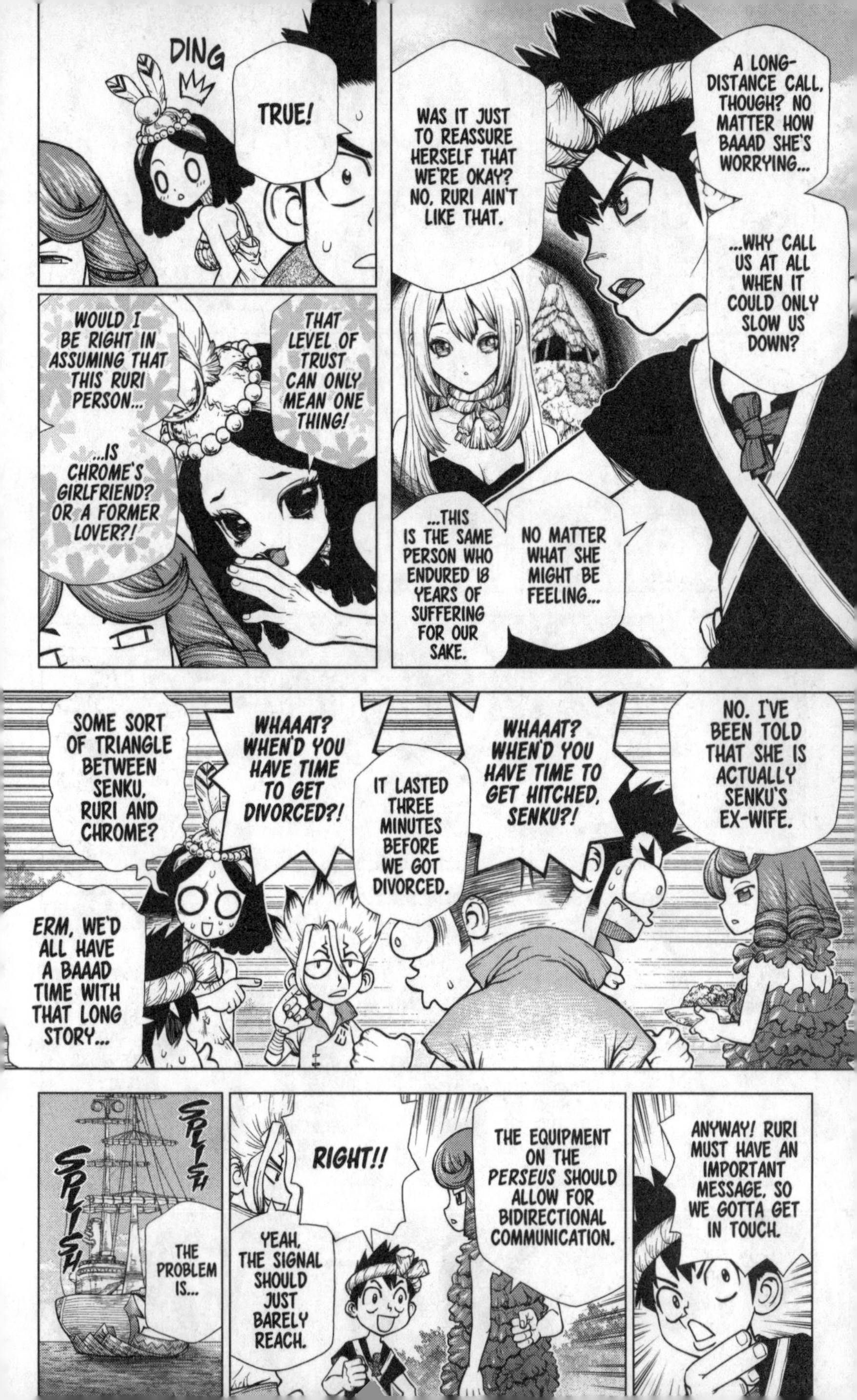
A LONG-DISTANCE CALL, THOUGH? NO MATTER HOW BAAAD SHE'S WORRYING...
...WHY CALL US AT ALL WHEN IT COULD ONLY SLOW US DOWN?
WAS IT JUST TO REASSURE HERSELF THAT WE'RE OKAY? NO, RURI AIN'T LIKE THAT.
NO MATTER WHAT SHE MIGHT BE FEELING...
...THIS IS THE SAME PERSON WHO ENDURED 18 YEARS OF SUFFERING FOR OUR SAKE.
DING
TRUE!
THAT LEVEL OF TRUST CAN ONLY MEAN ONE THING!
WOULD I BE RIGHT IN ASSUMING THAT THIS RURI PERSON...
...IS CHROME'S GIRLFRIEND? OR A FORMER LOVER?!
NO. I'VE BEEN TOLD THAT SHE IS ACTUALLY SENKU'S EX-WIFE.
WHAAAT? WHEN'D YOU HAVE TIME TO GET HITCHED, SENKU?!
IT LASTED THREE MINUTES BEFORE WE GOT DIVORCED.
WHAAAT? WHEN'D YOU HAVE TIME TO GET DIVORCED?!
SOME SORT OF TRIANGLE BETWEEN SENKU, RURI AND CHROME?
ERM, WE'D ALL HAVE A BAAAD TIME WITH THAT LONG STORY...
ANYWAY! RURI MUST HAVE AN IMPORTANT MESSAGE, SO WE GOTTA GET IN TOUCH.
THE EQUIPMENT ON THE PERSEUS SHOULD ALLOW FOR BIDIRECTIONAL COMMUNICATION.
RIGHT!!
YEAH, THE SIGNAL SHOULD JUST BARELY REACH.
SPLISH
SPLISH
THE PROBLEM IS...

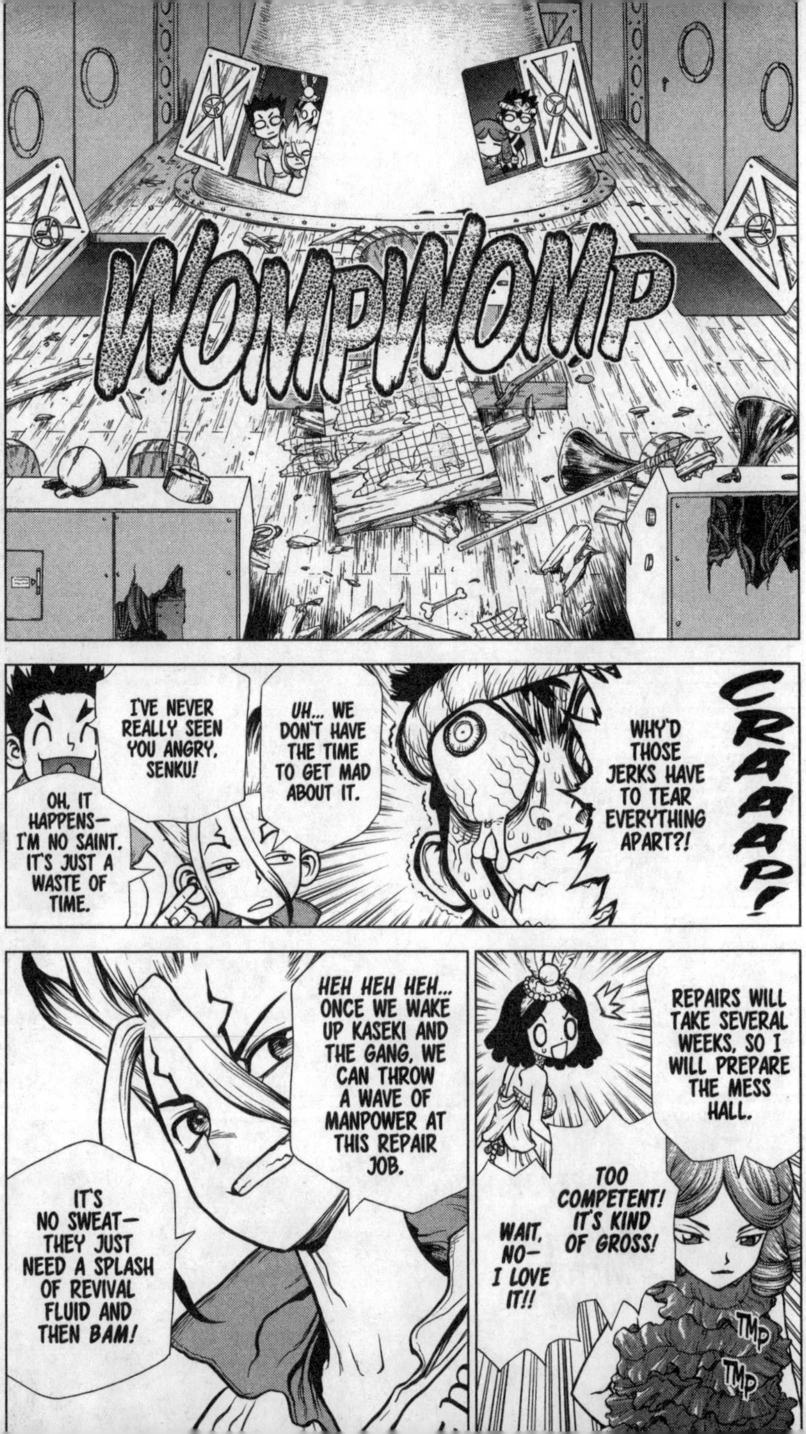
WOMPWOMP
CRAAAP!
WHY'D THOSE JERKS HAVE TO TEAR EVERYTHING APART?!
UH... WE DON'T HAVE THE TIME TO GET MAD ABOUT IT.
I'VE NEVER REALLY SEEN YOU ANGRY, SENKU!
OH, IT HAPPENS— I'M NO SAINT. IT'S JUST A WASTE OF TIME.
REPAIRS WILL TAKE SEVERAL WEEKS, SO I WILL PREPARE THE MESS HALL.
TOO COMPETENT! IT'S KIND OF GROSS!
WAIT, NO— I LOVE IT!!
TMP
TMP
HEH HEH HEH... ONCE WE WAKE UP KASEKI AND THE GANG, WE CAN THROW A WAVE OF MANPOWER AT THIS REPAIR JOB.
IT'S NO SWEAT— THEY JUST NEED A SPLASH OF REVIVAL FLUID AND THEN BAM!

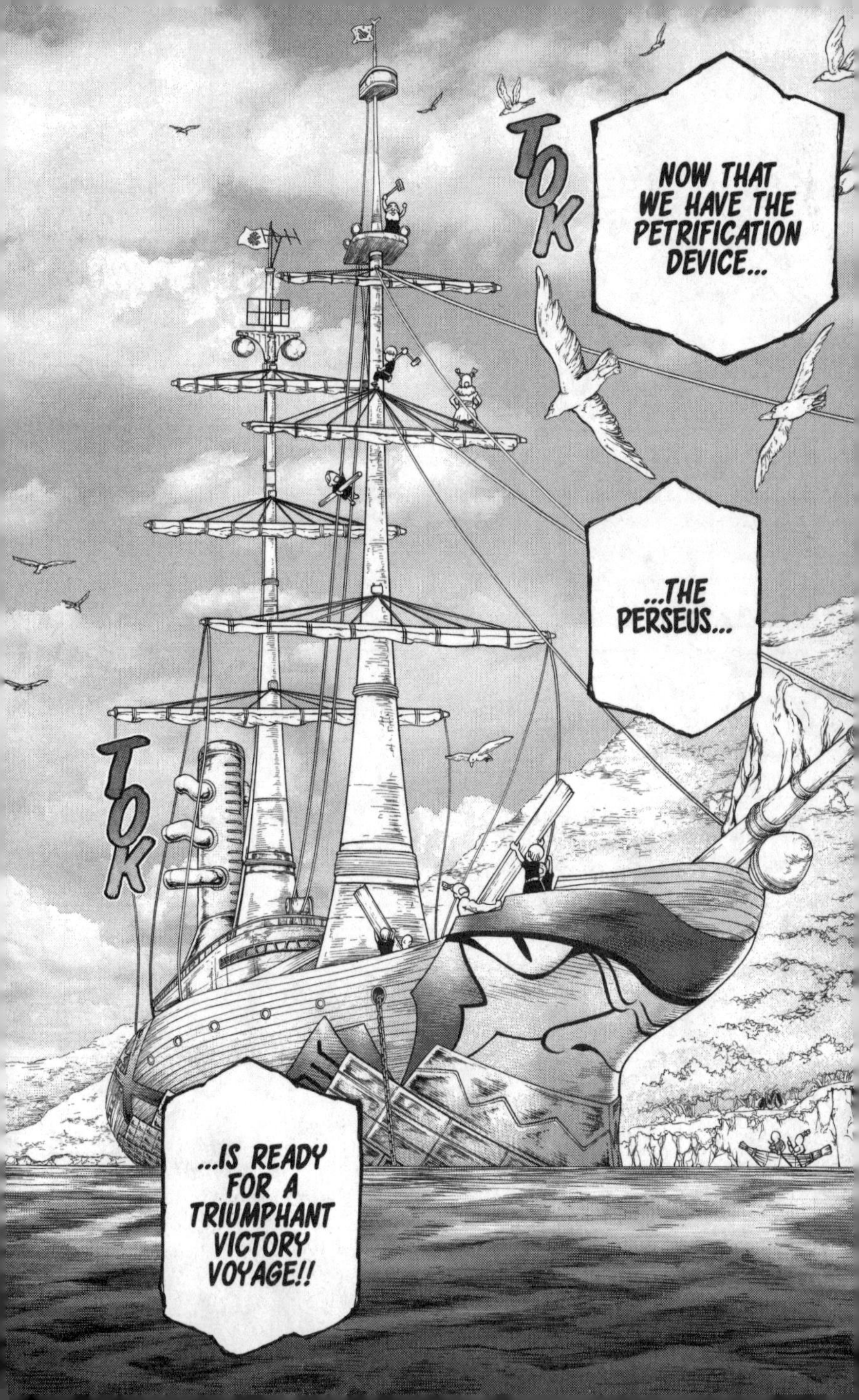
TOK
NOW THAT WE HAVE THE PETRIFICATION DEVICE...
...THE PERSEUS...
TOK
...IS READY FOR A TRIUMPHANT VICTORY VOYAGE!!

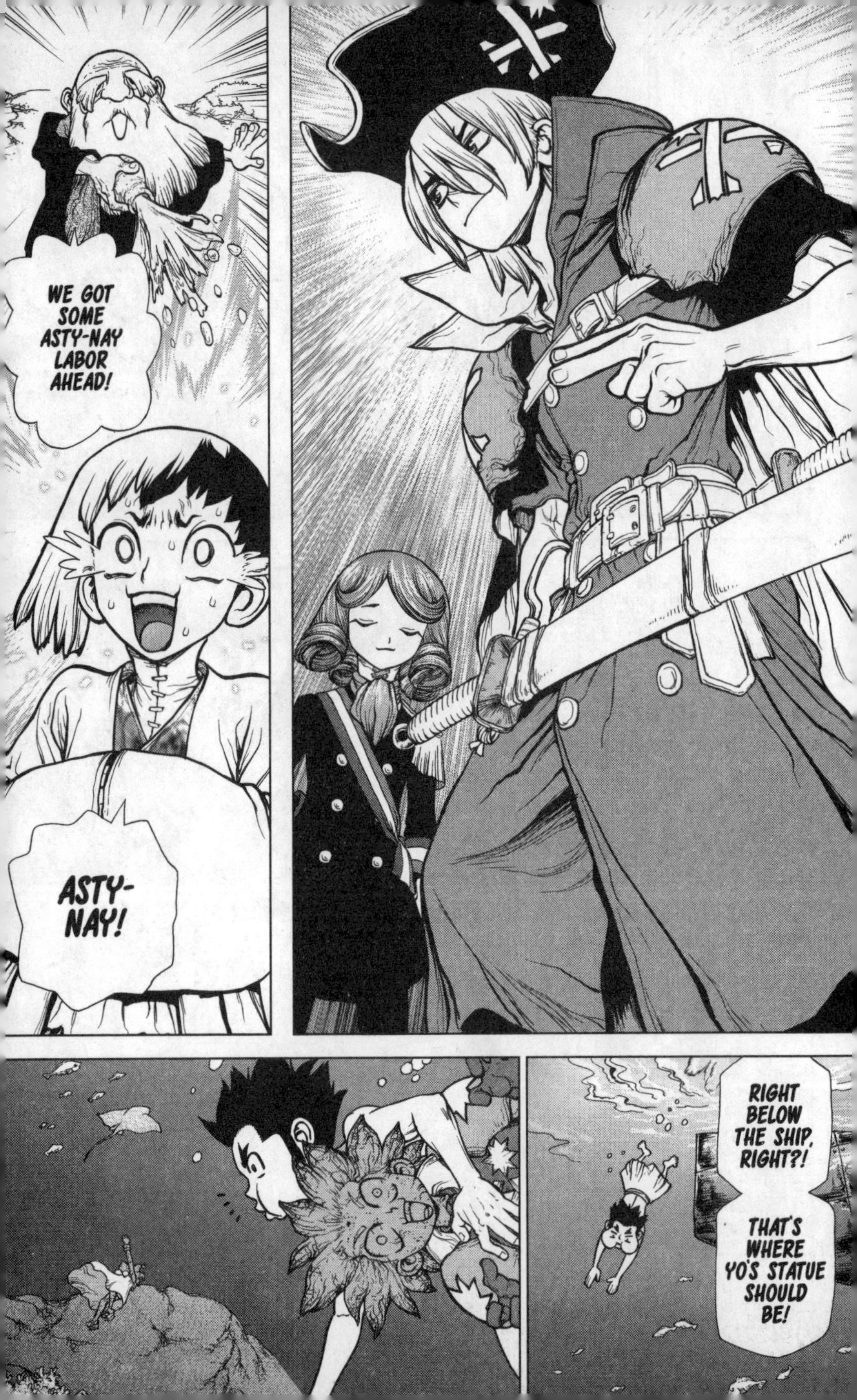
WE GOT SOME ASTY-NAY LABOR AHEAD!
ASTY-NAY!
RIGHT BELOW THE SHIP, RIGHT?!
THAT'S WHERE YO'S STATUE SHOULD BE!

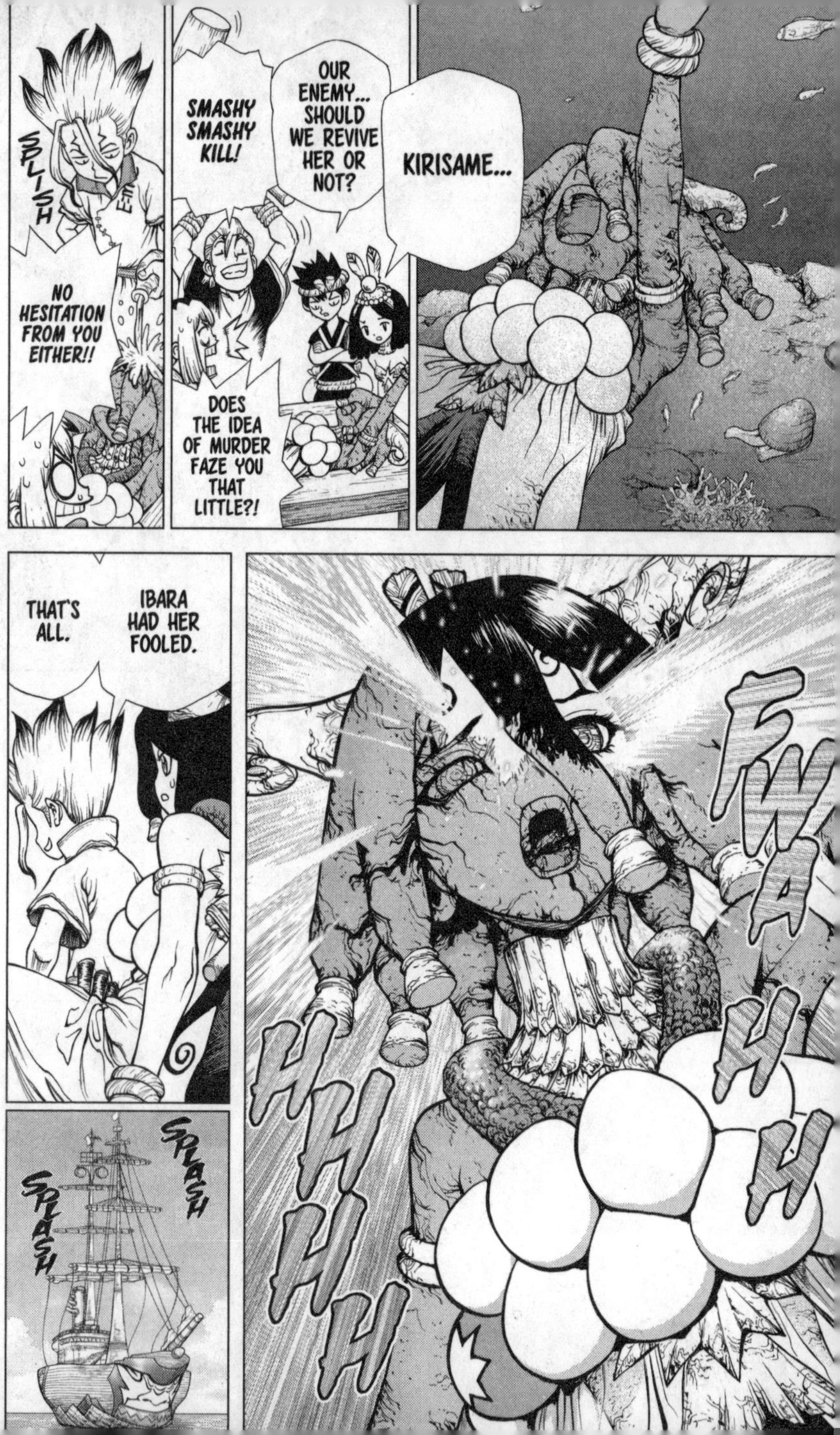
KIRISAME...
OUR ENEMY... SHOULD WE REVIVE HER OR NOT?
SMASHY SMASHY KILL!
DOES THE IDEA OF MURDER FAZE YOU THAT LITTLE?!
SPLISH
NO HESITATION FROM YOU EITHER!!
FWAHHHHHHHHHHH
THAT'S ALL.
IBARA HAD HER FOOLED.
SPLASH
SPLASH

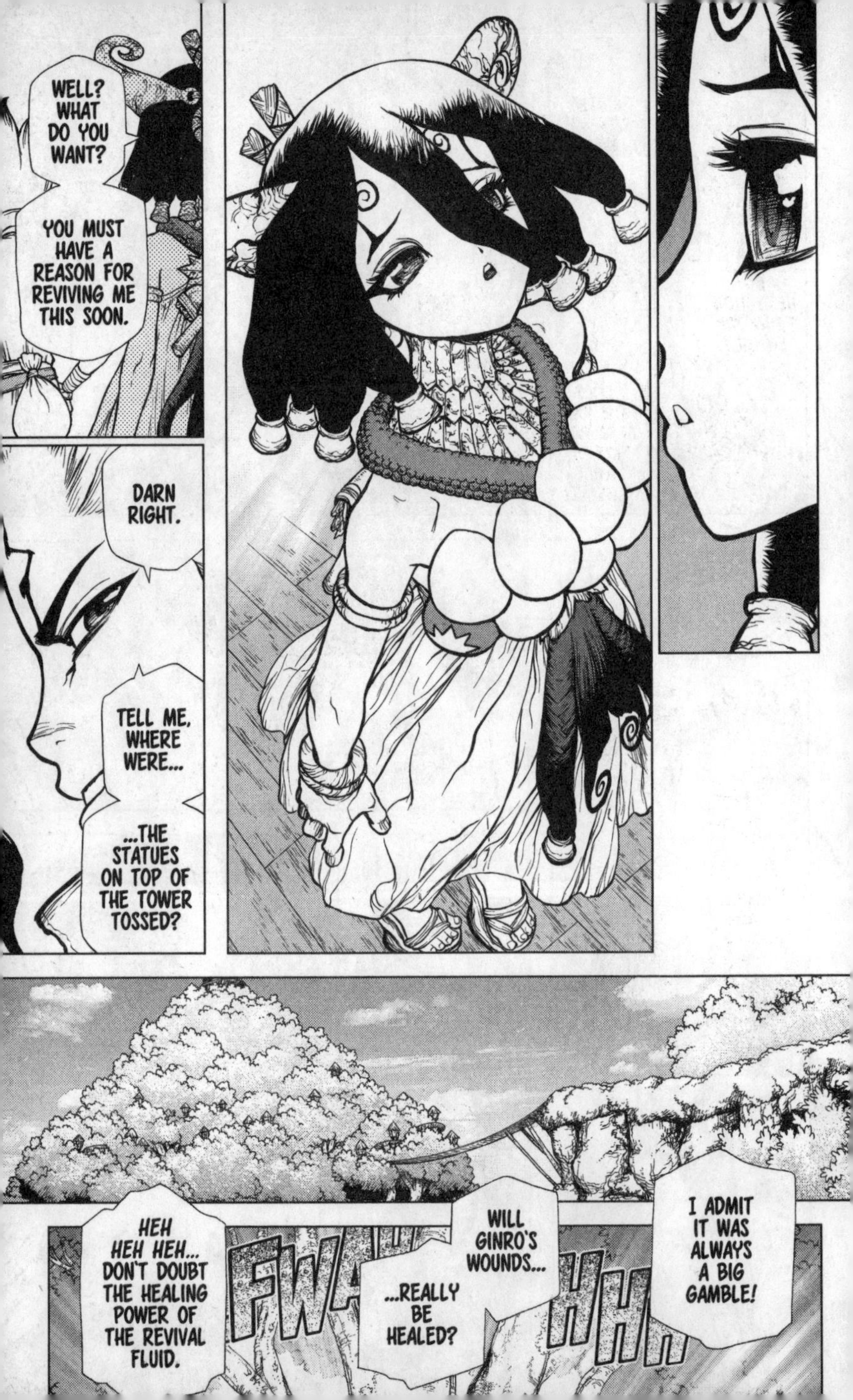
WELL? WHAT DO YOU WANT?
YOU MUST HAVE A REASON FOR REVIVING ME THIS SOON.
DARN RIGHT.
TELL ME, WHERE WERE...
...THE STATUES ON TOP OF THE TOWER TOSSED?
I ADMIT IT WAS ALWAYS A BIG GAMBLE!
WILL GINRO'S WOUNDS...
...REALLY BE HEALED?
FWAHHH
HEH HEH HEH... DON'T DOUBT THE HEALING POWER OF THE REVIVAL FLUID.

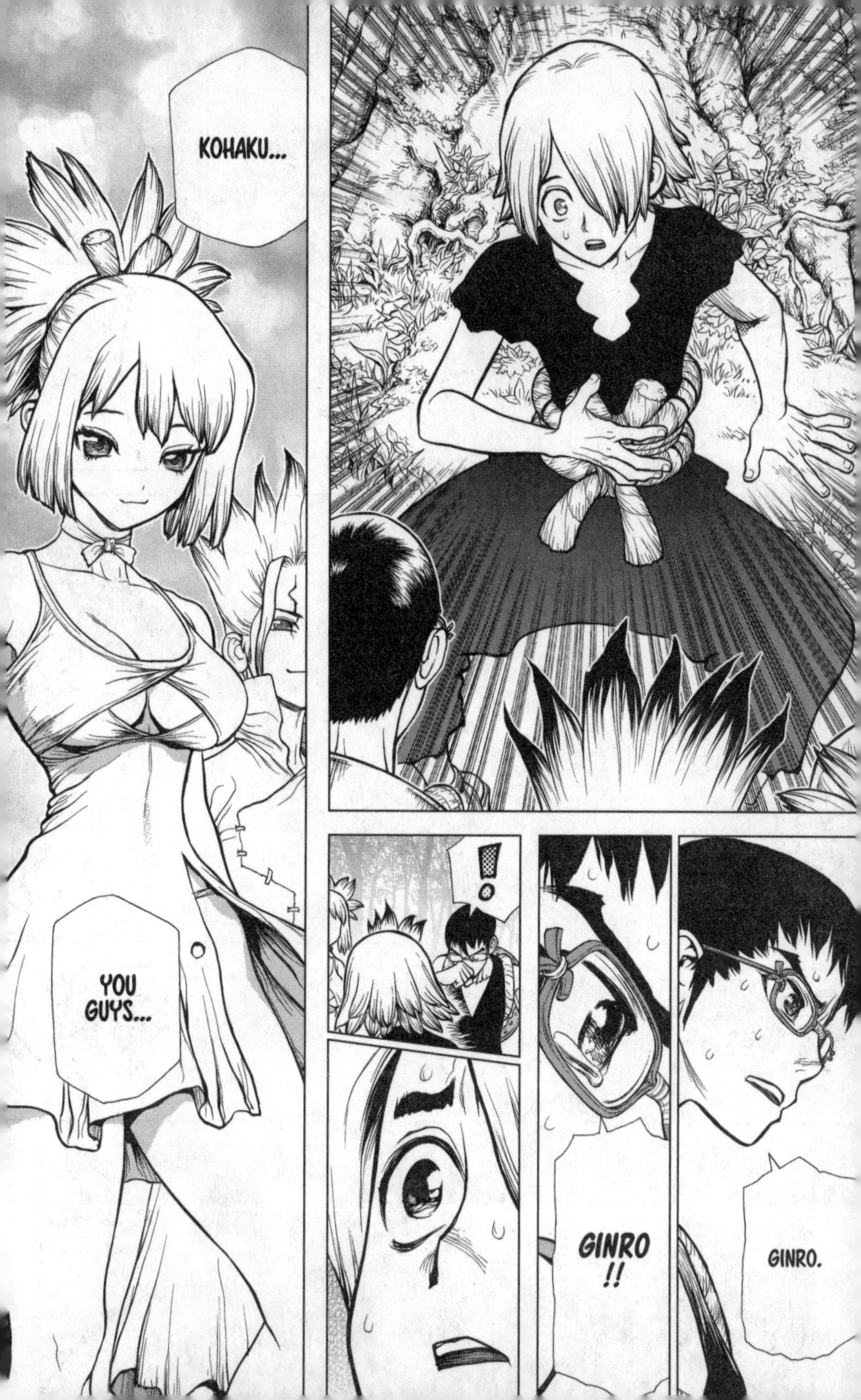
GINRO.
GINRO !!
!?
KOHAKU...
YOU GUYS...

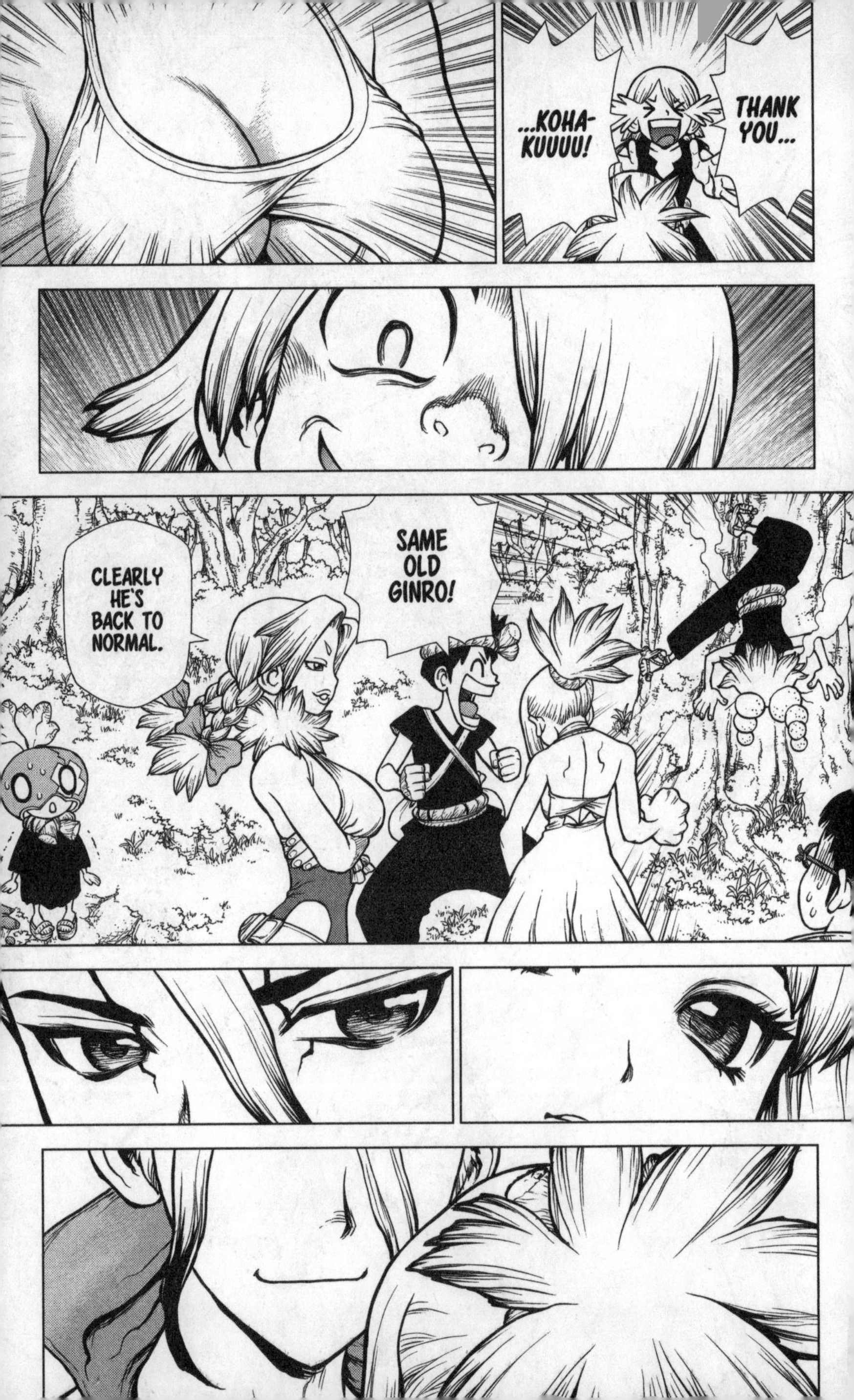
THANK YOU...
...KOHA-KUUUU!
SAME OLD GINRO!
CLEARLY HE'S BACK TO NORMAL.

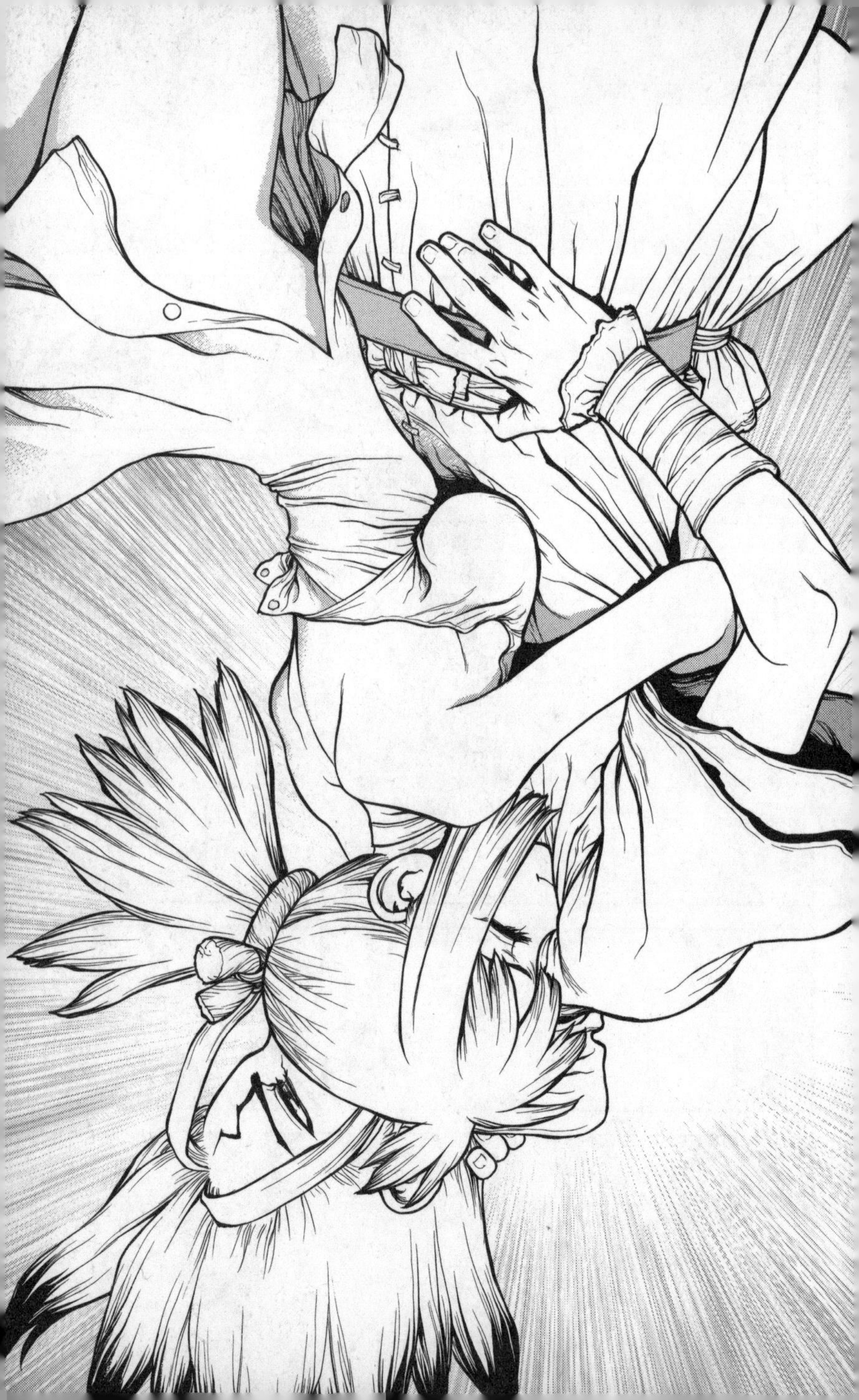

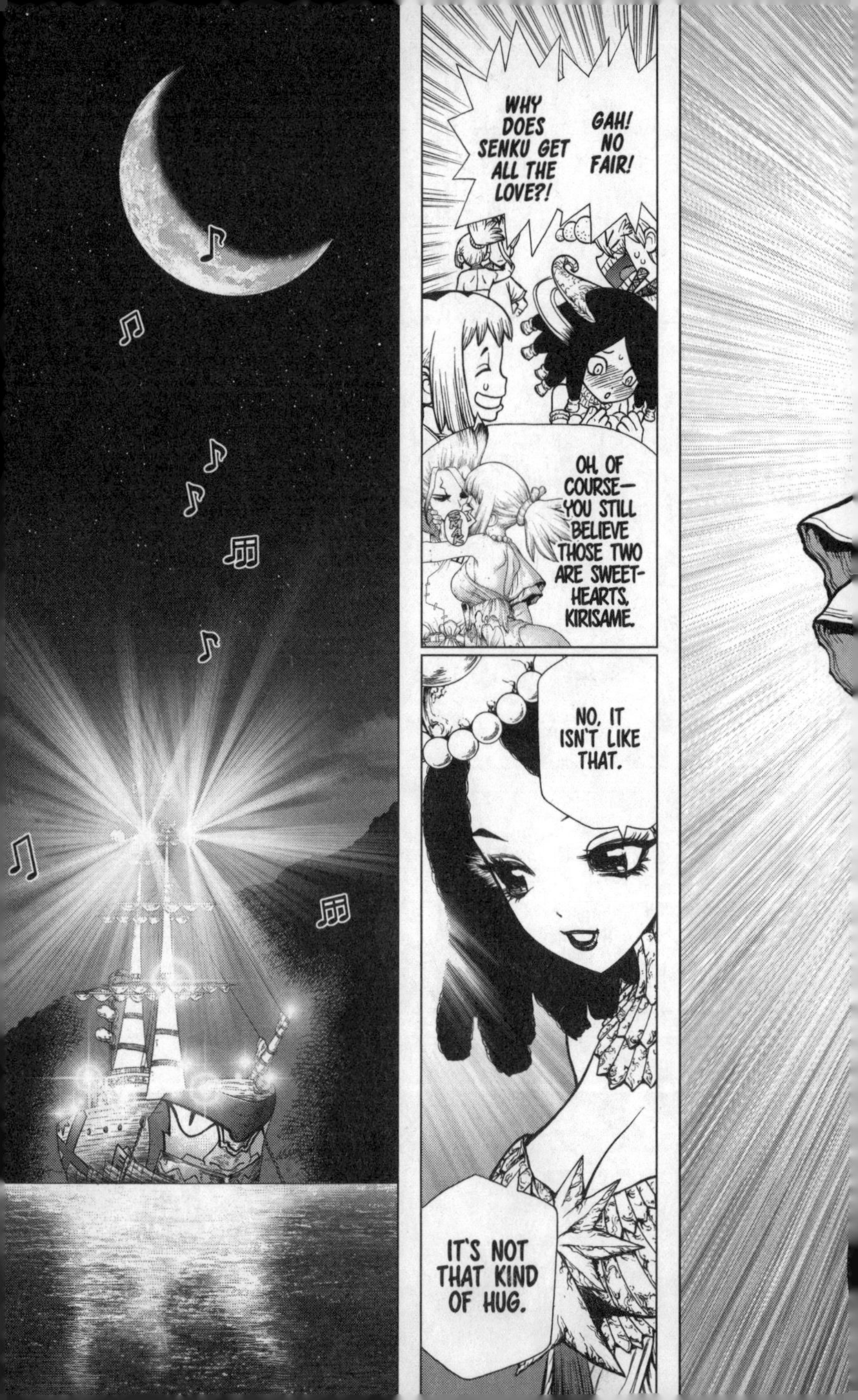
GAH! NO FAIR!
WHY DOES SENKU GET ALL THE LOVE?!
OH, OF COURSE—YOU STILL BELIEVE THOSE TWO ARE SWEET-HEARTS, KIRISAME.
NO, IT ISN'T LIKE THAT.
IT'S NOT THAT KIND OF HUG.

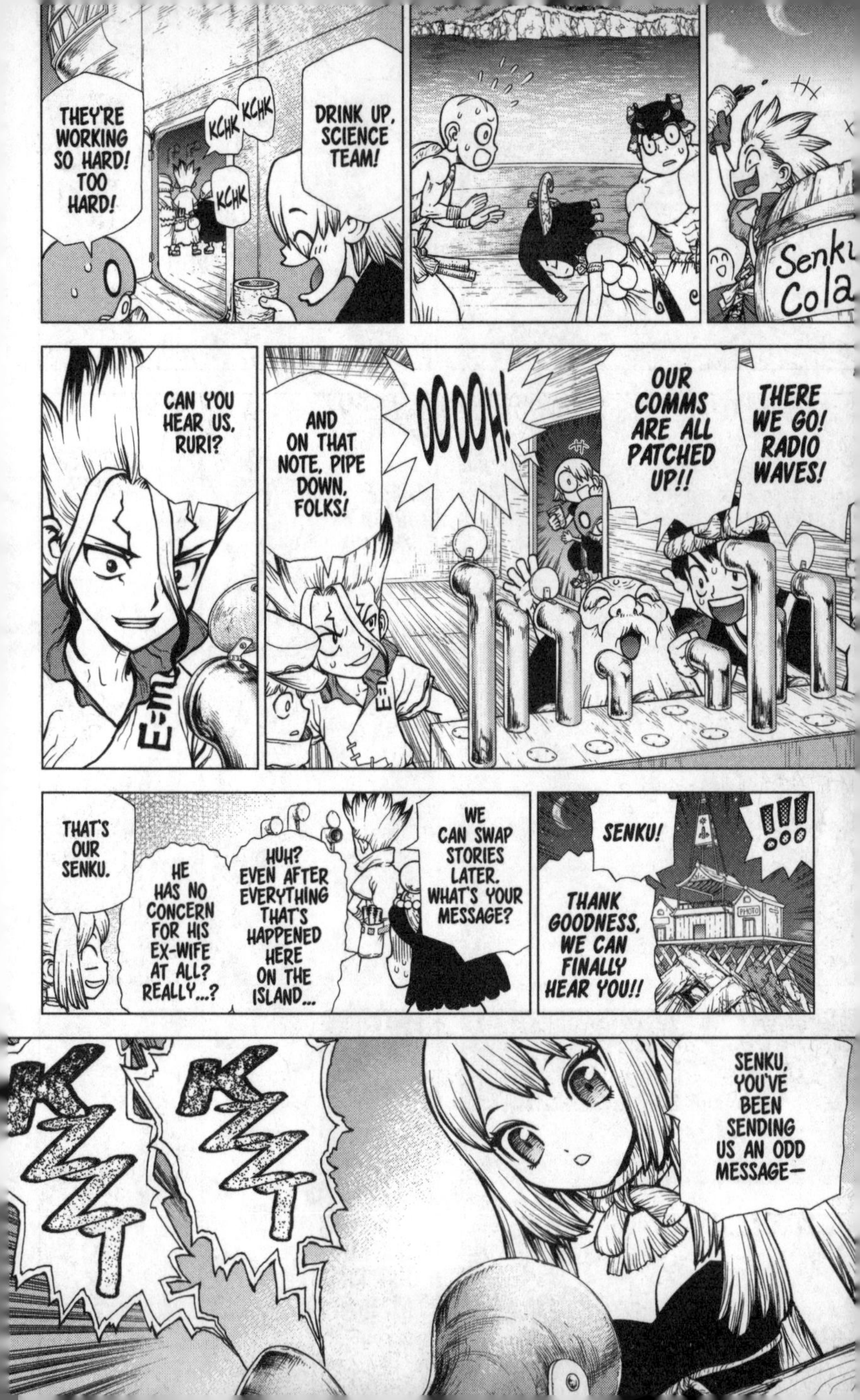
Senku Cola
DRINK UP, SCIENCE TEAM!
KCHK
KCHK
KCHK
THEY'RE WORKING SO HARD! TOO HARD!
THERE WE GO! RADIO WAVES!
OUR COMMS ARE ALL PATCHED UP!!
OOOOH!
AND ON THAT NOTE, PIPE DOWN, FOLKS!
CAN YOU HEAR US, RURI?
!!!
SENKU!
THANK GOODNESS, WE CAN FINALLY HEAR YOU!!
WE CAN SWAP STORIES LATER. WHAT'S YOUR MESSAGE?
HUH? EVEN AFTER EVERYTHING THAT'S HAPPENED HERE ON THE ISLAND...
HE HAS NO CONCERN FOR HIS EX-WIFE AT ALL? REALLY...?
THAT'S OUR SENKU.
SENKU, YOU'VE BEEN SENDING US AN ODD MESSAGE—
KZZZT
KZZZT

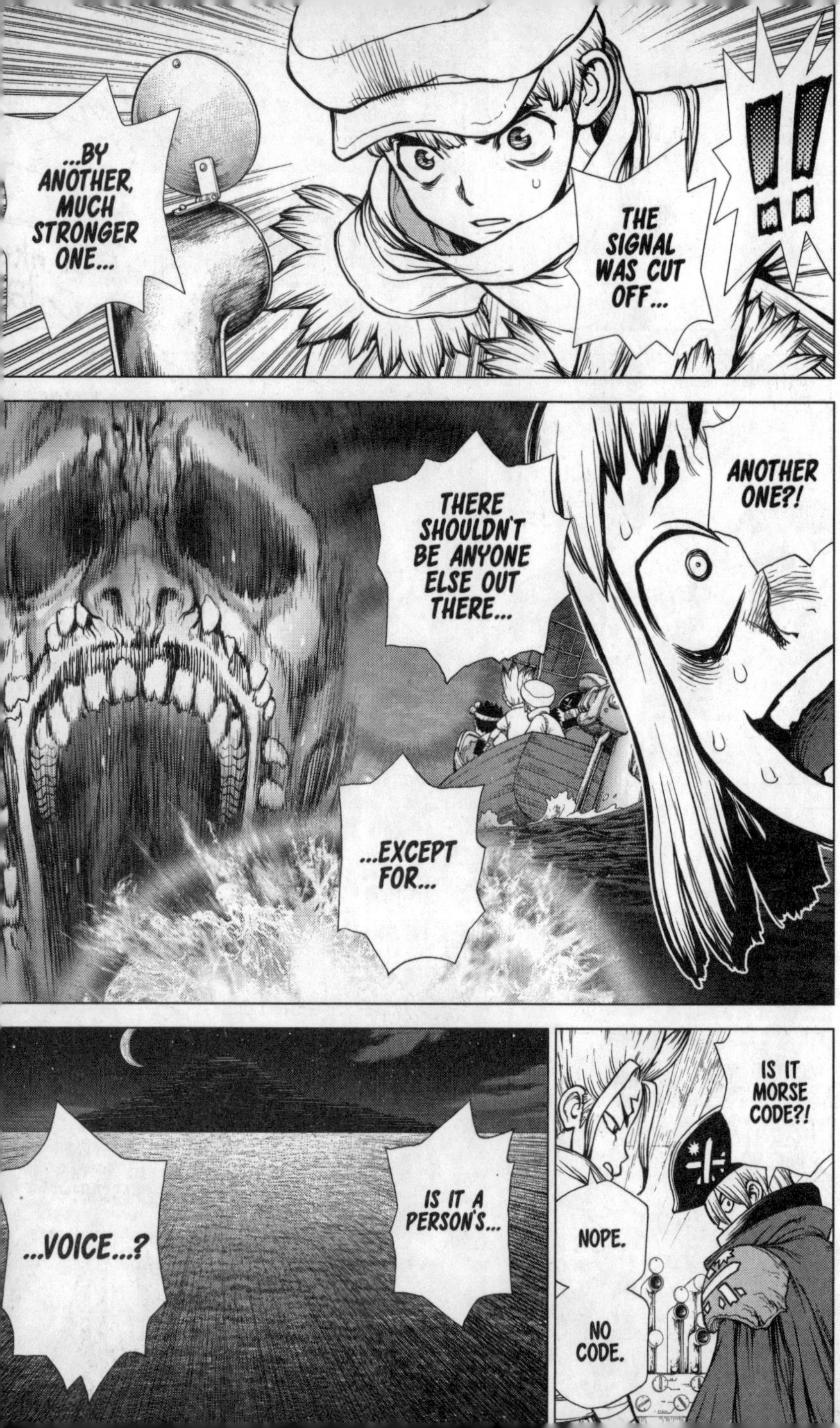
!!
THE SIGNAL WAS CUT OFF...
...BY ANOTHER, MUCH STRONGER ONE...
ANOTHER ONE?!
THERE SHOULDN'T BE ANYONE ELSE OUT THERE...
...EXCEPT FOR...
IS IT MORSE CODE?!
NOPE.
NO CODE.
IS IT A PERSON'S...
...VOICE...?

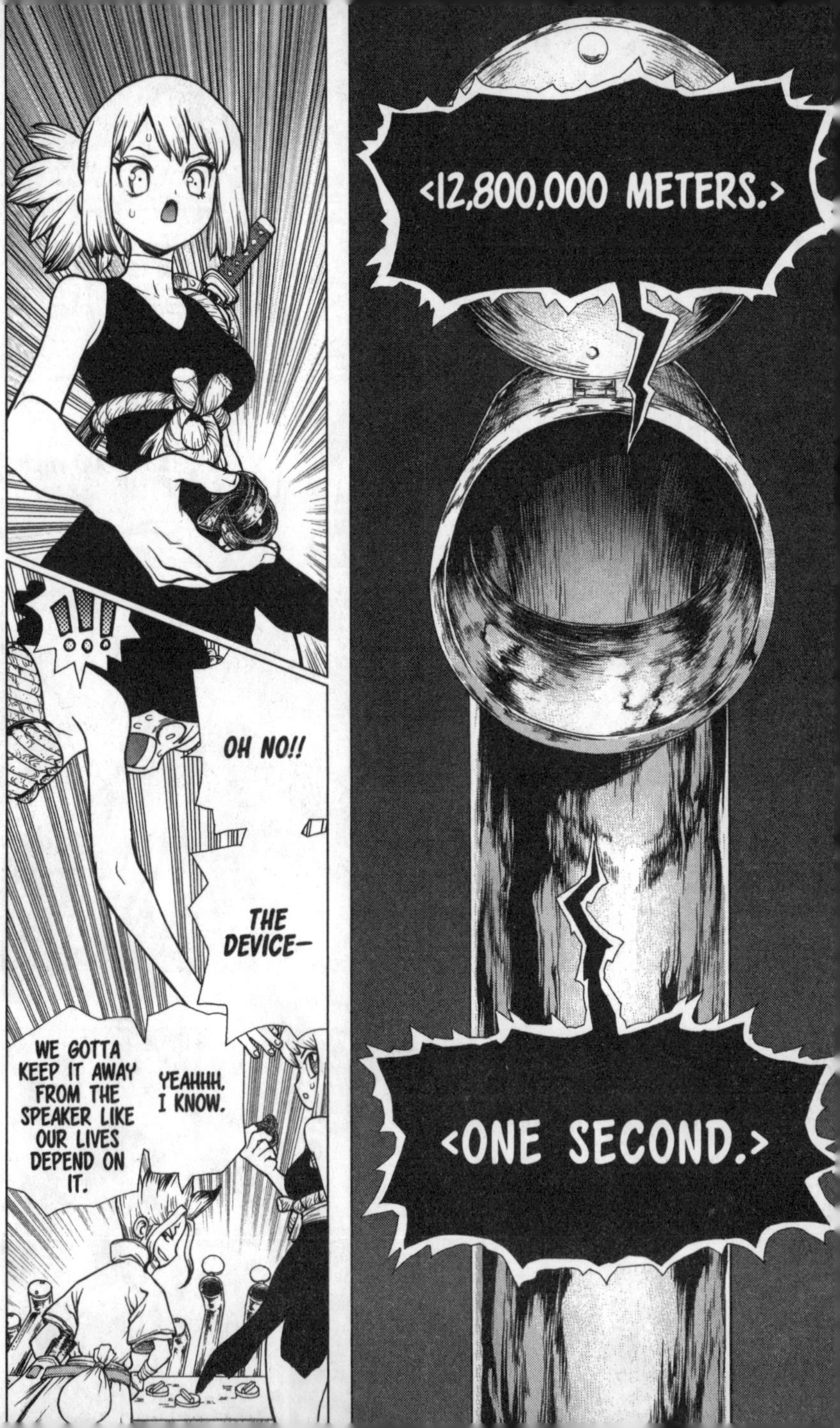

<12,800,000 METERS.>
<ONE SECOND.>
!!!
OH NO!!
THE DEVICE—
WE GOTTA KEEP IT AWAY FROM THE SPEAKER LIKE OUR LIVES DEPEND ON IT.
YEAHHH, I KNOW.

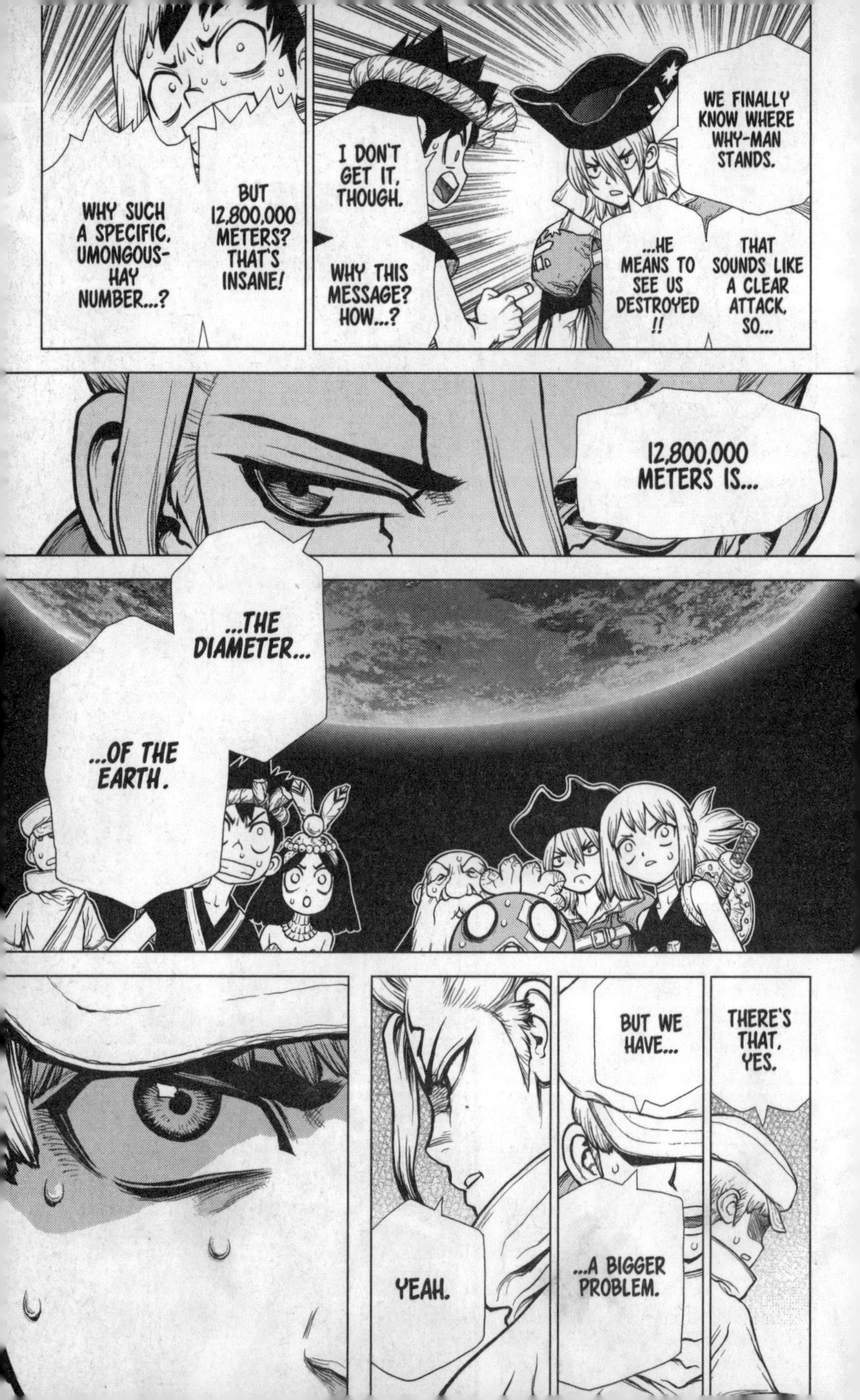
WE FINALLY KNOW WHERE WHY-MAN STANDS.
THAT SOUNDS LIKE A CLEAR ATTACK, SO...
...HE MEANS TO SEE US DESTROYED !!
I DON'T GET IT, THOUGH.
WHY THIS MESSAGE? HOW...?
BUT 12,800,000 METERS? THAT'S INSANE!
WHY SUCH A SPECIFIC, UMONGOUS-HAY NUMBER...?
12,800,000 METERS IS...
...THE DIAMETER...
...OF THE EARTH.
THERE'S THAT, YES.
BUT WE HAVE...
...A BIGGER PROBLEM.
YEAH.

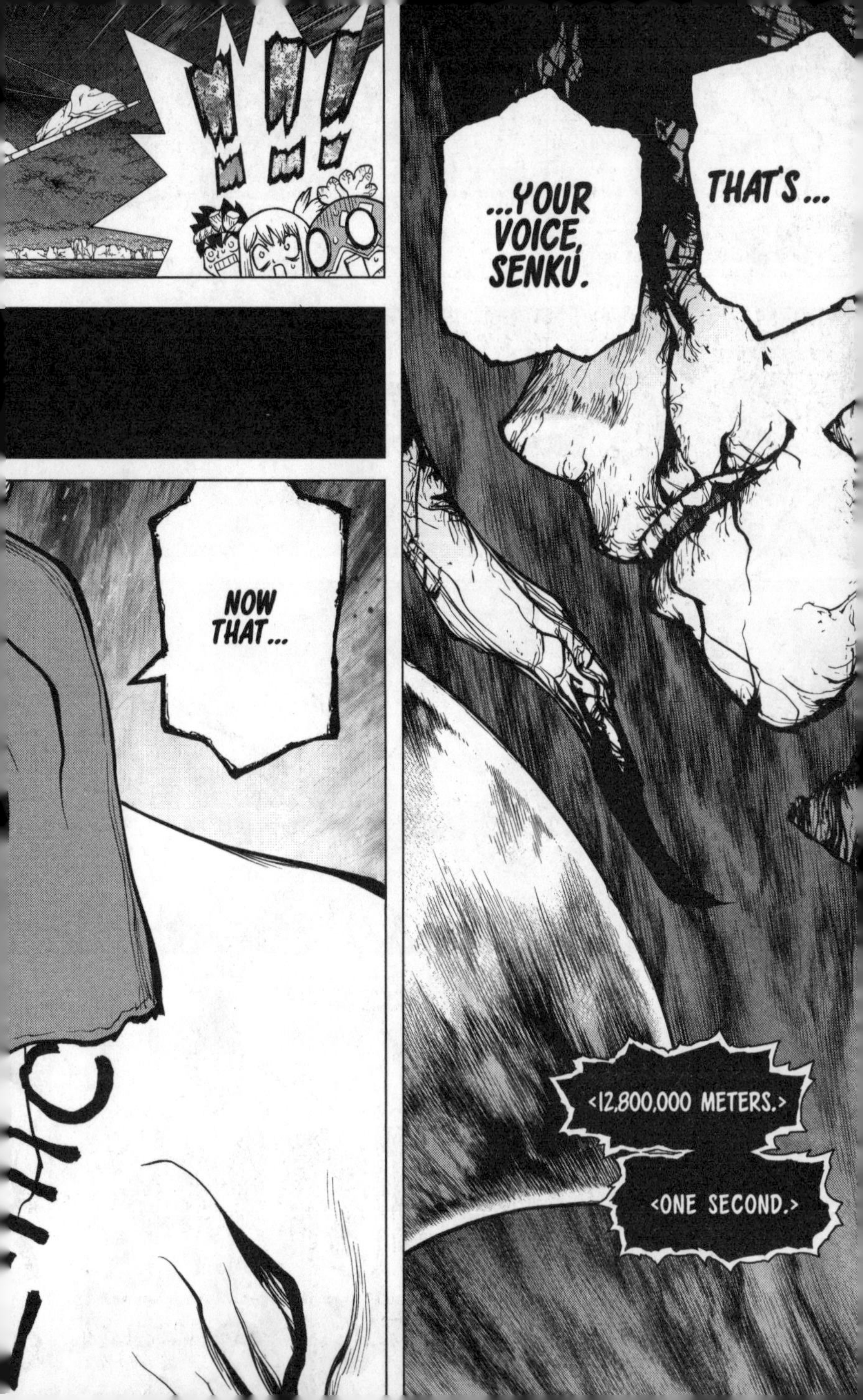
THAT'S...
...YOUR VOICE, SENKU.
<12,800,000 METERS.>
<ONE SECOND.>
NOW THAT...

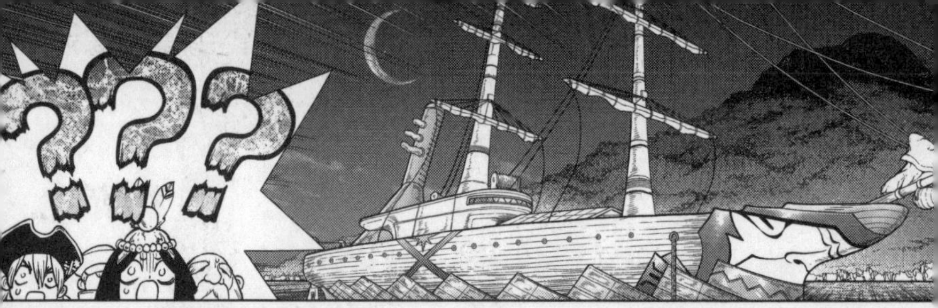
???

Z = 138: Epilogue of Part 3
(End of Part 3)

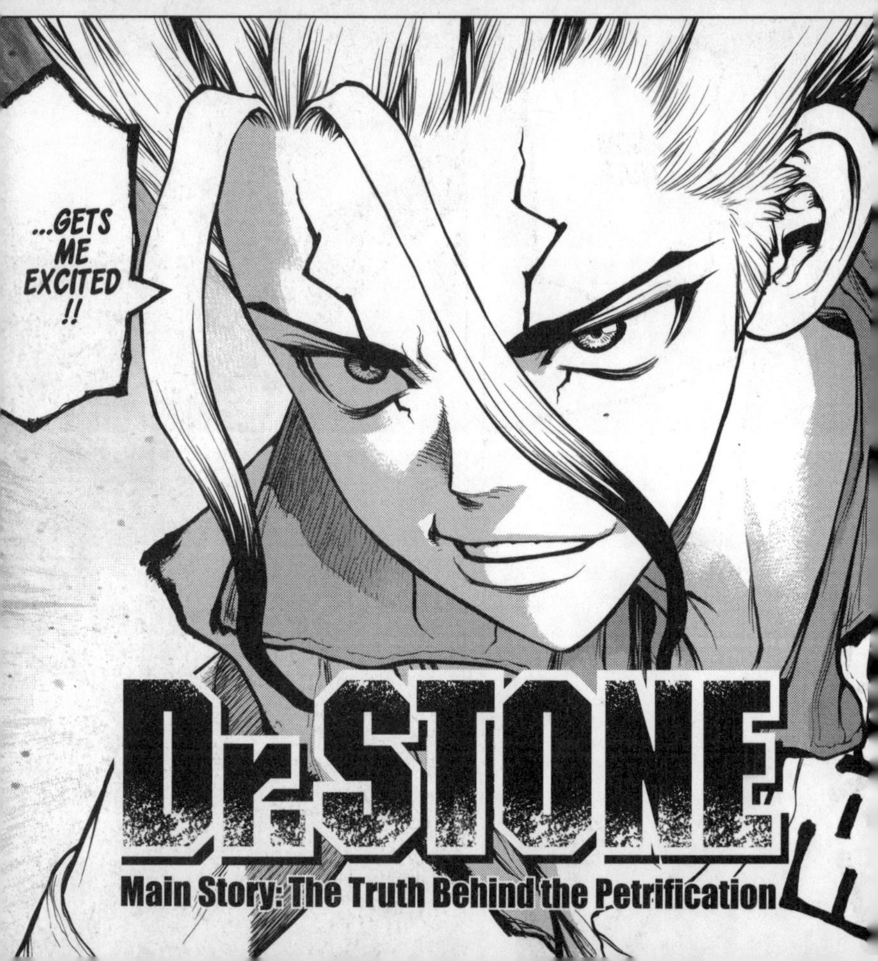
...GETS ME EXCITED !!
Dr.STONE
Main Story: The Truth Behind the Petrification

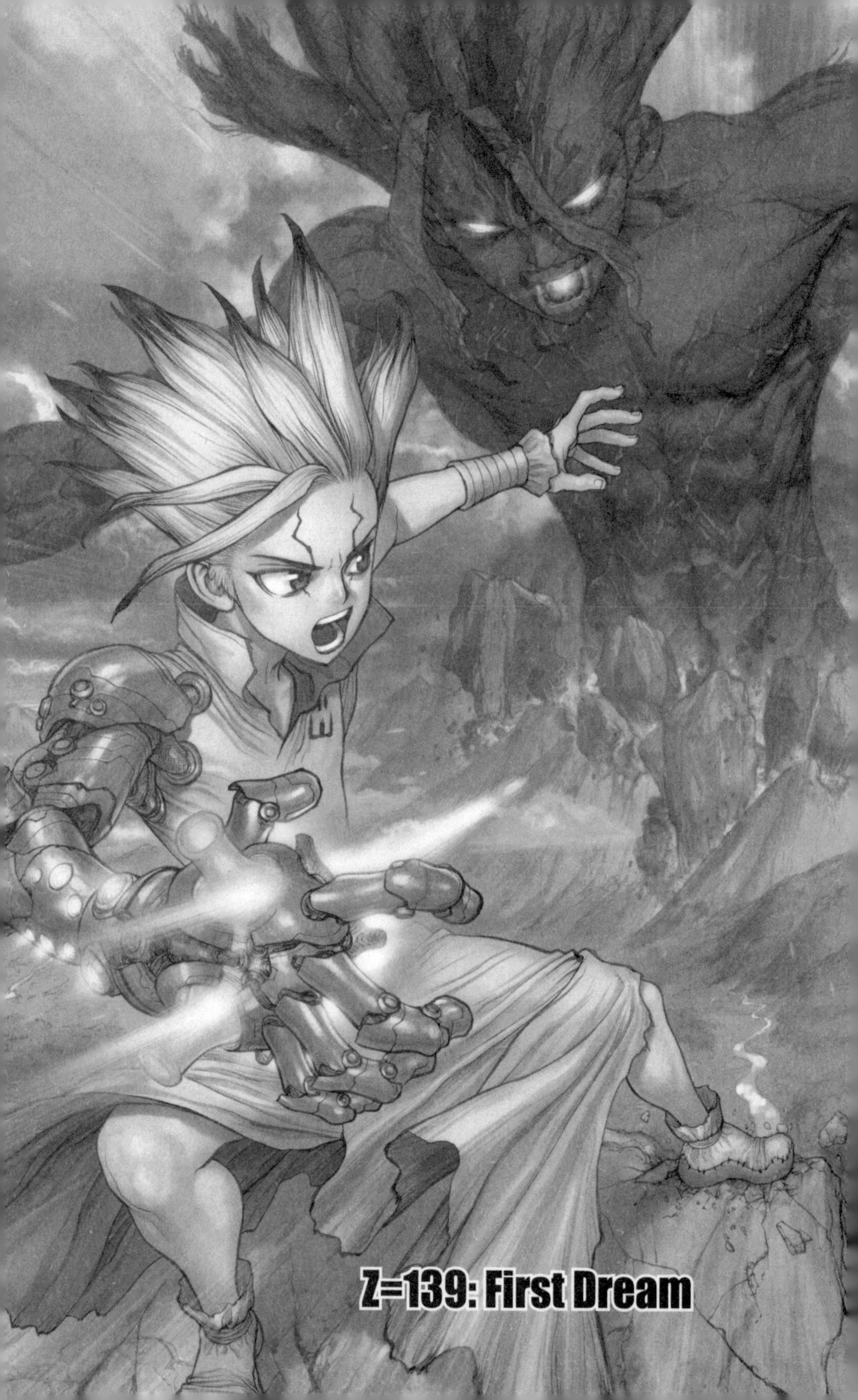
Z=139: First Dream

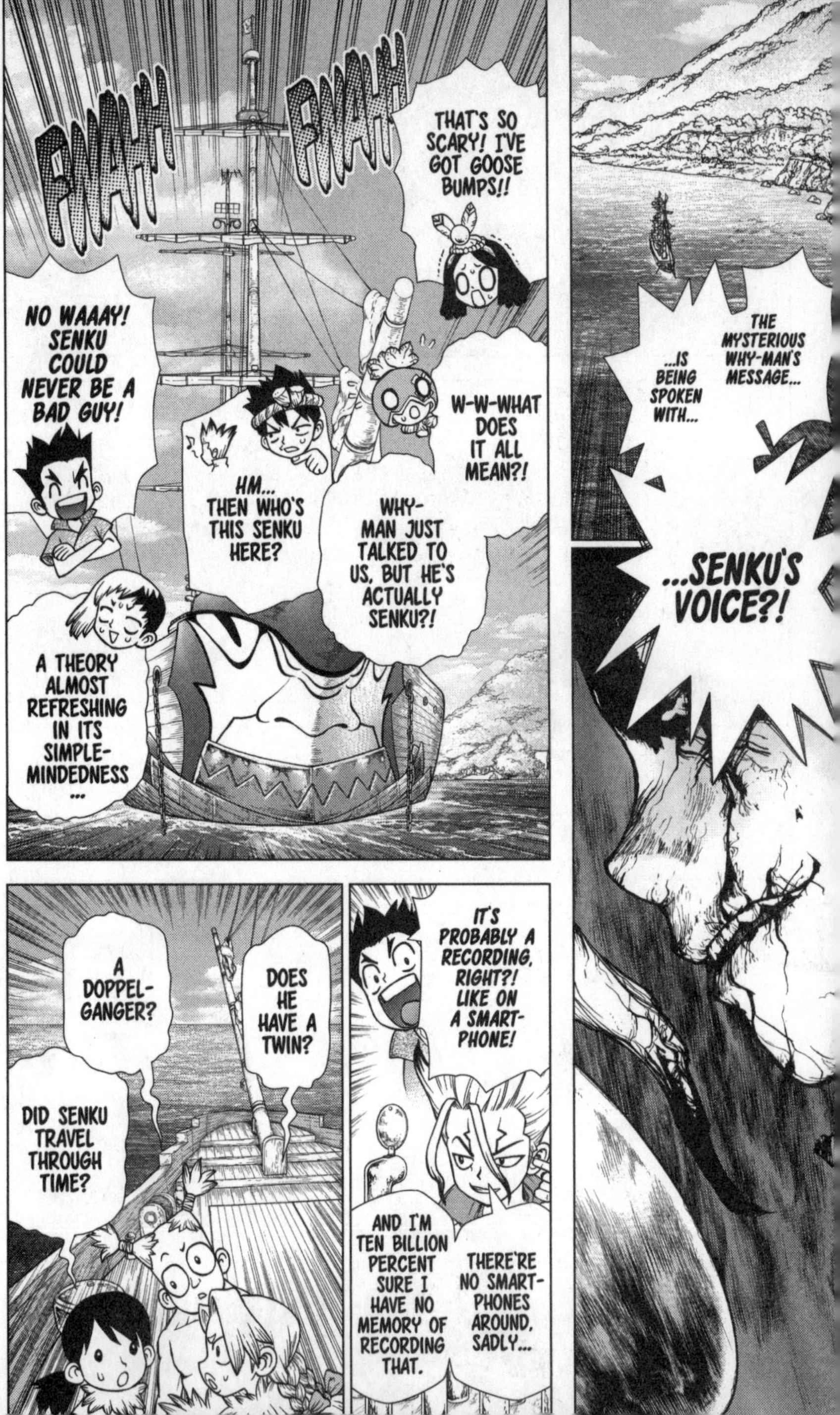
THE MYSTERIOUS WHY-MAN'S MESSAGE...
...IS BEING SPOKEN WITH...
...SENKU'S VOICE?!
THAT'S SO SCARY! I'VE GOT GOOSE BUMPS!!
W-W-WHAT DOES IT ALL MEAN?!
WHY-MAN JUST TALKED TO US, BUT HE'S ACTUALLY SENKU?!
HM... THEN WHO'S THIS SENKU HERE?
NO WAAAY! SENKU COULD NEVER BE A BAD GUY!
A THEORY ALMOST REFRESHING IN ITS SIMPLE-MINDEDNESS...
IT'S PROBABLY A RECORDING, RIGHT?! LIKE ON A SMART-PHONE!
THERE'RE NO SMART-PHONES AROUND, SADLY...
AND I'M TEN BILLION PERCENT SURE I HAVE NO MEMORY OF RECORDING THAT.
DOES HE HAVE A TWIN?
A DOPPEL-GANGER?
DID SENKU TRAVEL THROUGH TIME?

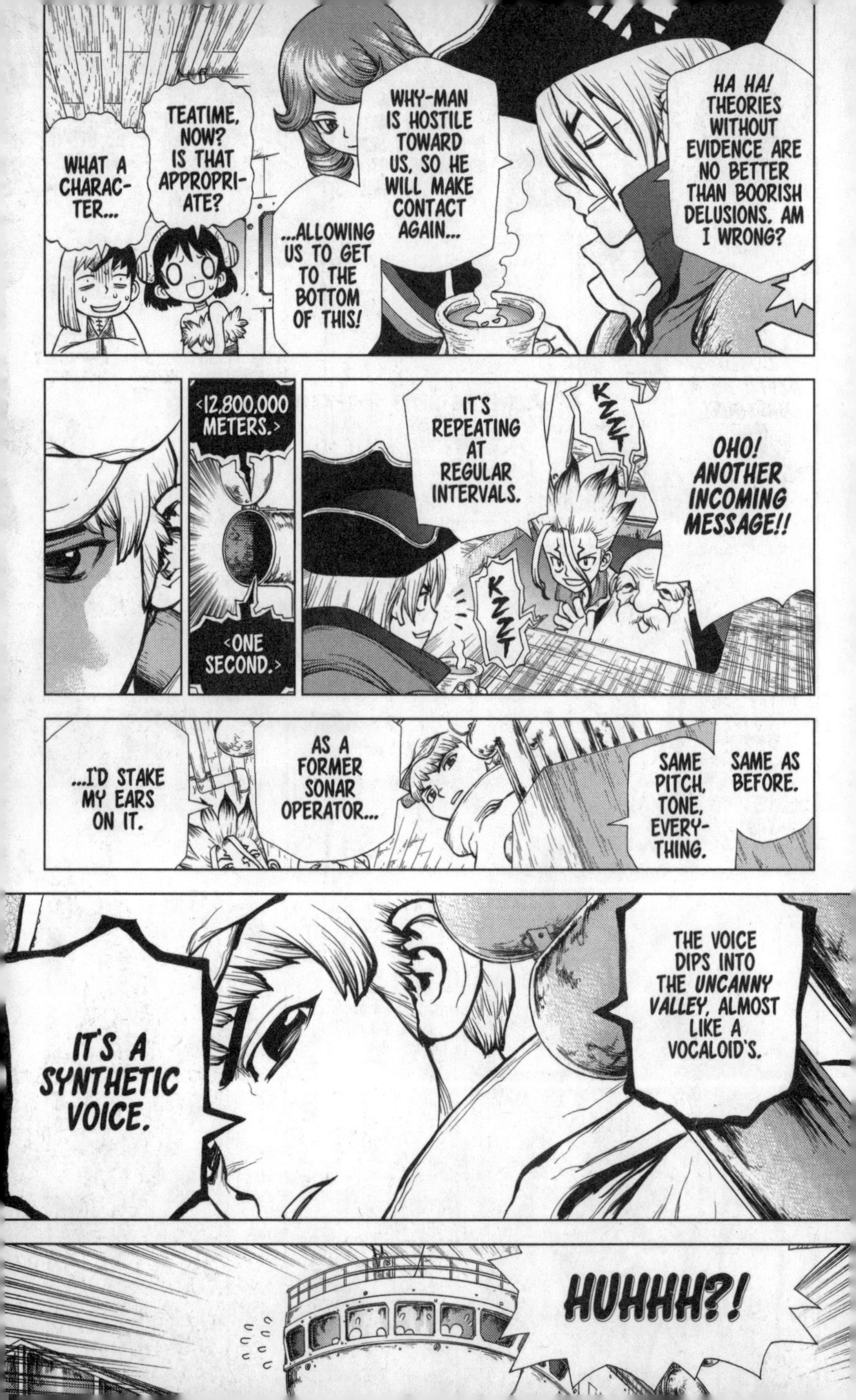
HA HA! THEORIES WITHOUT EVIDENCE ARE NO BETTER THAN BOORISH DELUSIONS. AM I WRONG?
WHY-MAN IS HOSTILE TOWARD US, SO HE WILL MAKE CONTACT AGAIN...
...ALLOWING US TO GET TO THE BOTTOM OF THIS!
TEATIME, NOW? IS THAT APPROPRIATE?
WHAT A CHARACTER...
OHO! ANOTHER INCOMING MESSAGE!!
KZZT
IT'S REPEATING AT REGULAR INTERVALS.
KZZT
<12,800,000 METERS.>
<ONE SECOND.>
SAME AS BEFORE.
SAME PITCH, TONE, EVERYTHING.
AS A FORMER SONAR OPERATOR...
...I'D STAKE MY EARS ON IT.
THE VOICE DIPS INTO THE UNCANNY VALLEY, ALMOST LIKE A VOCALOID'S.
IT'S A SYNTHETIC VOICE.
HUHHH?!

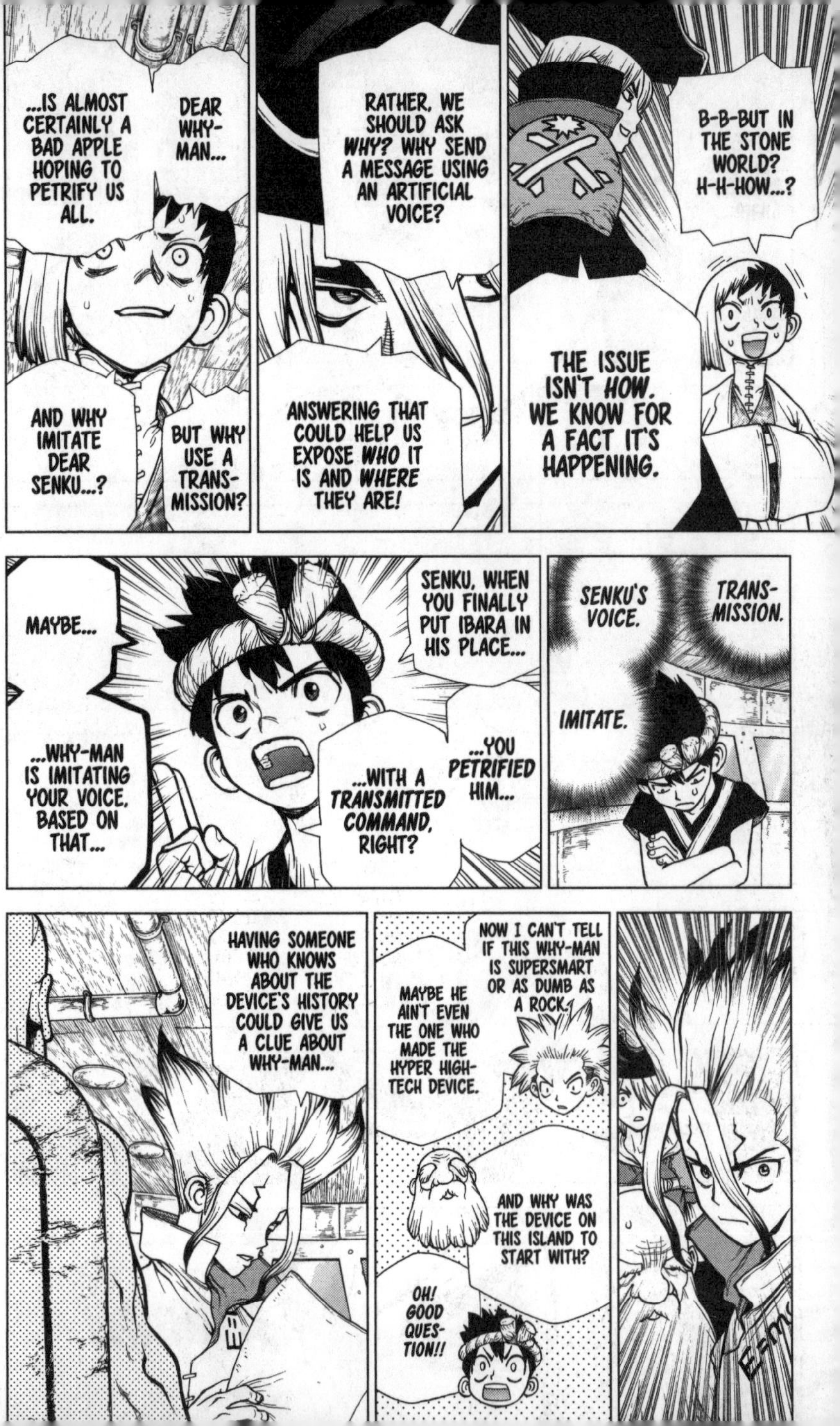
B-B-BUT IN THE STONE WORLD? H-H-HOW...?
THE ISSUE ISN'T *HOW*. WE KNOW FOR A FACT IT'S HAPPENING.
RATHER, WE SHOULD ASK *WHY?* WHY SEND A MESSAGE USING AN ARTIFICIAL VOICE?
ANSWERING THAT COULD HELP US EXPOSE *WHO* IT IS AND *WHERE* THEY ARE!
DEAR WHY-MAN...
...IS ALMOST CERTAINLY A BAD APPLE HOPING TO PETRIFY US ALL.
BUT WHY USE A TRANSMISSION?
AND WHY IMITATE DEAR SENKU...?
TRANS-MISSION.
SENKU'S VOICE.
IMITATE.
SENKU, WHEN YOU FINALLY PUT IBARA IN HIS PLACE...
...YOU PETRIFIED HIM...
...WITH A *TRANSMITTED COMMAND*, RIGHT?
MAYBE...
...WHY-MAN IS IMITATING YOUR VOICE, BASED ON THAT...
NOW I CAN'T TELL IF THIS WHY-MAN IS SUPERSMART OR AS DUMB AS A ROCK.
MAYBE HE AIN'T EVEN THE ONE WHO MADE THE HYPER HIGH-TECH DEVICE.
AND WHY WAS THE DEVICE ON THIS ISLAND TO START WITH?
OH! GOOD QUES-TION!!
HAVING SOMEONE WHO KNOWS ABOUT THE DEVICE'S HISTORY COULD GIVE US A CLUE ABOUT WHY-MAN...

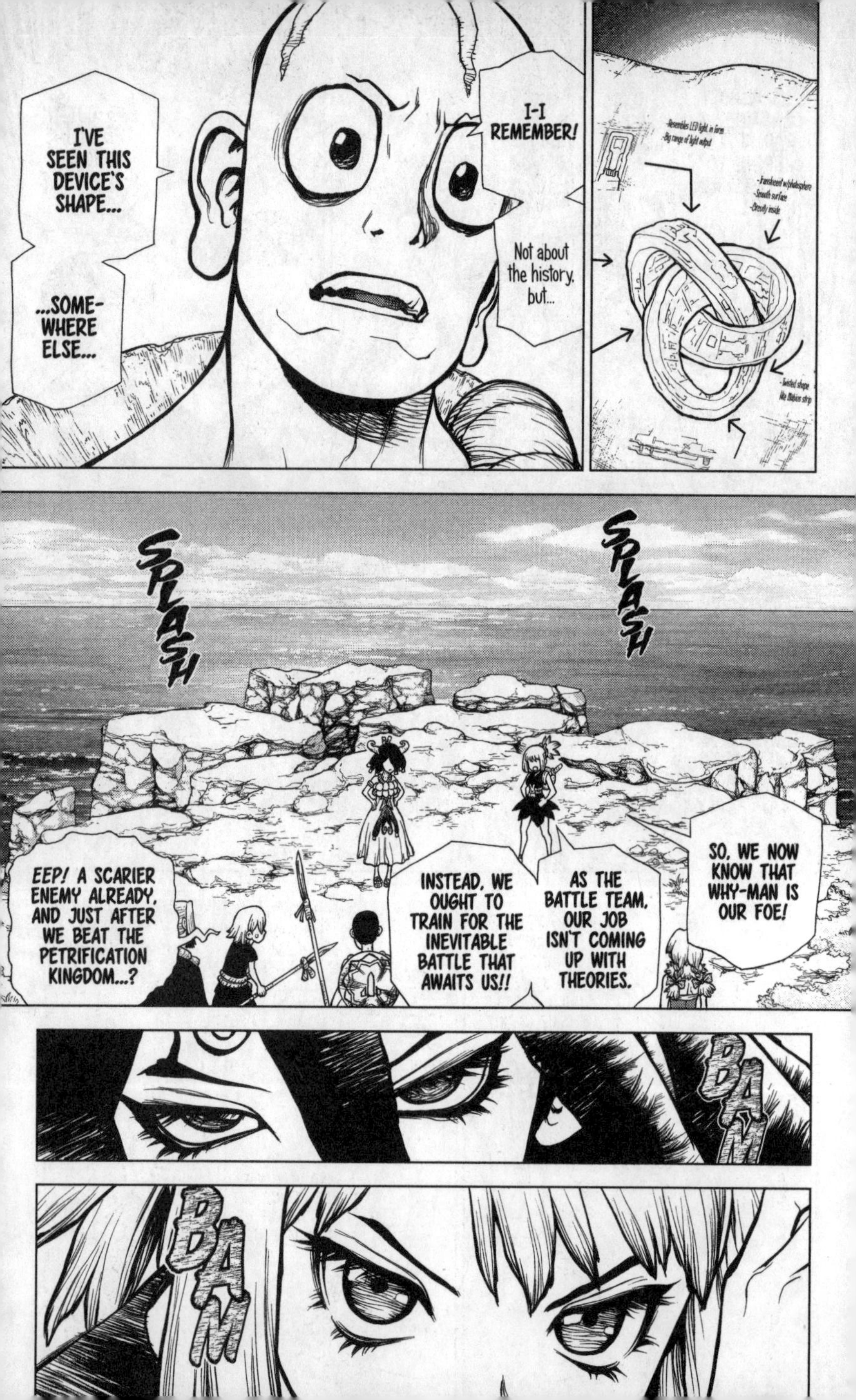
-Resembles LED light, in form
-Big range of light output
-Smooth surface
-Circuitry inside
-Twisted shape like Mobius strip
I-I REMEMBER!
Not about the history, but...
I'VE SEEN THIS DEVICE'S SHAPE...
...SOME-WHERE ELSE...
SPLASH
SPLASH
SO, WE NOW KNOW THAT WHY-MAN IS OUR FOE!
AS THE BATTLE TEAM, OUR JOB ISN'T COMING UP WITH THEORIES.
INSTEAD, WE OUGHT TO TRAIN FOR THE INEVITABLE BATTLE THAT AWAITS US!!
EEP! A SCARIER ENEMY ALREADY, AND JUST AFTER WE BEAT THE PETRIFICATION KINGDOM...?
BAM
BAM

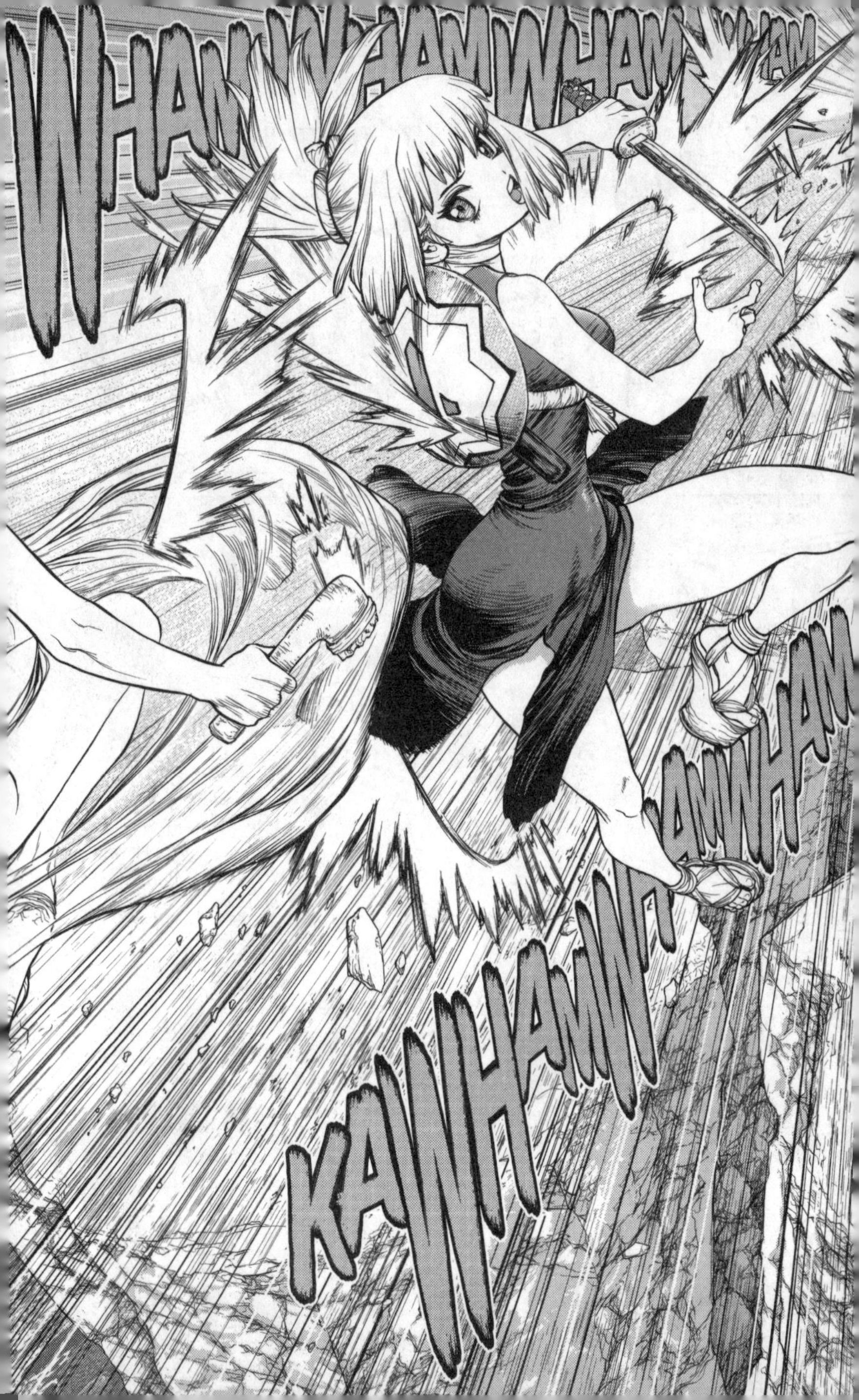
WHAM WHAM WHAM WHAM
KAWHAM WHAM WHAM

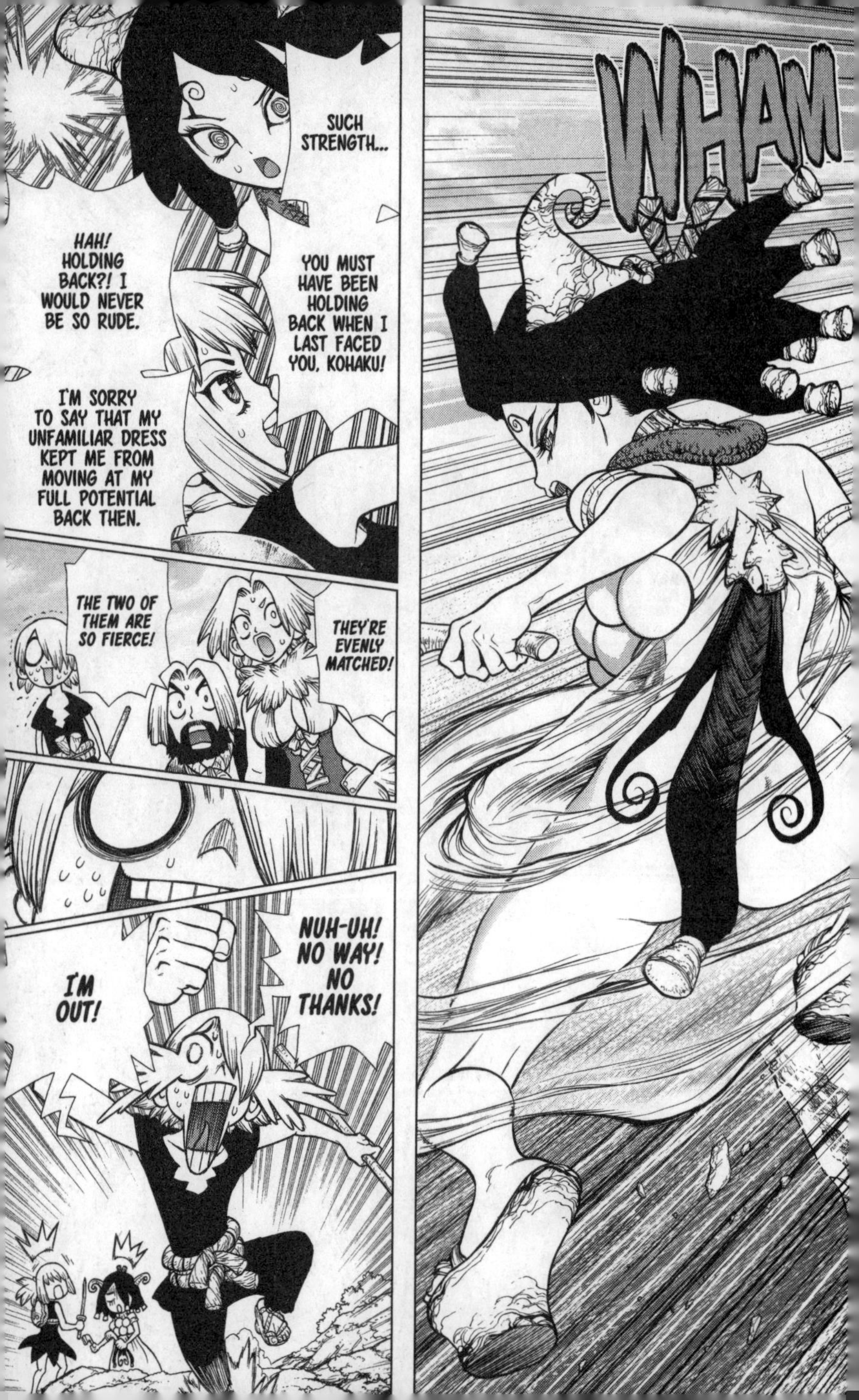
WHAM
SUCH STRENGTH...
YOU MUST HAVE BEEN HOLDING BACK WHEN I LAST FACED YOU, KOHAKU!
HAH! HOLDING BACK?! I WOULD NEVER BE SO RUDE.
I'M SORRY TO SAY THAT MY UNFAMILIAR DRESS KEPT ME FROM MOVING AT MY FULL POTENTIAL BACK THEN.
THEY'RE EVENLY MATCHED!
THE TWO OF THEM ARE SO FIERCE!
NUH-UH! NO WAY! NO THANKS!
I'M OUT!

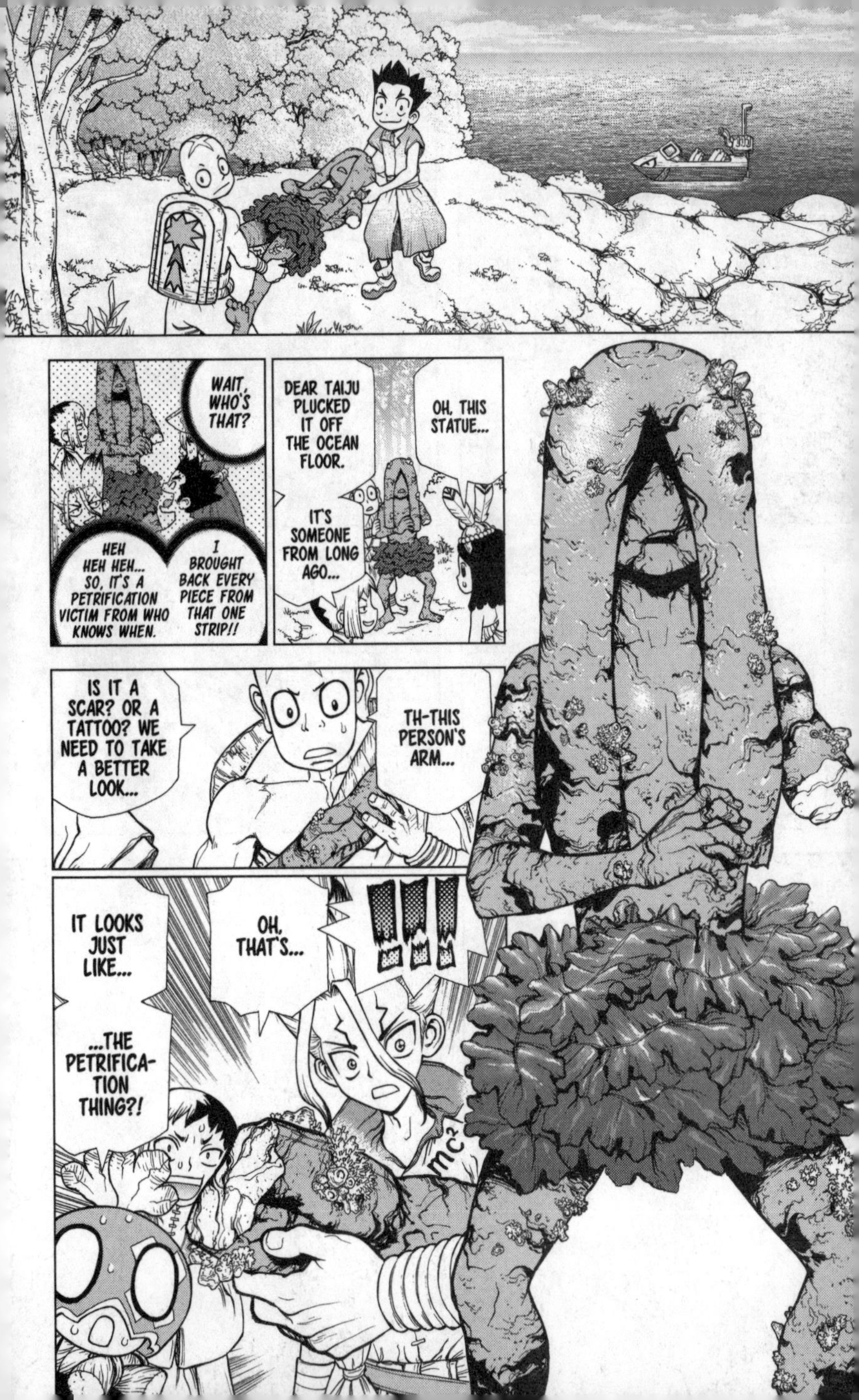
OH, THIS STATUE...
DEAR TAIJU PLUCKED IT OFF THE OCEAN FLOOR.
IT'S SOMEONE FROM LONG AGO...
WAIT, WHO'S THAT?
I BROUGHT BACK EVERY PIECE FROM THAT ONE STRIP!!
HEH HEH HEH... SO, IT'S A PETRIFICATION VICTIM FROM WHO KNOWS WHEN.
TH-THIS PERSON'S ARM...
IS IT A SCAR? OR A TATTOO? WE NEED TO TAKE A BETTER LOOK...
!!!
OH, THAT'S...
IT LOOKS JUST LIKE...
...THE PETRIFICATION THING?!
mc²

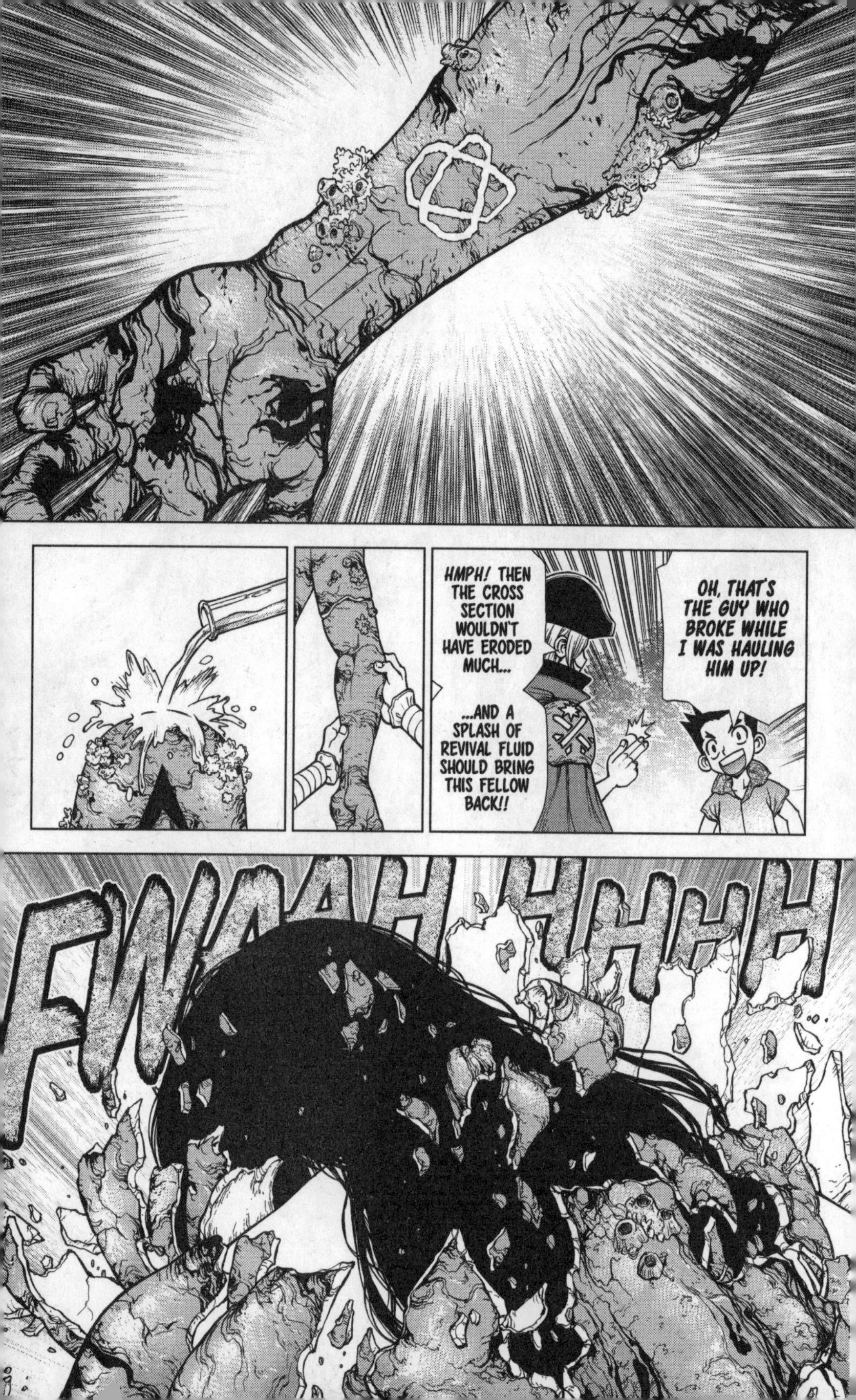
OH, THAT'S THE GUY WHO BROKE WHILE I WAS HAULING HIM UP!
HMPH! THEN THE CROSS SECTION WOULDN'T HAVE ERODED MUCH...
...AND A SPLASH OF REVIVAL FLUID SHOULD BRING THIS FELLOW BACK!!
FWAHHHHHH

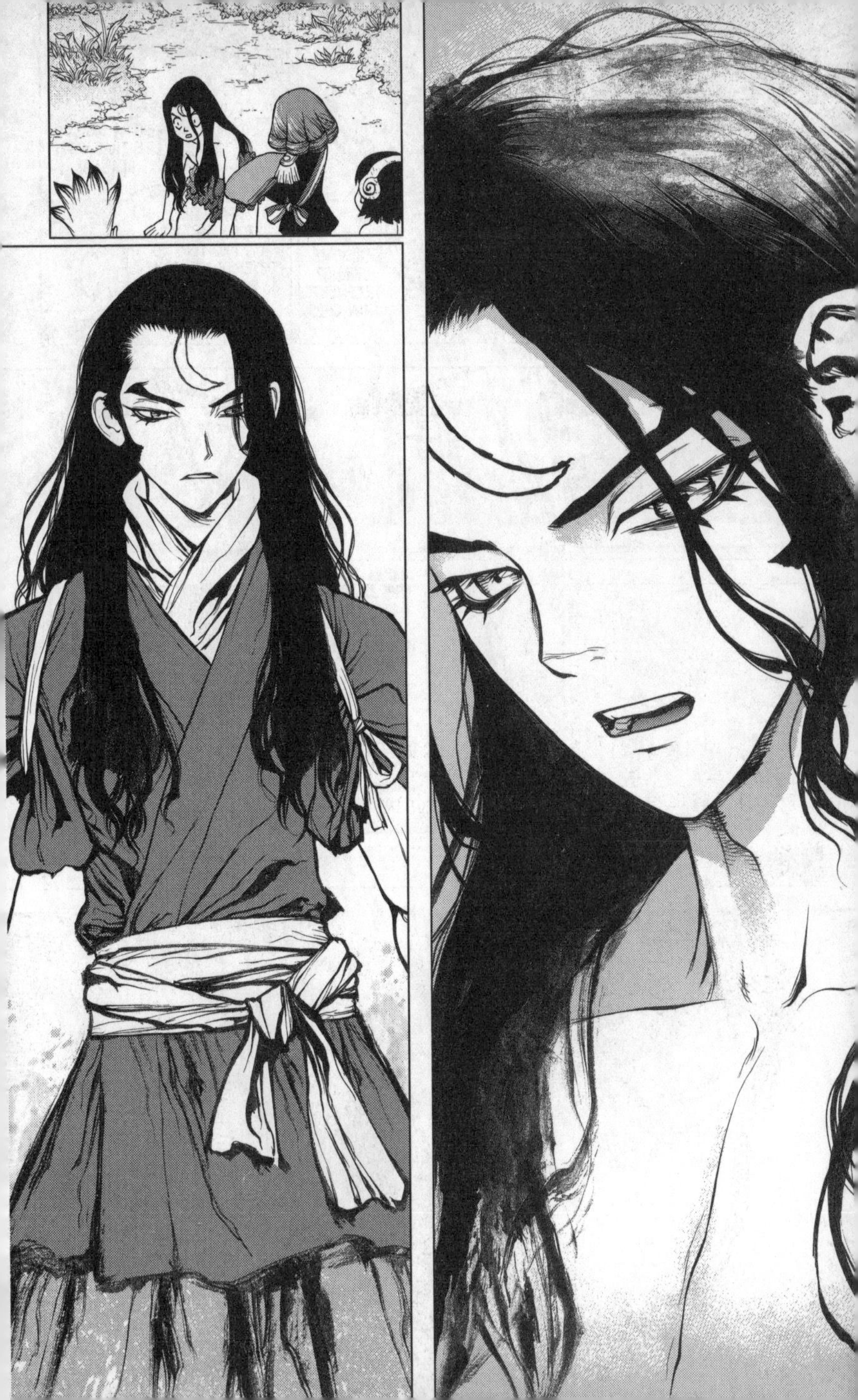

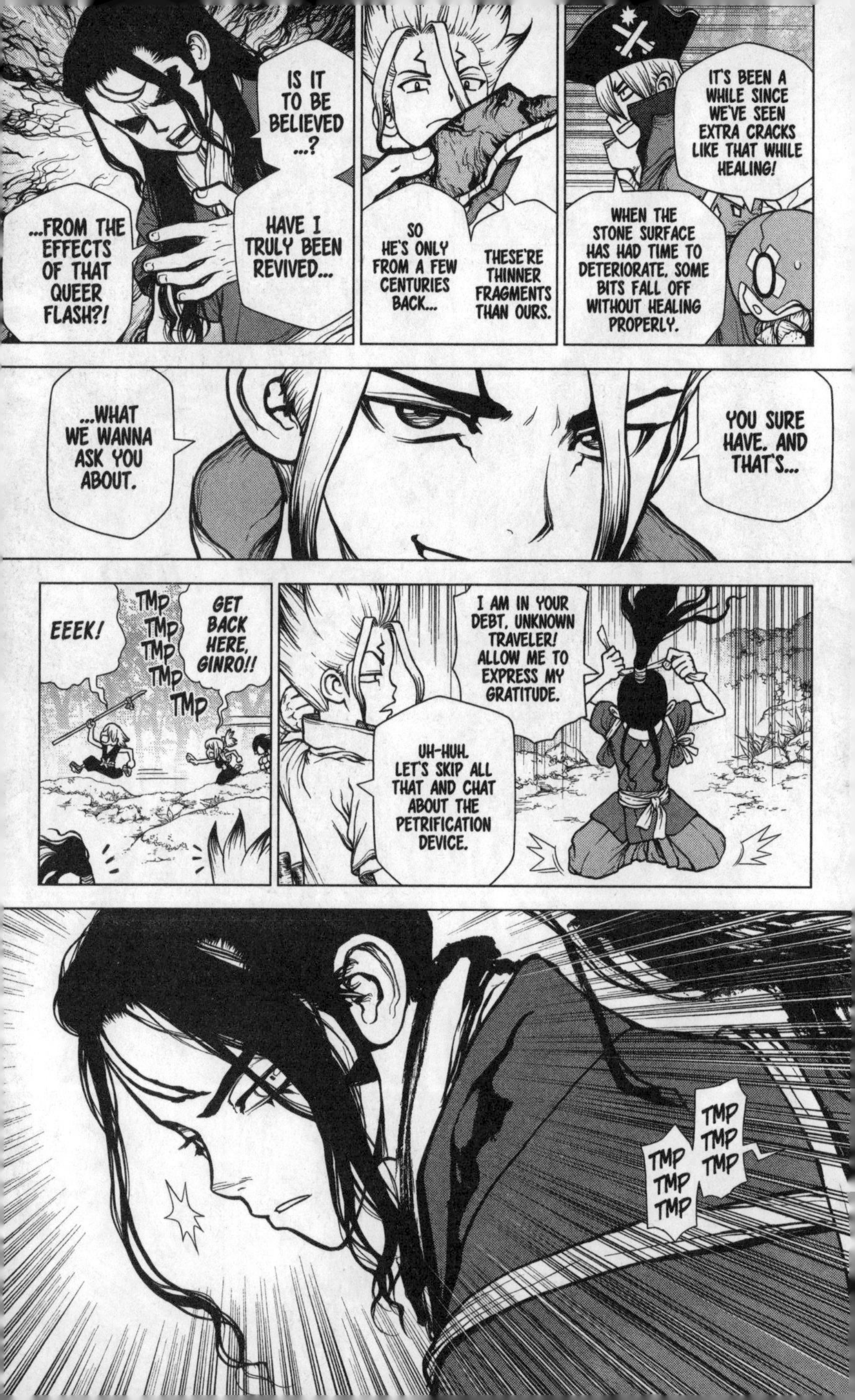

IT'S BEEN A WHILE SINCE WE'VE SEEN EXTRA CRACKS LIKE THAT WHILE HEALING!
WHEN THE STONE SURFACE HAS HAD TIME TO DETERIORATE, SOME BITS FALL OFF WITHOUT HEALING PROPERLY.
THESE'RE THINNER FRAGMENTS THAN OURS.
SO HE'S ONLY FROM A FEW CENTURIES BACK...
IS IT TO BE BELIEVED ...?
HAVE I TRULY BEEN REVIVED...
...FROM THE EFFECTS OF THAT QUEER FLASH?!
YOU SURE HAVE. AND THAT'S...
...WHAT WE WANNA ASK YOU ABOUT.
I AM IN YOUR DEBT, UNKNOWN TRAVELER! ALLOW ME TO EXPRESS MY GRATITUDE.
UH-HUH. LET'S SKIP ALL THAT AND CHAT ABOUT THE PETRIFICATION DEVICE.
GET BACK HERE, GINRO!!
TMP TMP TMP TMP TMP
EEEK!
TMP TMP TMP
TMP TMP TMP

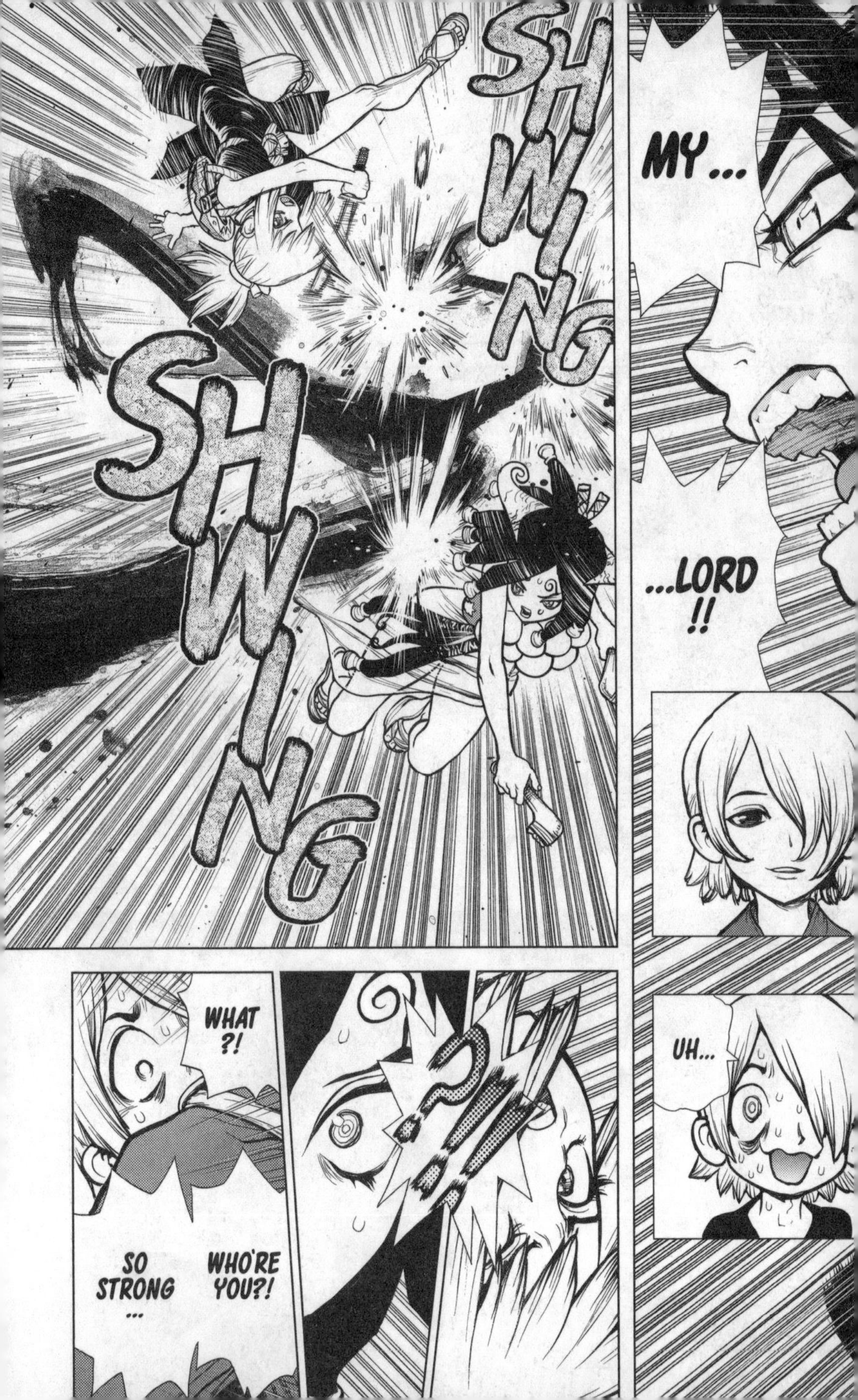
MY...
...LORD!!
UH...
SHWING
SHWING
?!!
WHAT?!
WHO'RE YOU?!
SO STRONG...

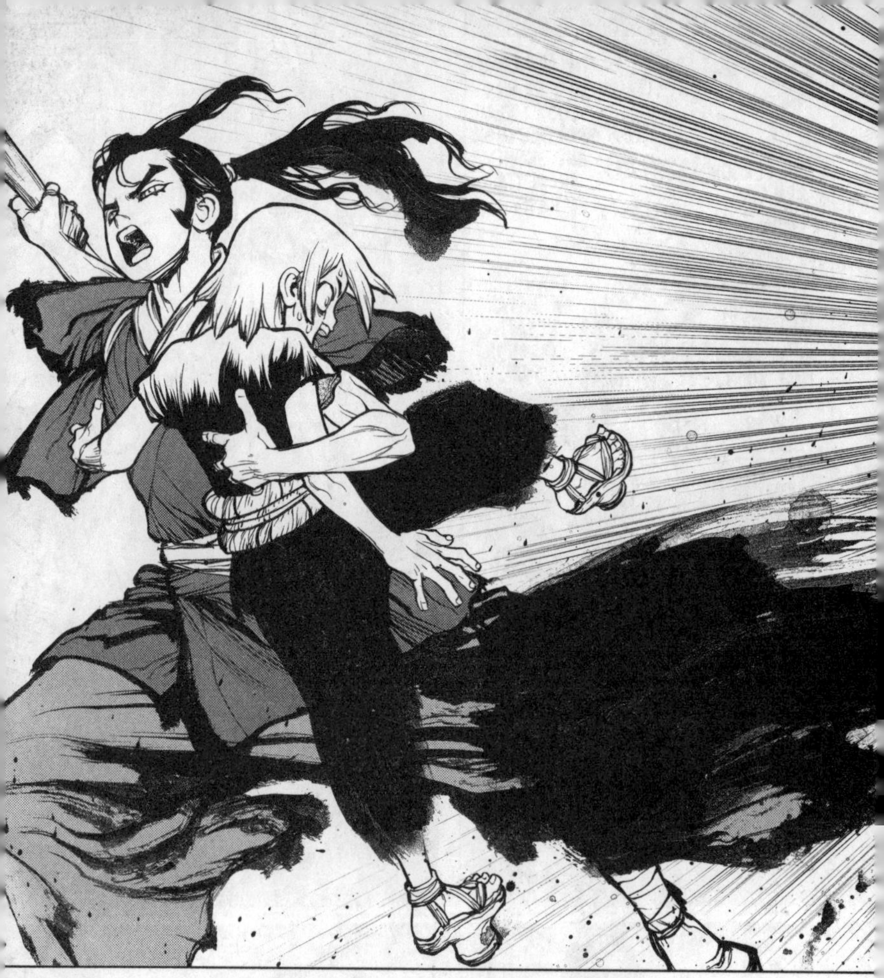

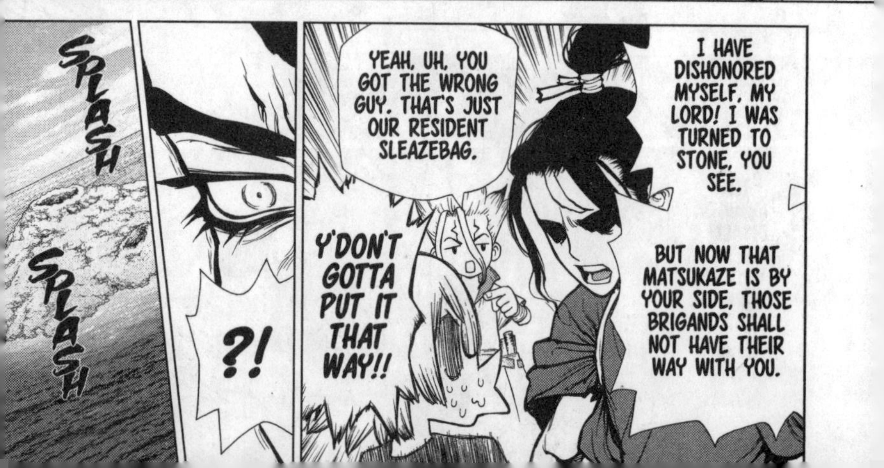
I HAVE DISHONORED MYSELF, MY LORD! I WAS TURNED TO STONE, YOU SEE.
BUT NOW THAT MATSUKAZE IS BY YOUR SIDE, THOSE BRIGANDS SHALL NOT HAVE THEIR WAY WITH YOU.
YEAH, UH, YOU GOT THE WRONG GUY. THAT'S JUST OUR RESIDENT SLEAZEBAG.
Y'DON'T GOTTA PUT IT THAT WAY!!
?!
SPLASH
SPLASH

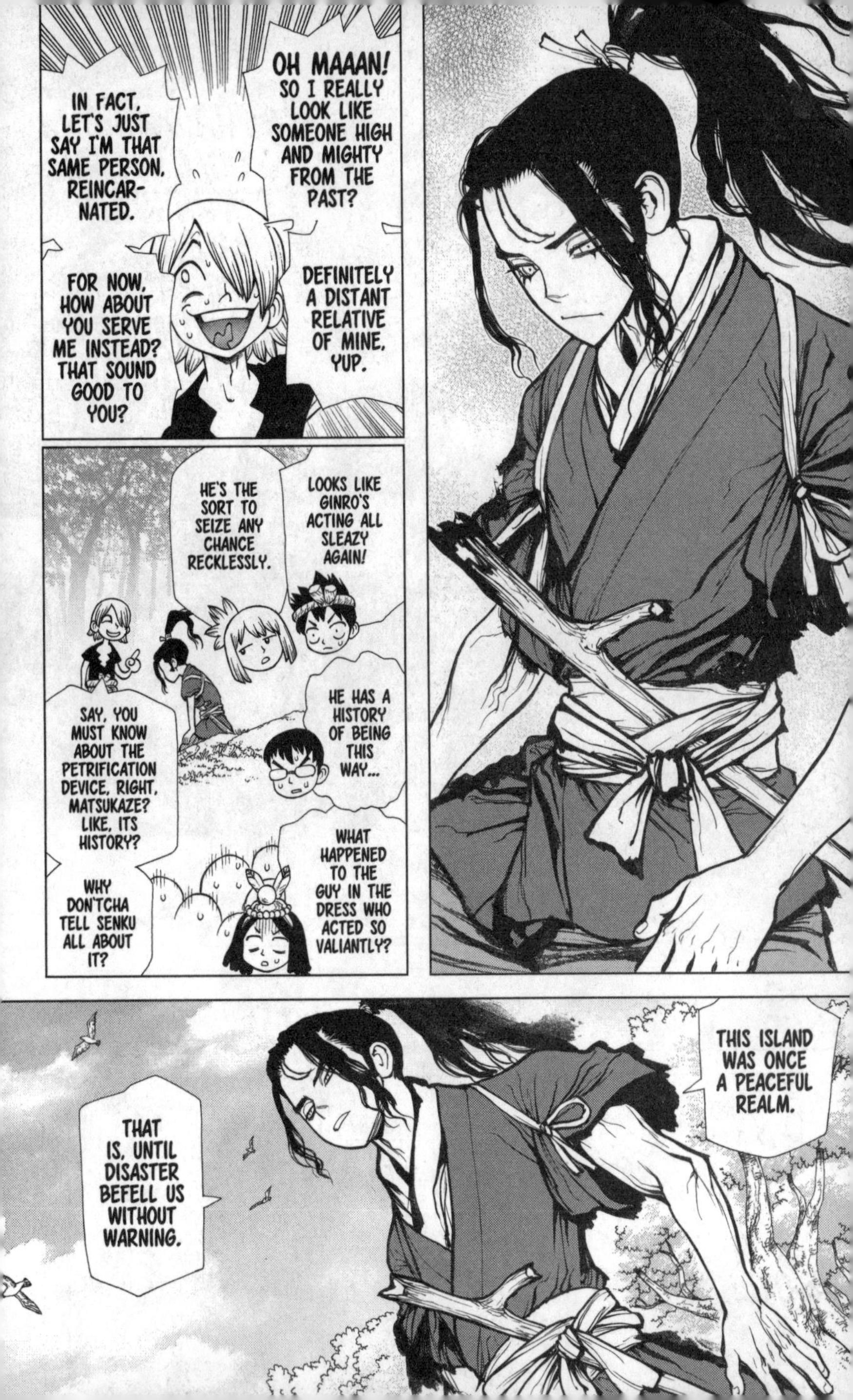
OH MAAAN! SO I REALLY LOOK LIKE SOMEONE HIGH AND MIGHTY FROM THE PAST?
IN FACT, LET'S JUST SAY I'M THAT SAME PERSON, REINCARNATED.
DEFINITELY A DISTANT RELATIVE OF MINE, YUP.
FOR NOW, HOW ABOUT YOU SERVE ME INSTEAD? THAT SOUND GOOD TO YOU?
LOOKS LIKE GINRO'S ACTING ALL SLEAZY AGAIN!
HE'S THE SORT TO SEIZE ANY CHANCE RECKLESSLY.
HE HAS A HISTORY OF BEING THIS WAY...
SAY, YOU MUST KNOW ABOUT THE PETRIFICATION DEVICE, RIGHT, MATSUKAZE? LIKE, ITS HISTORY?
WHAT HAPPENED TO THE GUY IN THE DRESS WHO ACTED SO VALIANTLY?
WHY DON'TCHA TELL SENKU ALL ABOUT IT?
THIS ISLAND WAS ONCE A PEACEFUL REALM.
THAT IS, UNTIL DISASTER BEFELL US WITHOUT WARNING.

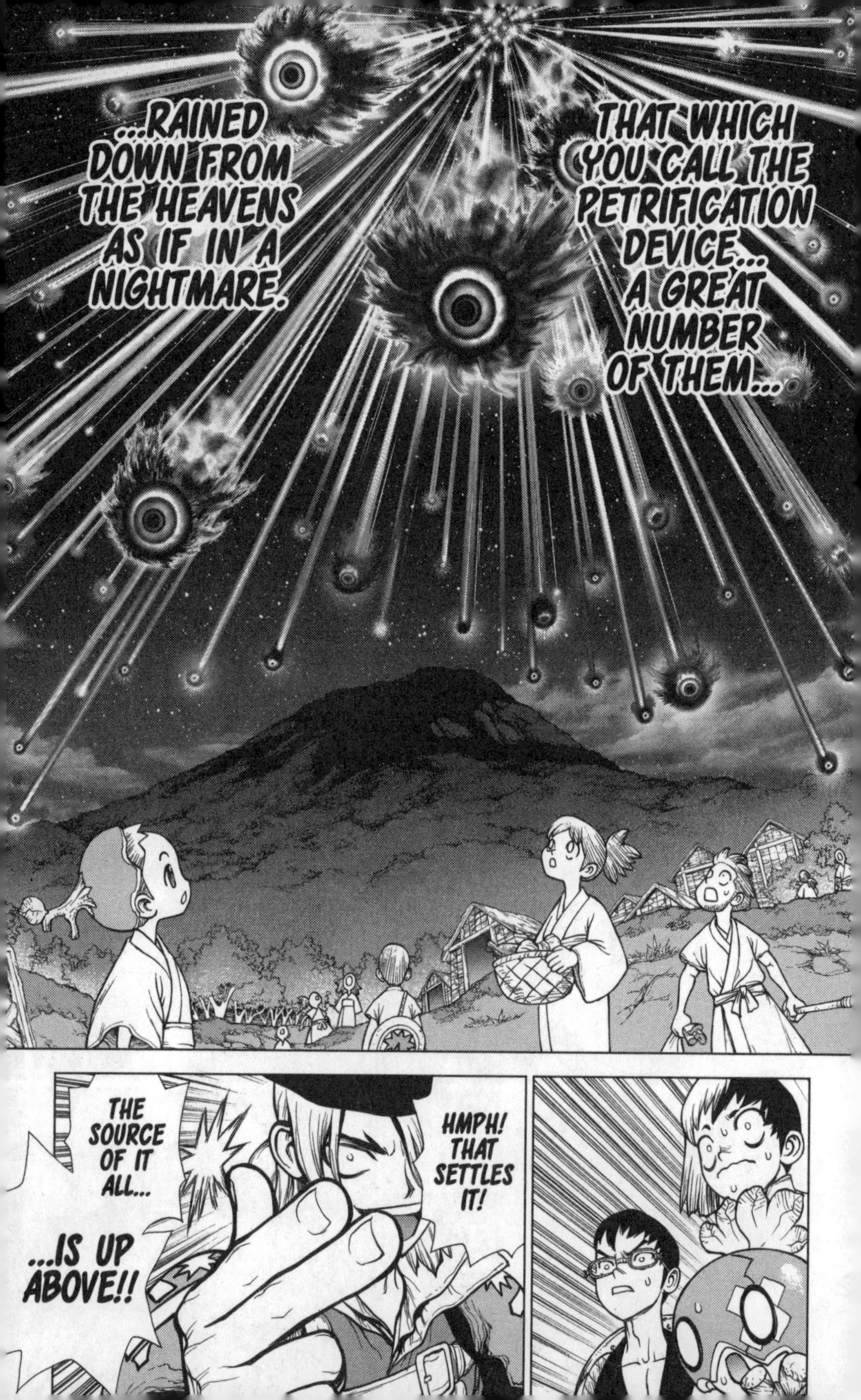
THAT WHICH YOU CALL THE PETRIFICATION DEVICE... A GREAT NUMBER OF THEM...
...RAINED DOWN FROM THE HEAVENS AS IF IN A NIGHTMARE.
HMPH! THAT SETTLES IT!
THE SOURCE OF IT ALL...
...IS UP ABOVE!!

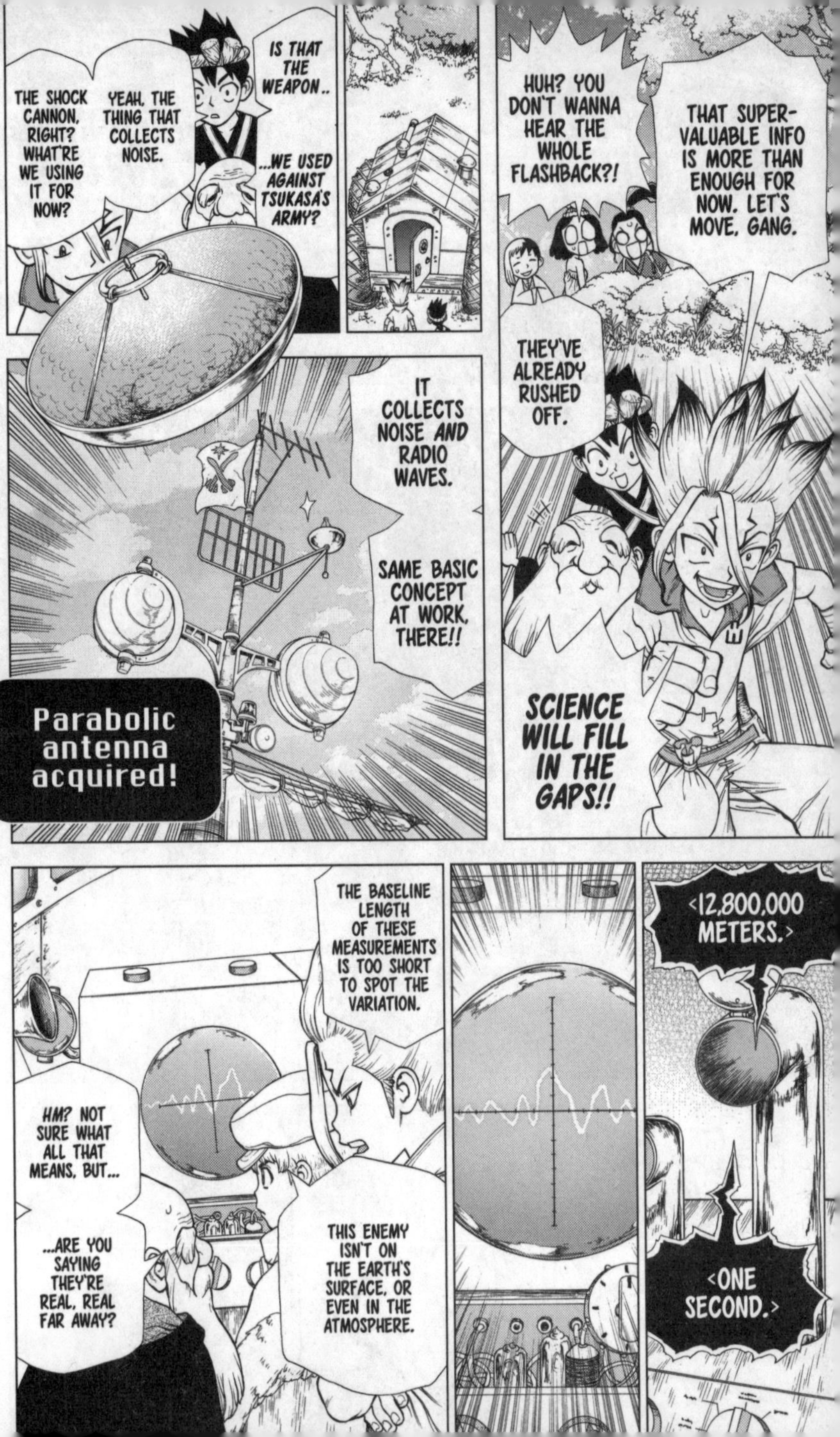
THAT SUPER-VALUABLE INFO IS MORE THAN ENOUGH FOR NOW. LET'S MOVE, GANG.
HUH? YOU DON'T WANNA HEAR THE WHOLE FLASHBACK?!
THEY'VE ALREADY RUSHED OFF.
SCIENCE WILL FILL IN THE GAPS!!
IS THAT THE WEAPON..
...WE USED AGAINST TSUKASA'S ARMY?
YEAH, THE THING THAT COLLECTS NOISE.
THE SHOCK CANNON, RIGHT? WHAT'RE WE USING IT FOR NOW?
IT COLLECTS NOISE AND RADIO WAVES.
SAME BASIC CONCEPT AT WORK, THERE!!
Parabolic antenna acquired!
<12,800,000 METERS.>
<ONE SECOND.>
THE BASELINE LENGTH OF THESE MEASUREMENTS IS TOO SHORT TO SPOT THE VARIATION.
THIS ENEMY ISN'T ON THE EARTH'S SURFACE, OR EVEN IN THE ATMOSPHERE.
HM? NOT SURE WHAT ALL THAT MEANS, BUT...
...ARE YOU SAYING THEY'RE REAL, REAL FAR AWAY?

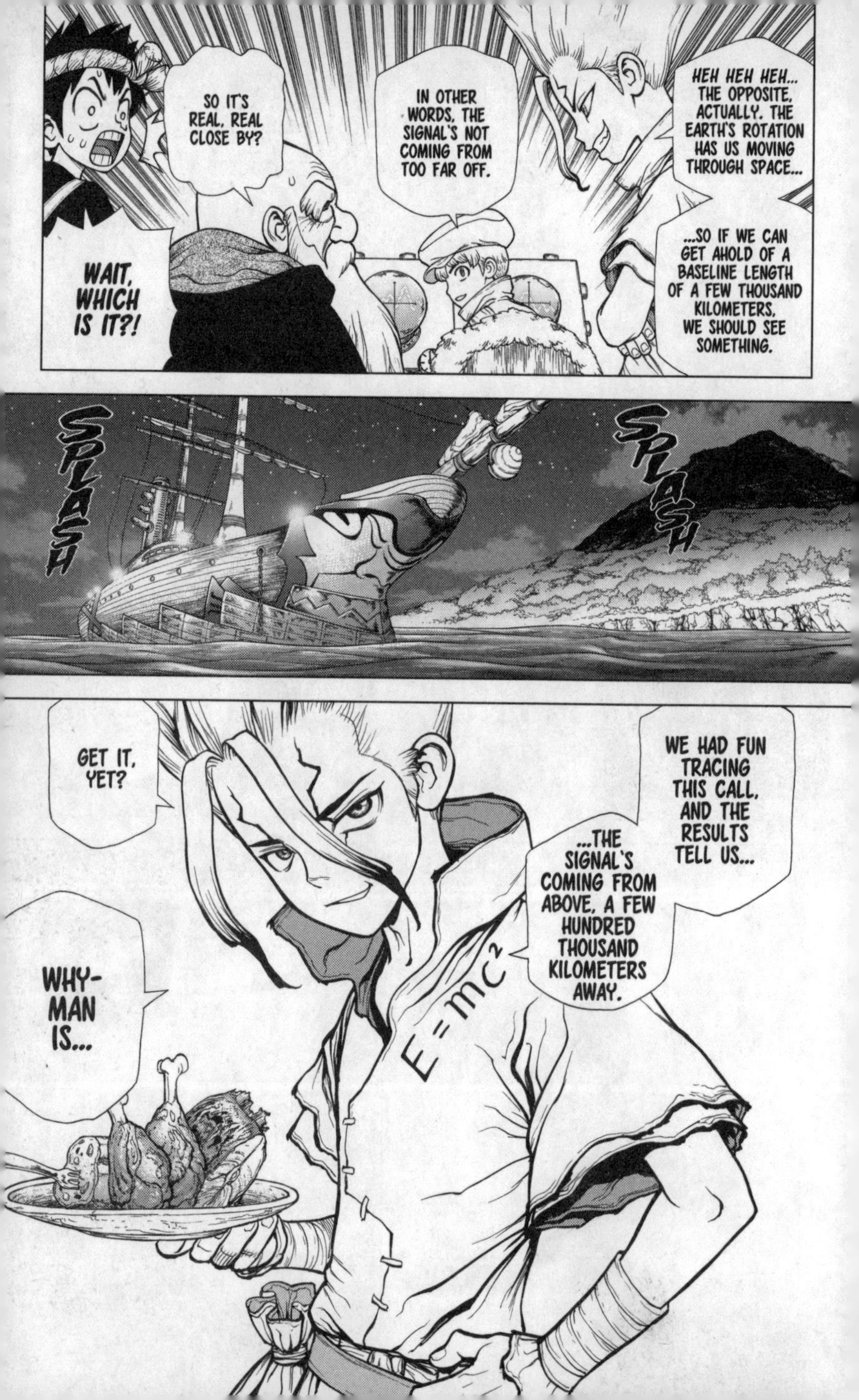
HEH HEH HEH... THE OPPOSITE, ACTUALLY. THE EARTH'S ROTATION HAS US MOVING THROUGH SPACE...
...SO IF WE CAN GET AHOLD OF A BASELINE LENGTH OF A FEW THOUSAND KILOMETERS, WE SHOULD SEE SOMETHING.
IN OTHER WORDS, THE SIGNAL'S NOT COMING FROM TOO FAR OFF.
SO IT'S REAL, REAL CLOSE BY?
WAIT, WHICH IS IT?!
SPLASH
SPLASH
WE HAD FUN TRACING THIS CALL, AND THE RESULTS TELL US...
...THE SIGNAL'S COMING FROM ABOVE, A FEW HUNDRED THOUSAND KILOMETERS AWAY.
E=mc²
GET IT, YET?
WHY-MAN IS...

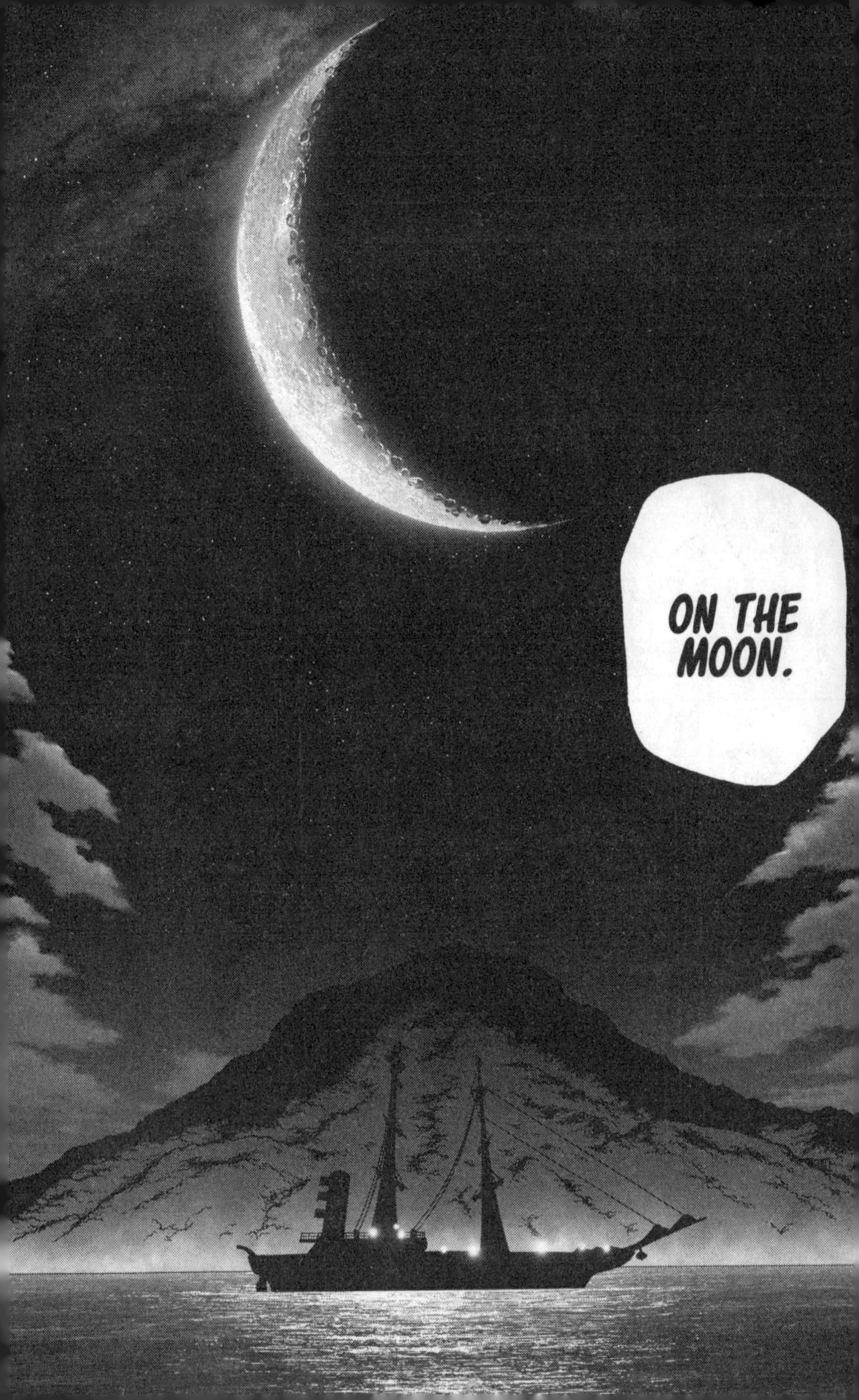
ON THE MOON.

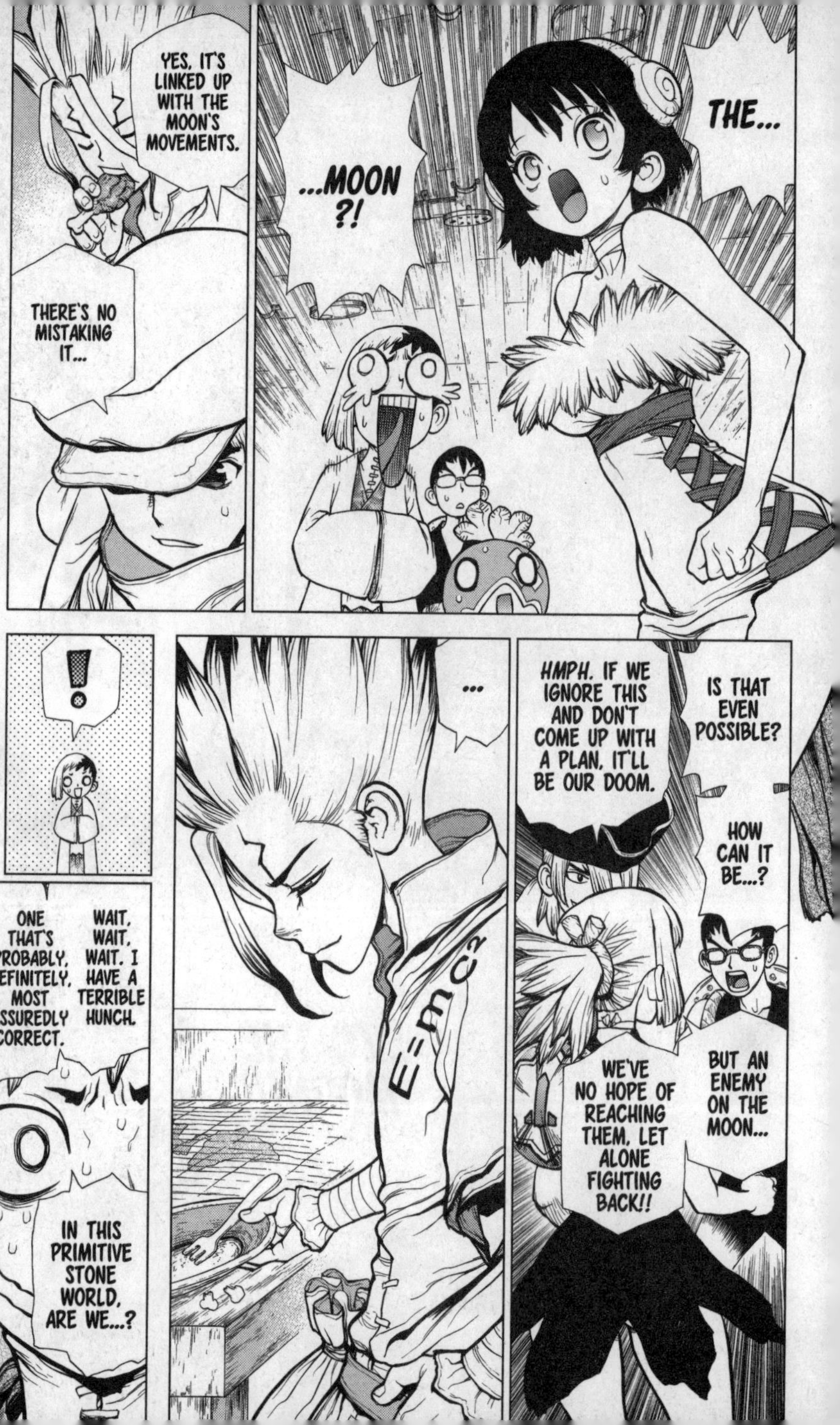
THE...
...MOON ?!
YES, IT'S LINKED UP WITH THE MOON'S MOVEMENTS.
THERE'S NO MISTAKING IT...
IS THAT EVEN POSSIBLE?
HMPH. IF WE IGNORE THIS AND DON'T COME UP WITH A PLAN, IT'LL BE OUR DOOM.
HOW CAN IT BE...?
BUT AN ENEMY ON THE MOON...
WE'VE NO HOPE OF REACHING THEM, LET ALONE FIGHTING BACK!!
...
E=mc2
!
WAIT, WAIT, WAIT. I HAVE A TERRIBLE HUNCH.
ONE THAT'S PROBABLY, DEFINITELY, MOST ASSUREDLY CORRECT.
IN THIS PRIMITIVE STONE WORLD, ARE WE...?

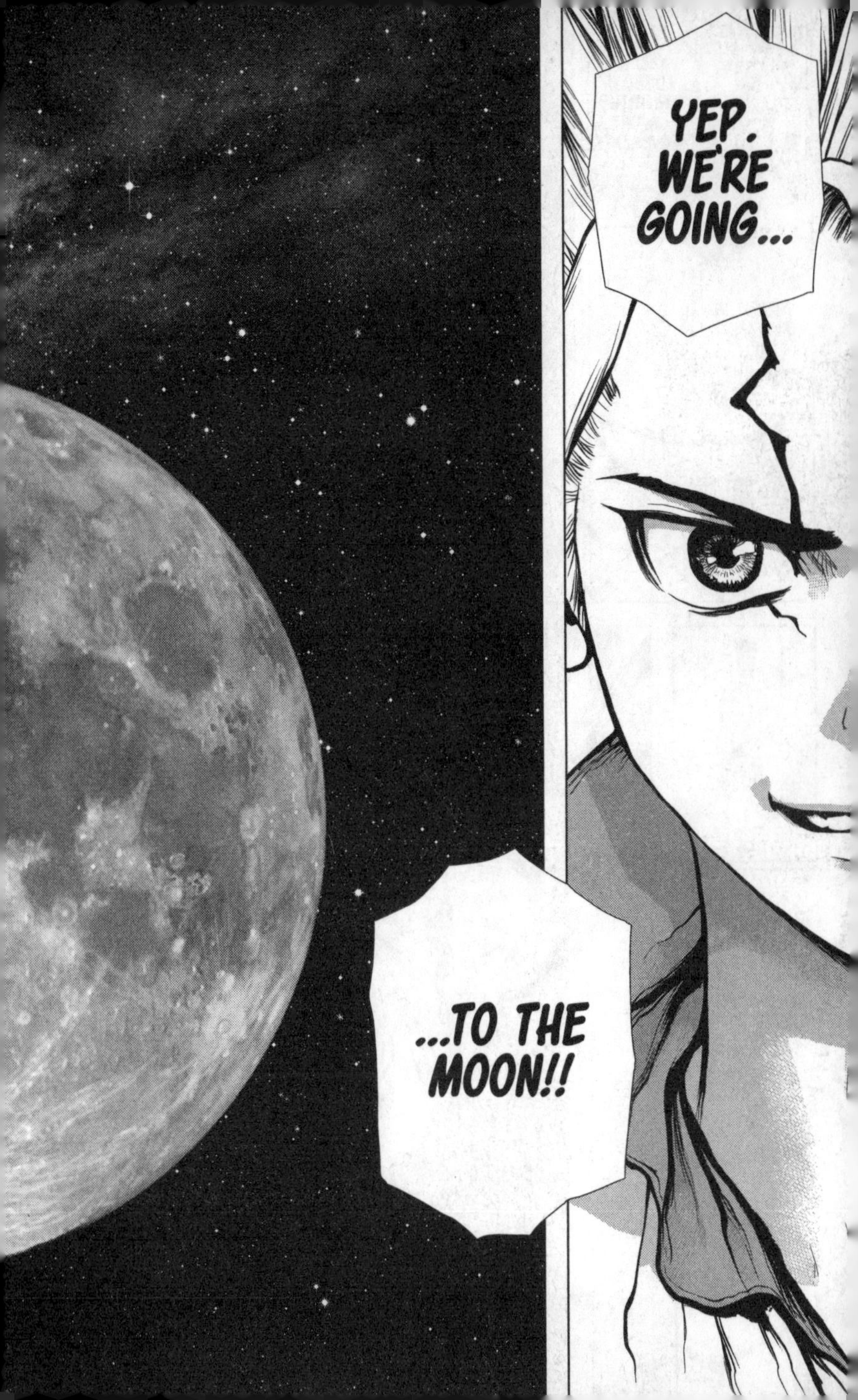
YEP. WE'RE GOING...
...TO THE MOON!!

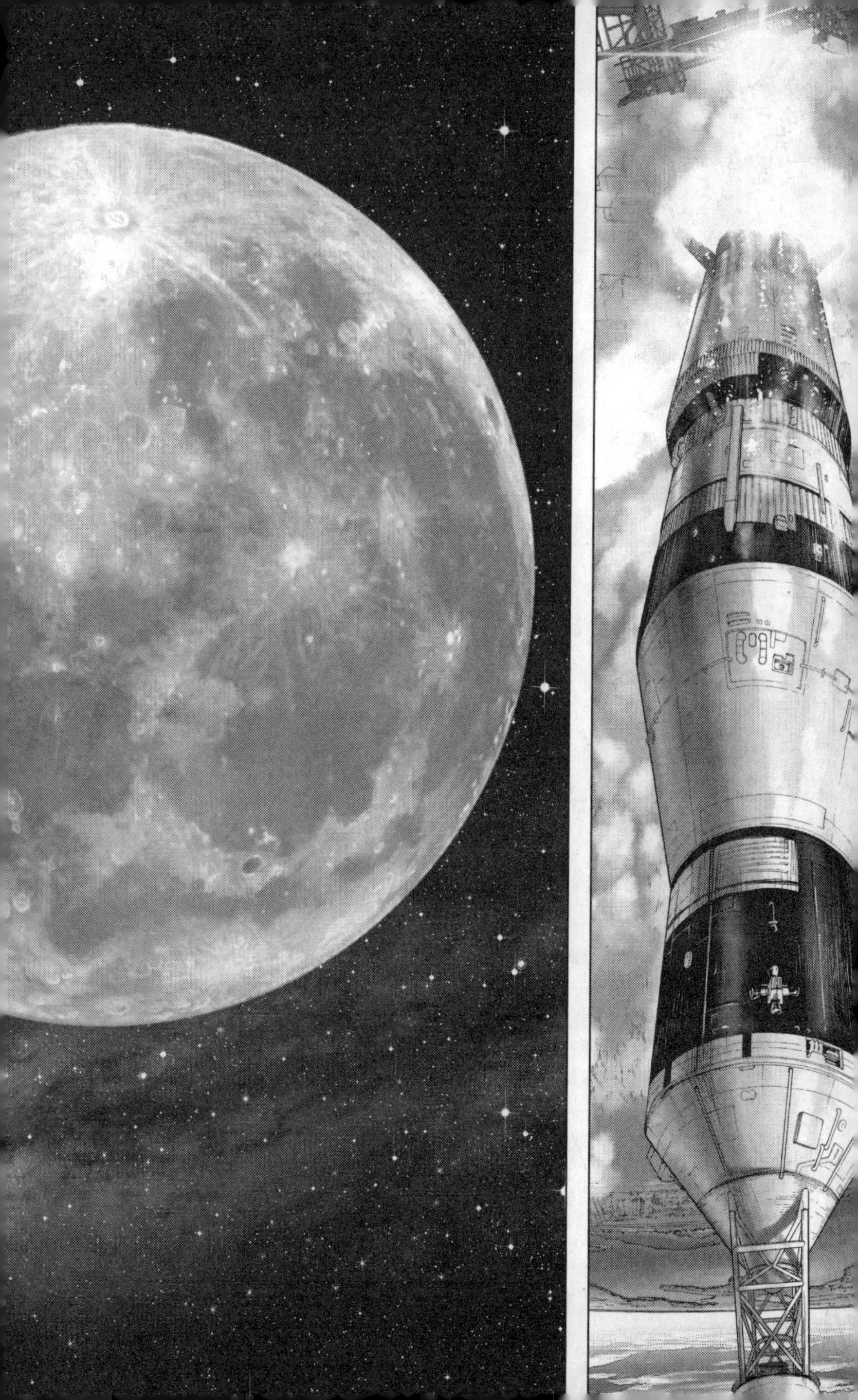

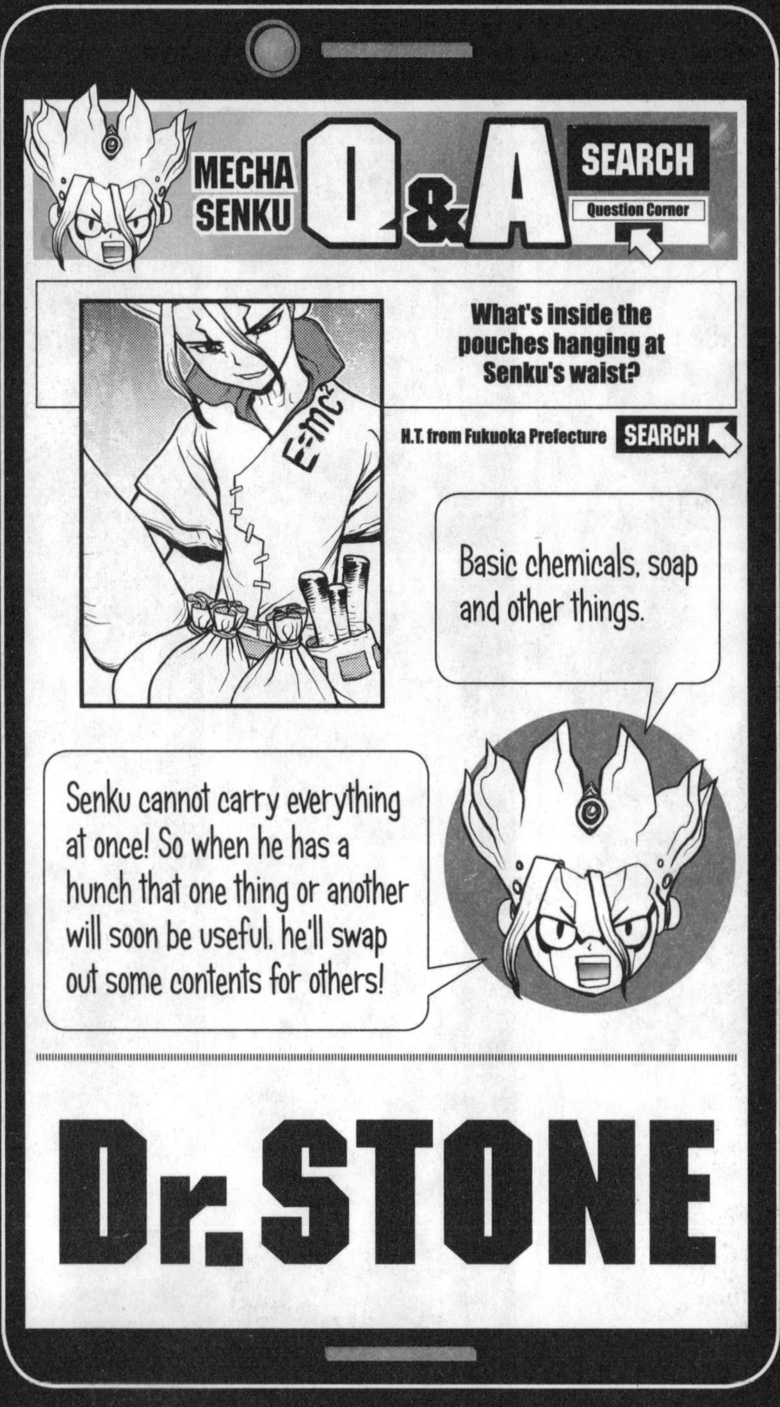
MECHA SENKU Q&A
SEARCH
Question Corner
What's inside the pouches hanging at Senku's waist?
H.T. from Fukuoka Prefecture
SEARCH
E=mc²
Basic chemicals, soap and other things.
Senku cannot carry everything at once! So when he has a hunch that one thing or another will soon be useful, he'll swap out some contents for others!
Dr.STONE

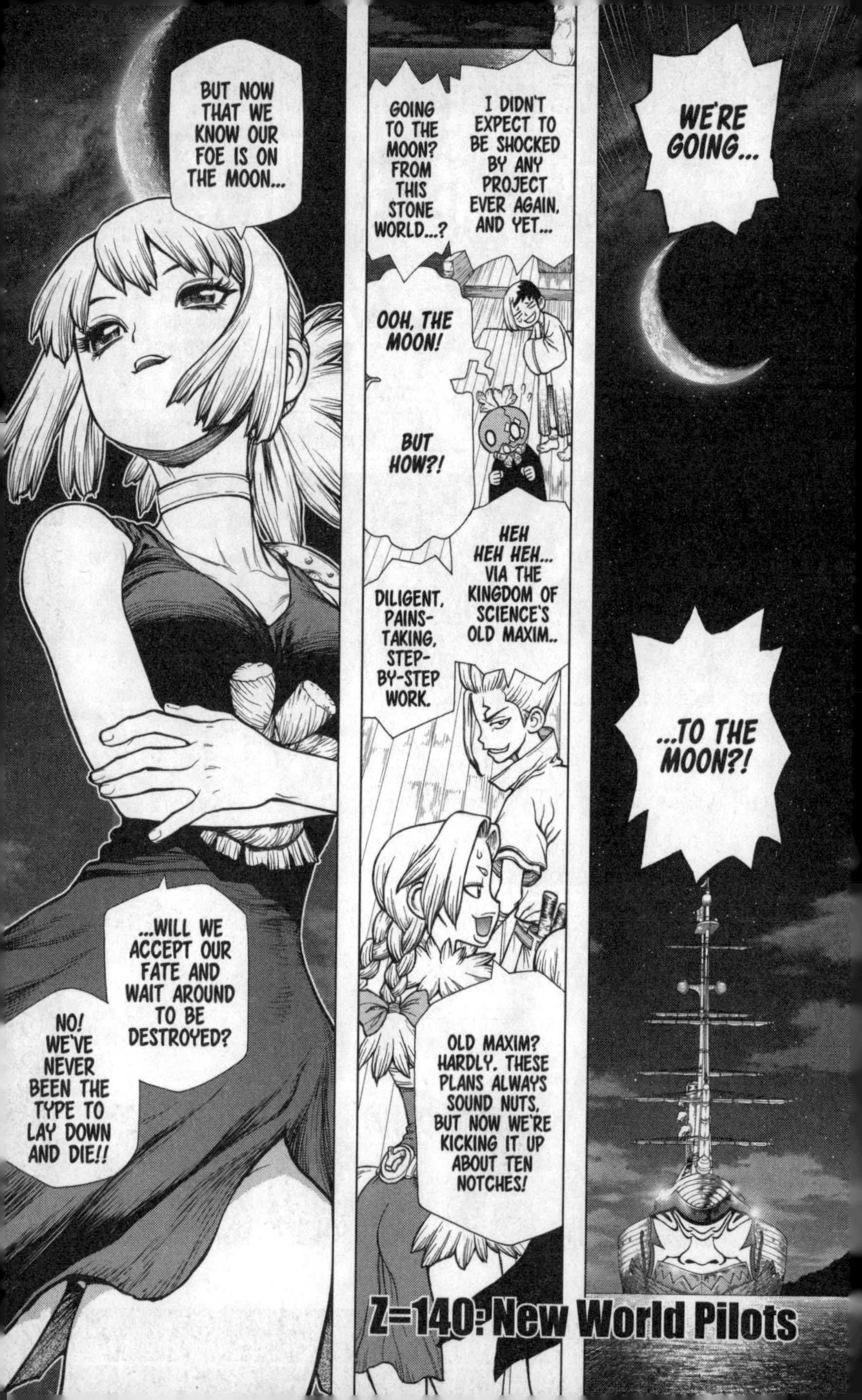
WE'RE GOING...
...TO THE MOON?!
Z=140: New World Pilots
I DIDN'T EXPECT TO BE SHOCKED BY ANY PROJECT EVER AGAIN, AND YET...
GOING TO THE MOON? FROM THIS STONE WORLD...?
OOH, THE MOON!
BUT HOW?!
HEH HEH HEH... VIA THE KINGDOM OF SCIENCE'S OLD MAXIM..
DILIGENT, PAINS-TAKING, STEP-BY-STEP WORK.
OLD MAXIM? HARDLY. THESE PLANS ALWAYS SOUND NUTS, BUT NOW WE'RE KICKING IT UP ABOUT TEN NOTCHES!
BUT NOW THAT WE KNOW OUR FOE IS ON THE MOON...
...WILL WE ACCEPT OUR FATE AND WAIT AROUND TO BE DESTROYED?
NO! WE'VE NEVER BEEN THE TYPE TO LAY DOWN AND DIE!!

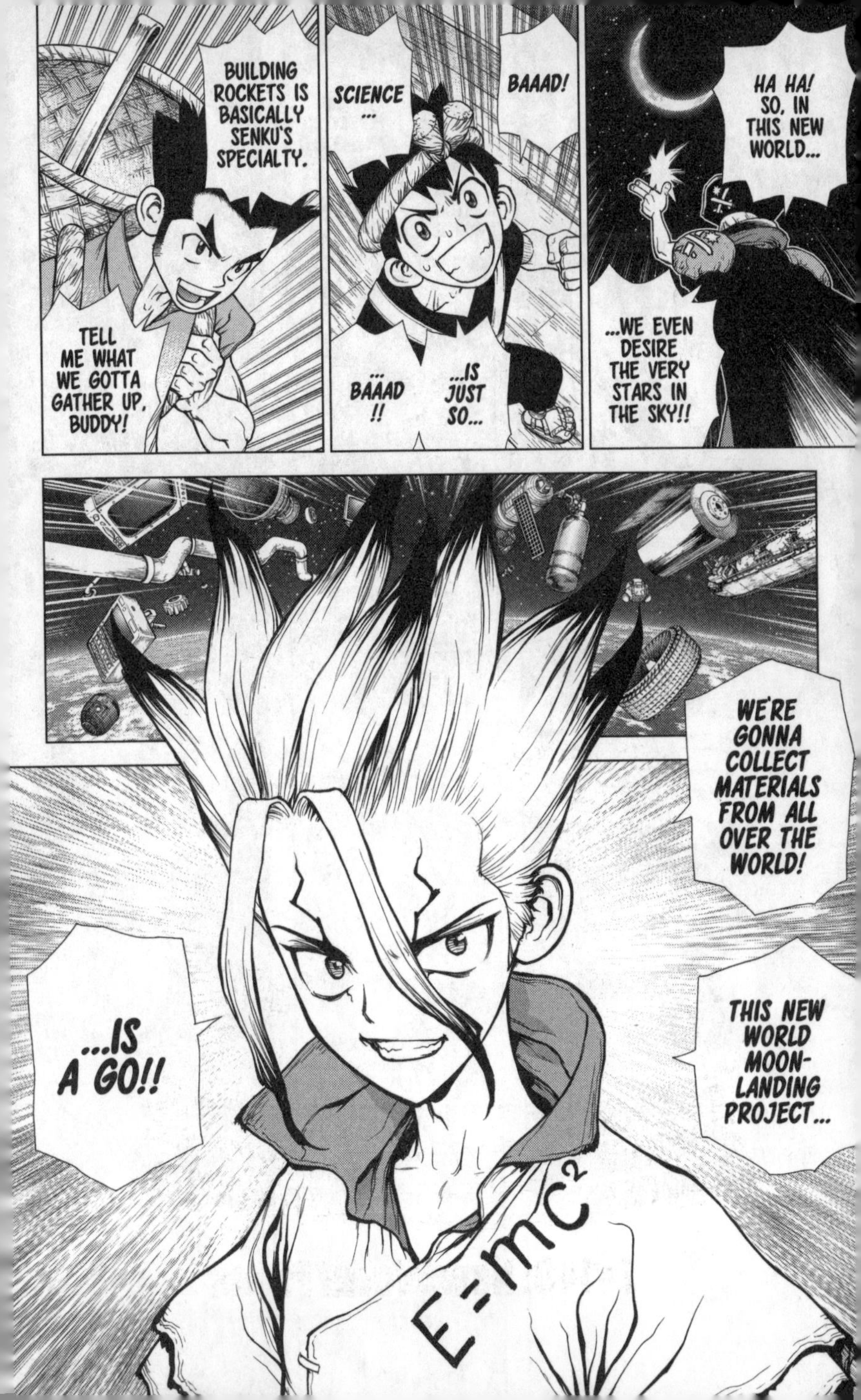
HA HA! SO, IN THIS NEW WORLD...
...WE EVEN DESIRE THE VERY STARS IN THE SKY!!
BAAAD!
SCIENCE ...
...IS JUST SO...
... BAAAD !!
BUILDING ROCKETS IS BASICALLY SENKU'S SPECIALTY.
TELL ME WHAT WE GOTTA GATHER UP, BUDDY!
WE'RE GONNA COLLECT MATERIALS FROM ALL OVER THE WORLD!
THIS NEW WORLD MOON-LANDING PROJECT...
...IS A GO!!
E=mc²

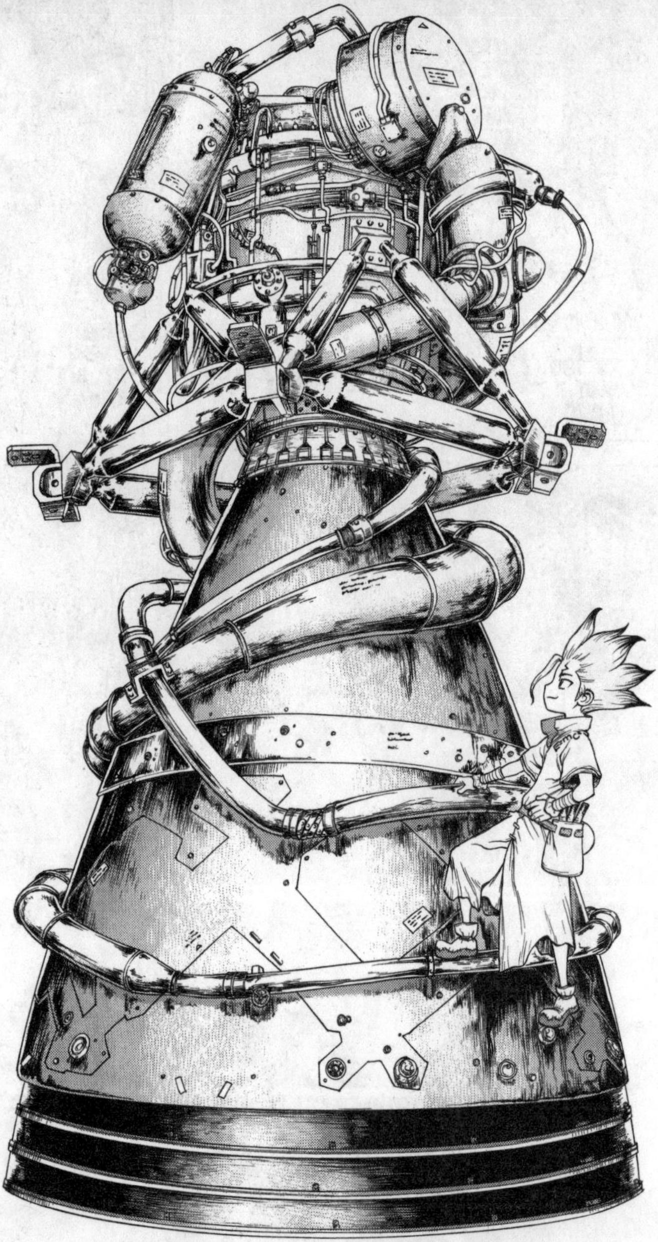

Z=140: New World Pilots

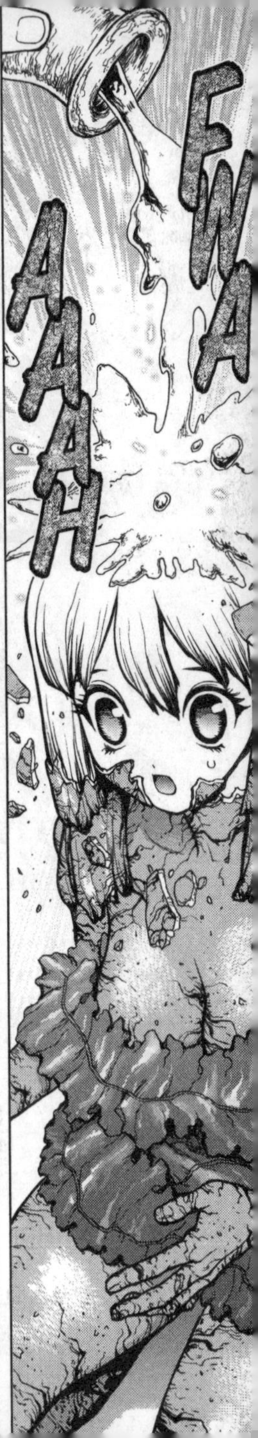
FWAAAAH
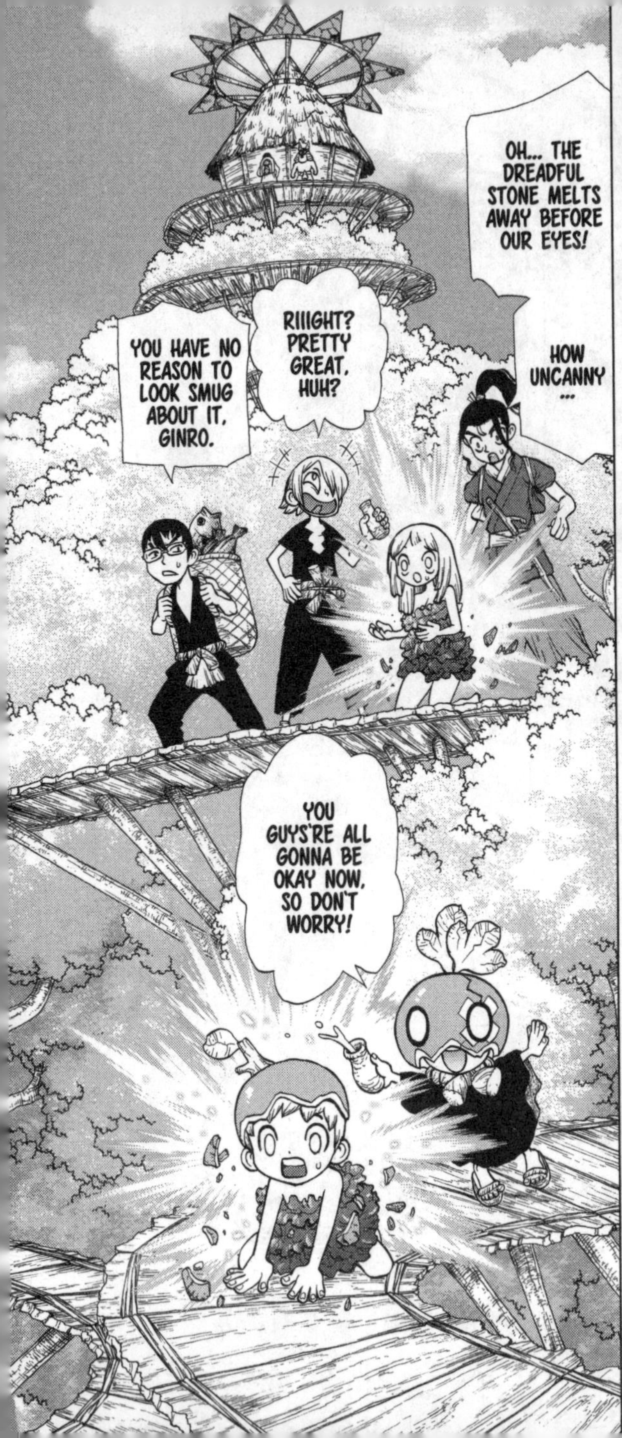
OH... THE DREADFUL STONE MELTS AWAY BEFORE OUR EYES!
HOW UNCANNY ...
RIIIGHT? PRETTY GREAT, HUH?
YOU HAVE NO REASON TO LOOK SMUG ABOUT IT, GINRO.
YOU GUYS'RE ALL GONNA BE OKAY NOW, SO DON'T WORRY!

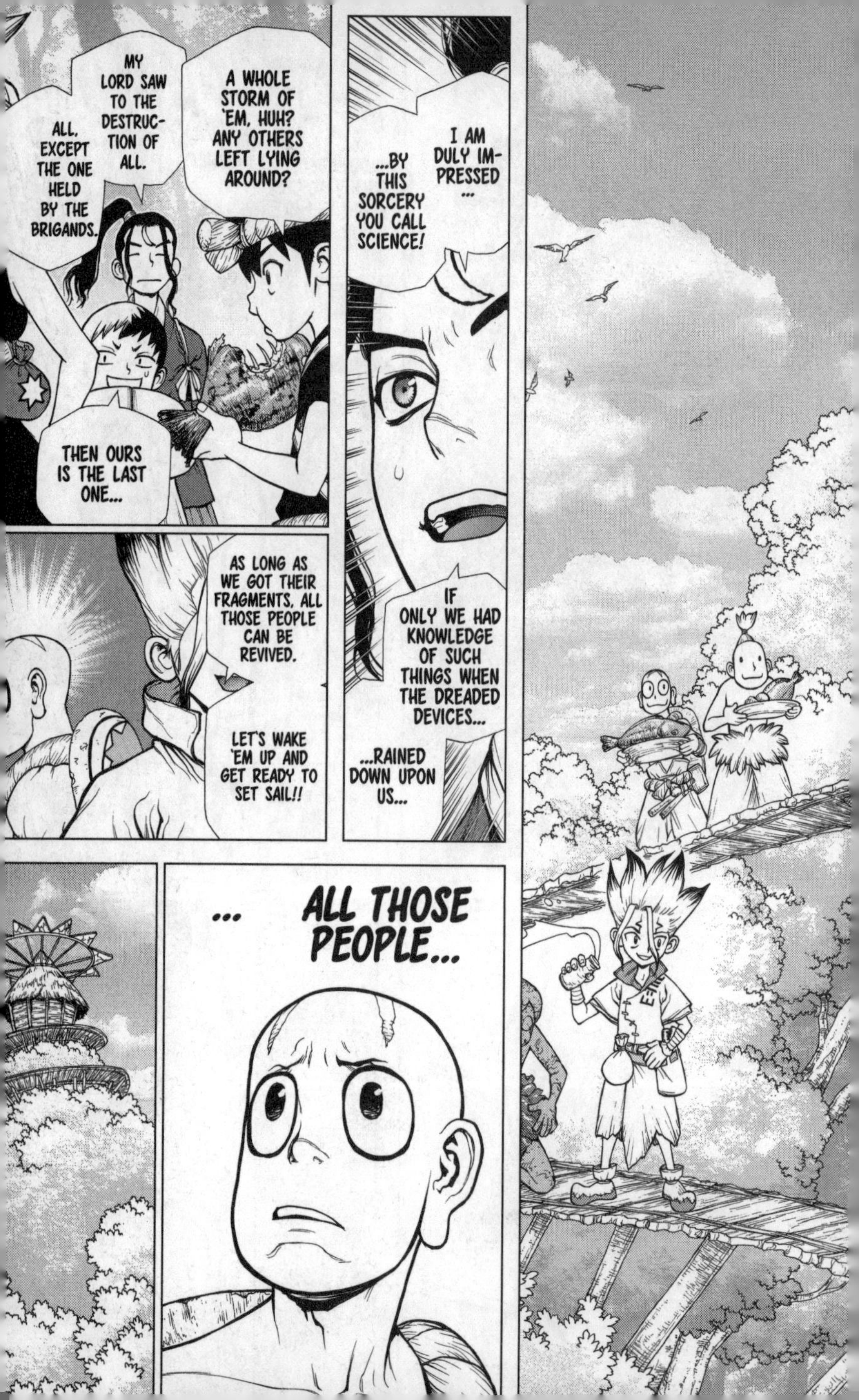
I AM DULY IM-PRESSED ...
...BY THIS SORCERY YOU CALL SCIENCE!
IF ONLY WE HAD KNOWLEDGE OF SUCH THINGS WHEN THE DREADED DEVICES...
...RAINED DOWN UPON US...
A WHOLE STORM OF 'EM, HUH? ANY OTHERS LEFT LYING AROUND?
MY LORD SAW TO THE DESTRUC-TION OF ALL.
ALL, EXCEPT THE ONE HELD BY THE BRIGANDS.
THEN OURS IS THE LAST ONE...
AS LONG AS WE GOT THEIR FRAGMENTS, ALL THOSE PEOPLE CAN BE REVIVED.
LET'S WAKE 'EM UP AND GET READY TO SET SAIL!!
... ALL THOSE PEOPLE...

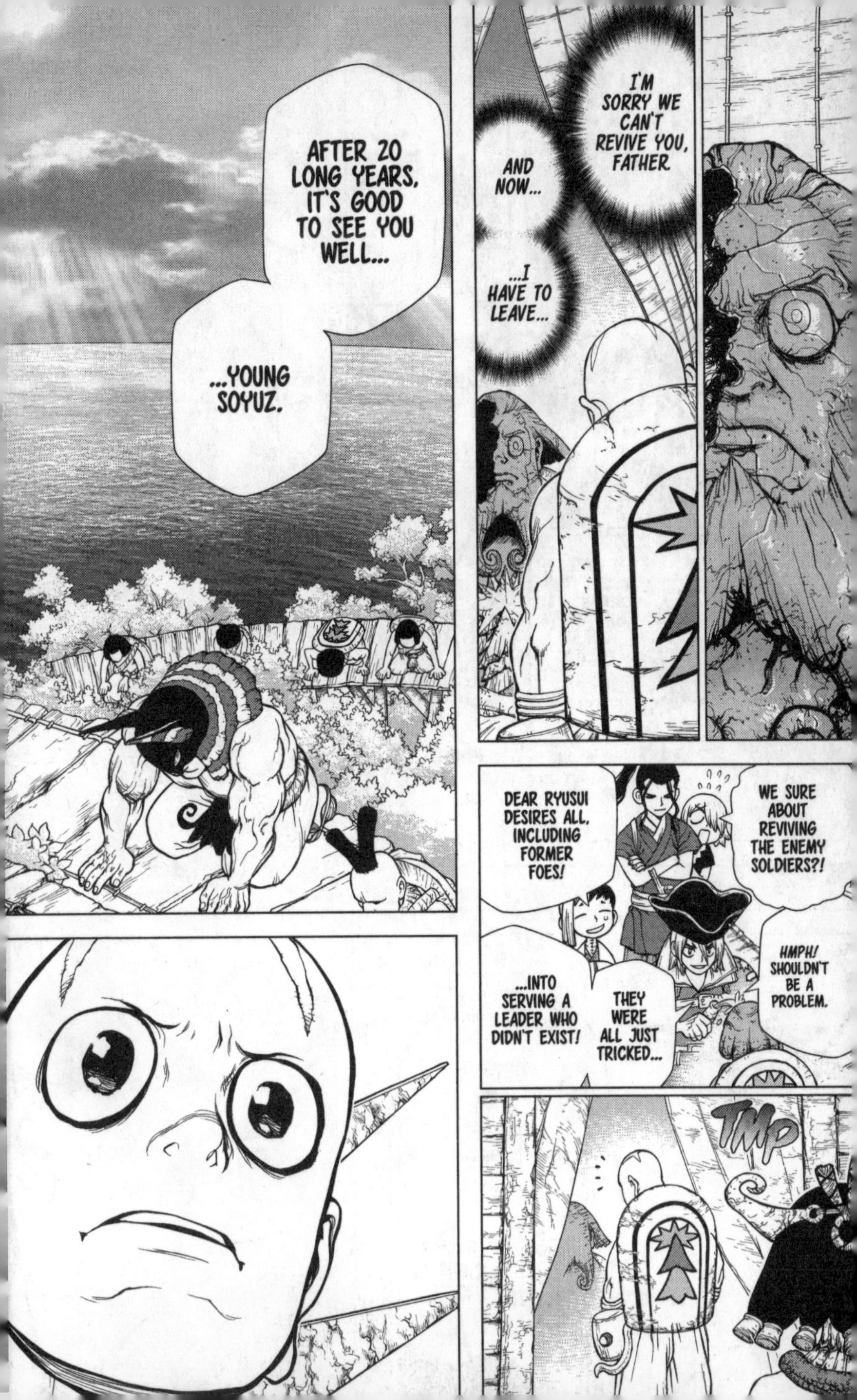
I'M SORRY WE CAN'T REVIVE YOU, FATHER.
AND NOW...
...I HAVE TO LEAVE...
WE SURE ABOUT REVIVING THE ENEMY SOLDIERS?!
DEAR RYUSUI DESIRES ALL, INCLUDING FORMER FOES!
HMPH! SHOULDN'T BE A PROBLEM.
THEY WERE ALL JUST TRICKED...
...INTO SERVING A LEADER WHO DIDN'T EXIST!
TMP
AFTER 20 LONG YEARS, IT'S GOOD TO SEE YOU WELL...
...YOUNG SOYUZ.

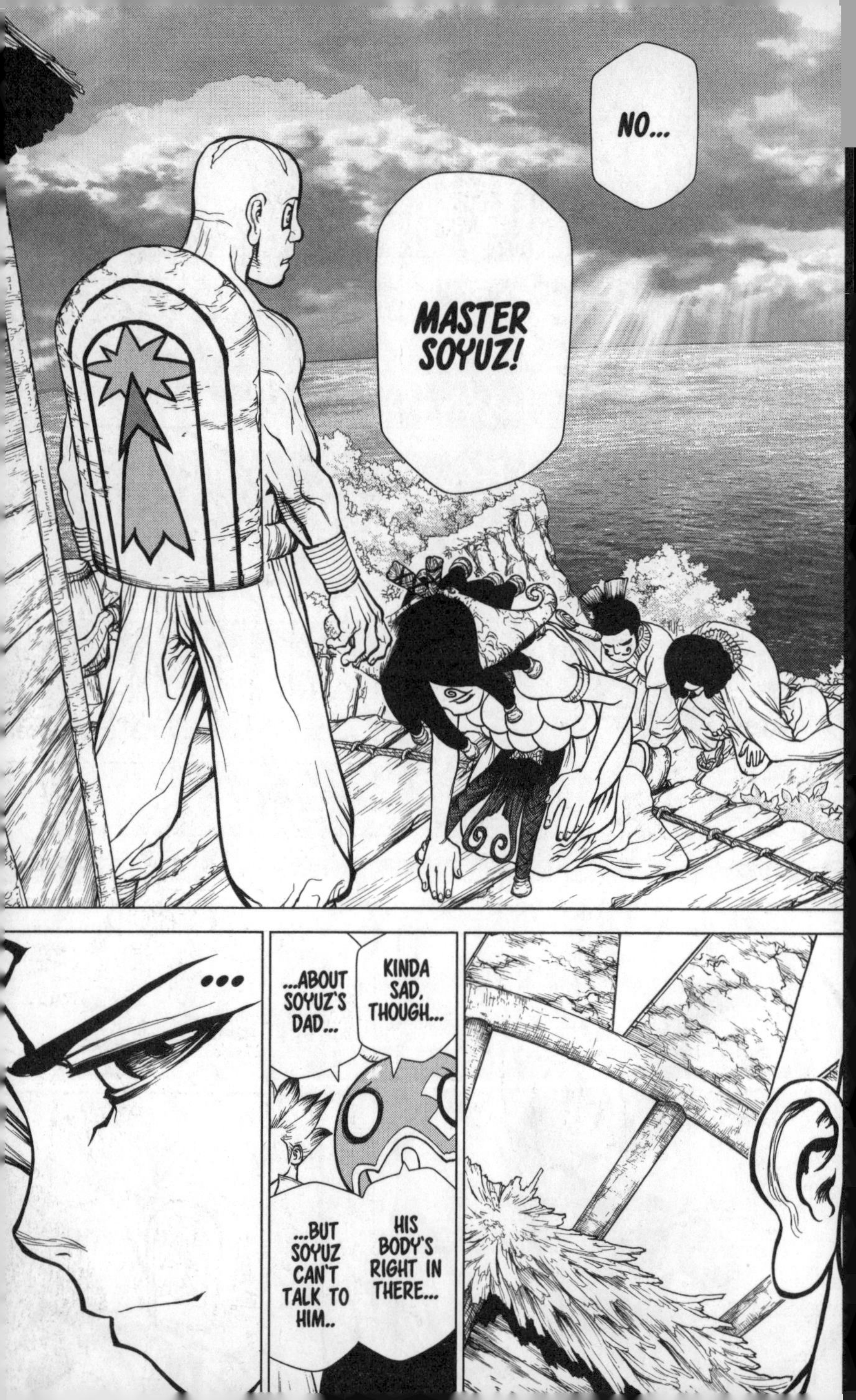
NO...
MASTER SOYUZ!
KINDA SAD, THOUGH...
...ABOUT SOYUZ'S DAD...
HIS BODY'S RIGHT IN THERE...
...BUT SOYUZ CAN'T TALK TO HIM..
...

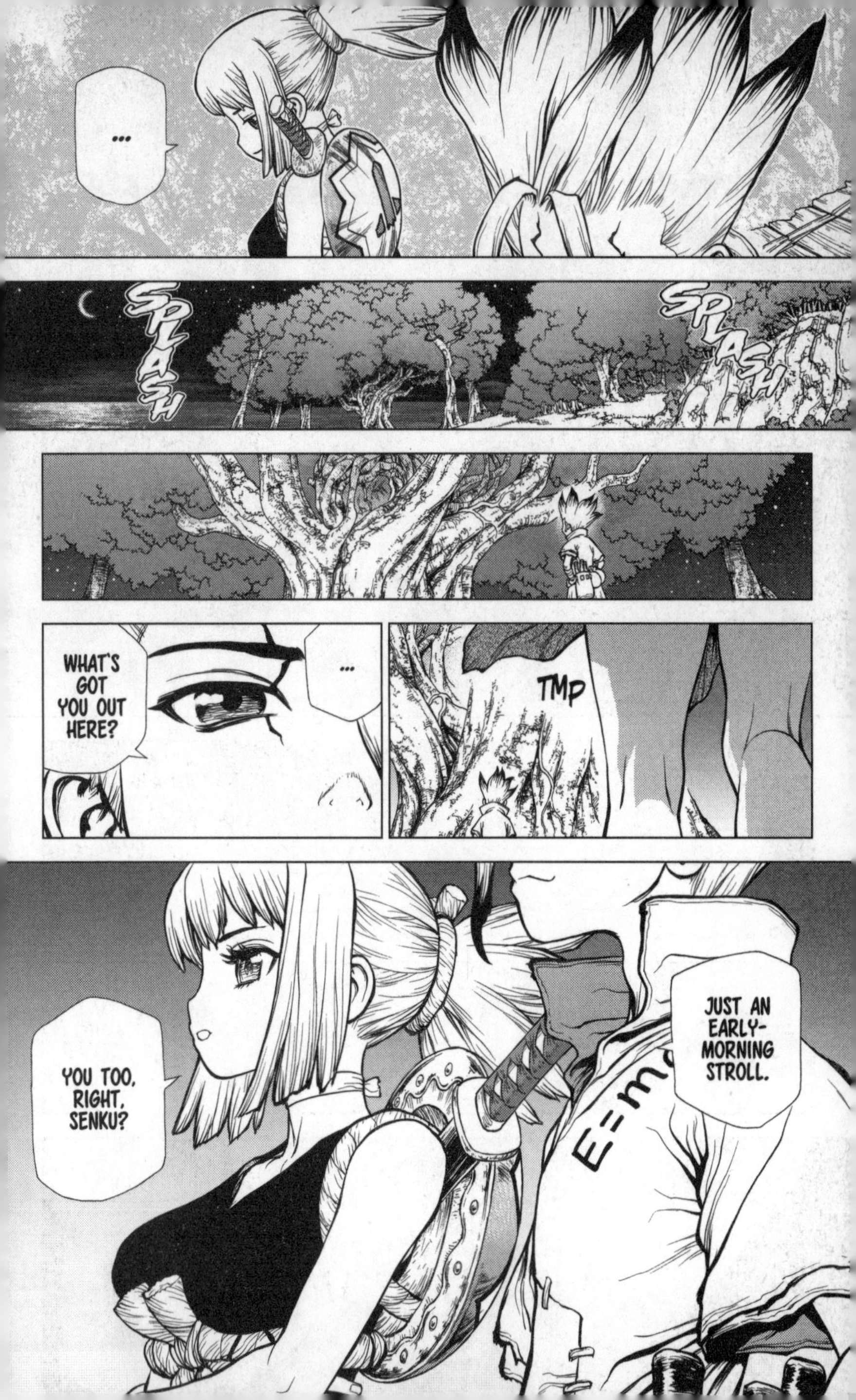
...
SPLASH
SPLASH
TMP
...
WHAT'S GOT YOU OUT HERE?
JUST AN EARLY-MORNING STROLL.
YOU TOO, RIGHT, SENKU?

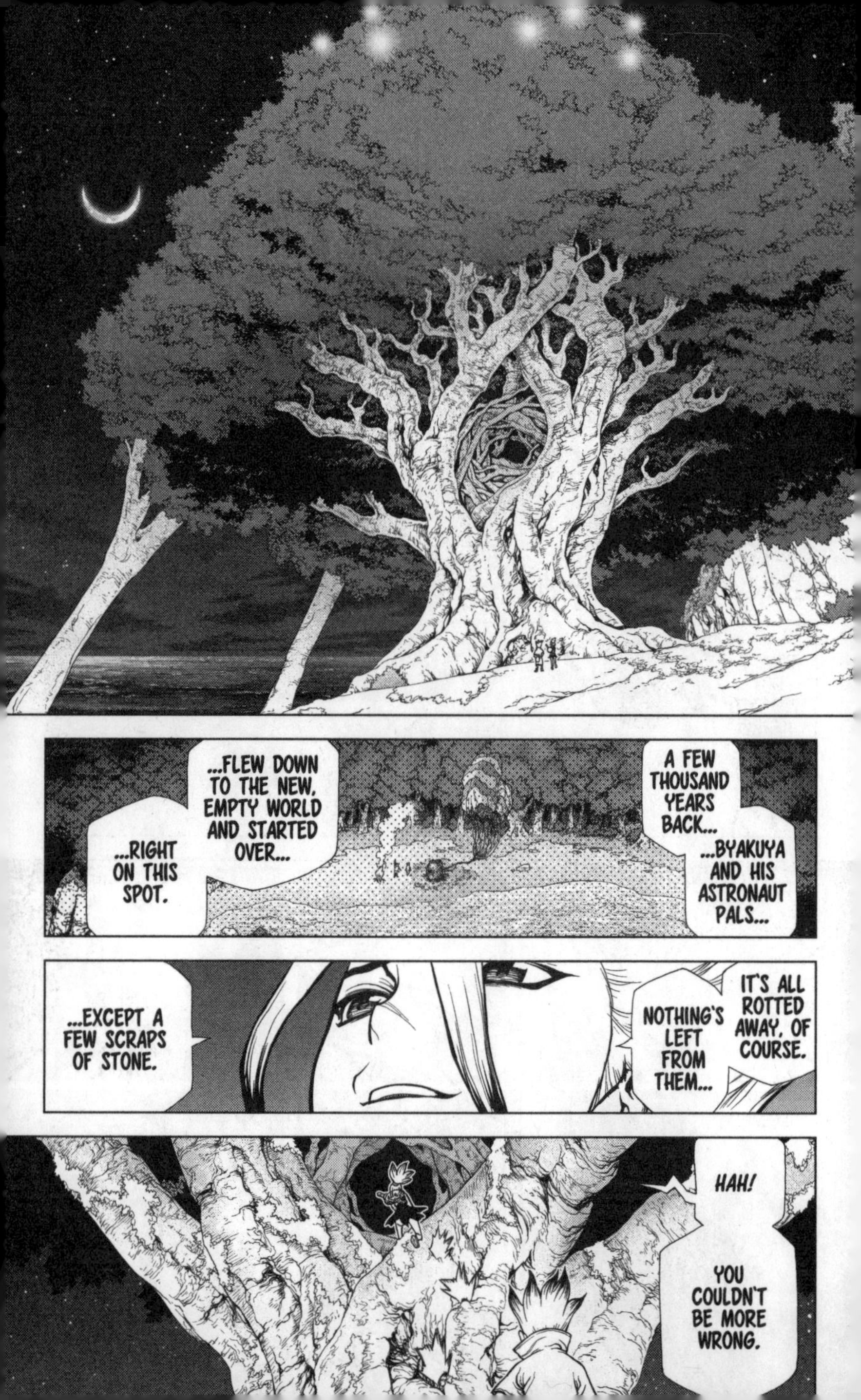
A FEW THOUSAND YEARS BACK...
...BYAKUYA AND HIS ASTRONAUT PALS...
...FLEW DOWN TO THE NEW, EMPTY WORLD AND STARTED OVER...
...RIGHT ON THIS SPOT.
IT'S ALL ROTTED AWAY, OF COURSE.
NOTHING'S LEFT FROM THEM...
...EXCEPT A FEW SCRAPS OF STONE.
HAH!
YOU COULDN'T BE MORE WRONG.

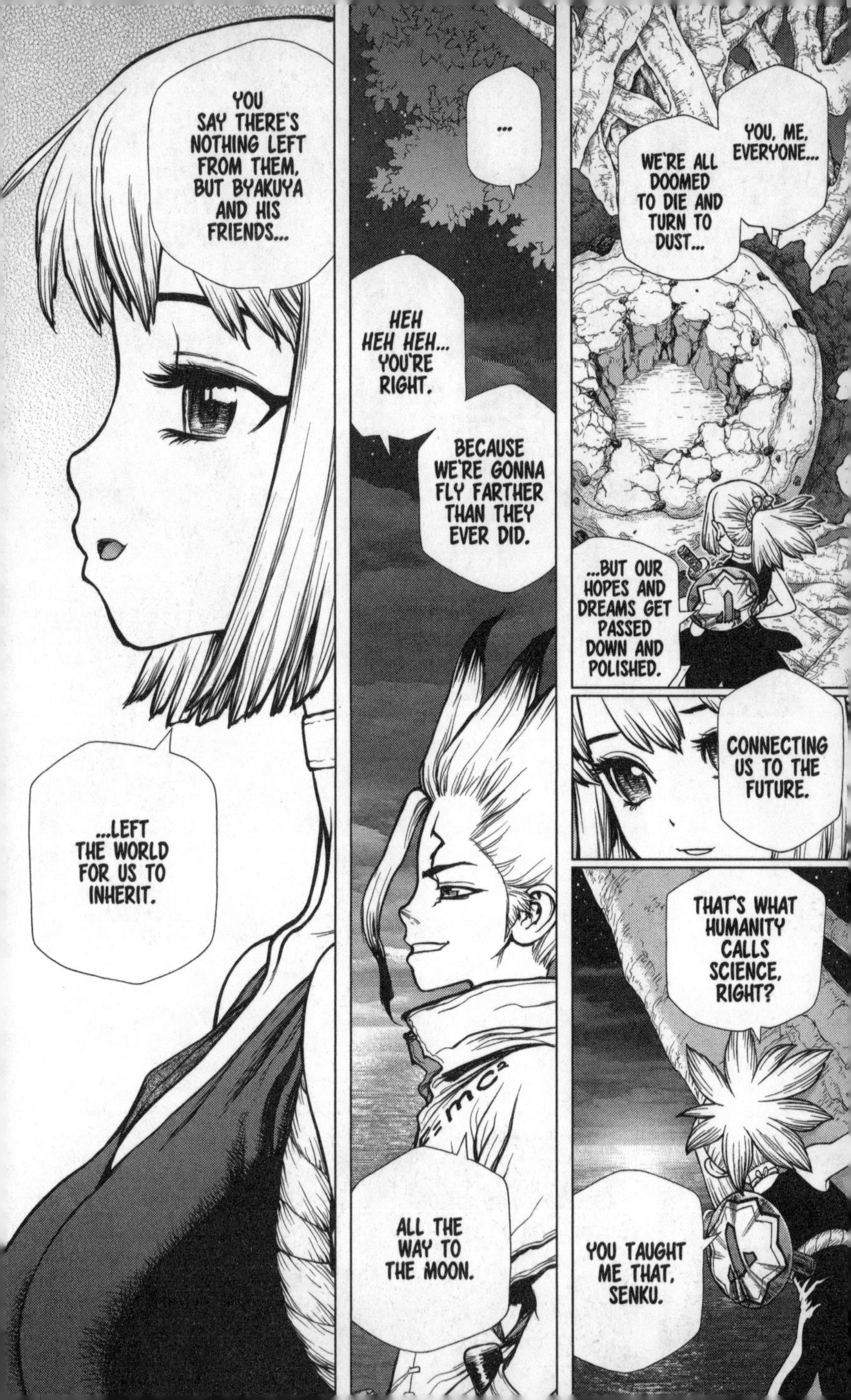
YOU, ME, EVERYONE...
WE'RE ALL DOOMED TO DIE AND TURN TO DUST...
...BUT OUR HOPES AND DREAMS GET PASSED DOWN AND POLISHED.
CONNECTING US TO THE FUTURE.
THAT'S WHAT HUMANITY CALLS SCIENCE, RIGHT?
YOU TAUGHT ME THAT, SENKU.
...
HEH HEH HEH... YOU'RE RIGHT.
BECAUSE WE'RE GONNA FLY FARTHER THAN THEY EVER DID.
ALL THE WAY TO THE MOON.
YOU SAY THERE'S NOTHING LEFT FROM THEM, BUT BYAKUYA AND HIS FRIENDS...
...LEFT THE WORLD FOR US TO INHERIT.

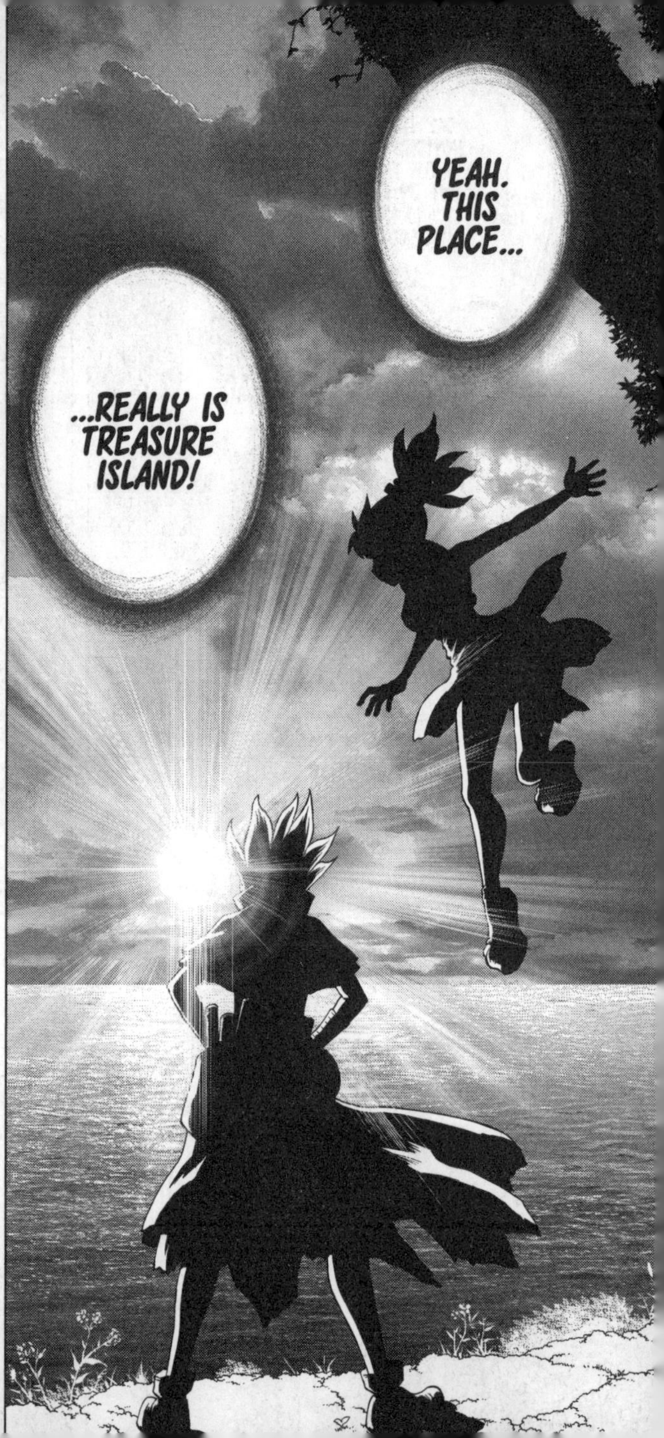
YEAH. THIS PLACE...
...REALLY IS TREASURE ISLAND!
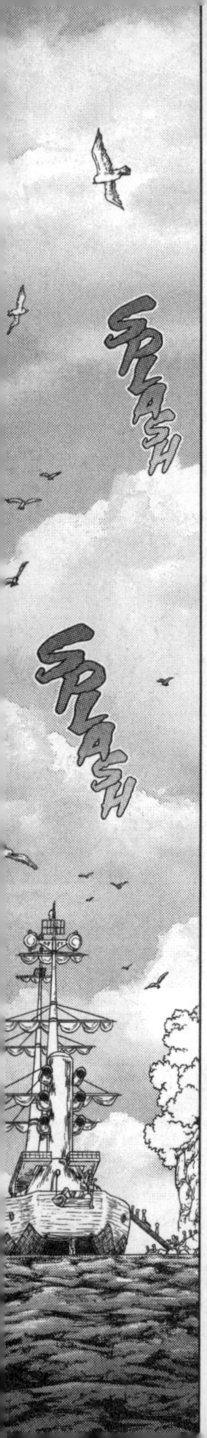
SPLASH
SPLASH

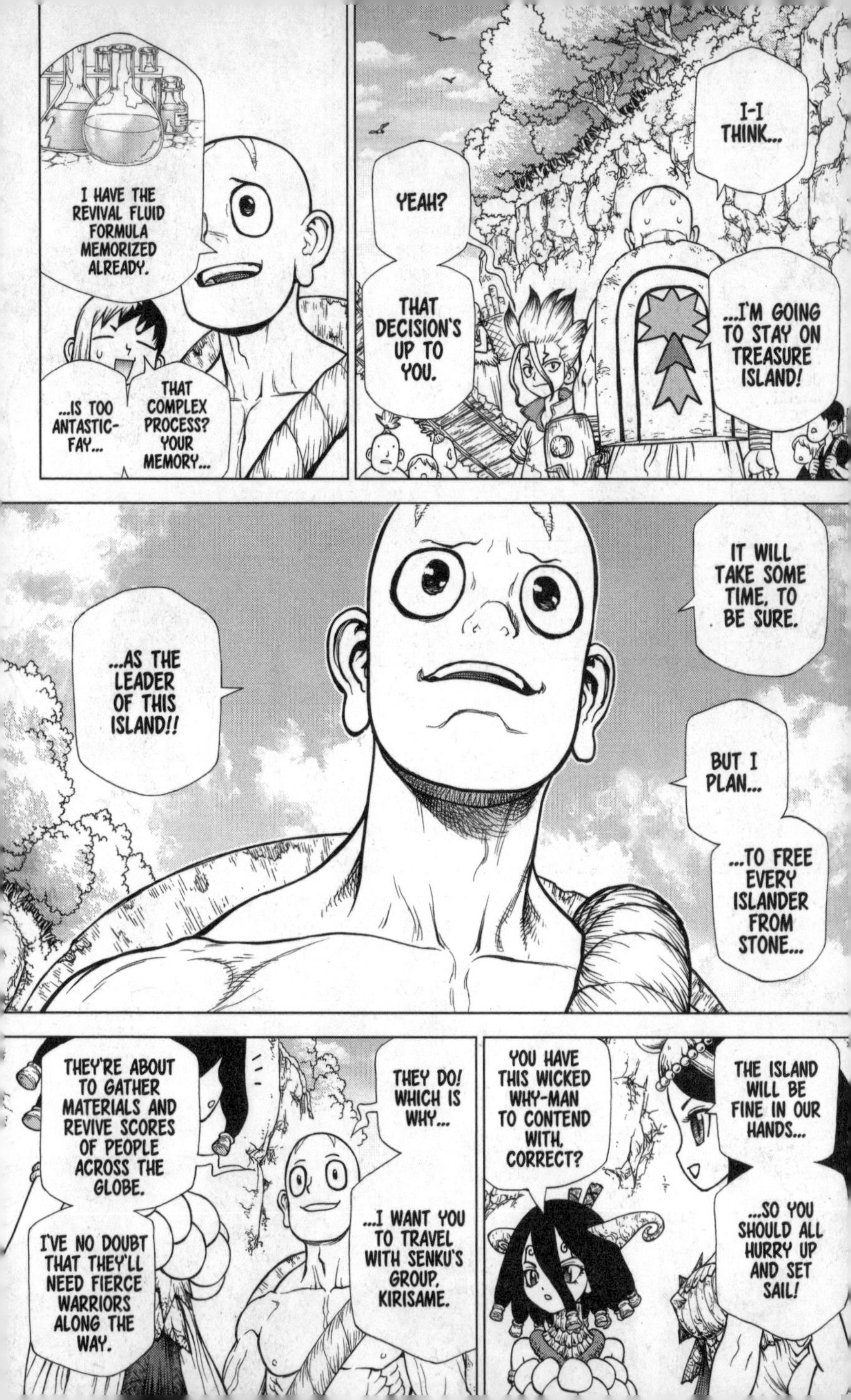
I-I THINK...
...I'M GOING TO STAY ON TREASURE ISLAND!
YEAH?
THAT DECISION'S UP TO YOU.
I HAVE THE REVIVAL FLUID FORMULA MEMORIZED ALREADY.
THAT COMPLEX PROCESS? YOUR MEMORY...
...IS TOO ANTASTIC-FAY...
IT WILL TAKE SOME TIME, TO BE SURE.
BUT I PLAN...
...TO FREE EVERY ISLANDER FROM STONE...
...AS THE LEADER OF THIS ISLAND!!
THE ISLAND WILL BE FINE IN OUR HANDS...
...SO YOU SHOULD ALL HURRY UP AND SET SAIL!
YOU HAVE THIS WICKED WHY-MAN TO CONTEND WITH, CORRECT?
THEY DO! WHICH IS WHY...
...I WANT YOU TO TRAVEL WITH SENKU'S GROUP, KIRISAME.
THEY'RE ABOUT TO GATHER MATERIALS AND REVIVE SCORES OF PEOPLE ACROSS THE GLOBE.
I'VE NO DOUBT THAT THEY'LL NEED FIERCE WARRIORS ALONG THE WAY.

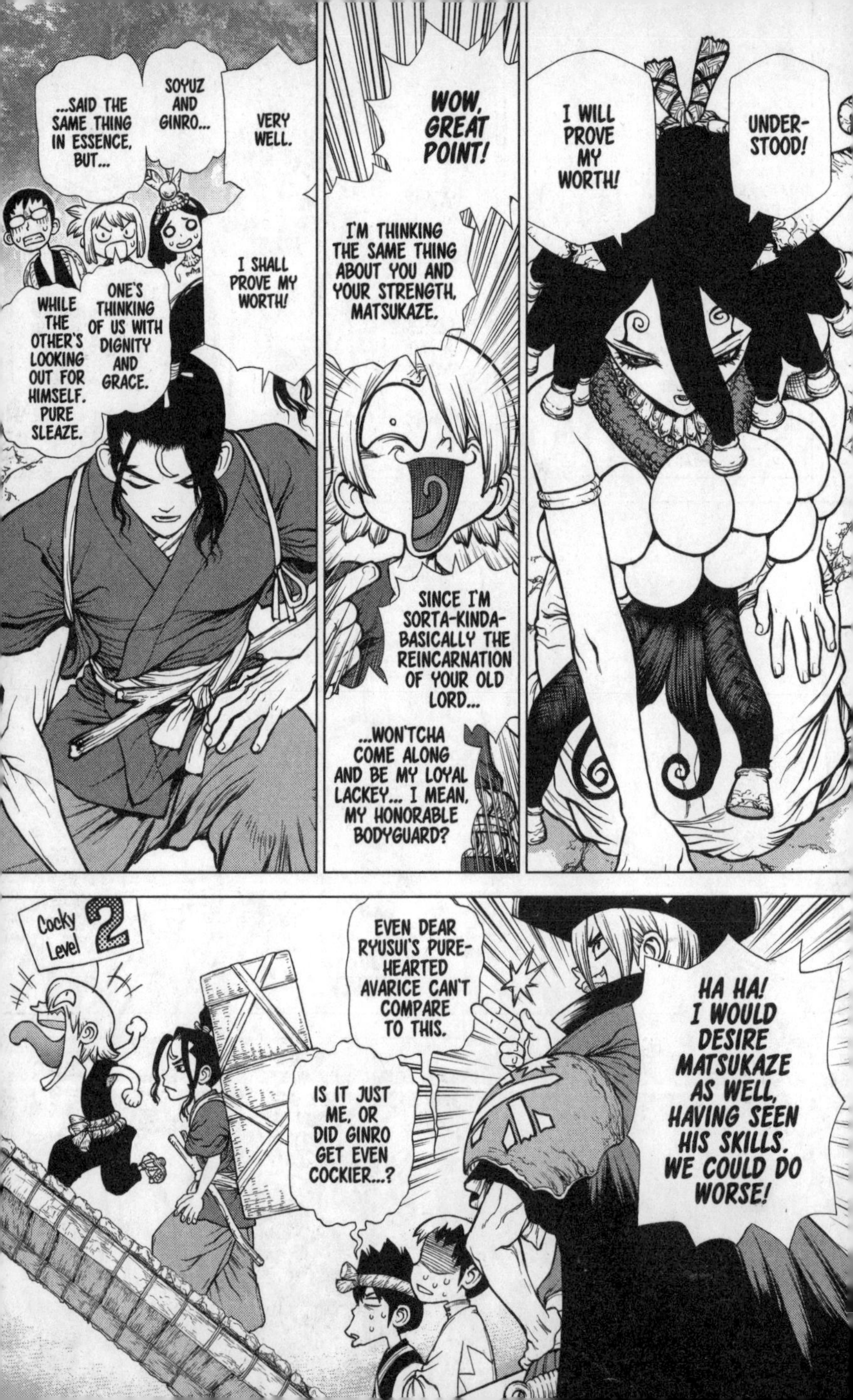
UNDER-STOOD!
I WILL PROVE MY WORTH!
WOW, GREAT POINT!
I'M THINKING THE SAME THING ABOUT YOU AND YOUR STRENGTH, MATSUKAZE.
SINCE I'M SORTA-KINDA-BASICALLY THE REINCARNATION OF YOUR OLD LORD...
...WON'TCHA COME ALONG AND BE MY LOYAL LACKEY... I MEAN, MY HONORABLE BODYGUARD?
VERY WELL.
I SHALL PROVE MY WORTH!
SOYUZ AND GINRO...
...SAID THE SAME THING IN ESSENCE, BUT...
ONE'S THINKING OF US WITH DIGNITY AND GRACE.
WHILE THE OTHER'S LOOKING OUT FOR HIMSELF. PURE SLEAZE.
HA HA! I WOULD DESIRE MATSUKAZE AS WELL, HAVING SEEN HIS SKILLS. WE COULD DO WORSE!
EVEN DEAR RYUSUI'S PURE-HEARTED AVARICE CAN'T COMPARE TO THIS.
IS IT JUST ME, OR DID GINRO GET EVEN COCKIER...?
Cocky Level 2

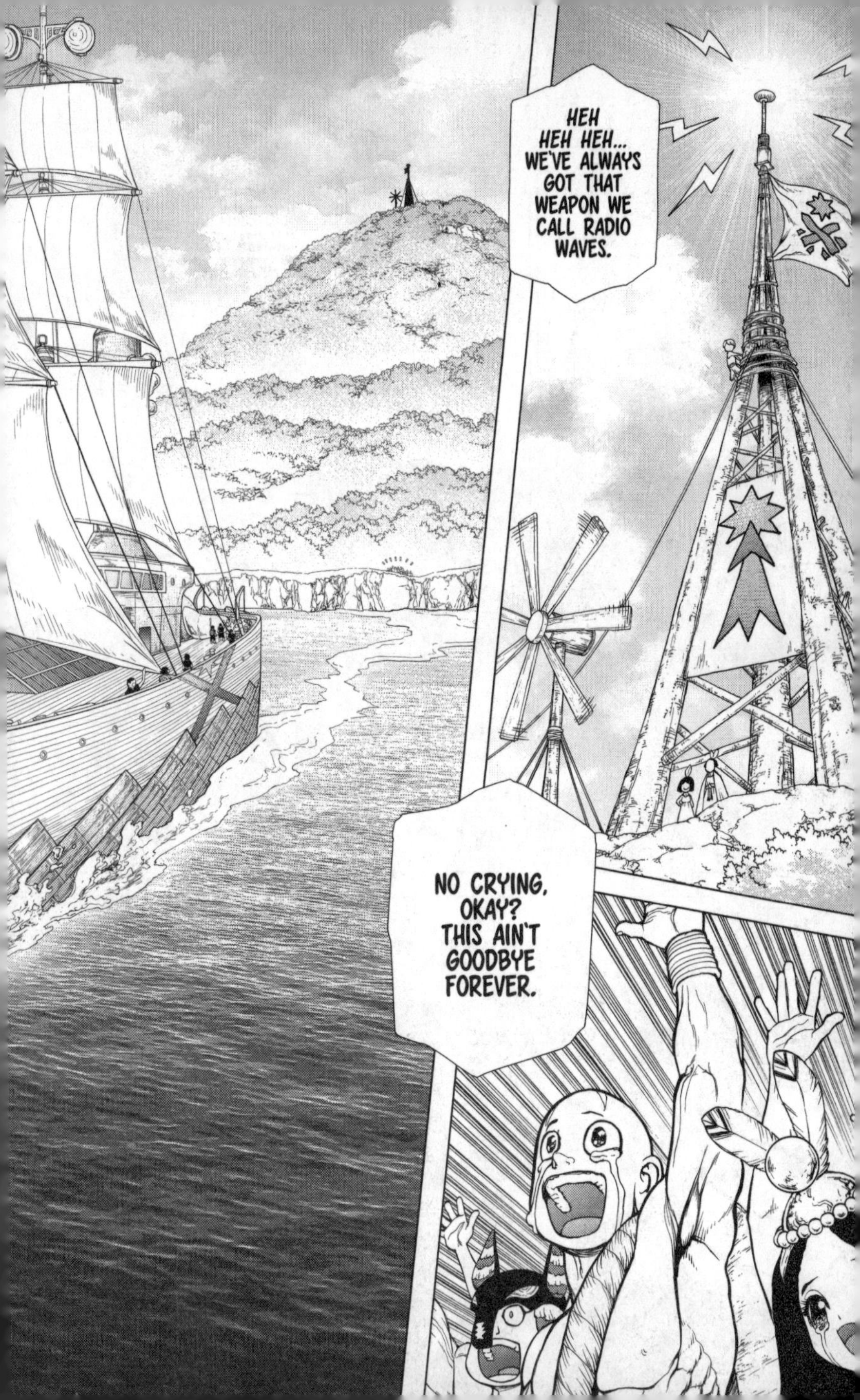
HEH HEH HEH... WE'VE ALWAYS GOT THAT WEAPON WE CALL RADIO WAVES.
NO CRYING, OKAY? THIS AIN'T GOODBYE FOREVER.

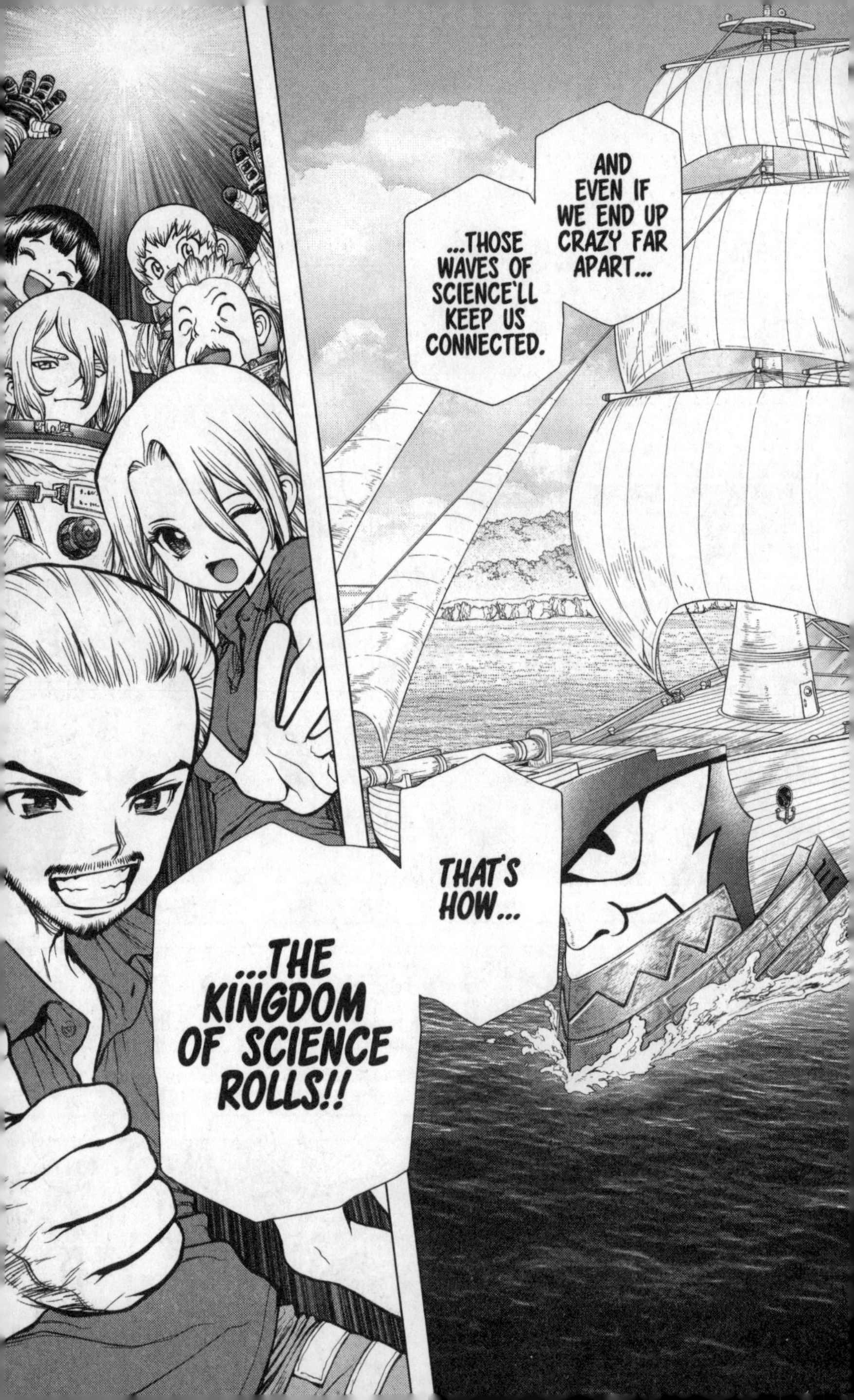
AND EVEN IF WE END UP CRAZY FAR APART...
...THOSE WAVES OF SCIENCE'LL KEEP US CONNECTED.
THAT'S HOW...
...THE KINGDOM OF SCIENCE ROLLS!!

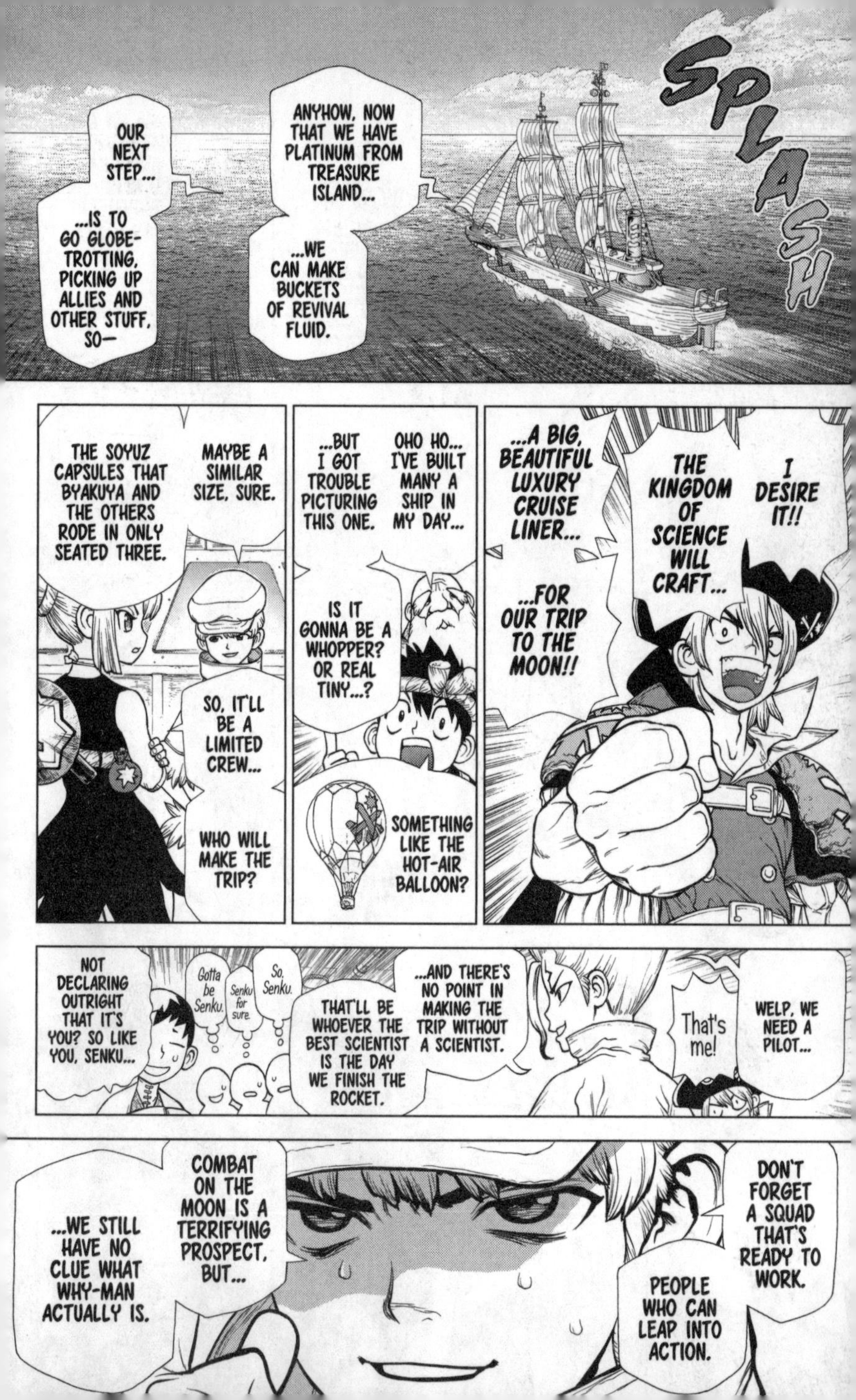
SPLASH
ANYHOW, NOW THAT WE HAVE PLATINUM FROM TREASURE ISLAND...
...WE CAN MAKE BUCKETS OF REVIVAL FLUID.
OUR NEXT STEP...
...IS TO GO GLOBE-TROTTING, PICKING UP ALLIES AND OTHER STUFF, SO—
I DESIRE IT!!
THE KINGDOM OF SCIENCE WILL CRAFT...
...A BIG, BEAUTIFUL LUXURY CRUISE LINER...
...FOR OUR TRIP TO THE MOON!!
OHO HO... I'VE BUILT MANY A SHIP IN MY DAY...
...BUT I GOT TROUBLE PICTURING THIS ONE.
IS IT GONNA BE A WHOPPER? OR REAL TINY...?
SOMETHING LIKE THE HOT-AIR BALLOON?
MAYBE A SIMILAR SIZE, SURE.
THE SOYUZ CAPSULES THAT BYAKUYA AND THE OTHERS RODE IN ONLY SEATED THREE.
SO, IT'LL BE A LIMITED CREW...
WHO WILL MAKE THE TRIP?
WELP, WE NEED A PILOT...
That's me!
...AND THERE'S NO POINT IN MAKING THE TRIP WITHOUT A SCIENTIST.
THAT'LL BE WHOEVER THE BEST SCIENTIST IS THE DAY WE FINISH THE ROCKET.
So, Senku.
Senku for sure.
Gotta be Senku.
NOT DECLARING OUTRIGHT THAT IT'S YOU? SO LIKE YOU, SENKU...
DON'T FORGET A SQUAD THAT'S READY TO WORK.
PEOPLE WHO CAN LEAP INTO ACTION.
COMBAT ON THE MOON IS A TERRIFYING PROSPECT, BUT...
...WE STILL HAVE NO CLUE WHAT WHY-MAN ACTUALLY IS.

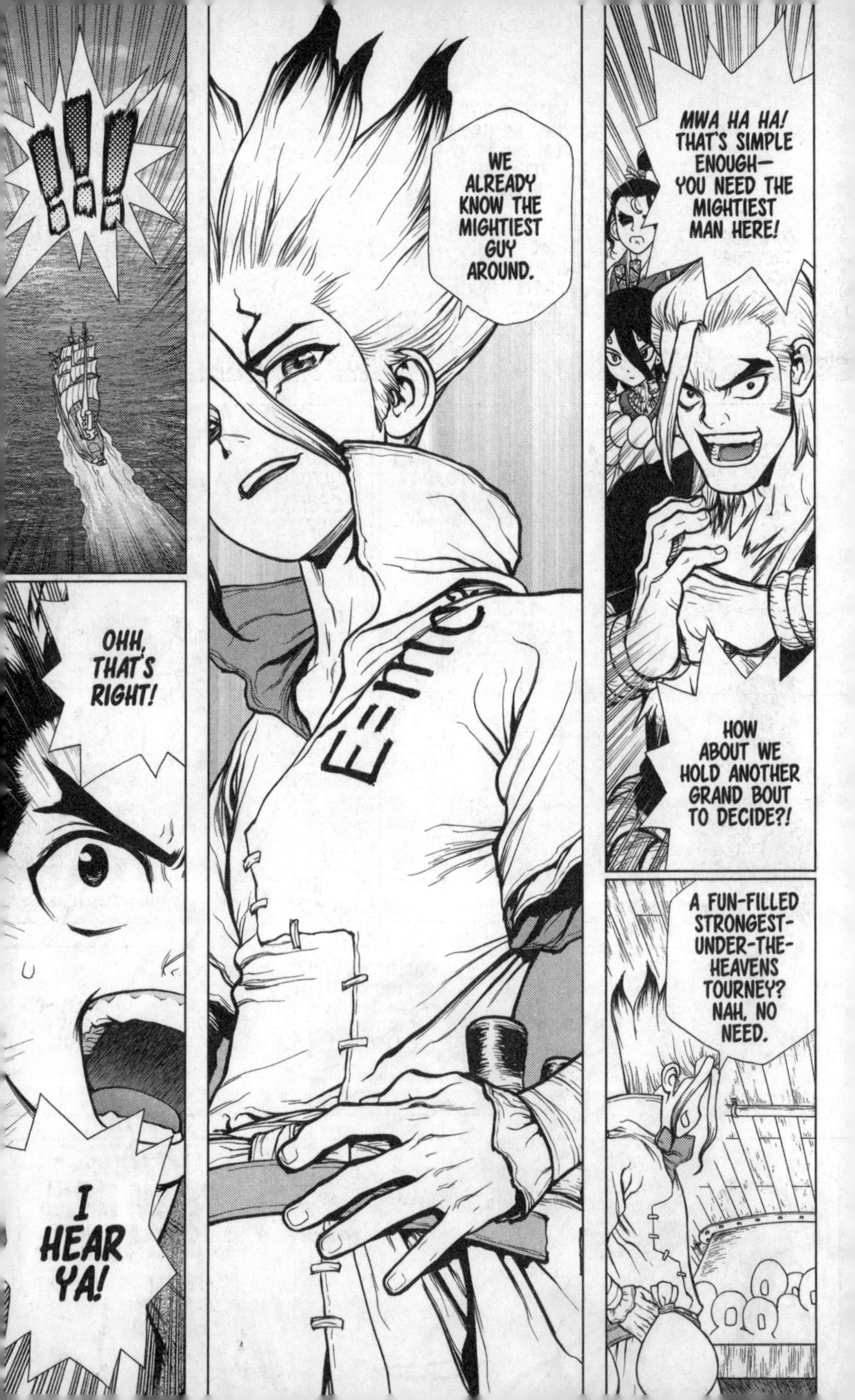
MWA HA HA! THAT'S SIMPLE ENOUGH—YOU NEED THE MIGHTIEST MAN HERE!
HOW ABOUT WE HOLD ANOTHER GRAND BOUT TO DECIDE?!
A FUN-FILLED STRONGEST-UNDER-THE-HEAVENS TOURNEY? NAH, NO NEED.
WE ALREADY KNOW THE MIGHTIEST GUY AROUND.
E=mc²
!!!
OHH, THAT'S RIGHT!
I HEAR YA!

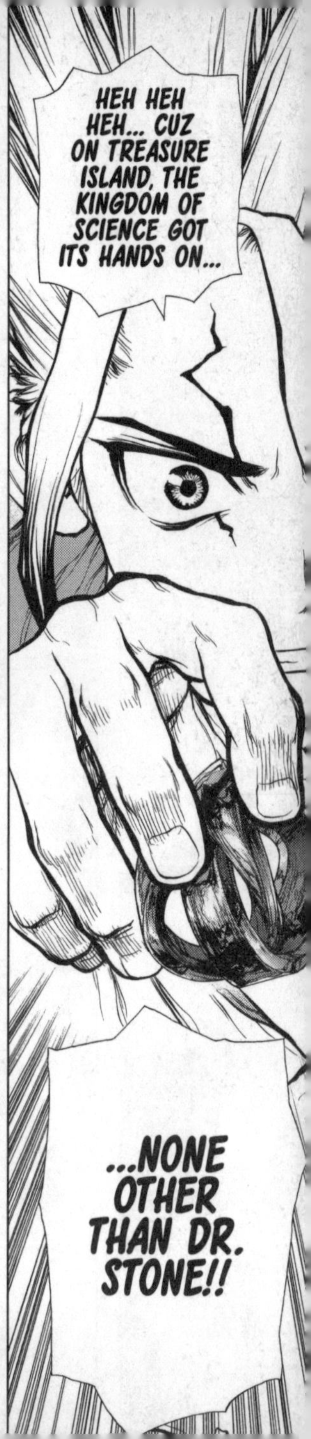
HEH HEH HEH... CUZ ON TREASURE ISLAND, THE KINGDOM OF SCIENCE GOT ITS HANDS ON...
...NONE OTHER THAN DR. STONE!!
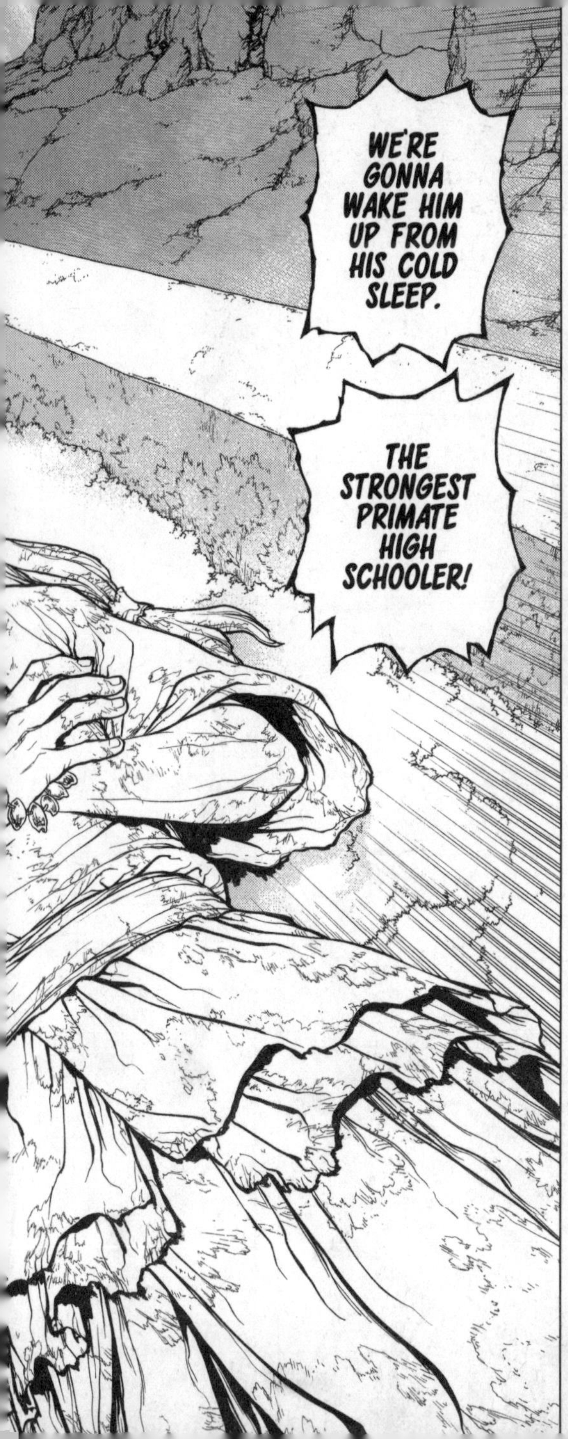
WE'RE GONNA WAKE HIM UP FROM HIS COLD SLEEP.
THE STRONGEST PRIMATE HIGH SCHOOLER!

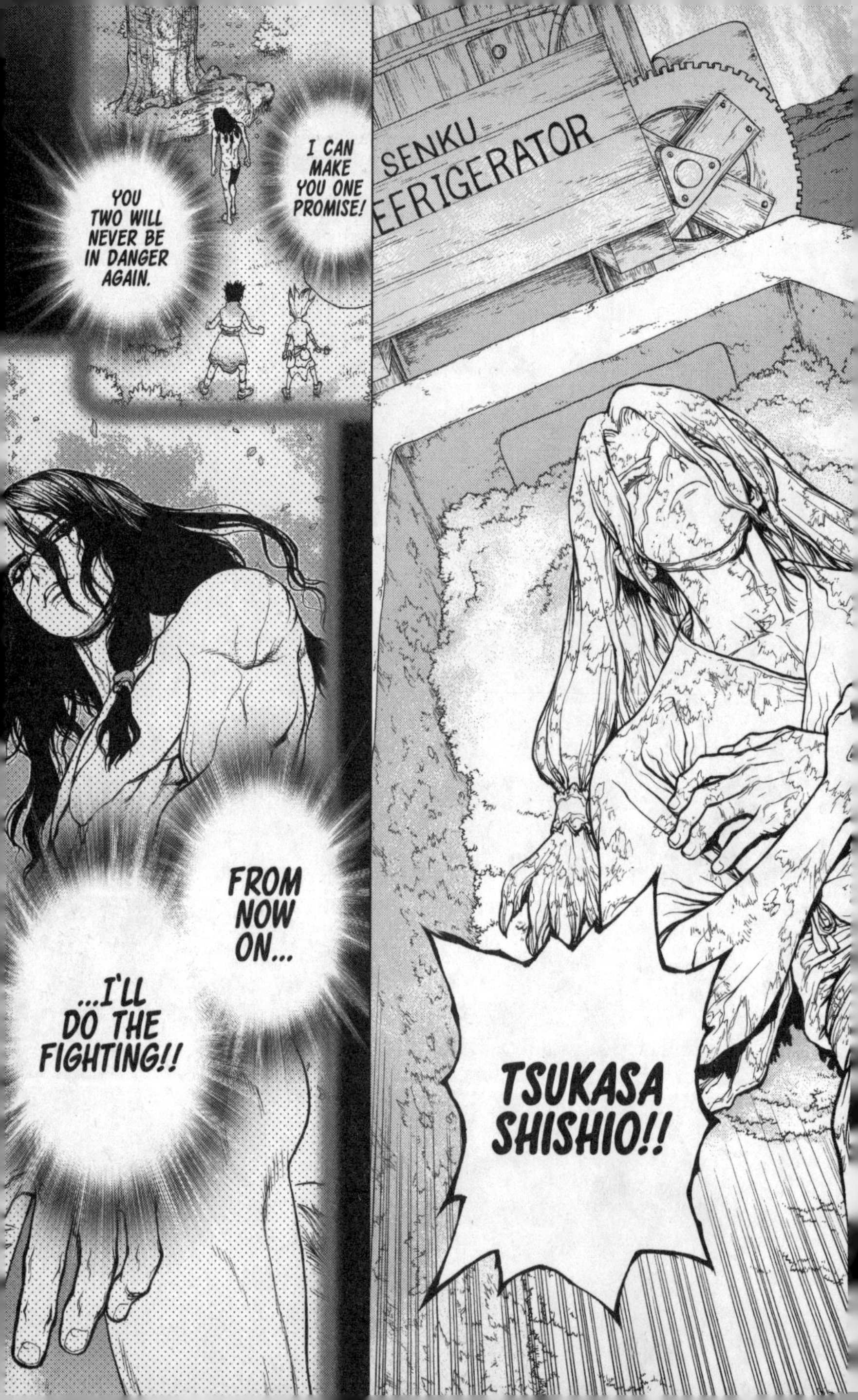
SENKU
EFRIGERATOR
TSUKASA SHISHIO!!
I CAN MAKE YOU ONE PROMISE!
YOU TWO WILL NEVER BE IN DANGER AGAIN.
FROM NOW ON...
...I'LL DO THE FIGHTING!!

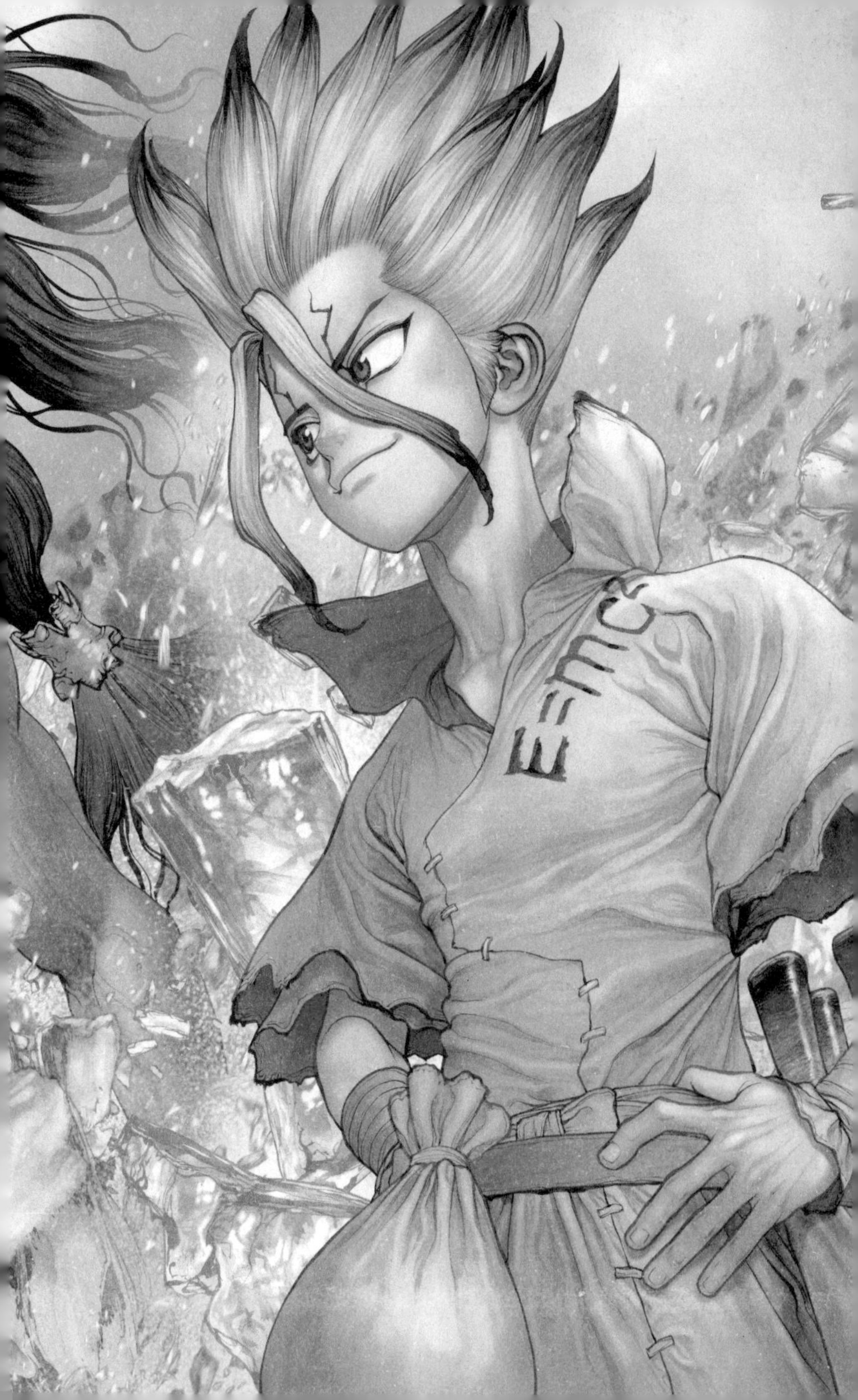
E=mc²

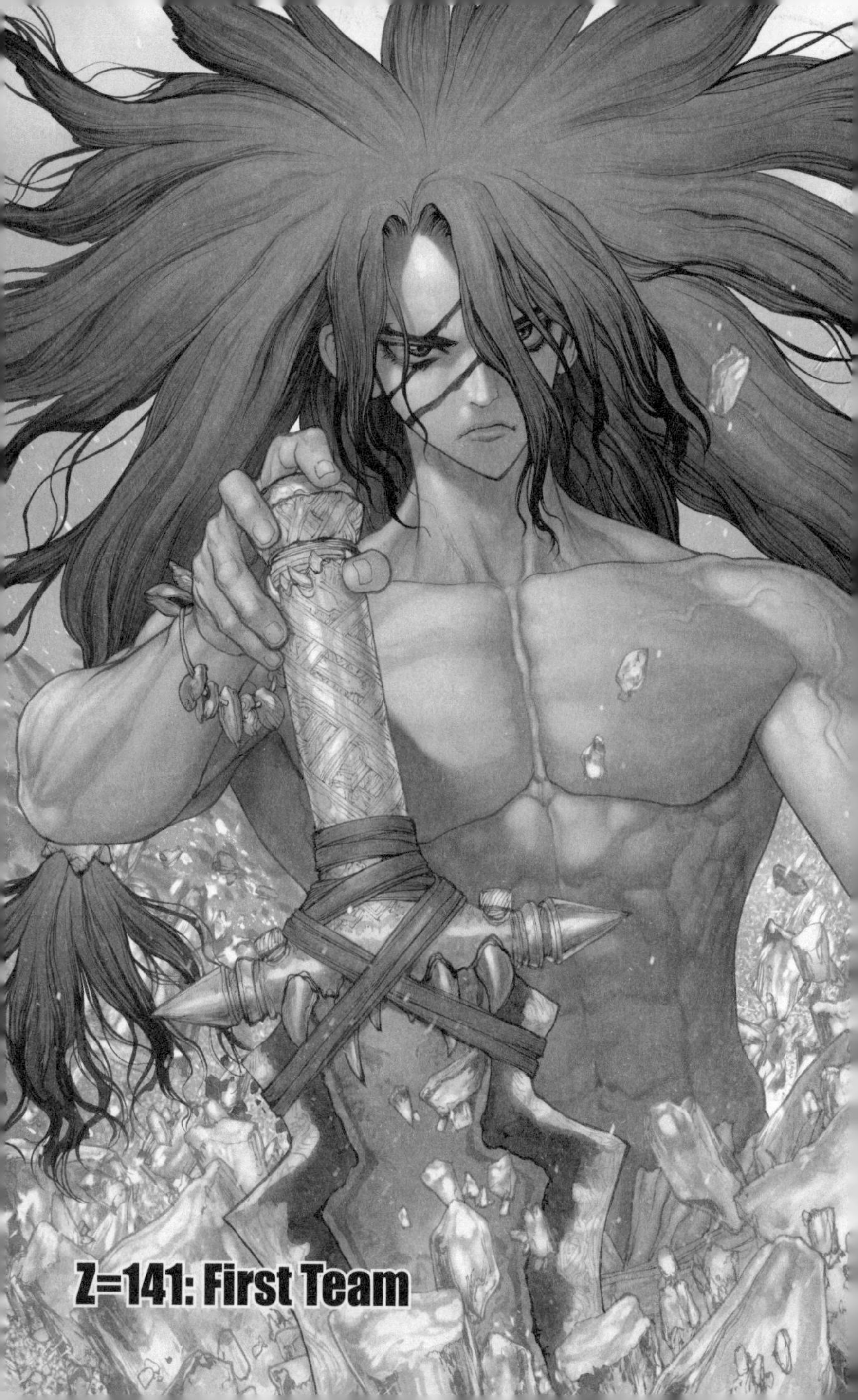
Z=141: First Team

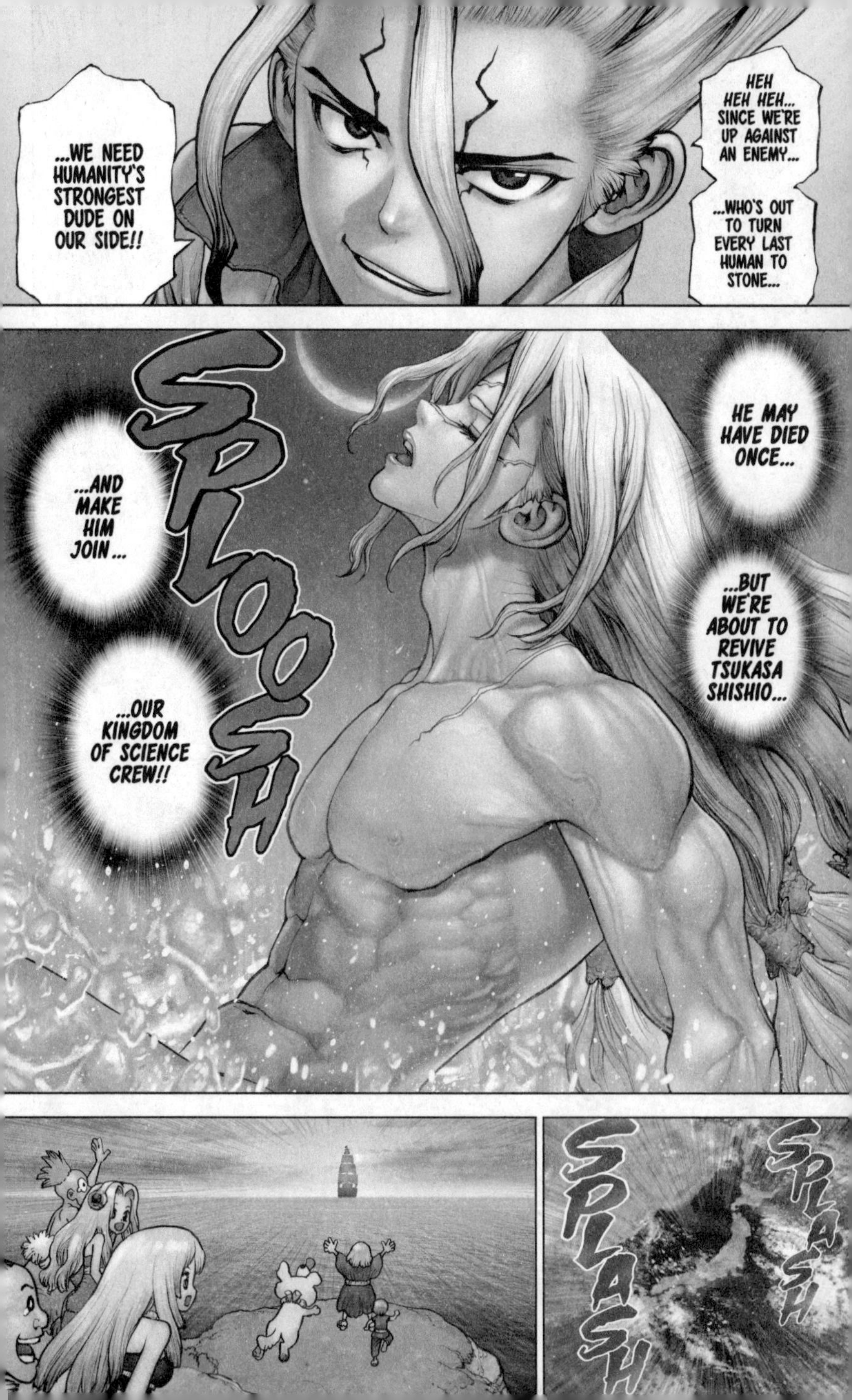
HEH HEH HEH... SINCE WE'RE UP AGAINST AN ENEMY...
...WHO'S OUT TO TURN EVERY LAST HUMAN TO STONE...
...WE NEED HUMANITY'S STRONGEST DUDE ON OUR SIDE!!
HE MAY HAVE DIED ONCE...
...BUT WE'RE ABOUT TO REVIVE TSUKASA SHISHIO...
...AND MAKE HIM JOIN...
SPLOOSH
...OUR KINGDOM OF SCIENCE CREW!!
SPLASH
SPLASH

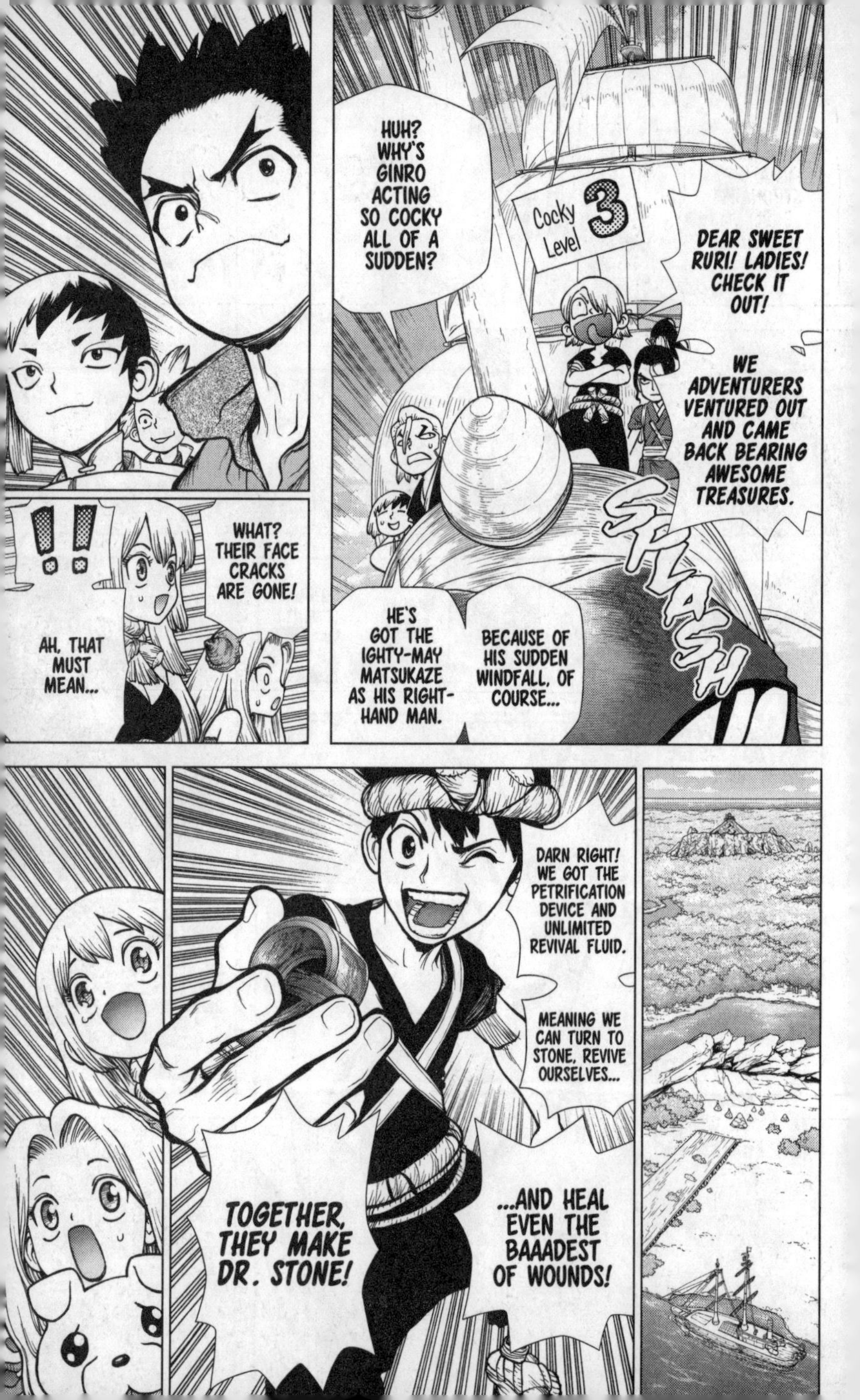
DEAR SWEET RURI! LADIES! CHECK IT OUT!
WE ADVENTURERS VENTURED OUT AND CAME BACK BEARING AWESOME TREASURES.
Cocky Level 3
SPLASH
HUH? WHY'S GINRO ACTING SO COCKY ALL OF A SUDDEN?
BECAUSE OF HIS SUDDEN WINDFALL, OF COURSE...
HE'S GOT THE IGHTY-MAY MATSUKAZE AS HIS RIGHT-HAND MAN.
WHAT? THEIR FACE CRACKS ARE GONE!
!!
AH, THAT MUST MEAN...
DARN RIGHT! WE GOT THE PETRIFICATION DEVICE AND UNLIMITED REVIVAL FLUID.
MEANING WE CAN TURN TO STONE, REVIVE OURSELVES...
...AND HEAL EVEN THE BAAADEST OF WOUNDS!
TOGETHER, THEY MAKE DR. STONE!

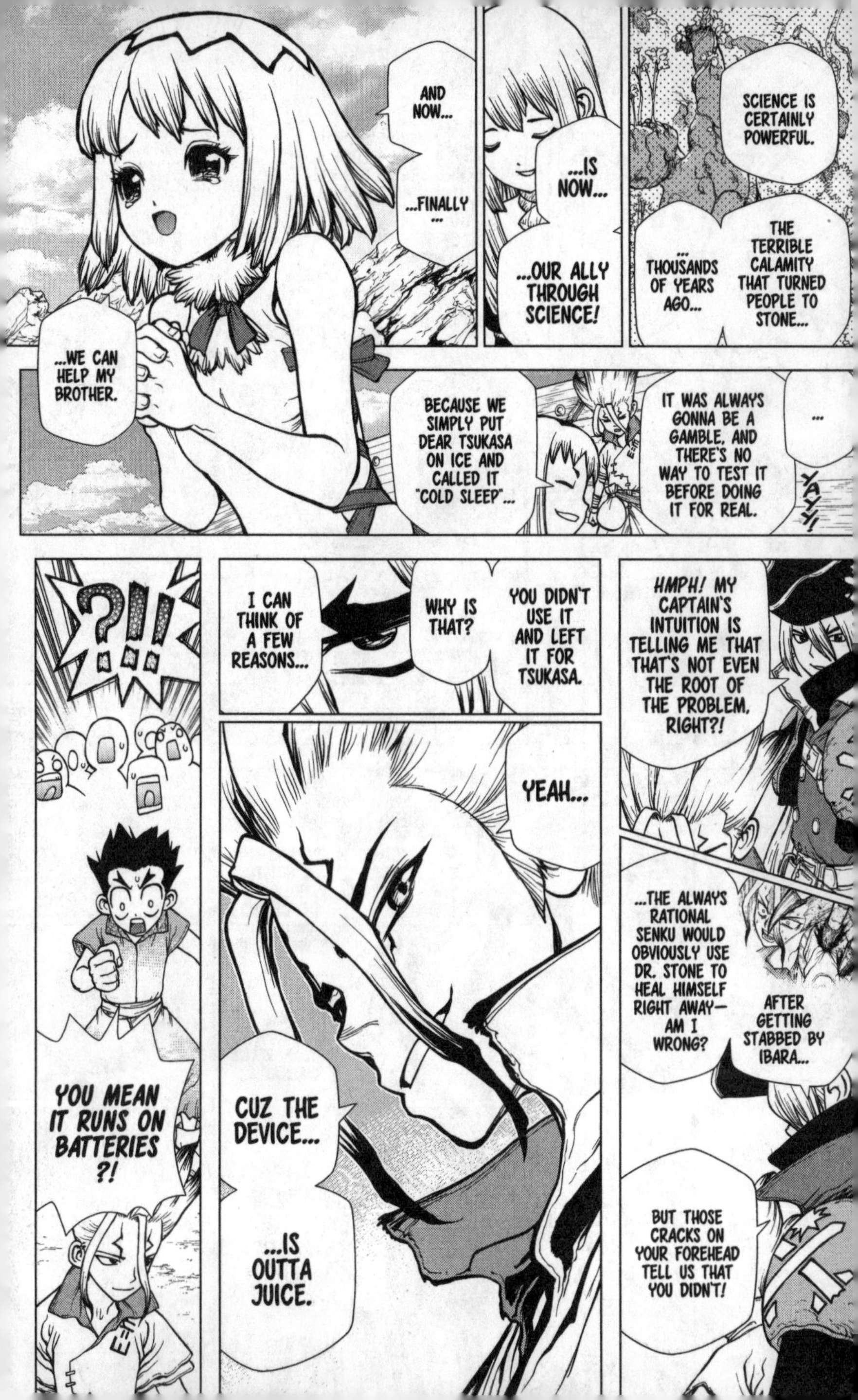
SCIENCE IS CERTAINLY POWERFUL.
THE TERRIBLE CALAMITY THAT TURNED PEOPLE TO STONE...
...THOUSANDS OF YEARS AGO...
...IS NOW...
...OUR ALLY THROUGH SCIENCE!
AND NOW...
...FINALLY...
...WE CAN HELP MY BROTHER.
...
IT WAS ALWAYS GONNA BE A GAMBLE, AND THERE'S NO WAY TO TEST IT BEFORE DOING IT FOR REAL.
YAY!
BECAUSE WE SIMPLY PUT DEAR TSUKASA ON ICE AND CALLED IT "COLD SLEEP"...
HMPH! MY CAPTAIN'S INTUITION IS TELLING ME THAT THAT'S NOT EVEN THE ROOT OF THE PROBLEM, RIGHT?!
AFTER GETTING STABBED BY IBARA...
...THE ALWAYS RATIONAL SENKU WOULD OBVIOUSLY USE DR. STONE TO HEAL HIMSELF RIGHT AWAY—AM I WRONG?
BUT THOSE CRACKS ON YOUR FOREHEAD TELL US THAT YOU DIDN'T!
YOU DIDN'T USE IT AND LEFT IT FOR TSUKASA.
WHY IS THAT?
I CAN THINK OF A FEW REASONS...
YEAH...
CUZ THE DEVICE...
...IS OUTTA JUICE.
?!!
YOU MEAN IT RUNS ON BATTERIES?!

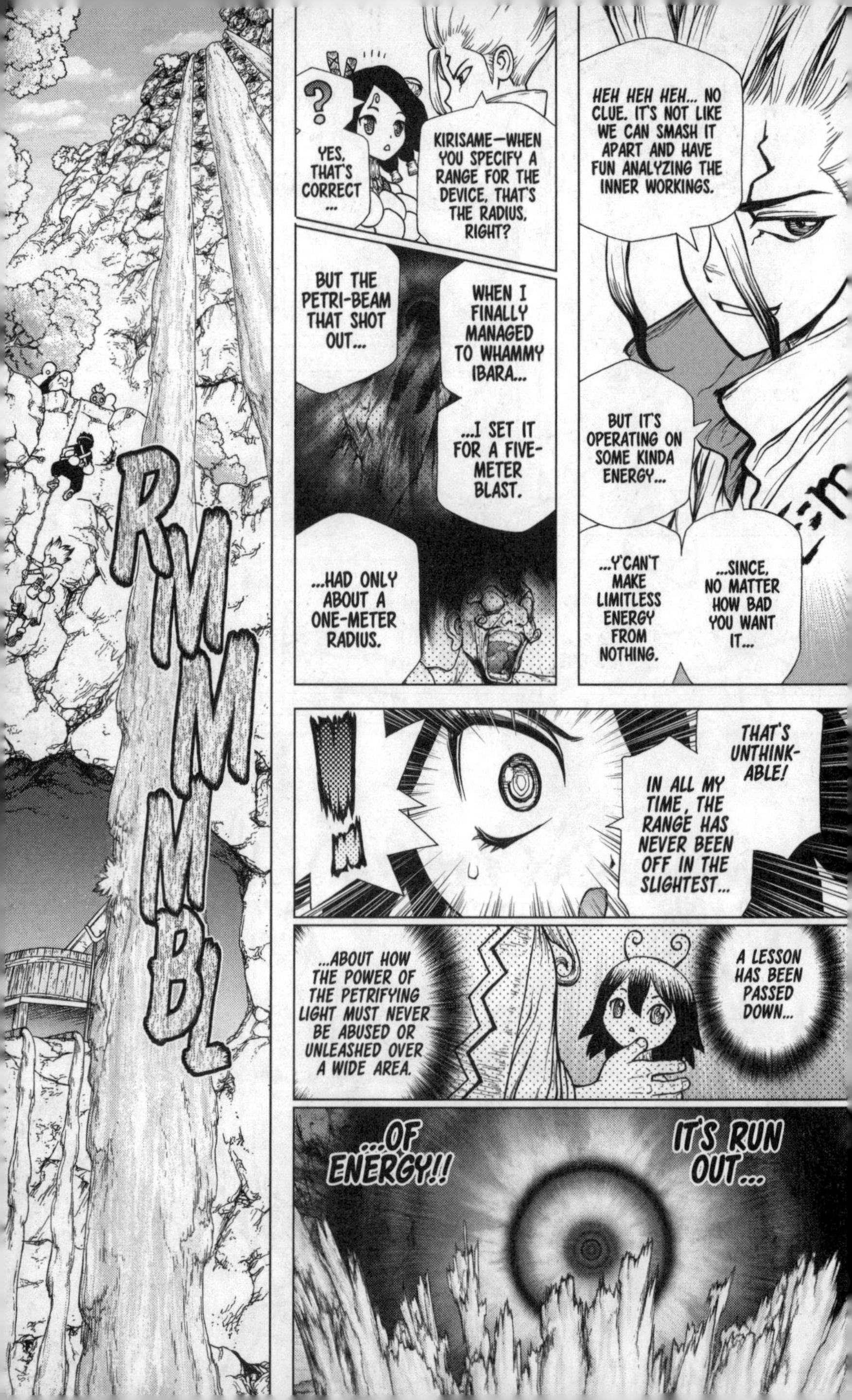
HEH HEH HEH... NO CLUE. IT'S NOT LIKE WE CAN SMASH IT APART AND HAVE FUN ANALYZING THE INNER WORKINGS.
BUT IT'S OPERATING ON SOME KINDA ENERGY...
...SINCE, NO MATTER HOW BAD YOU WANT IT...
...Y'CAN'T MAKE LIMITLESS ENERGY FROM NOTHING.
KIRISAME—WHEN YOU SPECIFY A RANGE FOR THE DEVICE, THAT'S THE RADIUS, RIGHT?
?
YES, THAT'S CORRECT ...
WHEN I FINALLY MANAGED TO WHAMMY IBARA...
...I SET IT FOR A FIVE-METER BLAST.
BUT THE PETRI-BEAM THAT SHOT OUT...
...HAD ONLY ABOUT A ONE-METER RADIUS.
THAT'S UNTHINK-ABLE!
IN ALL MY TIME, THE RANGE HAS NEVER BEEN OFF IN THE SLIGHTEST...
A LESSON HAS BEEN PASSED DOWN...
...ABOUT HOW THE POWER OF THE PETRIFYING LIGHT MUST NEVER BE ABUSED OR UNLEASHED OVER A WIDE AREA.
IT'S RUN OUT...
...OF ENERGY!!
RMMMMBL

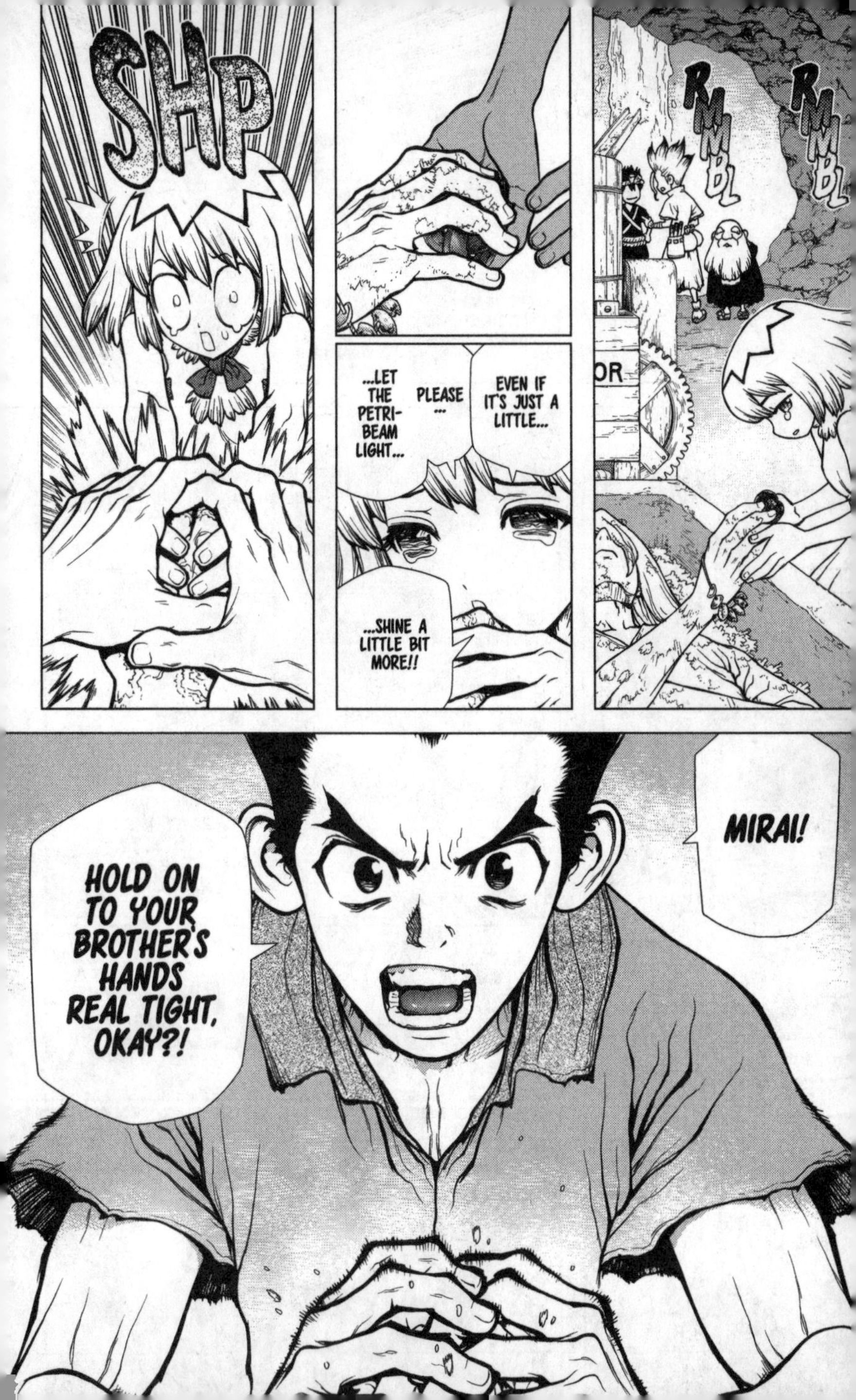
RMMBL
RMMBL
EVEN IF IT'S JUST A LITTLE...
PLEASE ...
...LET THE PETRI-BEAM LIGHT...
...SHINE A LITTLE BIT MORE!!
SHP
MIRAI!
HOLD ON TO YOUR BROTHER'S HANDS REAL TIGHT, OKAY?!

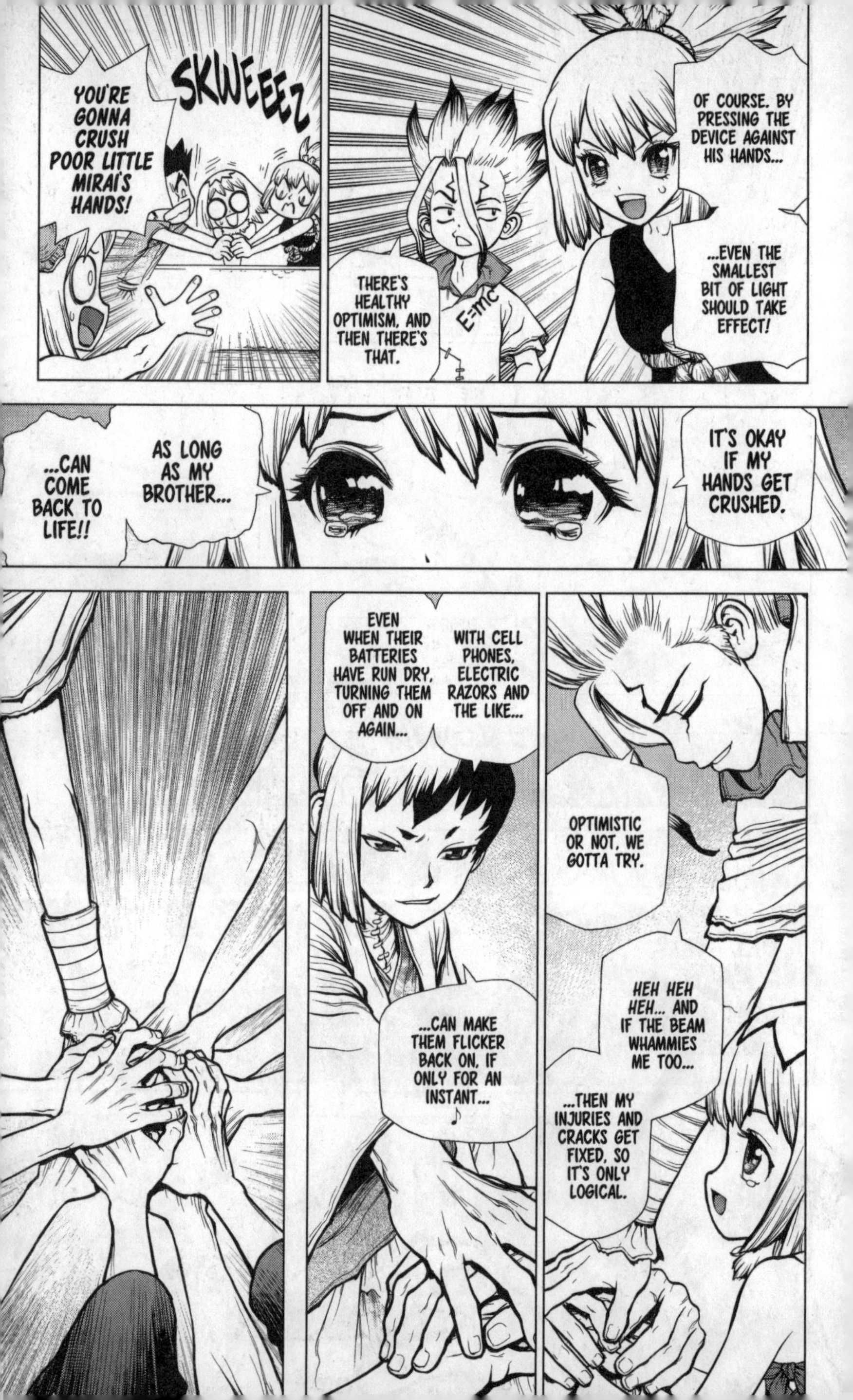
OF COURSE. BY PRESSING THE DEVICE AGAINST HIS HANDS...
...EVEN THE SMALLEST BIT OF LIGHT SHOULD TAKE EFFECT!
THERE'S HEALTHY OPTIMISM, AND THEN THERE'S THAT.
E=mc
YOU'RE GONNA CRUSH POOR LITTLE MIRAI'S HANDS!
SKWEEEZ
IT'S OKAY IF MY HANDS GET CRUSHED.
AS LONG AS MY BROTHER...
...CAN COME BACK TO LIFE!!
OPTIMISTIC OR NOT, WE GOTTA TRY.
HEH HEH HEH... AND IF THE BEAM WHAMMIES ME TOO...
...THEN MY INJURIES AND CRACKS GET FIXED, SO IT'S ONLY LOGICAL.
WITH CELL PHONES, ELECTRIC RAZORS AND THE LIKE...
EVEN WHEN THEIR BATTERIES HAVE RUN DRY, TURNING THEM OFF AND ON AGAIN...
...CAN MAKE THEM FLICKER BACK ON, IF ONLY FOR AN INSTANT... ♪

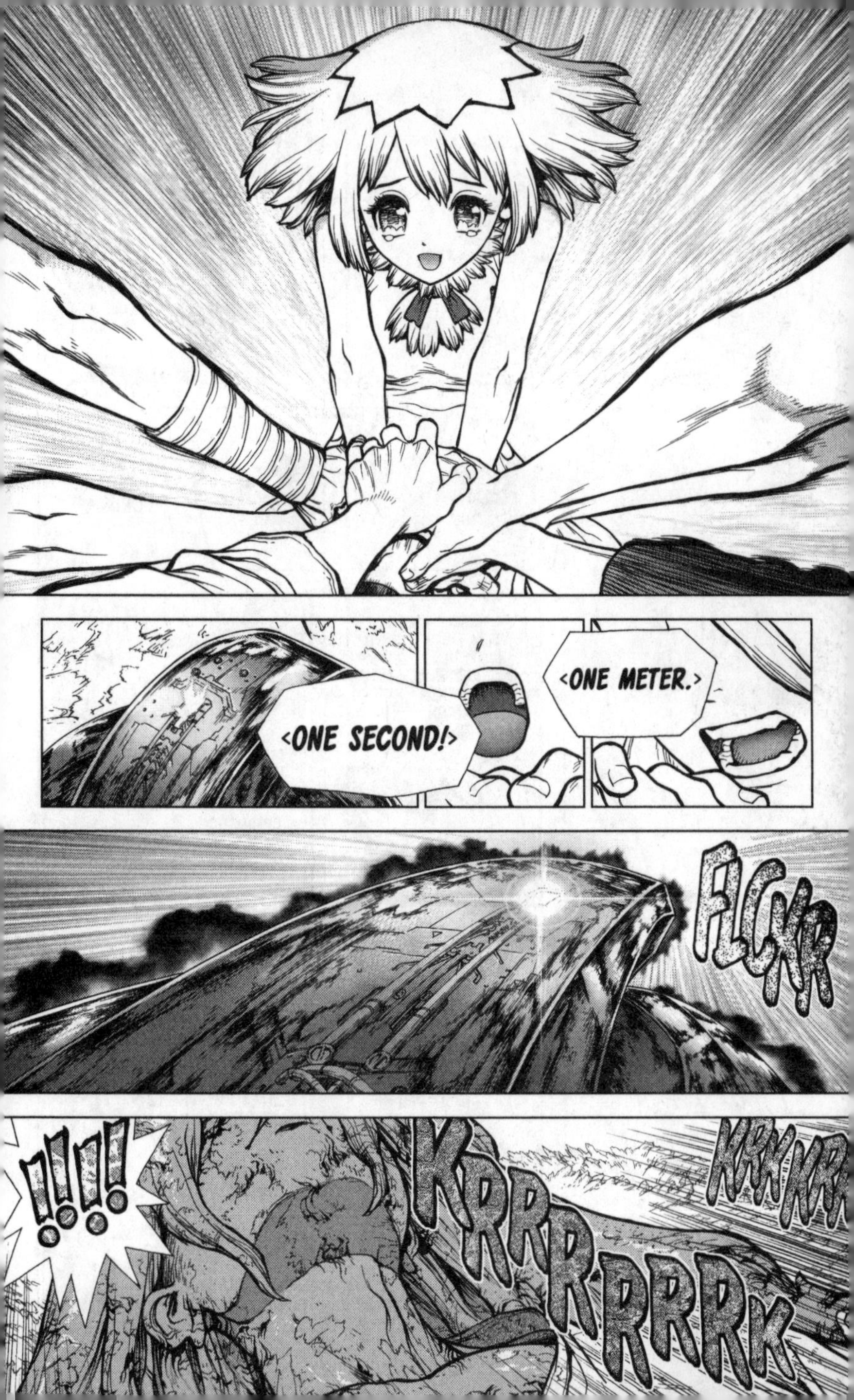

<ONE METER.>
<ONE SECOND!>
FLCKR
KRKKR
KRRRRRRRK
!!!!

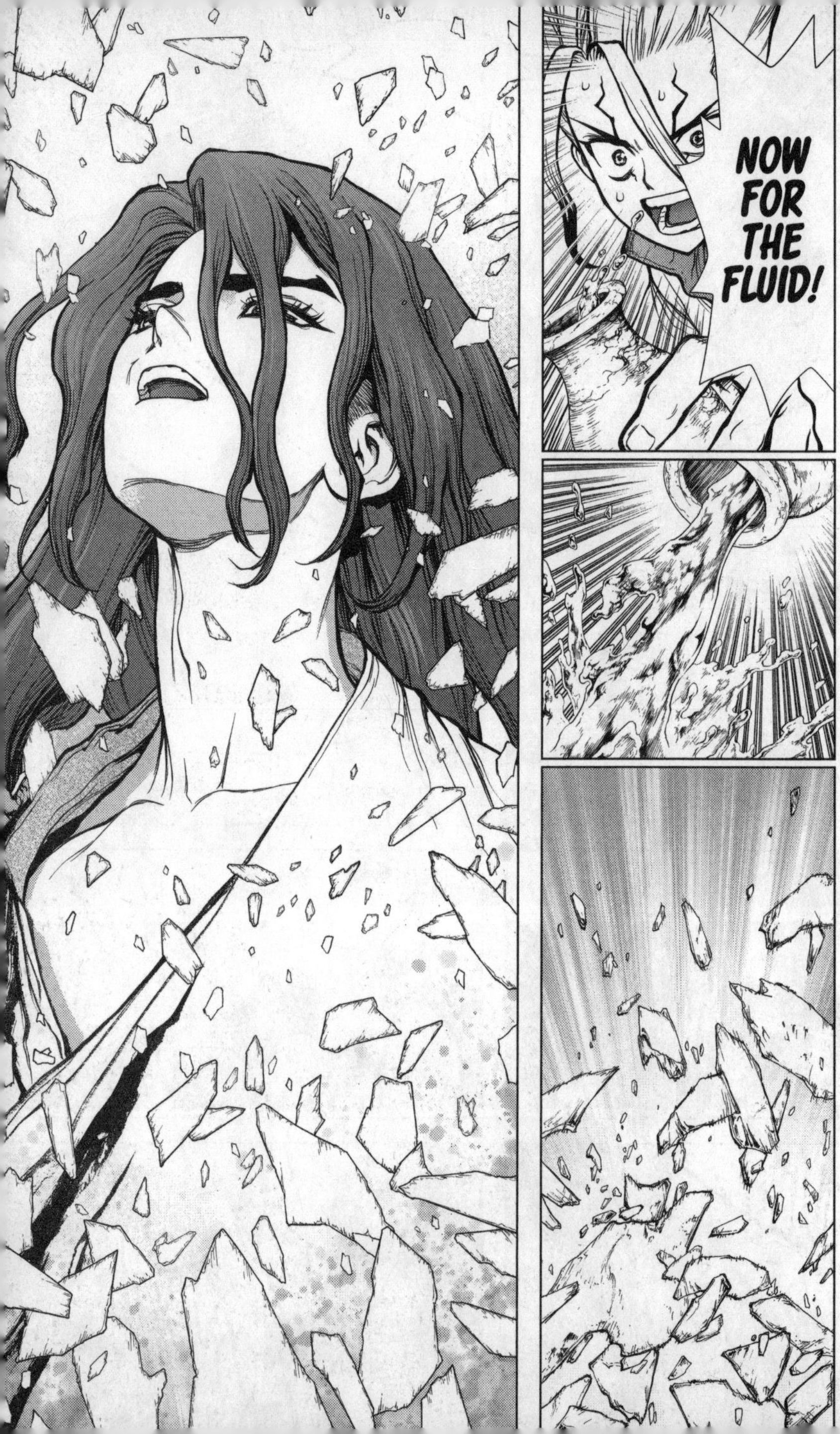
NOW FOR THE FLUID!

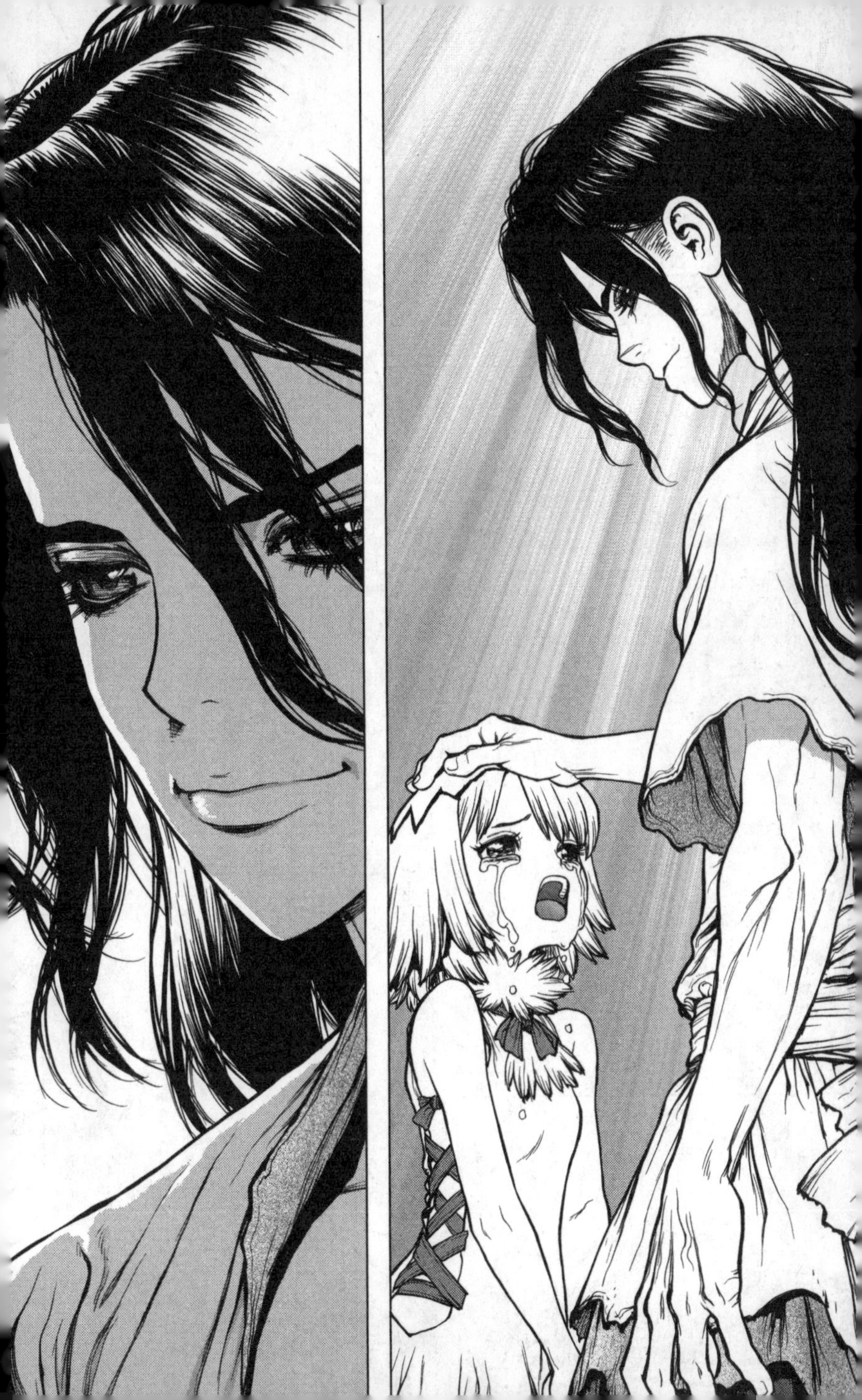

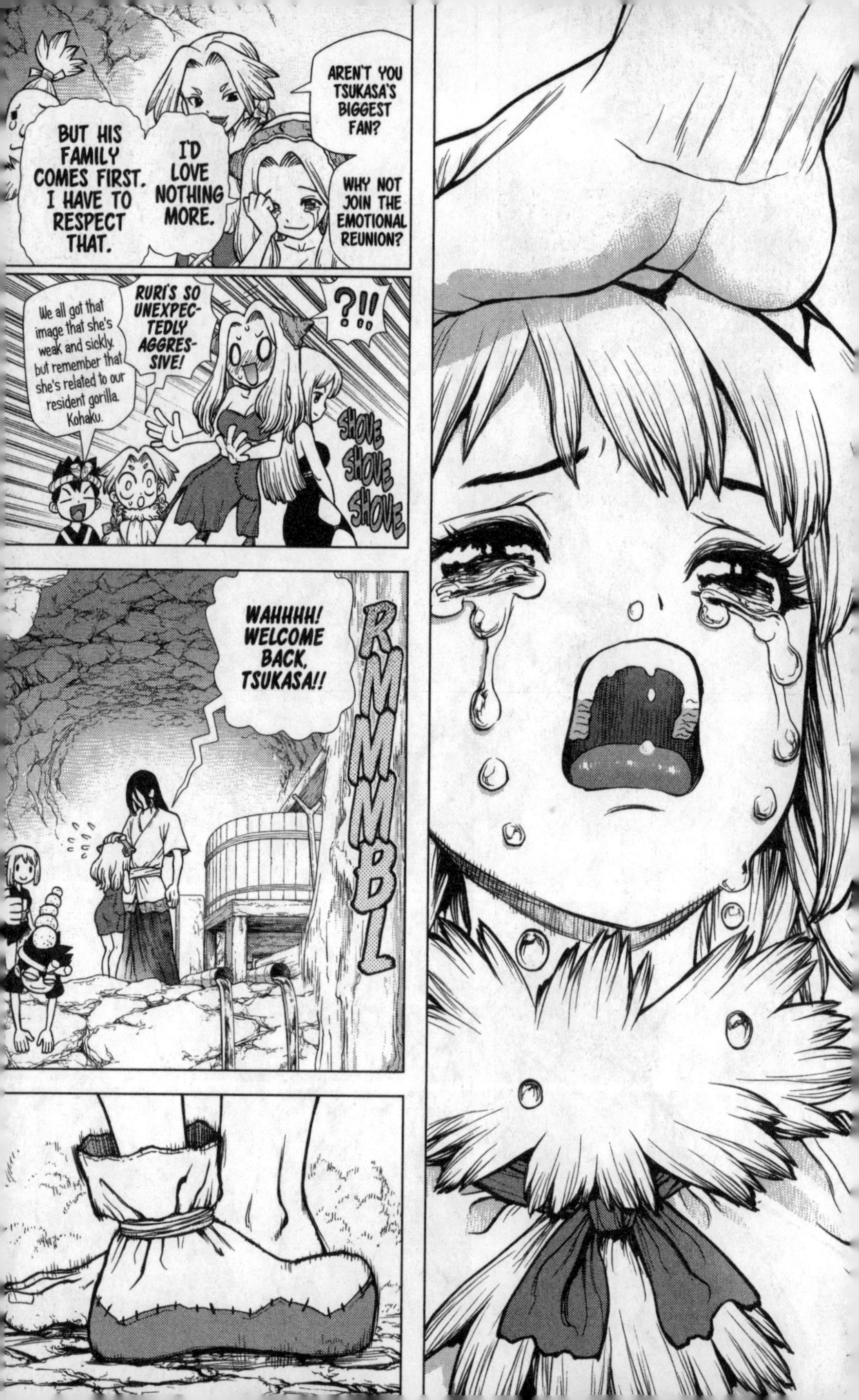
AREN'T YOU TSUKASA'S BIGGEST FAN?
WHY NOT JOIN THE EMOTIONAL REUNION?
I'D LOVE NOTHING MORE.
BUT HIS FAMILY COMES FIRST. I HAVE TO RESPECT THAT.
?!!
RURI'S SO UNEXPECTEDLY AGGRESSIVE!
We all got that image that she's weak and sickly, but remember that she's related to our resident gorilla, Kohaku.
SHOVE SHOVE SHOVE
RMMMBL
WAHHHH! WELCOME BACK, TSUKASA!!

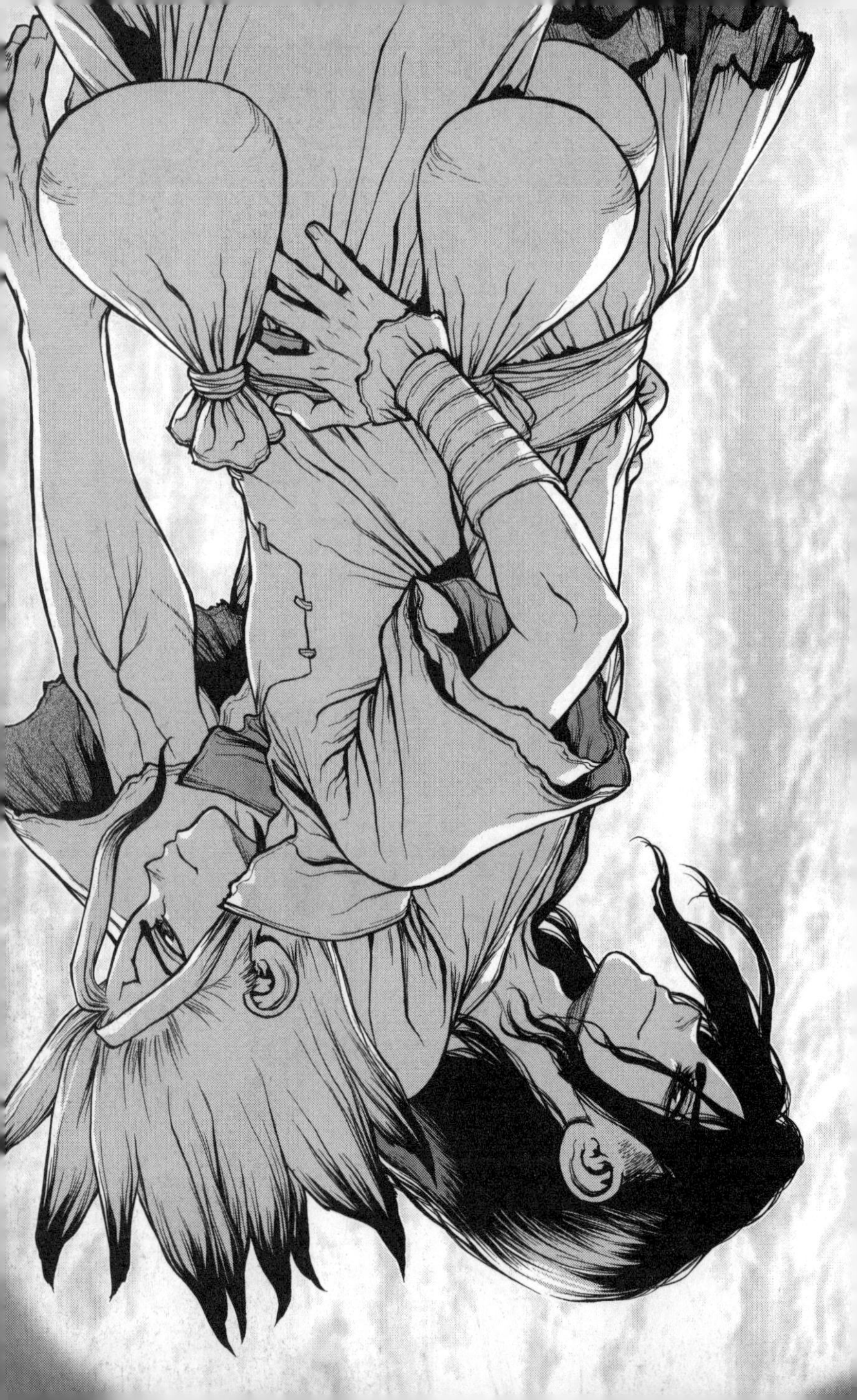

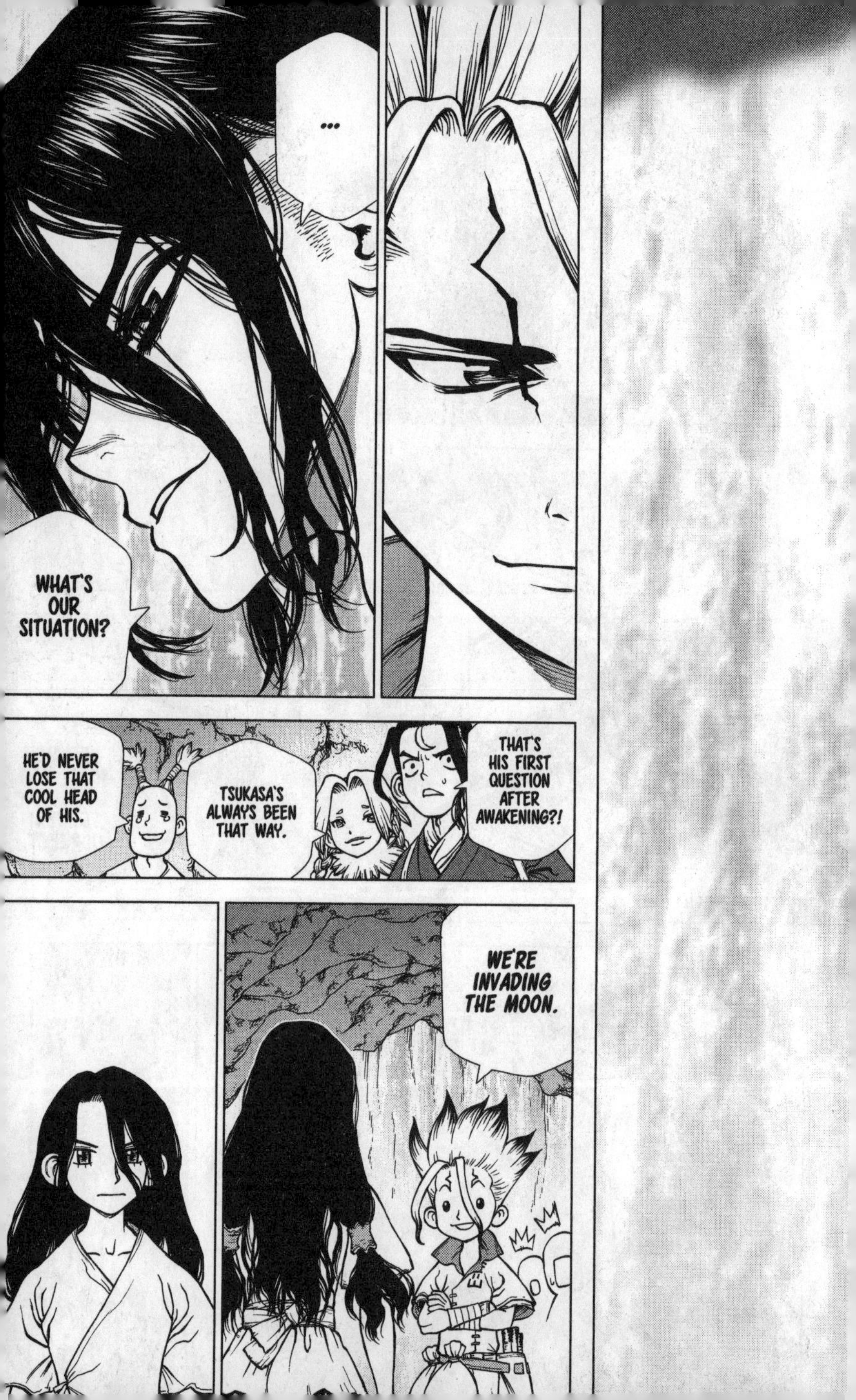
...
WHAT'S OUR SITUATION?
THAT'S HIS FIRST QUESTION AFTER AWAKENING?!
TSUKASA'S ALWAYS BEEN THAT WAY.
HE'D NEVER LOSE THAT COOL HEAD OF HIS.
WE'RE INVADING THE MOON.

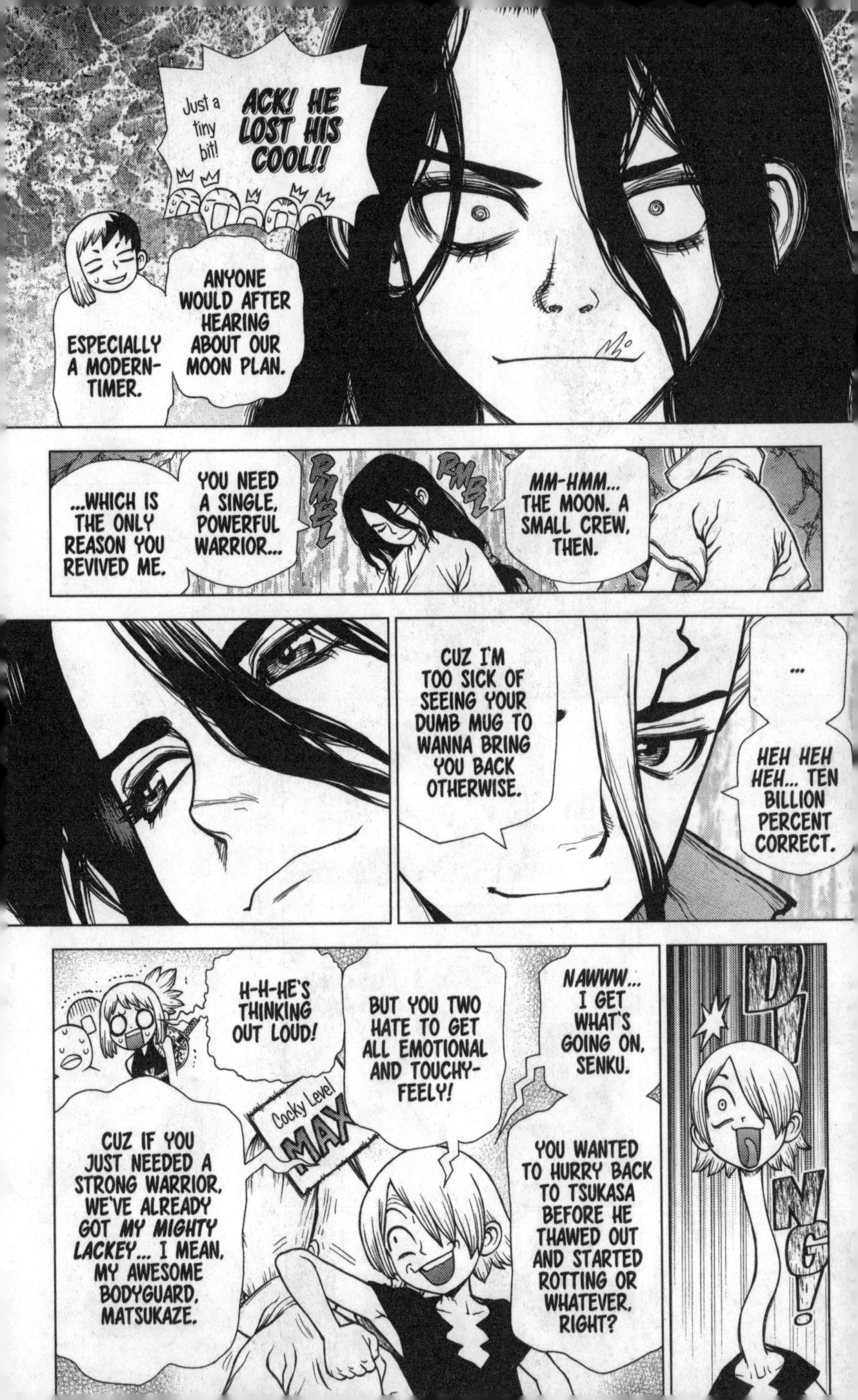
ACK! HE LOST HIS COOL!!
Just a tiny bit!
ANYONE WOULD AFTER HEARING ABOUT OUR MOON PLAN.
ESPECIALLY A MODERN-TIMER.
MM-HMM... THE MOON. A SMALL CREW, THEN.
RMBL RMBL
YOU NEED A SINGLE, POWERFUL WARRIOR...
...WHICH IS THE ONLY REASON YOU REVIVED ME.
...
HEH HEH HEH... TEN BILLION PERCENT CORRECT.
CUZ I'M TOO SICK OF SEEING YOUR DUMB MUG TO WANNA BRING YOU BACK OTHERWISE.
DING!
NAWWW... I GET WHAT'S GOING ON, SENKU.
YOU WANTED TO HURRY BACK TO TSUKASA BEFORE HE THAWED OUT AND STARTED ROTTING OR WHATEVER, RIGHT?
BUT YOU TWO HATE TO GET ALL EMOTIONAL AND TOUCHY-FEELY!
Cocky Level MAX
H-H-HE'S THINKING OUT LOUD!
CUZ IF YOU JUST NEEDED A STRONG WARRIOR, WE'VE ALREADY GOT MY MIGHTY LACKEY... I MEAN, MY AWESOME BODYGUARD, MATSUKAZE.

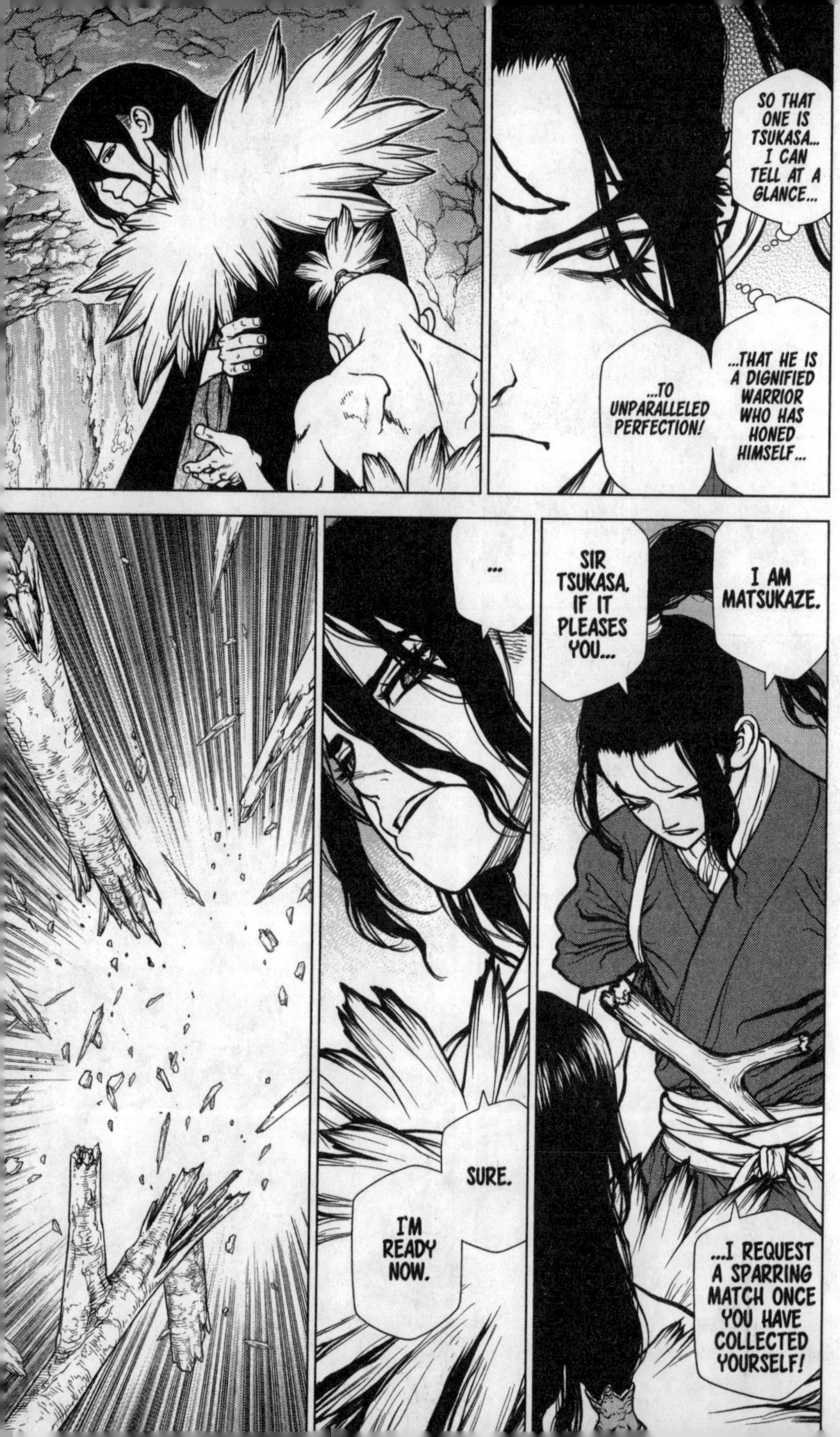
SO THAT ONE IS TSUKASA... I CAN TELL AT A GLANCE...
...THAT HE IS A DIGNIFIED WARRIOR WHO HAS HONED HIMSELF...
...TO UNPARALLELED PERFECTION!
I AM MATSUKAZE.
SIR TSUKASA, IF IT PLEASES YOU...
...I REQUEST A SPARRING MATCH ONCE YOU HAVE COLLECTED YOURSELF!
...
SURE.
I'M READY NOW.

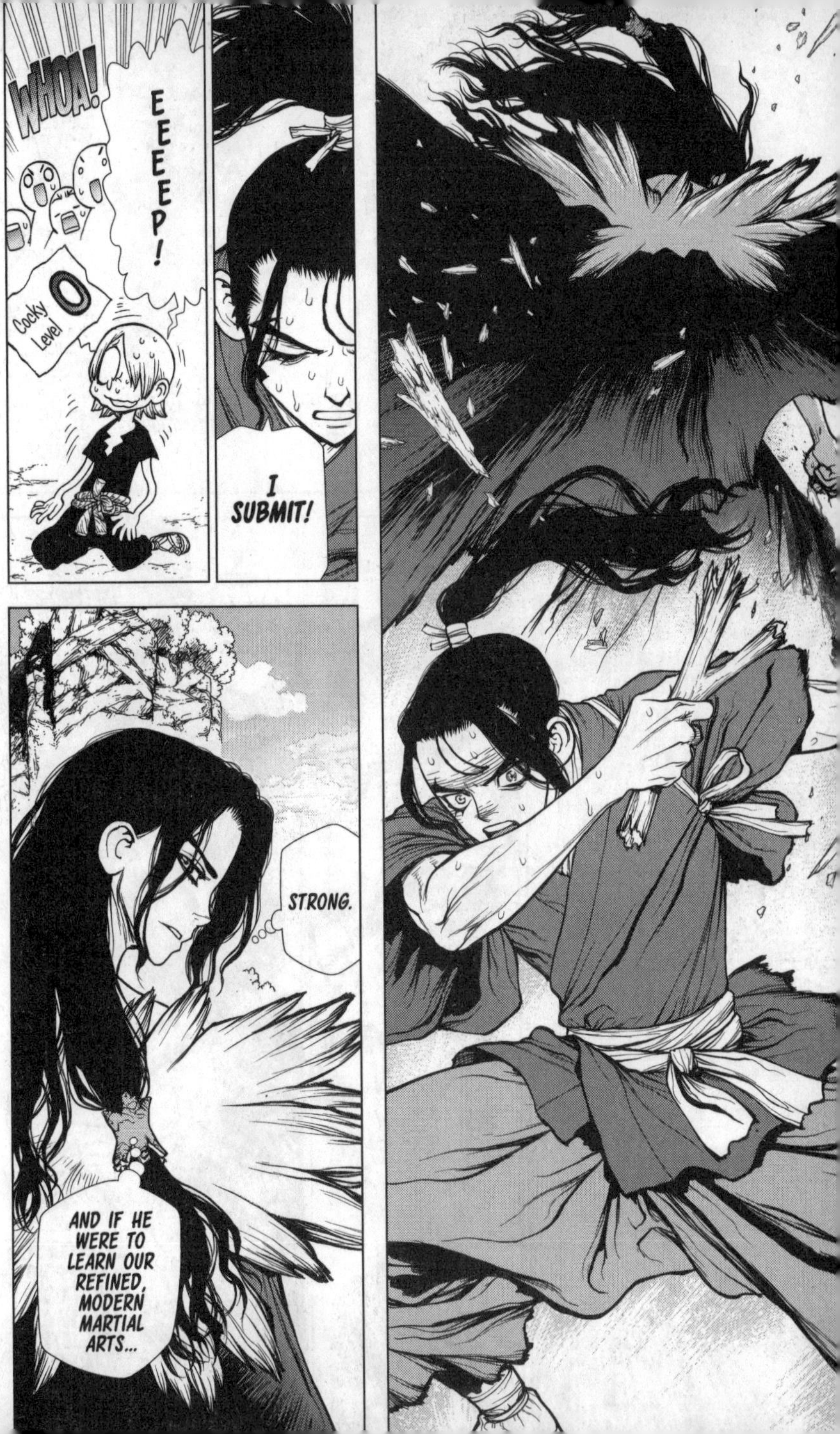
I SUBMIT!
WHOA!
EEEEEP!
Cocky Level 0
STRONG.
AND IF HE WERE TO LEARN OUR REFINED, MODERN MARTIAL ARTS...

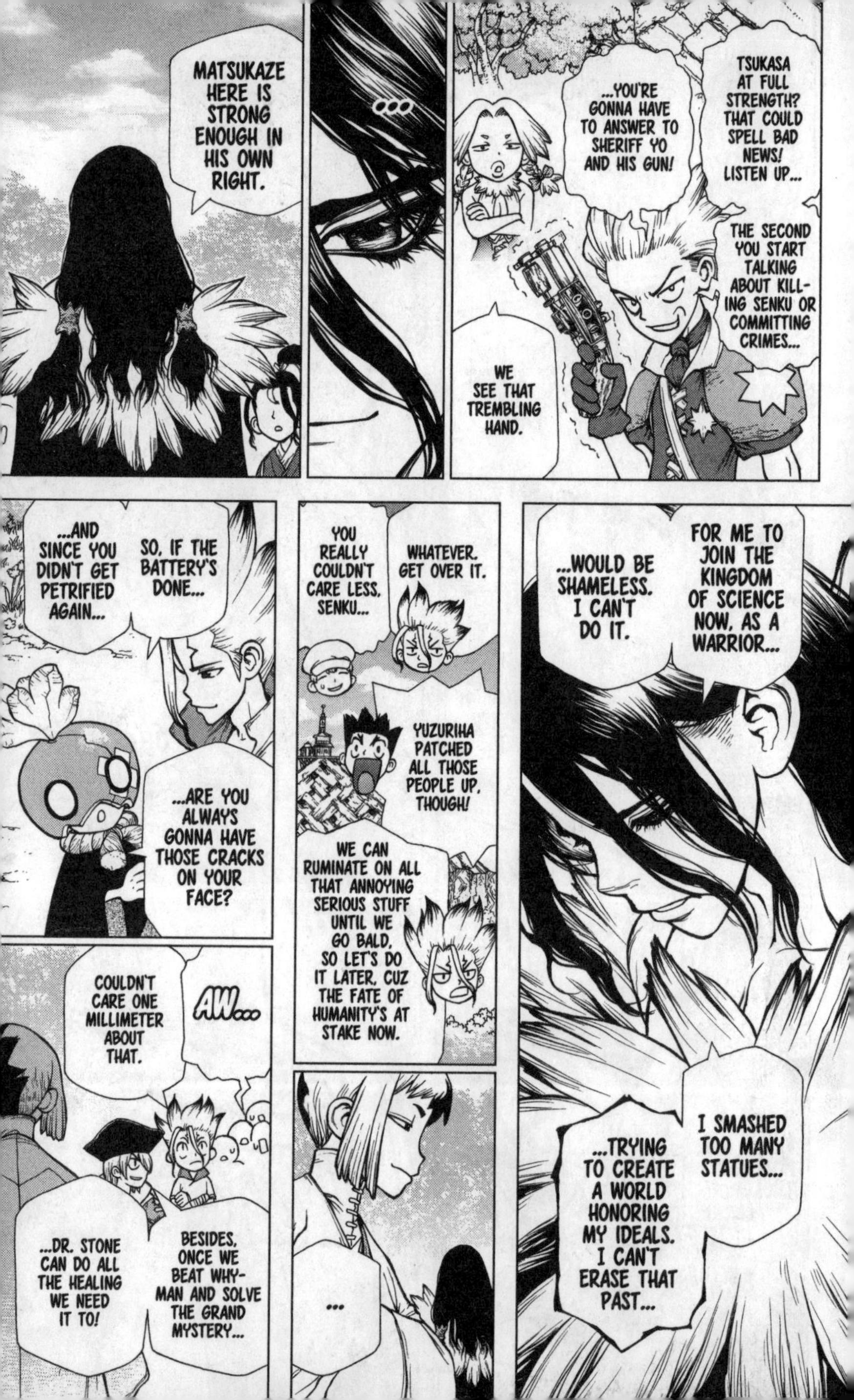
TSUKASA AT FULL STRENGTH? THAT COULD SPELL BAD NEWS! LISTEN UP...
...YOU'RE GONNA HAVE TO ANSWER TO SHERIFF YO AND HIS GUN!
THE SECOND YOU START TALKING ABOUT KILL-ING SENKU OR COMMITTING CRIMES...
WE SEE THAT TREMBLING HAND.
...
MATSUKAZE HERE IS STRONG ENOUGH IN HIS OWN RIGHT.
FOR ME TO JOIN THE KINGDOM OF SCIENCE NOW, AS A WARRIOR...
...WOULD BE SHAMELESS. I CAN'T DO IT.
I SMASHED TOO MANY STATUES...
...TRYING TO CREATE A WORLD HONORING MY IDEALS. I CAN'T ERASE THAT PAST...
WHATEVER. GET OVER IT.
YOU REALLY COULDN'T CARE LESS, SENKU...
YUZURIHA PATCHED ALL THOSE PEOPLE UP, THOUGH!
WE CAN RUMINATE ON ALL THAT ANNOYING SERIOUS STUFF UNTIL WE GO BALD, SO LET'S DO IT LATER, CUZ THE FATE OF HUMANITY'S AT STAKE NOW.
...
SO, IF THE BATTERY'S DONE...
...AND SINCE YOU DIDN'T GET PETRIFIED AGAIN...
...ARE YOU ALWAYS GONNA HAVE THOSE CRACKS ON YOUR FACE?
AW...
COULDN'T CARE ONE MILLIMETER ABOUT THAT.
BESIDES, ONCE WE BEAT WHY-MAN AND SOLVE THE GRAND MYSTERY...
...DR. STONE CAN DO ALL THE HEALING WE NEED IT TO!

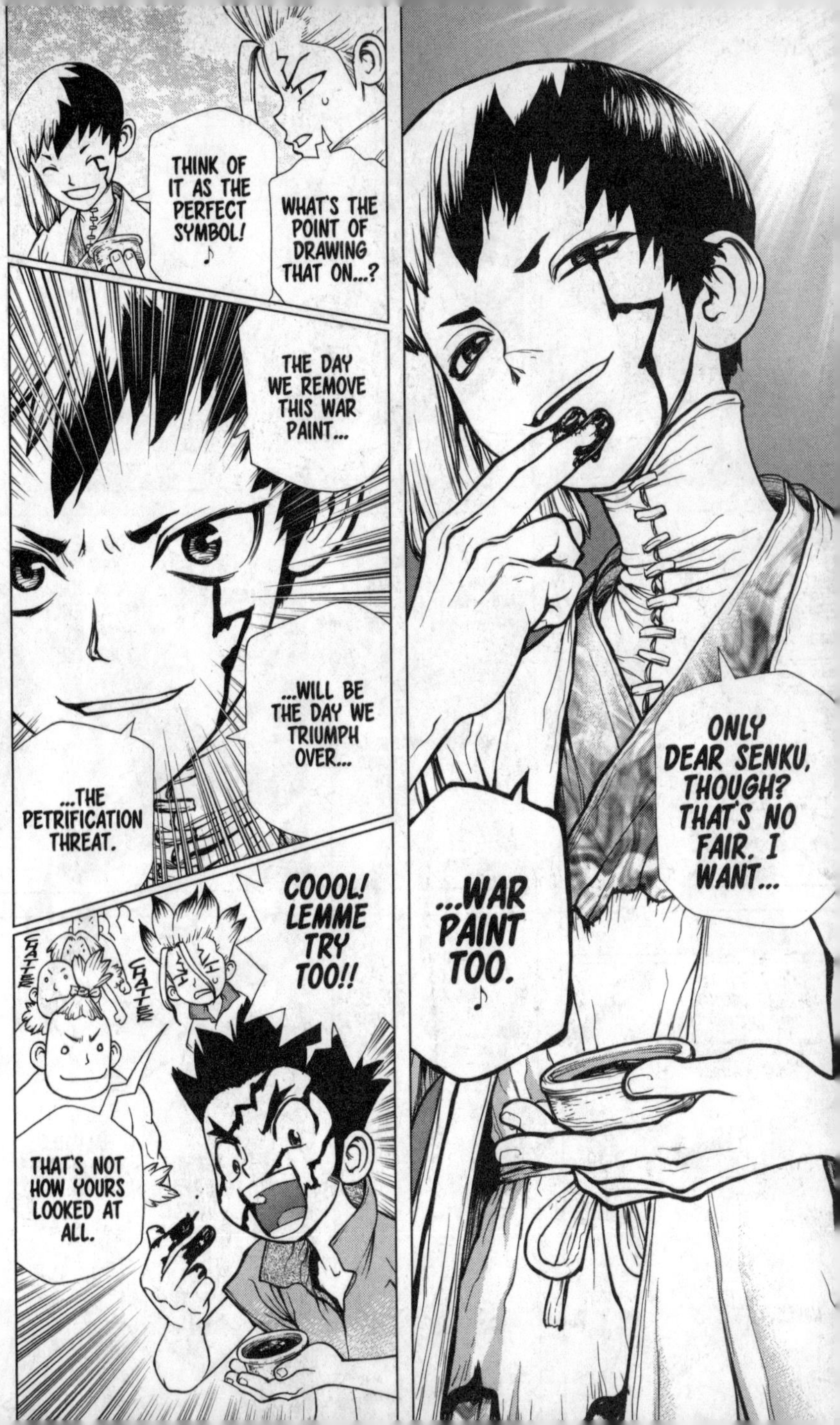
ONLY DEAR SENKU, THOUGH? THAT'S NO FAIR. I WANT...
...WAR PAINT TOO. ♪
THINK OF IT AS THE PERFECT SYMBOL! ♪
WHAT'S THE POINT OF DRAWING THAT ON...?
THE DAY WE REMOVE THIS WAR PAINT...
...WILL BE THE DAY WE TRIUMPH OVER...
...THE PETRIFICATION THREAT.
COOOL! LEMME TRY TOO!!
THAT'S NOT HOW YOURS LOOKED AT ALL.

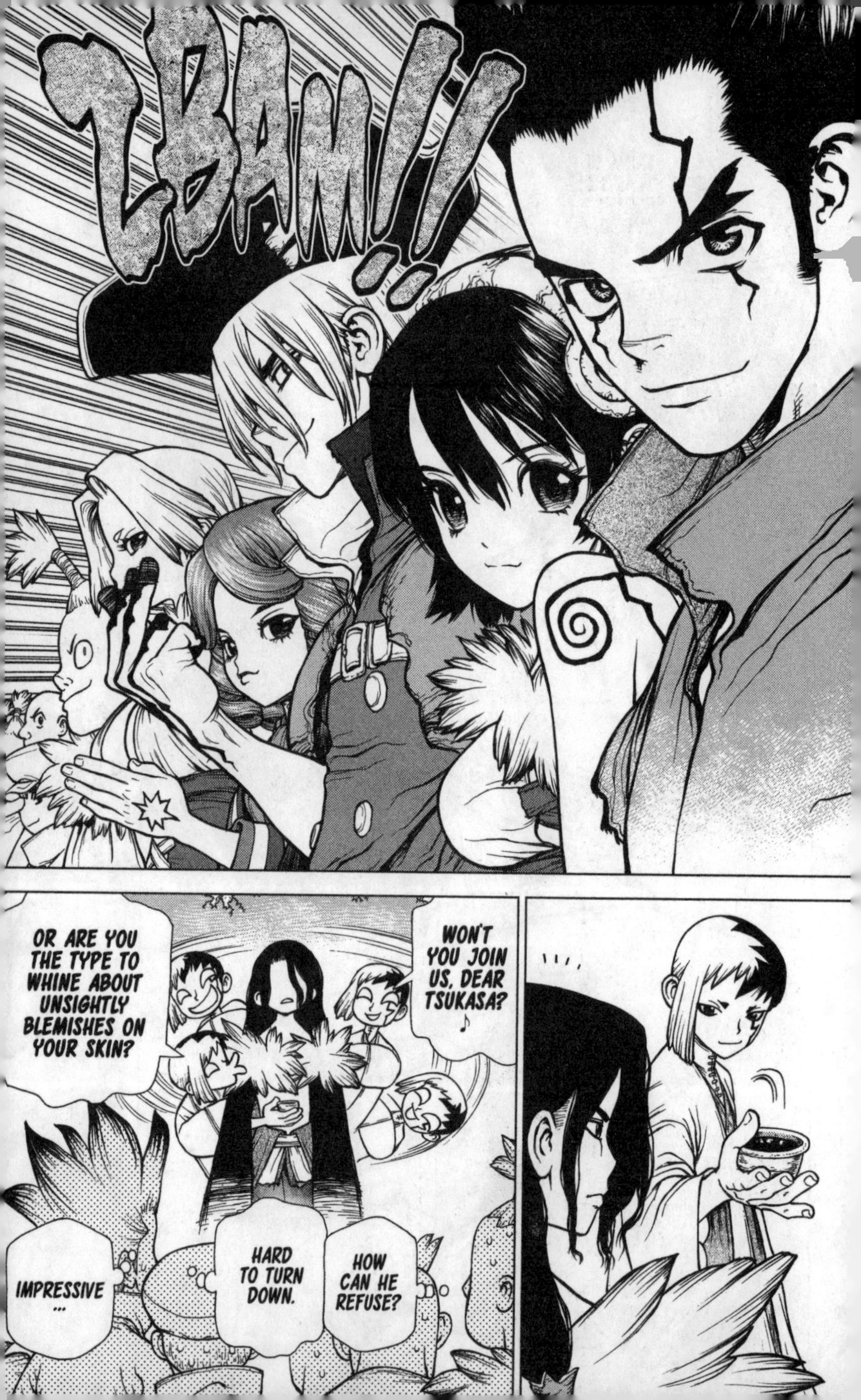
ZBAM!!
...!
WON'T YOU JOIN US, DEAR TSUKASA? ♪
OR ARE YOU THE TYPE TO WHINE ABOUT UNSIGHTLY BLEMISHES ON YOUR SKIN?
HOW CAN HE REFUSE?
HARD TO TURN DOWN.
IMPRESSIVE ...

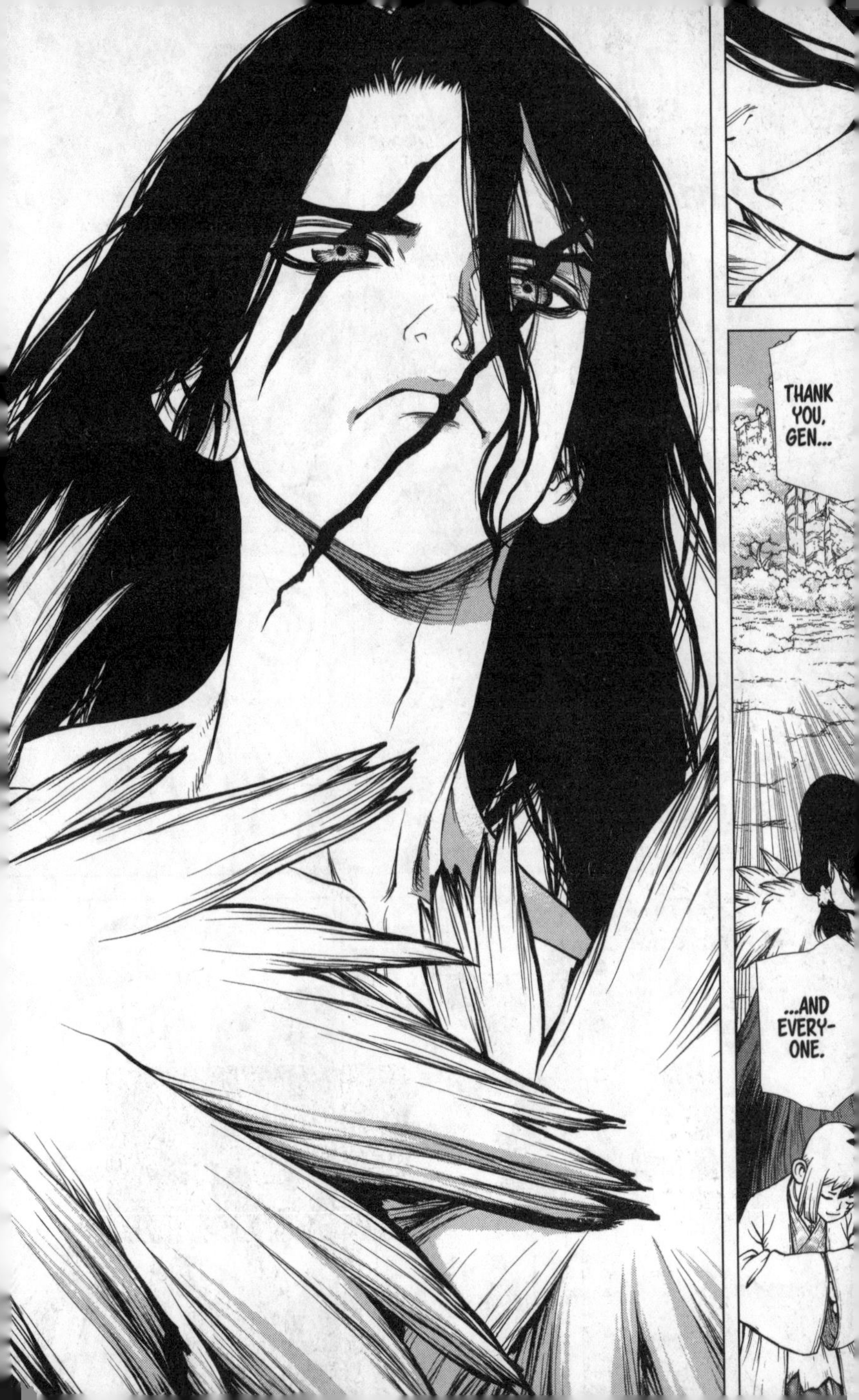
THANK YOU, GEN...
...AND EVERY-ONE.

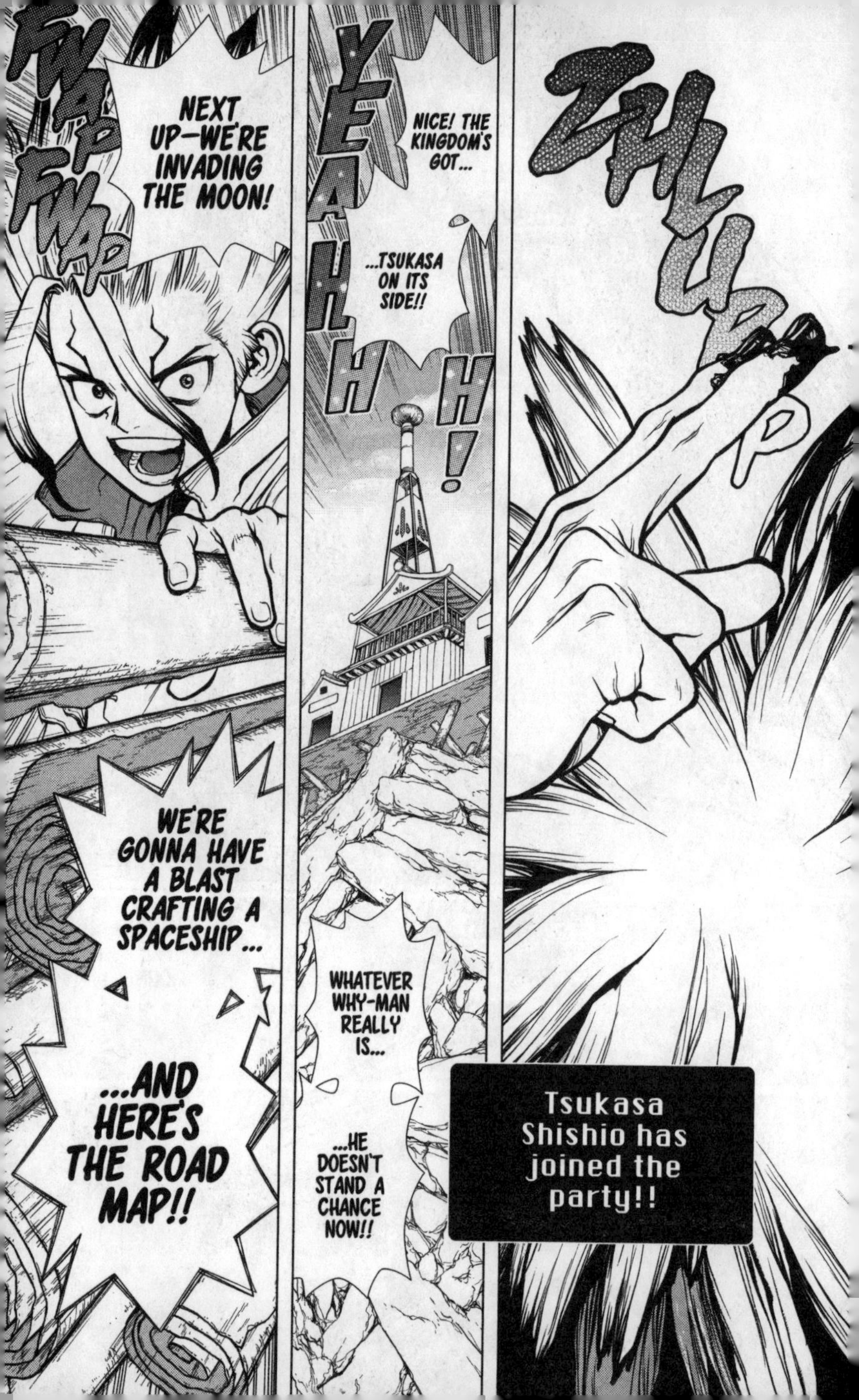
ZHWUP
Tsukasa Shishio has joined the party!!
YEAHHHH!
NICE! THE KINGDOM'S GOT...
...TSUKASA ON ITS SIDE!!
WHATEVER WHY-MAN REALLY IS...
...HE DOESN'T STAND A CHANCE NOW!!
FWAP FWAP
NEXT UP—WE'RE INVADING THE MOON!
WE'RE GONNA HAVE A BLAST CRAFTING A SPACESHIP...
...AND HERE'S THE ROAD MAP!!

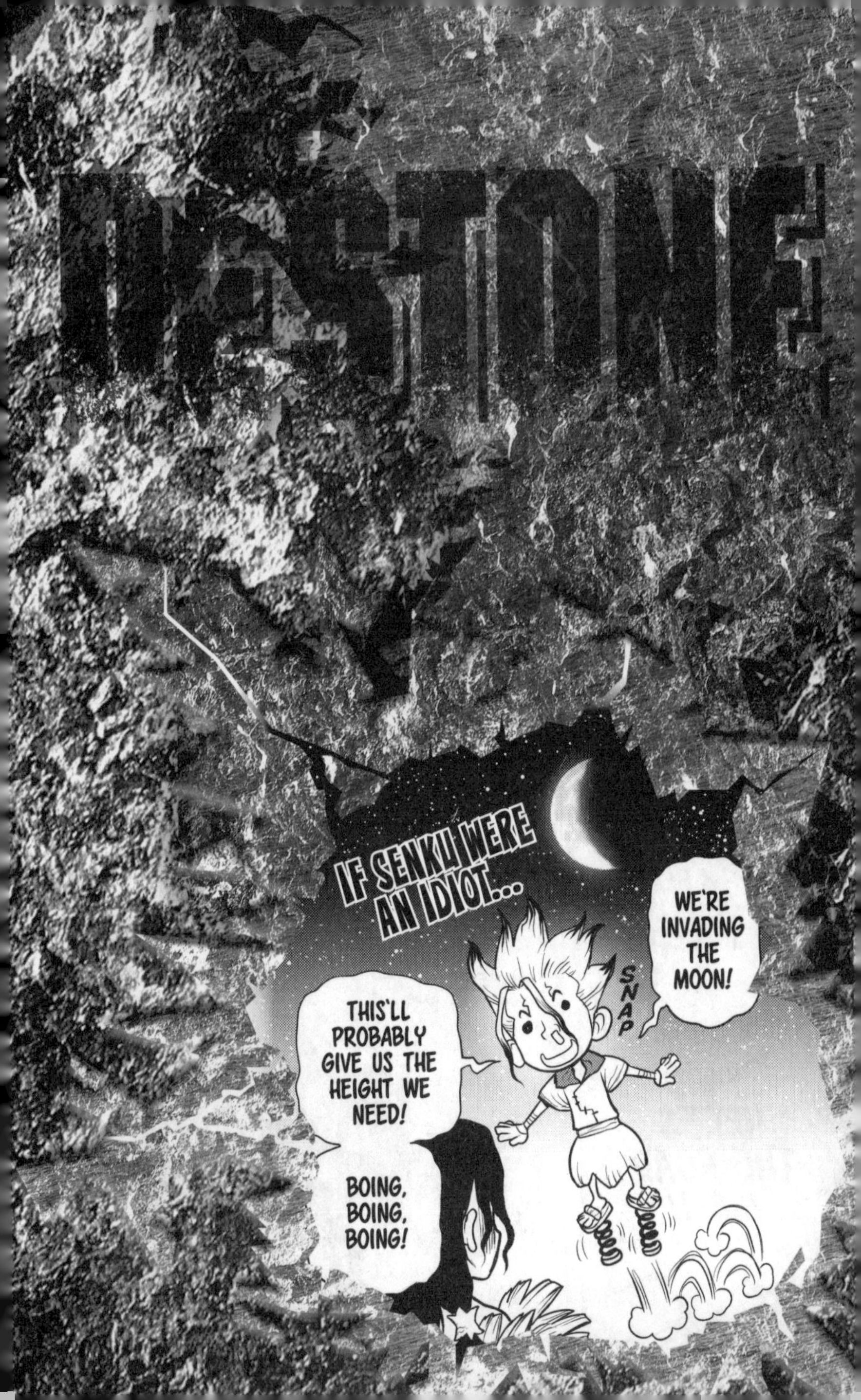
DR. STONE
IF SENKU WERE AN IDIOT...
WE'RE INVADING THE MOON!
SNAP
THIS'LL PROBABLY GIVE US THE HEIGHT WE NEED!
BOING, BOING, BOING!

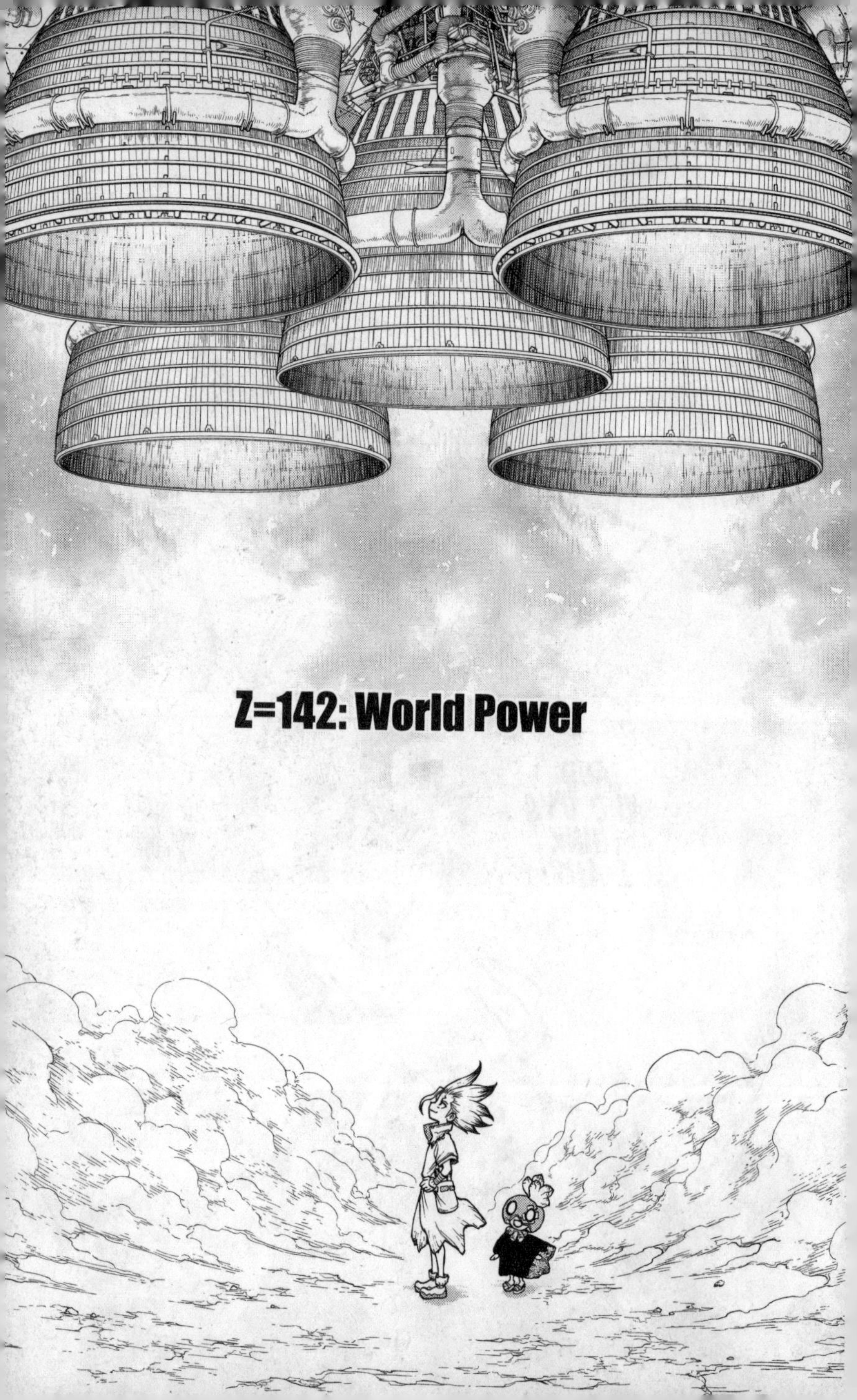
Z=142: World Power

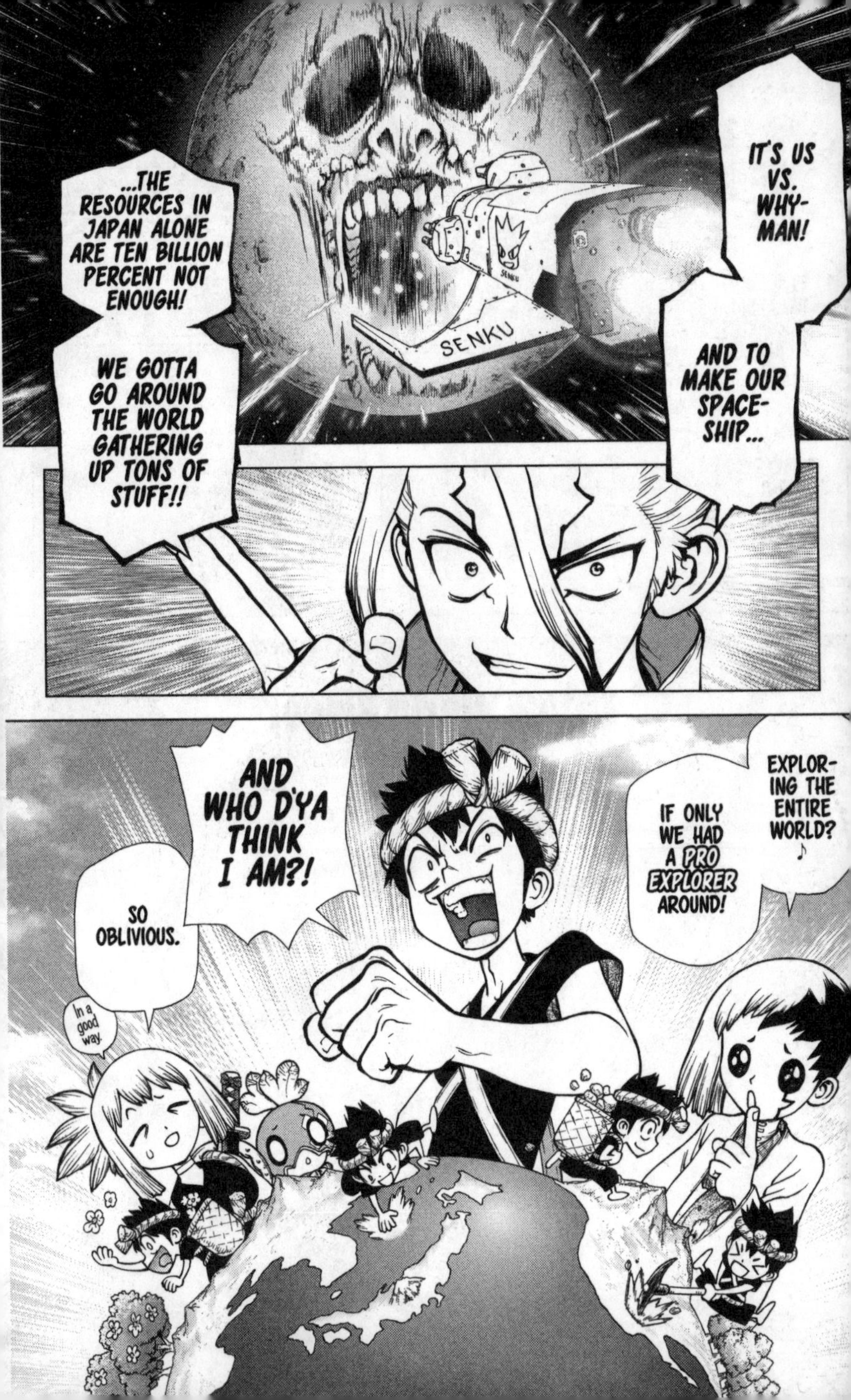
IT'S US VS. WHY-MAN!
AND TO MAKE OUR SPACE-SHIP...
...THE RESOURCES IN JAPAN ALONE ARE TEN BILLION PERCENT NOT ENOUGH!
WE GOTTA GO AROUND THE WORLD GATHERING UP TONS OF STUFF!!
SENKU
SENKU
EXPLORING THE ENTIRE WORLD? ♪
IF ONLY WE HAD A PRO EXPLORER AROUND!
AND WHO D'YA THINK I AM?!
SO OBLIVIOUS.
In a good way.

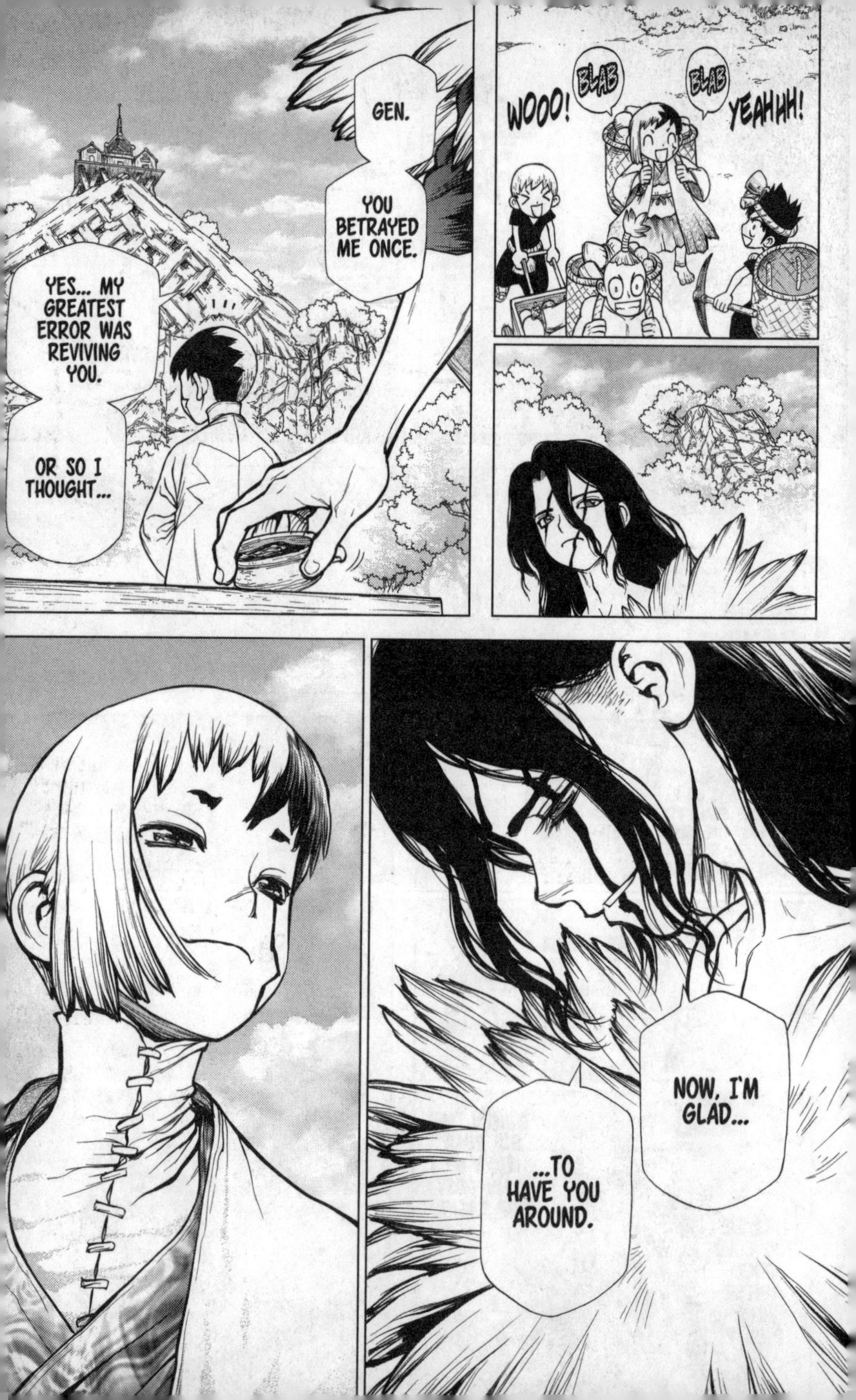
YEAHHH!
BLAB
BLAB
WOOO!
GEN.
YOU BETRAYED ME ONCE.
YES... MY GREATEST ERROR WAS REVIVING YOU.
OR SO I THOUGHT...
NOW, I'M GLAD...
...TO HAVE YOU AROUND.

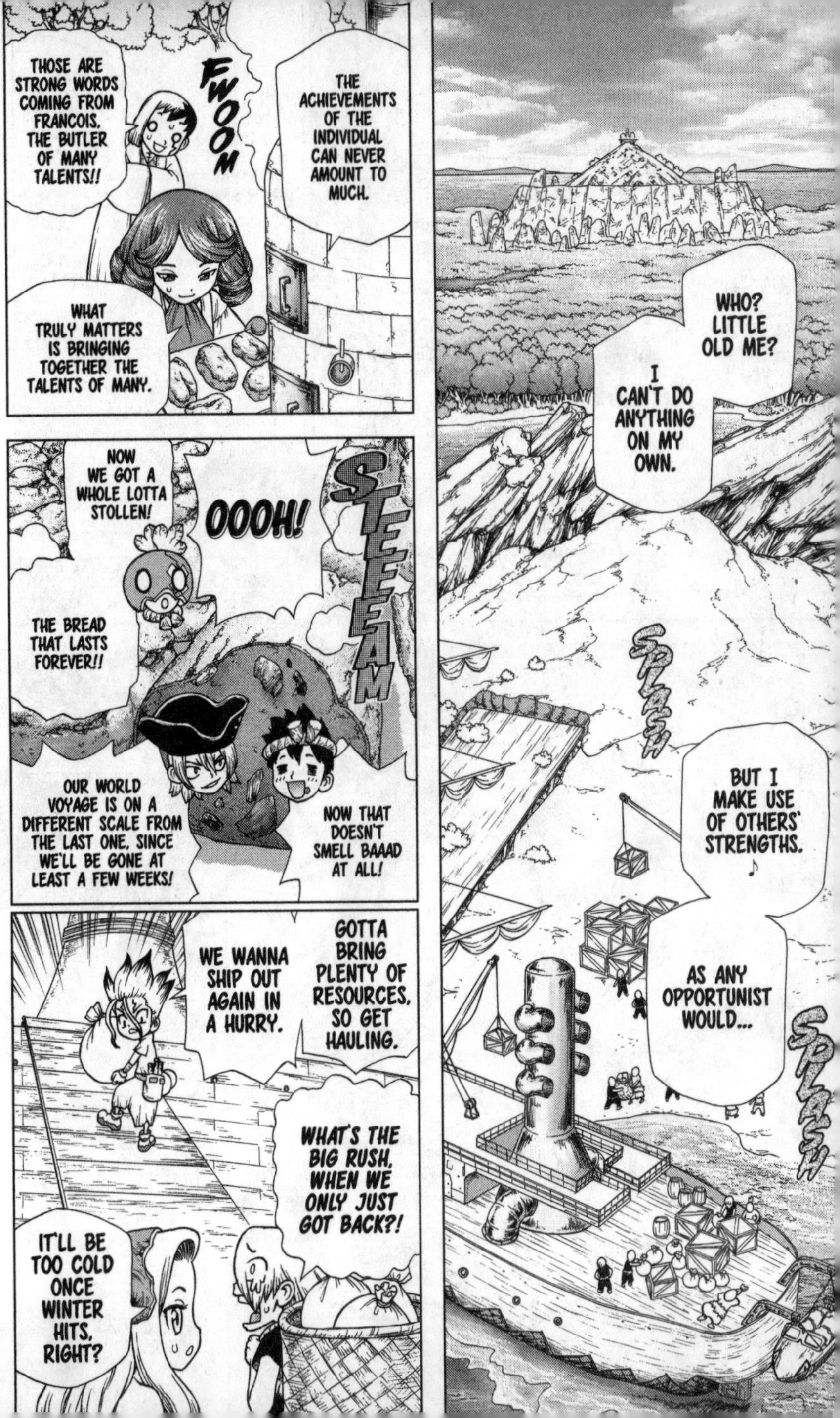
THOSE ARE STRONG WORDS COMING FROM FRANCOIS, THE BUTLER OF MANY TALENTS!!
FWOOM
THE ACHIEVEMENTS OF THE INDIVIDUAL CAN NEVER AMOUNT TO MUCH.
WHAT TRULY MATTERS IS BRINGING TOGETHER THE TALENTS OF MANY.
NOW WE GOT A WHOLE LOTTA STOLLEN!
OOOH!
STEEEEAM
THE BREAD THAT LASTS FOREVER!!
OUR WORLD VOYAGE IS ON A DIFFERENT SCALE FROM THE LAST ONE, SINCE WE'LL BE GONE AT LEAST A FEW WEEKS!
NOW THAT DOESN'T SMELL BAAAD AT ALL!
GOTTA BRING PLENTY OF RESOURCES, SO GET HAULING.
WE WANNA SHIP OUT AGAIN IN A HURRY.
WHAT'S THE BIG RUSH, WHEN WE ONLY JUST GOT BACK?!
IT'LL BE TOO COLD ONCE WINTER HITS, RIGHT?
WHO? LITTLE OLD ME?
I CAN'T DO ANYTHING ON MY OWN.
SPLASH
BUT I MAKE USE OF OTHERS' STRENGTHS. ♪
AS ANY OPPORTUNIST WOULD...
SPLASH

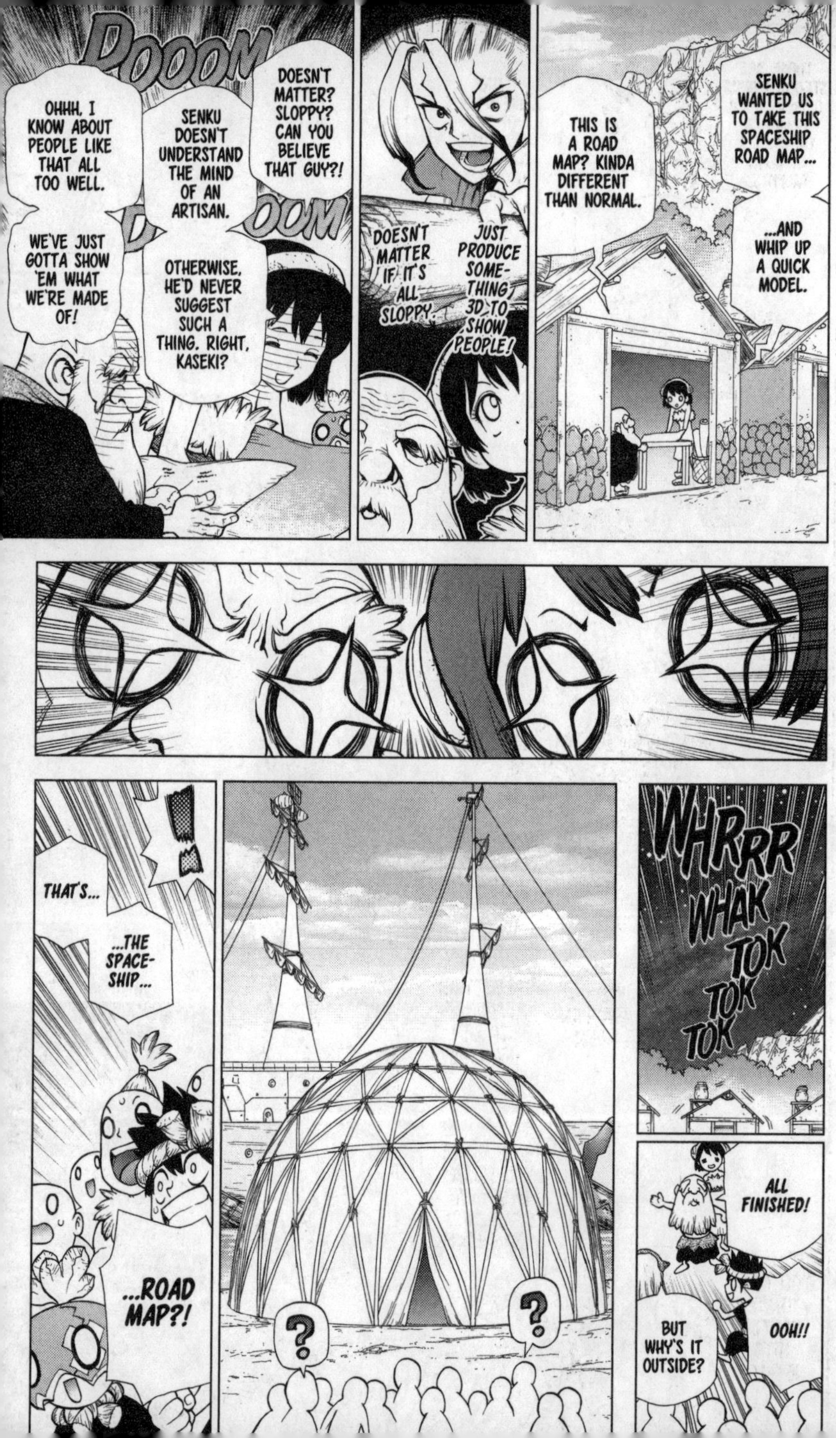
SENKU WANTED US TO TAKE THIS SPACESHIP ROAD MAP...
...AND WHIP UP A QUICK MODEL.
THIS IS A ROAD MAP? KINDA DIFFERENT THAN NORMAL.
JUST PRODUCE SOME-THING 3D TO SHOW PEOPLE!
DOESN'T MATTER IF IT'S ALL SLOPPY.
DOESN'T MATTER? SLOPPY? CAN YOU BELIEVE THAT GUY?!
DOOOM
DOOOM
SENKU DOESN'T UNDERSTAND THE MIND OF AN ARTISAN.
OTHERWISE, HE'D NEVER SUGGEST SUCH A THING. RIGHT, KASEKI?
OHHH, I KNOW ABOUT PEOPLE LIKE THAT ALL TOO WELL.
WE'VE JUST GOTTA SHOW 'EM WHAT WE'RE MADE OF!
WHRRR
WHAK
TOK
TOK
TOK
ALL FINISHED!
OOH!!
BUT WHY'S IT OUTSIDE?
?
?
THAT'S...
...THE SPACE-SHIP...
...ROAD MAP?!

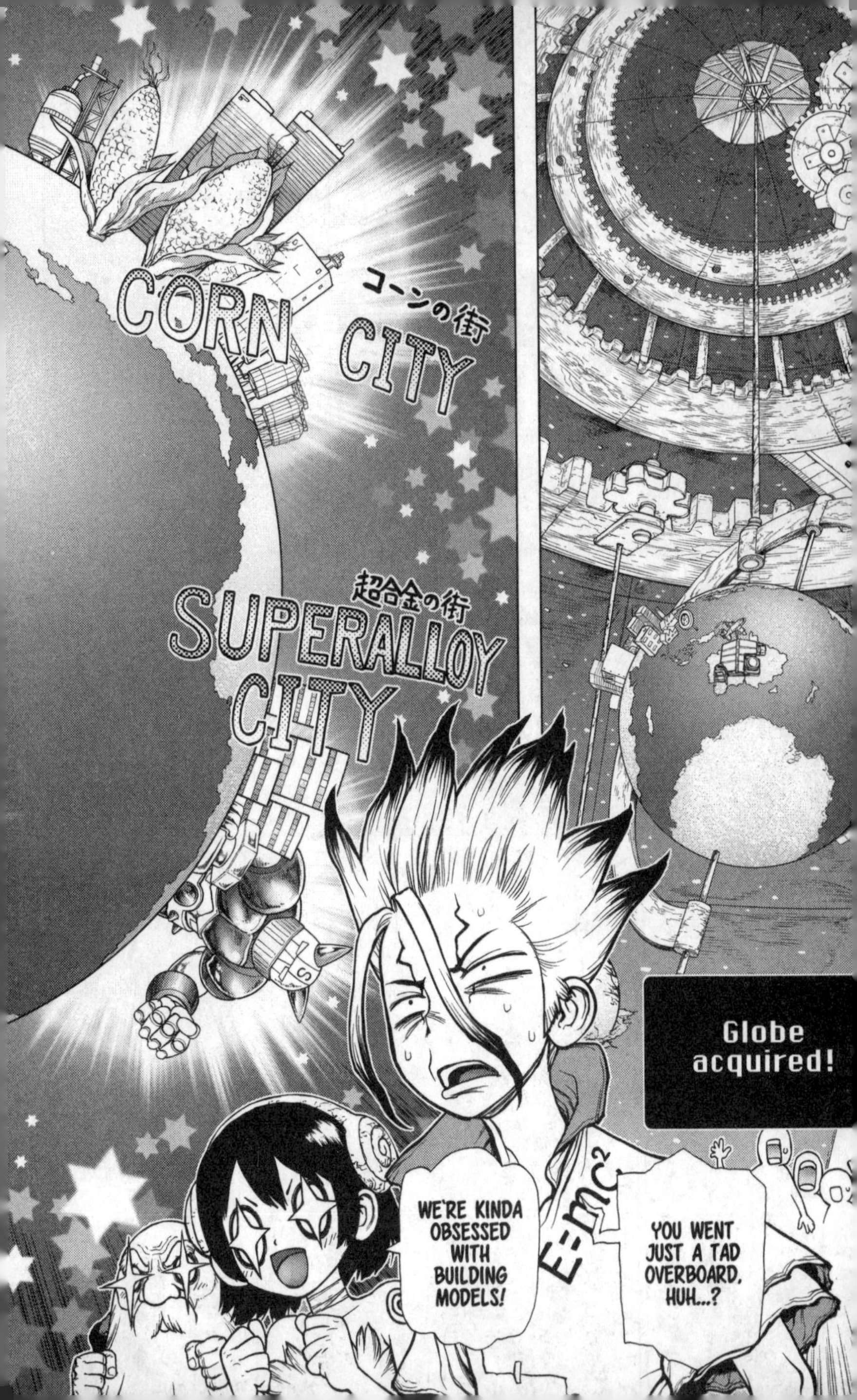
Globe acquired!
YOU WENT JUST A TAD OVERBOARD, HUH...?
E=mc²
WE'RE KINDA OBSESSED WITH BUILDING MODELS!
コーンの街
CORN CITY
超合金の街
SUPERALLOY CITY

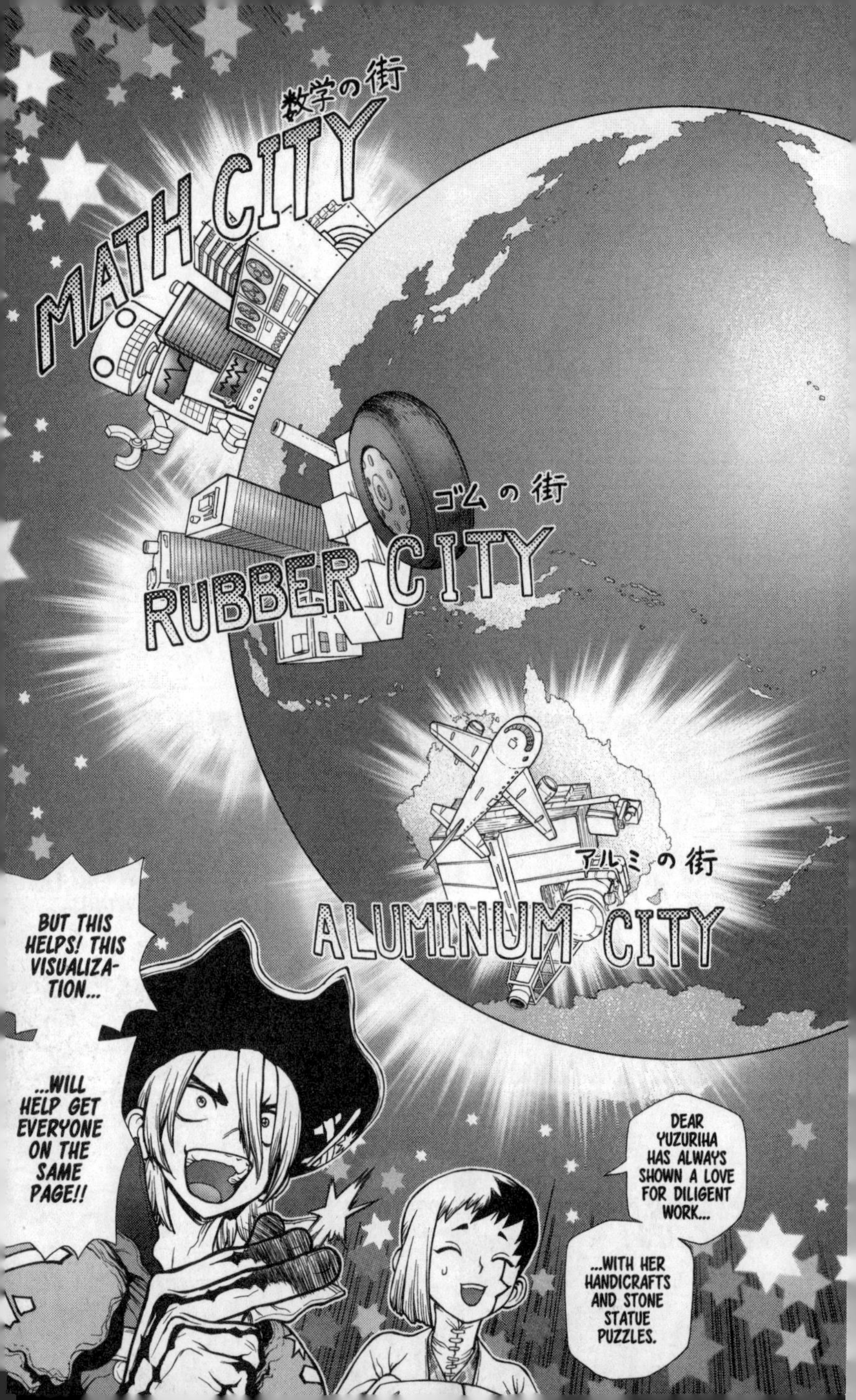
数学の街
MATH CITY
ゴムの街
RUBBER CITY
アルミの街
ALUMINUM CITY
DEAR YUZURIHA HAS ALWAYS SHOWN A LOVE FOR DILIGENT WORK...
...WITH HER HANDICRAFTS AND STONE STATUE PUZZLES.
BUT THIS HELPS! THIS VISUALIZA-TION...
...WILL HELP GET EVERYONE ON THE SAME PAGE!!

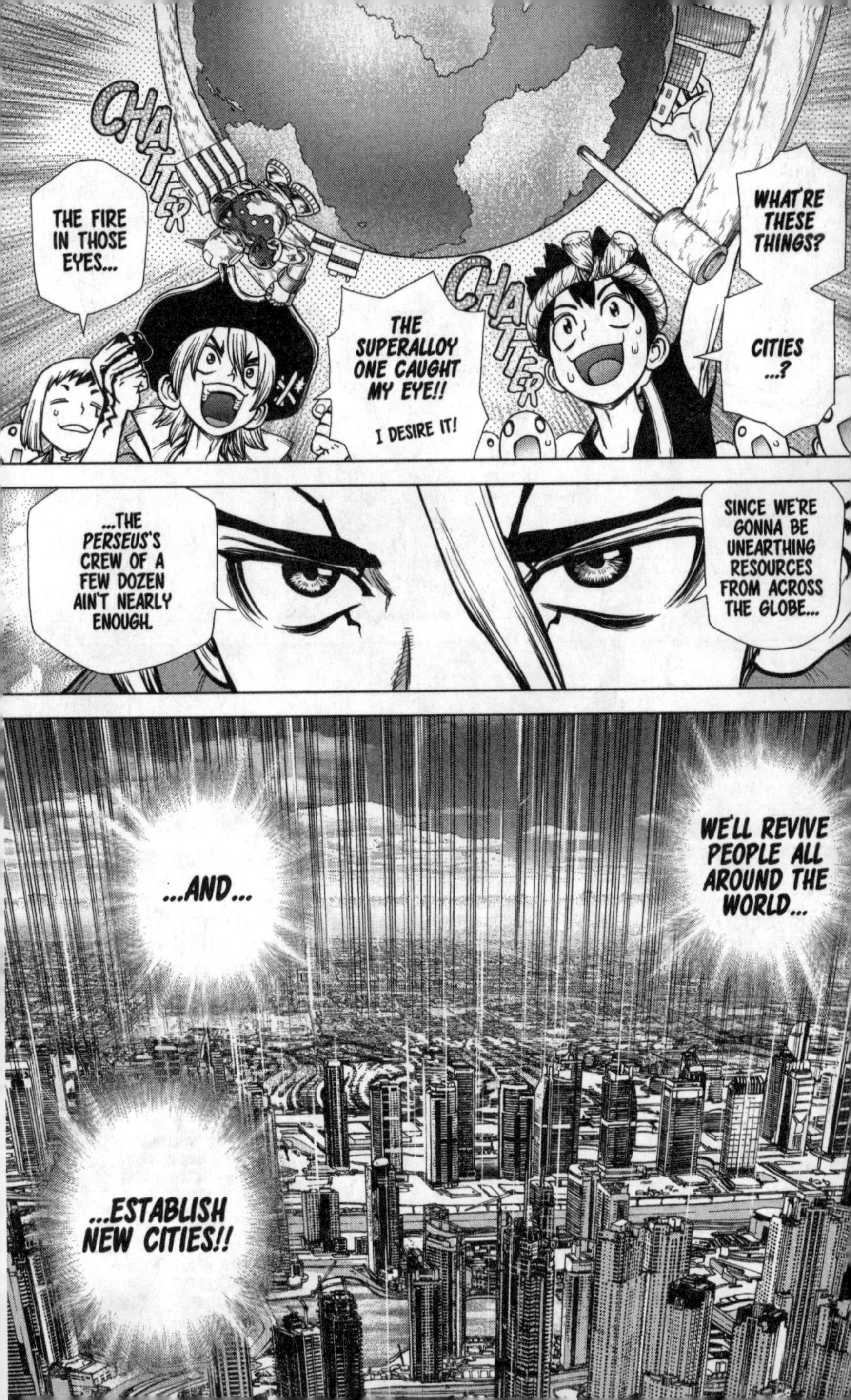
WHAT'RE THESE THINGS?
CITIES ...?
CHATTER
THE SUPERALLOY ONE CAUGHT MY EYE!!
I DESIRE IT!
CHATTER
THE FIRE IN THOSE EYES...
SINCE WE'RE GONNA BE UNEARTHING RESOURCES FROM ACROSS THE GLOBE...
...THE PERSEUS'S CREW OF A FEW DOZEN AIN'T NEARLY ENOUGH.
WE'LL REVIVE PEOPLE ALL AROUND THE WORLD...
...AND...
...ESTABLISH NEW CITIES!!

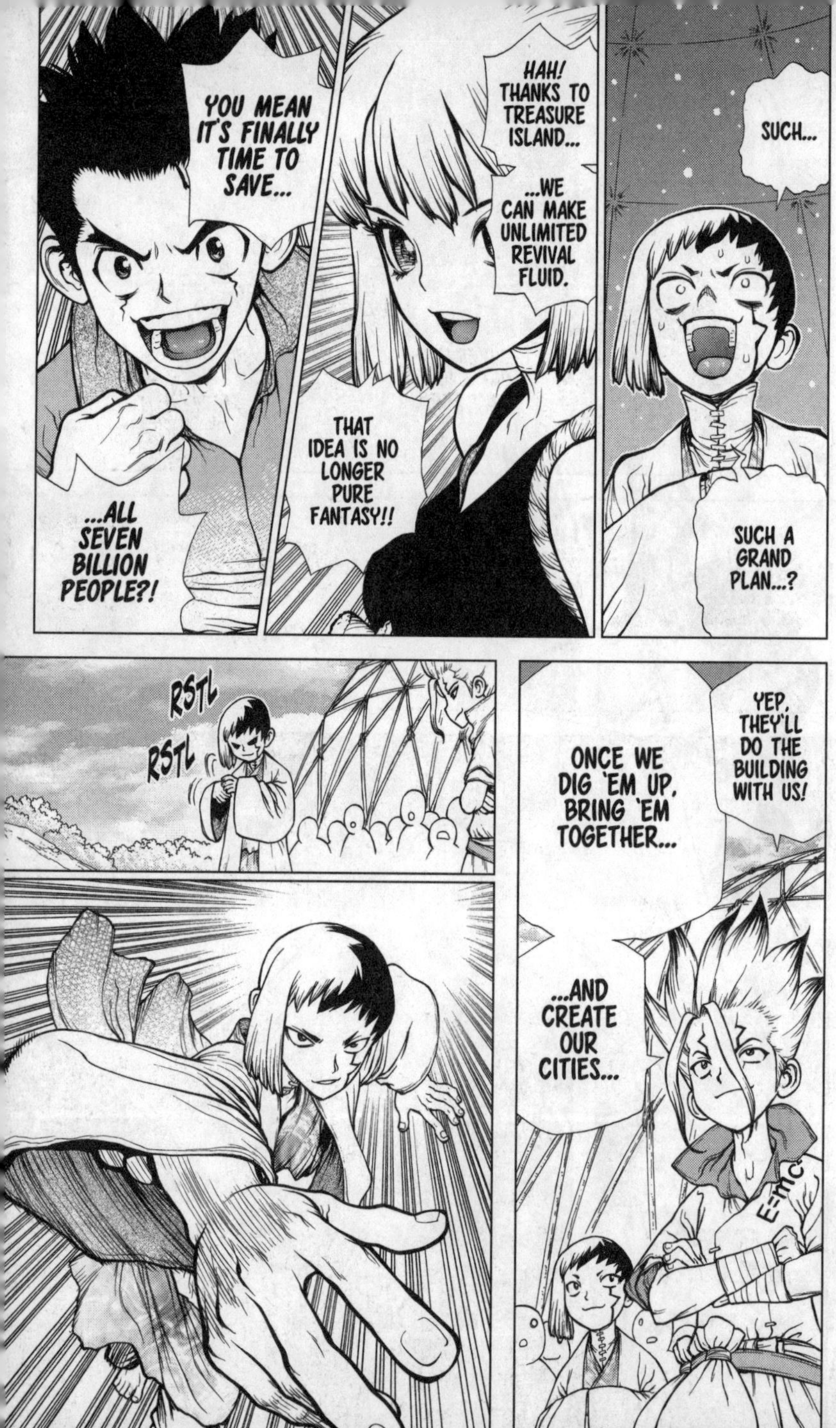
SUCH...
SUCH A GRAND PLAN...?
HAH! THANKS TO TREASURE ISLAND...
...WE CAN MAKE UNLIMITED REVIVAL FLUID.
THAT IDEA IS NO LONGER PURE FANTASY!!
YOU MEAN IT'S FINALLY TIME TO SAVE...
...ALL SEVEN BILLION PEOPLE?!
YEP, THEY'LL DO THE BUILDING WITH US!
ONCE WE DIG 'EM UP, BRING 'EM TOGETHER...
...AND CREATE OUR CITIES...
E=mc
RSTL
RSTL

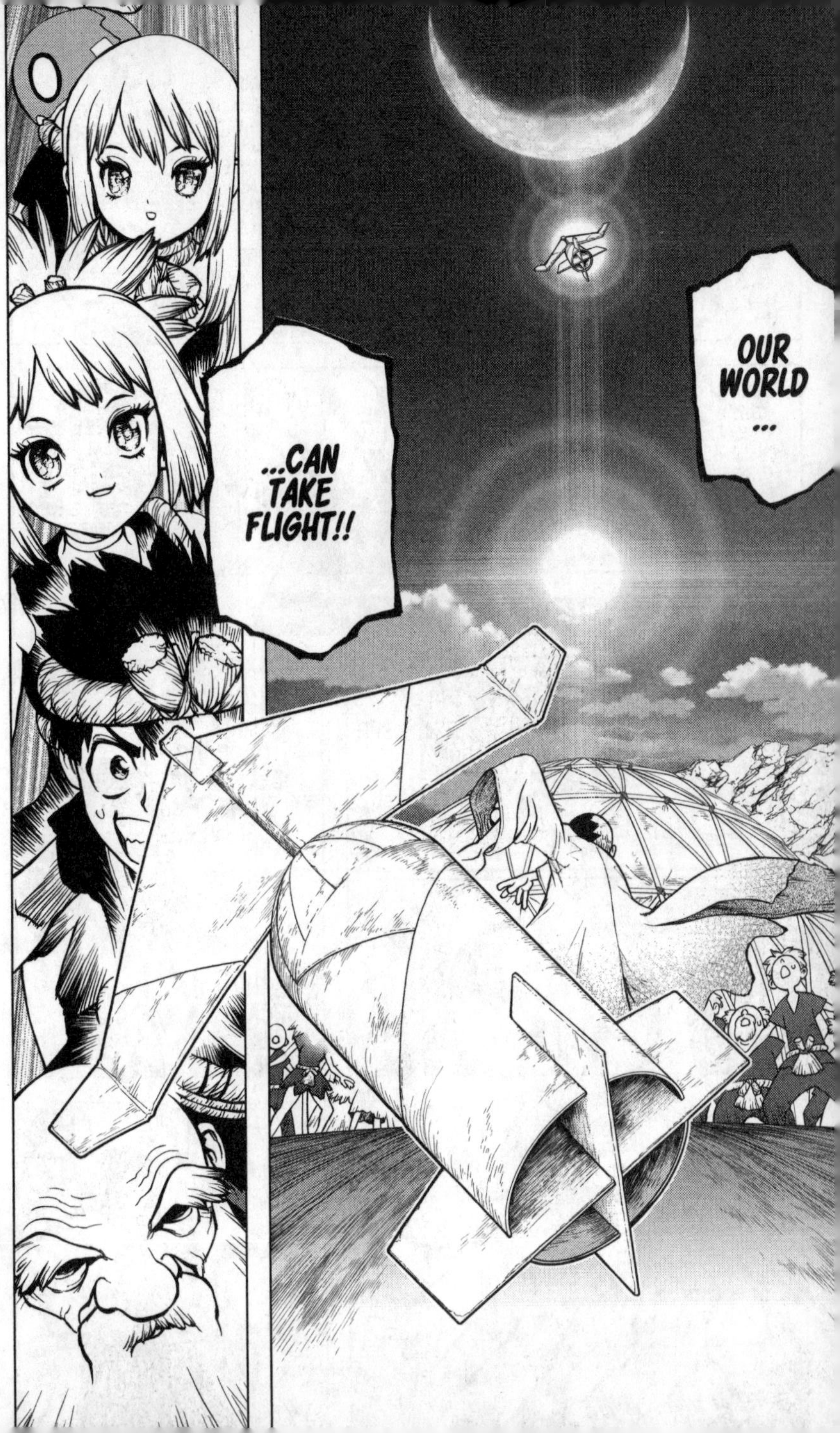
OUR WORLD...
...CAN TAKE FLIGHT!!

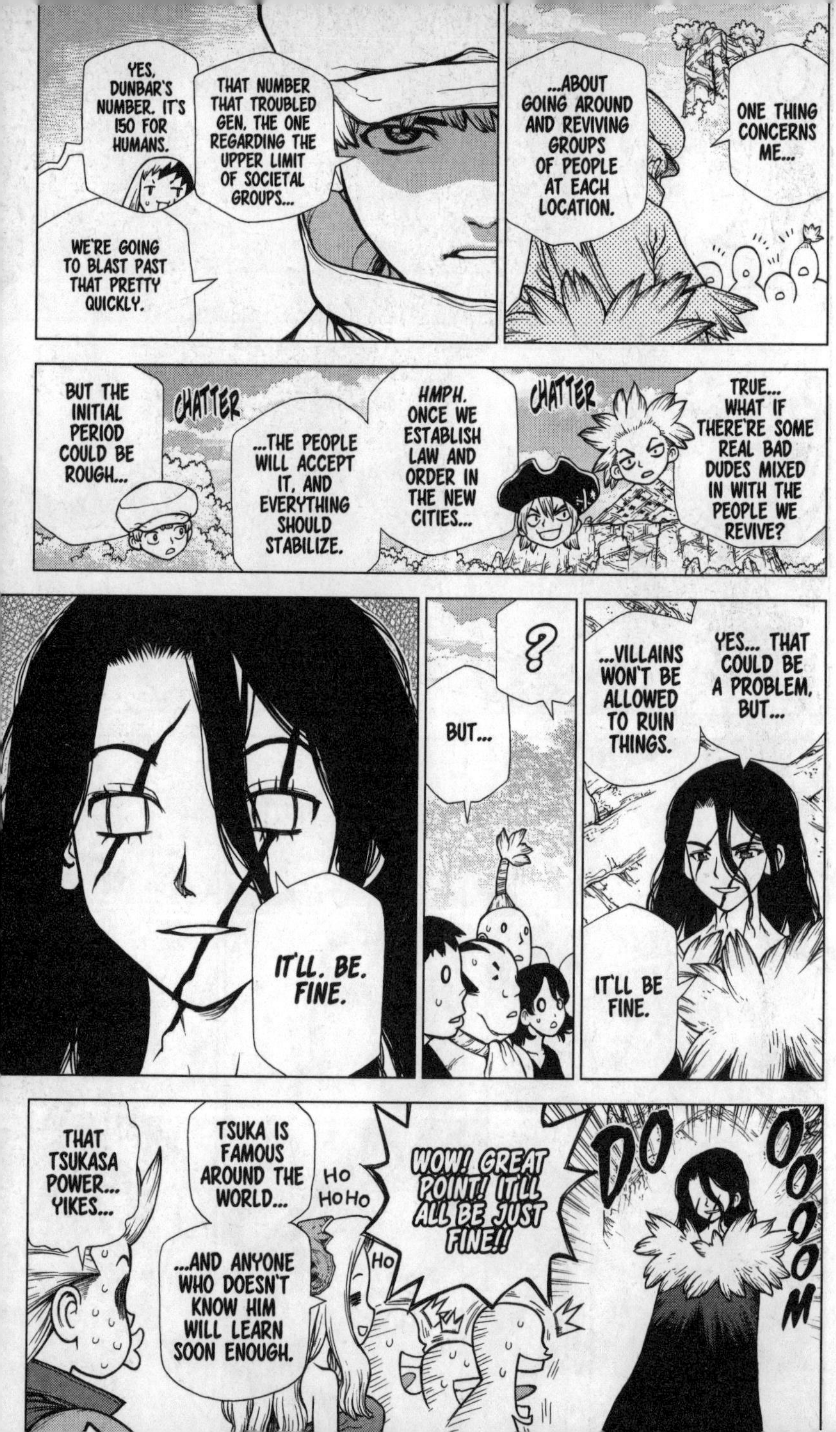
ONE THING CONCERNS ME...
...ABOUT GOING AROUND AND REVIVING GROUPS OF PEOPLE AT EACH LOCATION.
THAT NUMBER THAT TROUBLED GEN, THE ONE REGARDING THE UPPER LIMIT OF SOCIETAL GROUPS...
YES, DUNBAR'S NUMBER. IT'S 150 FOR HUMANS.
WE'RE GOING TO BLAST PAST THAT PRETTY QUICKLY.
TRUE... WHAT IF THERE'RE SOME REAL BAD DUDES MIXED IN WITH THE PEOPLE WE REVIVE?
CHATTER
HMPH. ONCE WE ESTABLISH LAW AND ORDER IN THE NEW CITIES...
...THE PEOPLE WILL ACCEPT IT, AND EVERYTHING SHOULD STABILIZE.
CHATTER
BUT THE INITIAL PERIOD COULD BE ROUGH...
YES... THAT COULD BE A PROBLEM, BUT...
...VILLAINS WON'T BE ALLOWED TO RUIN THINGS.
IT'LL BE FINE.
?
BUT...
IT'LL. BE. FINE.
DOOOOOOM
WOW! GREAT POINT! IT'LL ALL BE JUST FINE!!
HO HO HO HO
TSUKA IS FAMOUS AROUND THE WORLD...
...AND ANYONE WHO DOESN'T KNOW HIM WILL LEARN SOON ENOUGH.
THAT TSUKASA POWER... YIKES...

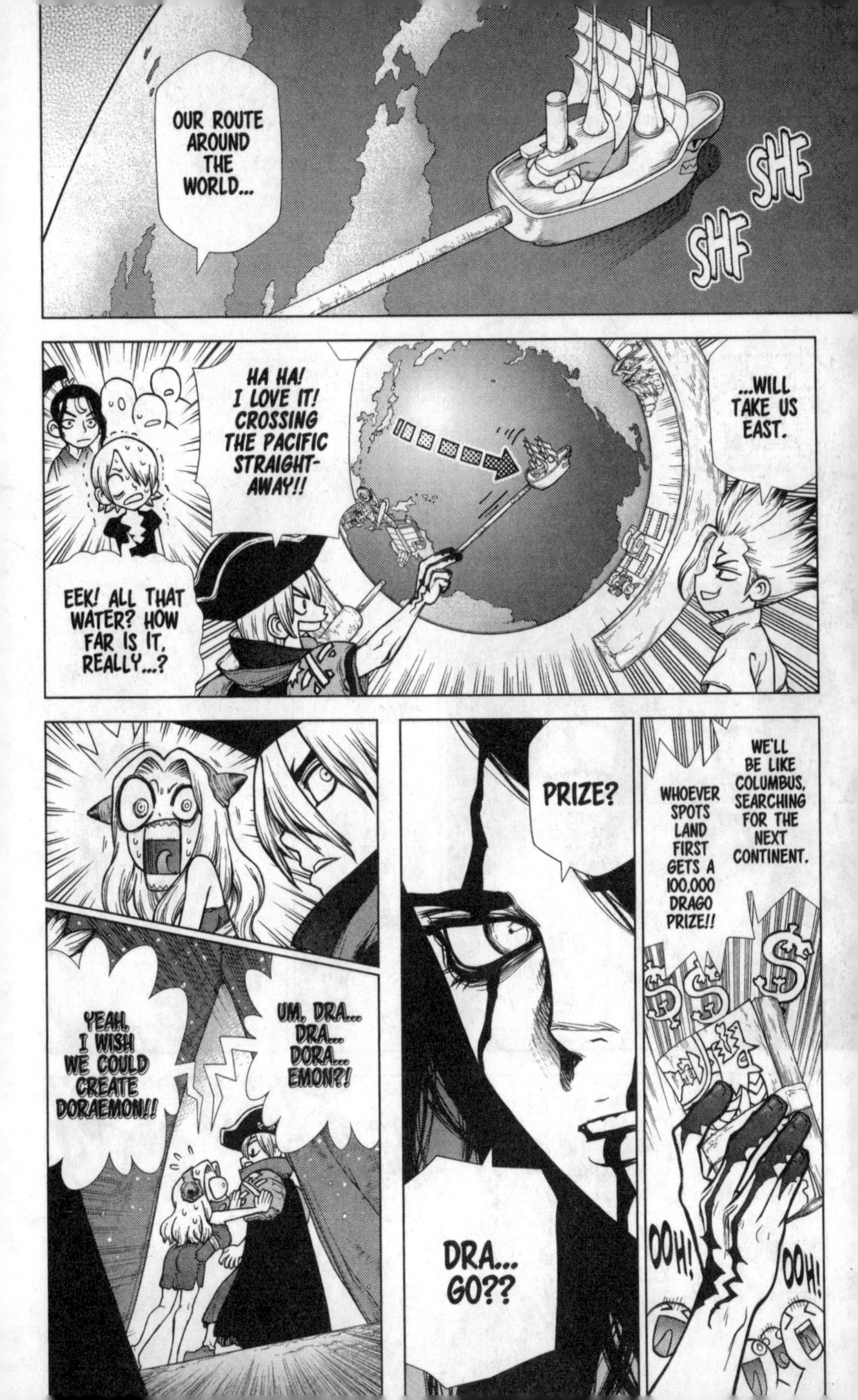
SHF SHF
OUR ROUTE AROUND THE WORLD...
...WILL TAKE US EAST.
HA HA! I LOVE IT! CROSSING THE PACIFIC STRAIGHT-AWAY!!
EEK! ALL THAT WATER? HOW FAR IS IT, REALLY...?
WE'LL BE LIKE COLUMBUS, SEARCHING FOR THE NEXT CONTINENT.
WHOEVER SPOTS LAND FIRST GETS A 100,000 DRAGO PRIZE!!
OOH!
OOH!
PRIZE?
DRA... GO??
UM, DRA... DRA... DORA... EMON?!
YEAH, I WISH WE COULD CREATE DORAEMON!!

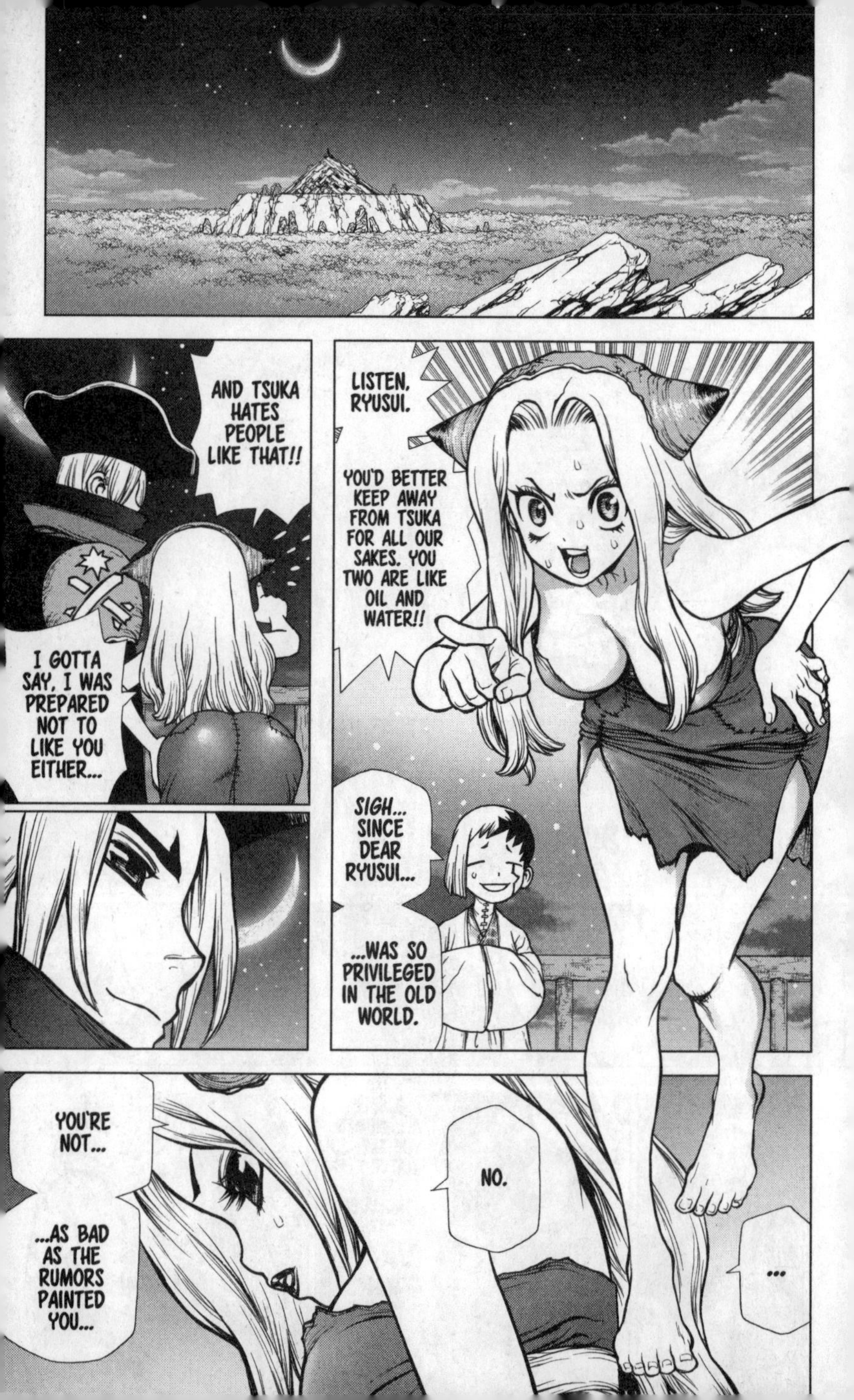
LISTEN, RYUSUI.
YOU'D BETTER KEEP AWAY FROM TSUKA FOR ALL OUR SAKES. YOU TWO ARE LIKE OIL AND WATER!!
SIGH... SINCE DEAR RYUSUI...
...WAS SO PRIVILEGED IN THE OLD WORLD.
AND TSUKA HATES PEOPLE LIKE THAT!!
I GOTTA SAY, I WAS PREPARED NOT TO LIKE YOU EITHER...
...
NO.
YOU'RE NOT...
...AS BAD AS THE RUMORS PAINTED YOU...

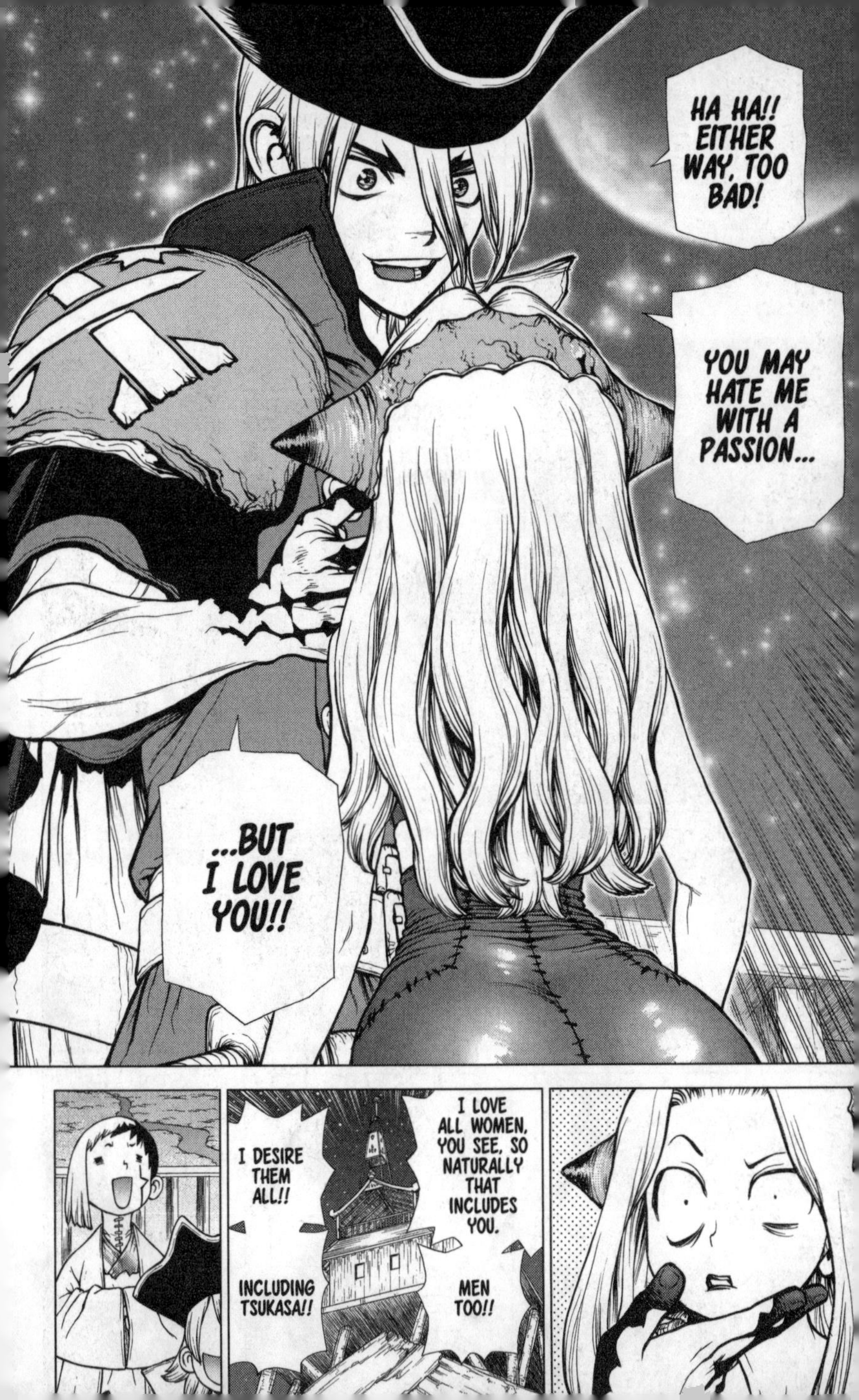
HA HA!! EITHER WAY, TOO BAD!
YOU MAY HATE ME WITH A PASSION...
...BUT I LOVE YOU!!
I LOVE ALL WOMEN, YOU SEE, SO NATURALLY THAT INCLUDES YOU.
MEN TOO!!
I DESIRE THEM ALL!!
INCLUDING TSUKASA!!

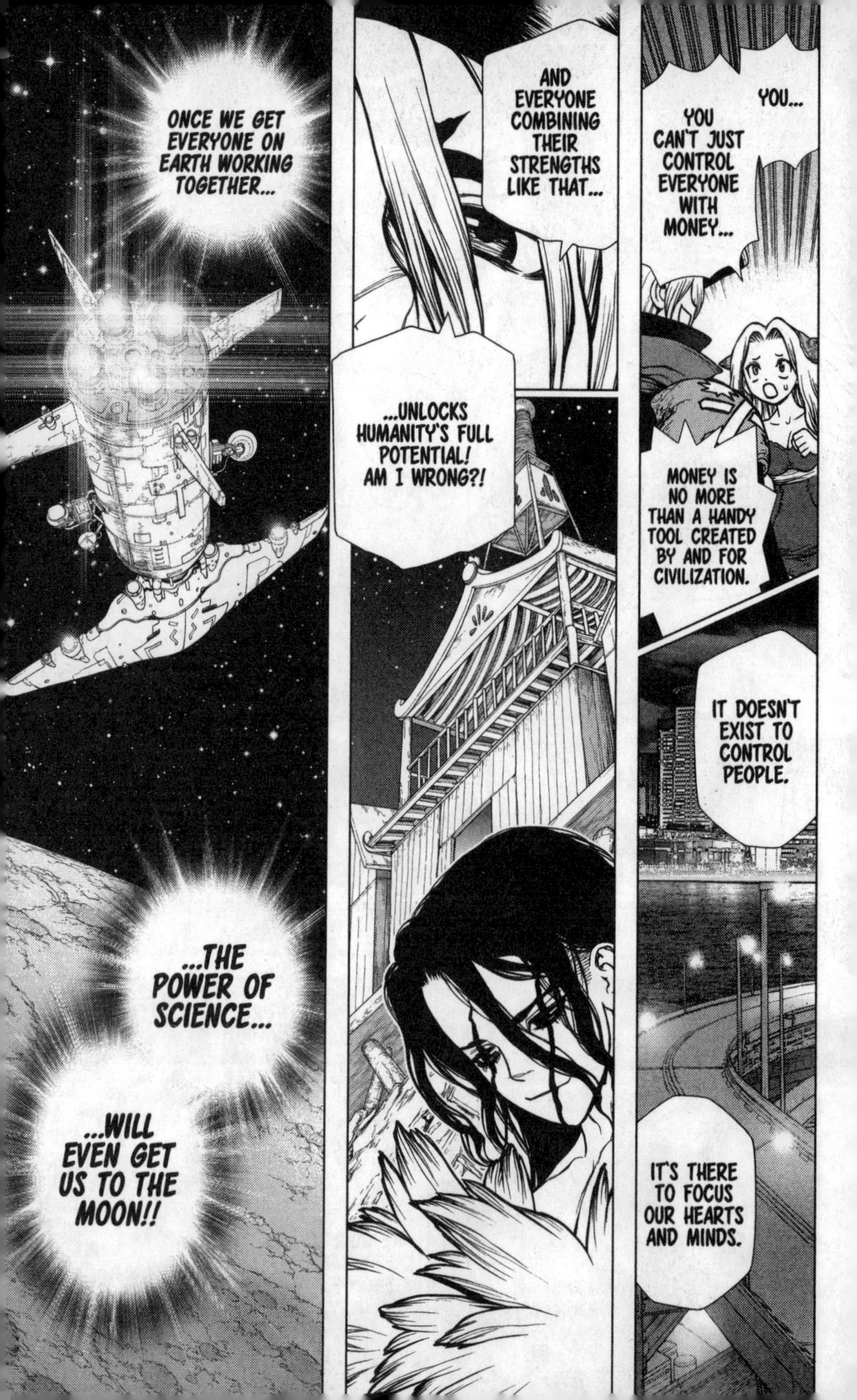
YOU...
YOU CAN'T JUST CONTROL EVERYONE WITH MONEY...
MONEY IS NO MORE THAN A HANDY TOOL CREATED BY AND FOR CIVILIZATION.
IT DOESN'T EXIST TO CONTROL PEOPLE.
IT'S THERE TO FOCUS OUR HEARTS AND MINDS.
AND EVERYONE COMBINING THEIR STRENGTHS LIKE THAT...
...UNLOCKS HUMANITY'S FULL POTENTIAL! AM I WRONG?!
ONCE WE GET EVERYONE ON EARTH WORKING TOGETHER...
...THE POWER OF SCIENCE...
...WILL EVEN GET US TO THE MOON!!

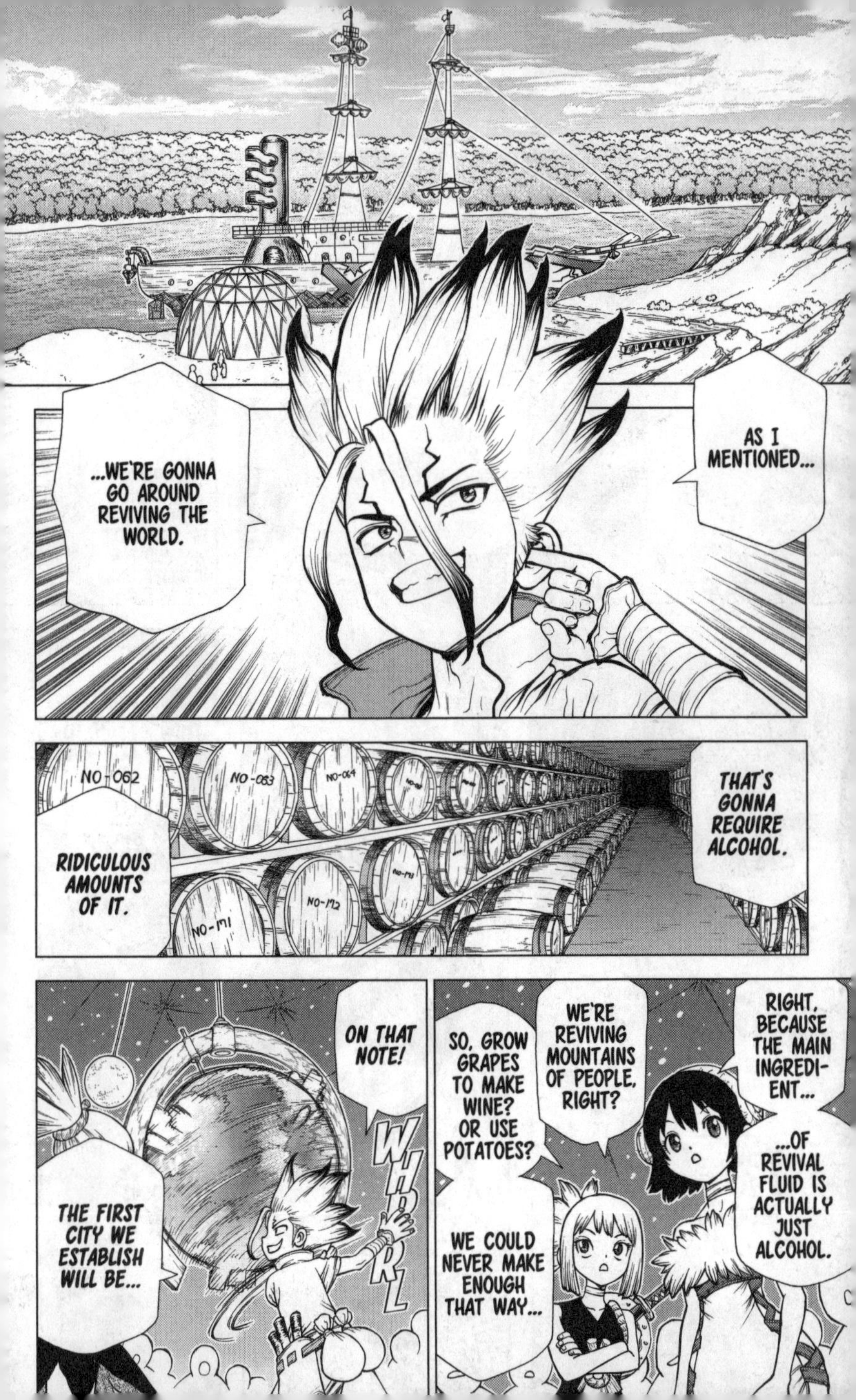
AS I MENTIONED...
...WE'RE GONNA GO AROUND REVIVING THE WORLD.
THAT'S GONNA REQUIRE ALCOHOL.
RIDICULOUS AMOUNTS OF IT.
NO-062
NO-063
NO-064
NO-171
NO-172
RIGHT, BECAUSE THE MAIN INGREDI-ENT...
...OF REVIVAL FLUID IS ACTUALLY JUST ALCOHOL.
WE'RE REVIVING MOUNTAINS OF PEOPLE, RIGHT?
SO, GROW GRAPES TO MAKE WINE? OR USE POTATOES?
WE COULD NEVER MAKE ENOUGH THAT WAY...
ON THAT NOTE!
WHHRRL
THE FIRST CITY WE ESTABLISH WILL BE...

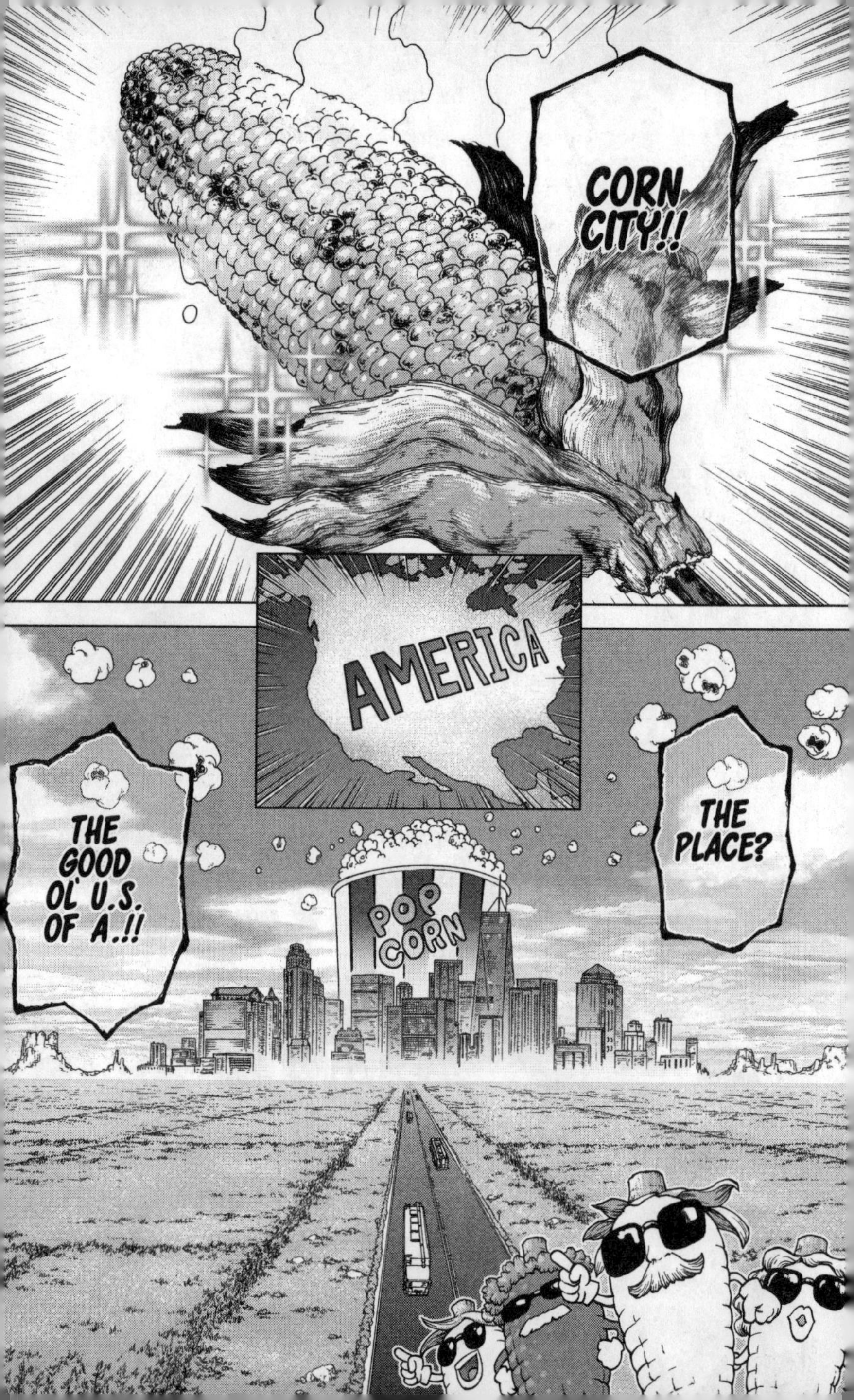
CORN CITY!!
AMERICA
THE PLACE?
THE GOOD OL' U.S. OF A.!!
POP CORN

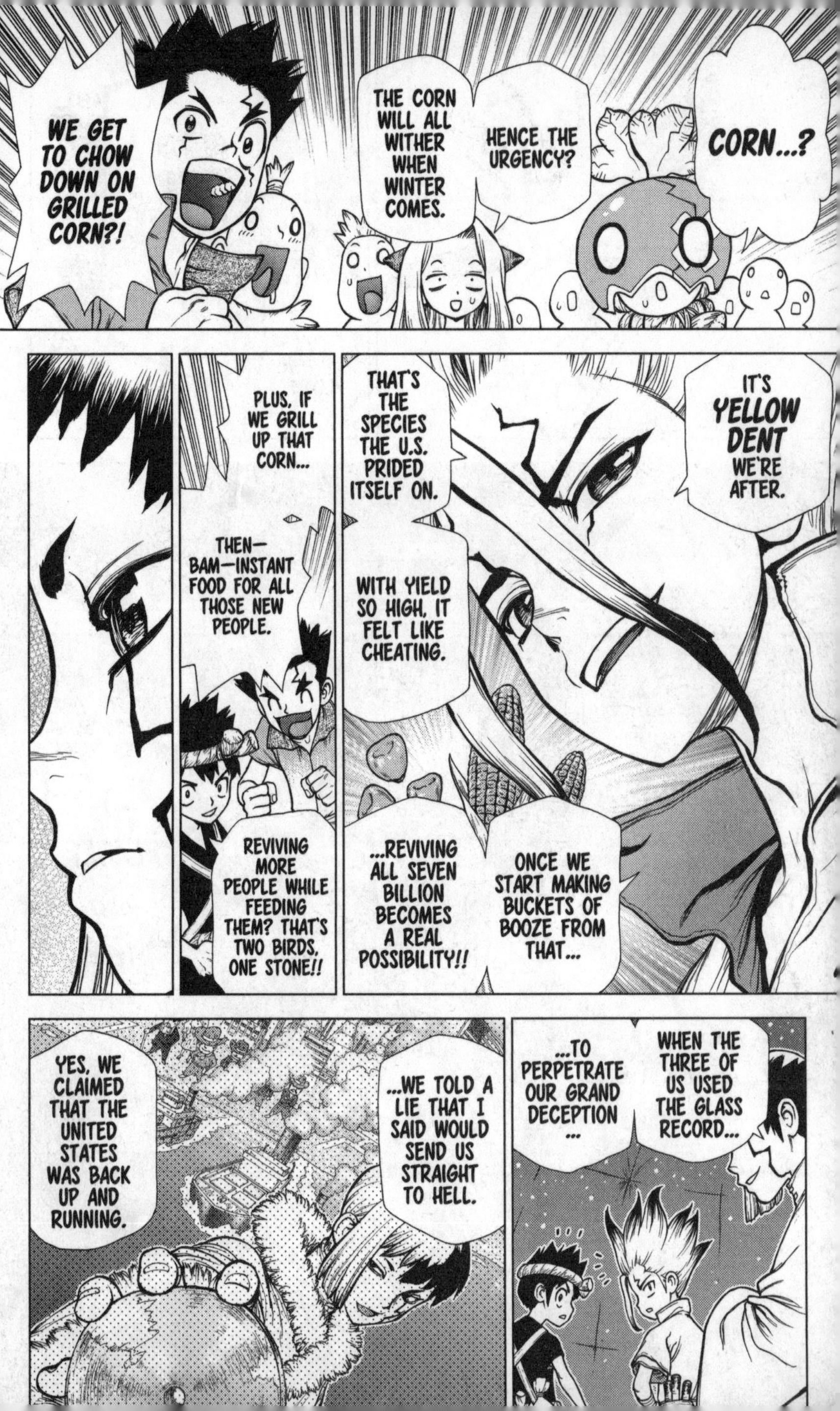
CORN...?
HENCE THE URGENCY?
THE CORN WILL ALL WITHER WHEN WINTER COMES.
WE GET TO CHOW DOWN ON GRILLED CORN?!
IT'S *YELLOW DENT* WE'RE AFTER.
THAT'S THE SPECIES THE U.S. PRIDED ITSELF ON.
WITH YIELD SO HIGH, IT FELT LIKE CHEATING.
ONCE WE START MAKING BUCKETS OF BOOZE FROM THAT...
...REVIVING ALL SEVEN BILLION BECOMES A REAL POSSIBILITY!!
PLUS, IF WE GRILL UP THAT CORN...
THEN—BAM—INSTANT FOOD FOR ALL THOSE NEW PEOPLE.
REVIVING MORE PEOPLE WHILE FEEDING THEM? THAT'S TWO BIRDS, ONE STONE!!
WHEN THE THREE OF US USED THE GLASS RECORD...
...TO PERPETRATE OUR GRAND DECEPTION...
...WE TOLD A LIE THAT I SAID WOULD SEND US STRAIGHT TO HELL.
YES, WE CLAIMED THAT THE UNITED STATES WAS BACK UP AND RUNNING.

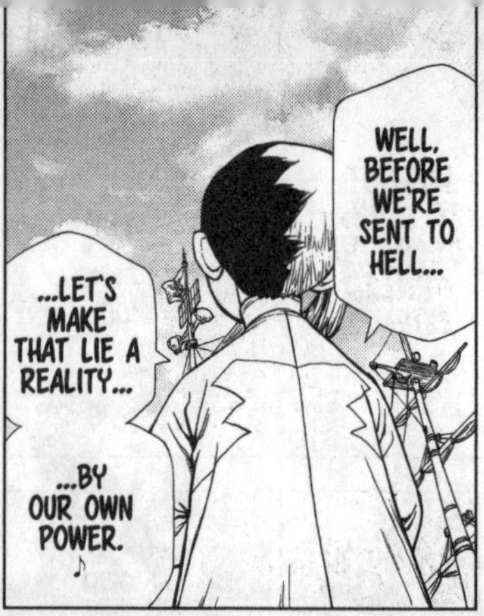
WELL, BEFORE WE'RE SENT TO HELL...
...LET'S MAKE THAT LIE A REALITY...
...BY OUR OWN POWER. ♪

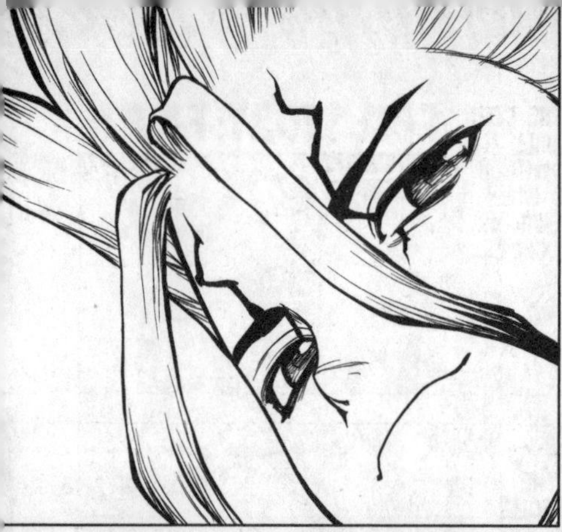

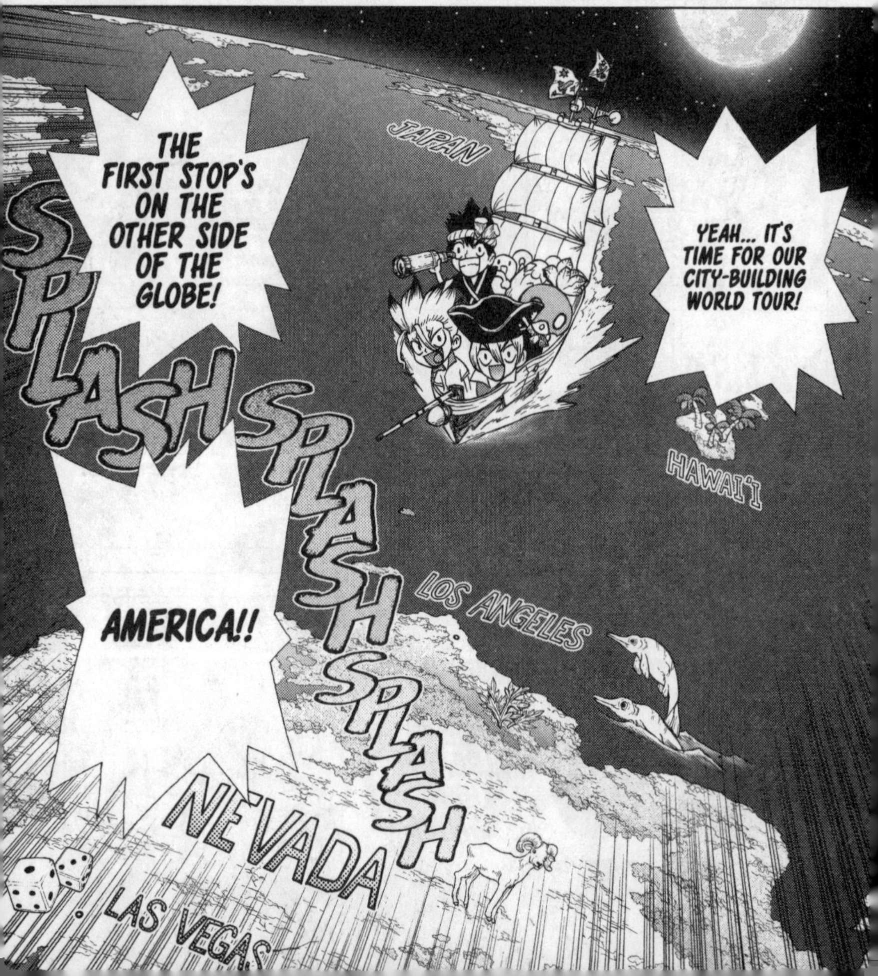
YEAH... IT'S TIME FOR OUR CITY-BUILDING WORLD TOUR!
JAPAN
HAWAI'I
THE FIRST STOP'S ON THE OTHER SIDE OF THE GLOBE!
SPLASH SPLASH SPLASH
AMERICA!!
LOS ANGELES
NEVADA
LAS VEGAS

SIDE STORY: F.A.A.N.

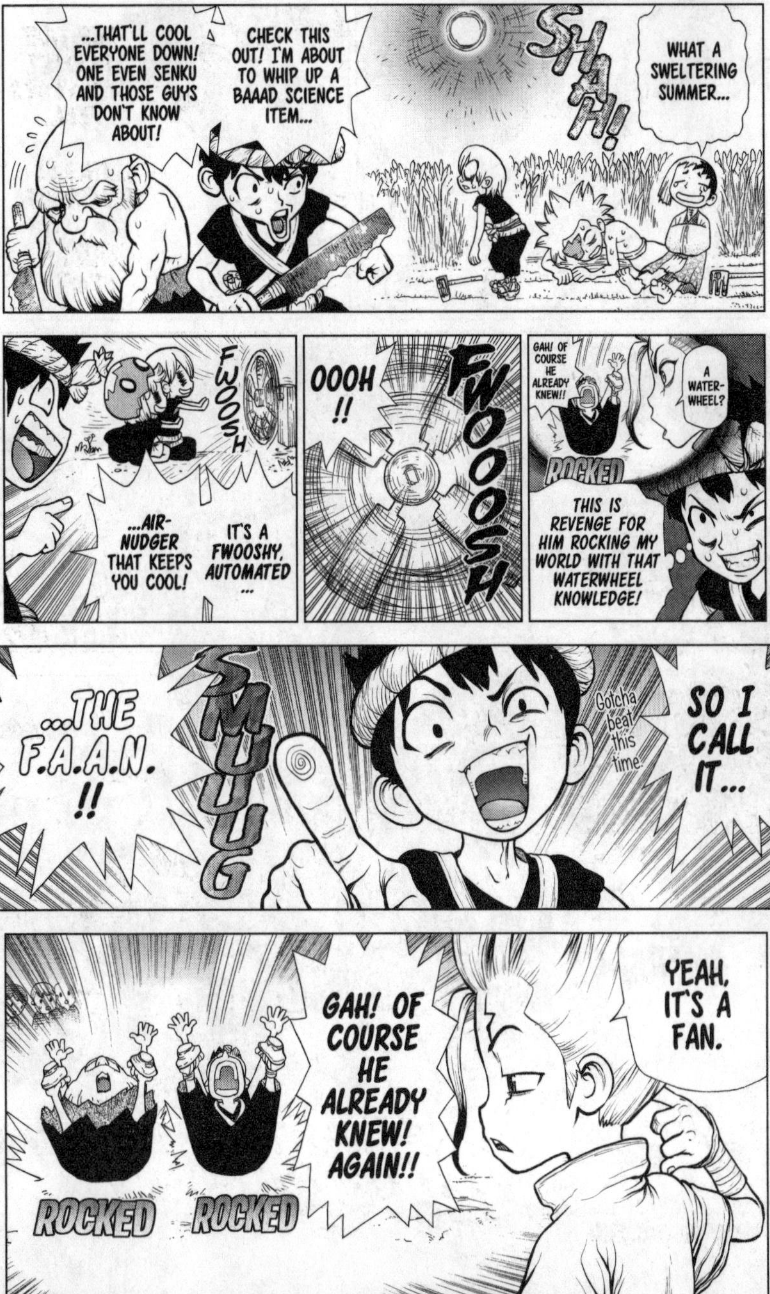
WHAT A SWELTERING SUMMER...
SHAH!
CHECK THIS OUT! I'M ABOUT TO WHIP UP A BAAAD SCIENCE ITEM...
...THAT'LL COOL EVERYONE DOWN! ONE EVEN SENKU AND THOSE GUYS DON'T KNOW ABOUT!
A WATER-WHEEL?
GAH! OF COURSE HE ALREADY KNEW!!
ROCKED
THIS IS REVENGE FOR HIM ROCKING MY WORLD WITH THAT WATERWHEEL KNOWLEDGE!
FWOOOOSH
OOOH !!
FWOOSH
IT'S A FWOOSHY, AUTOMATED ...
...AIR-NUDGER THAT KEEPS YOU COOL!
SO I CALL IT...
Gotcha beat this time.
SMUUUG
...THE F.A.A.N. !!
YEAH, IT'S A FAN.
GAH! OF COURSE HE ALREADY KNEW! AGAIN!!
ROCKED
ROCKED

SIDE STORY: KOTATSU

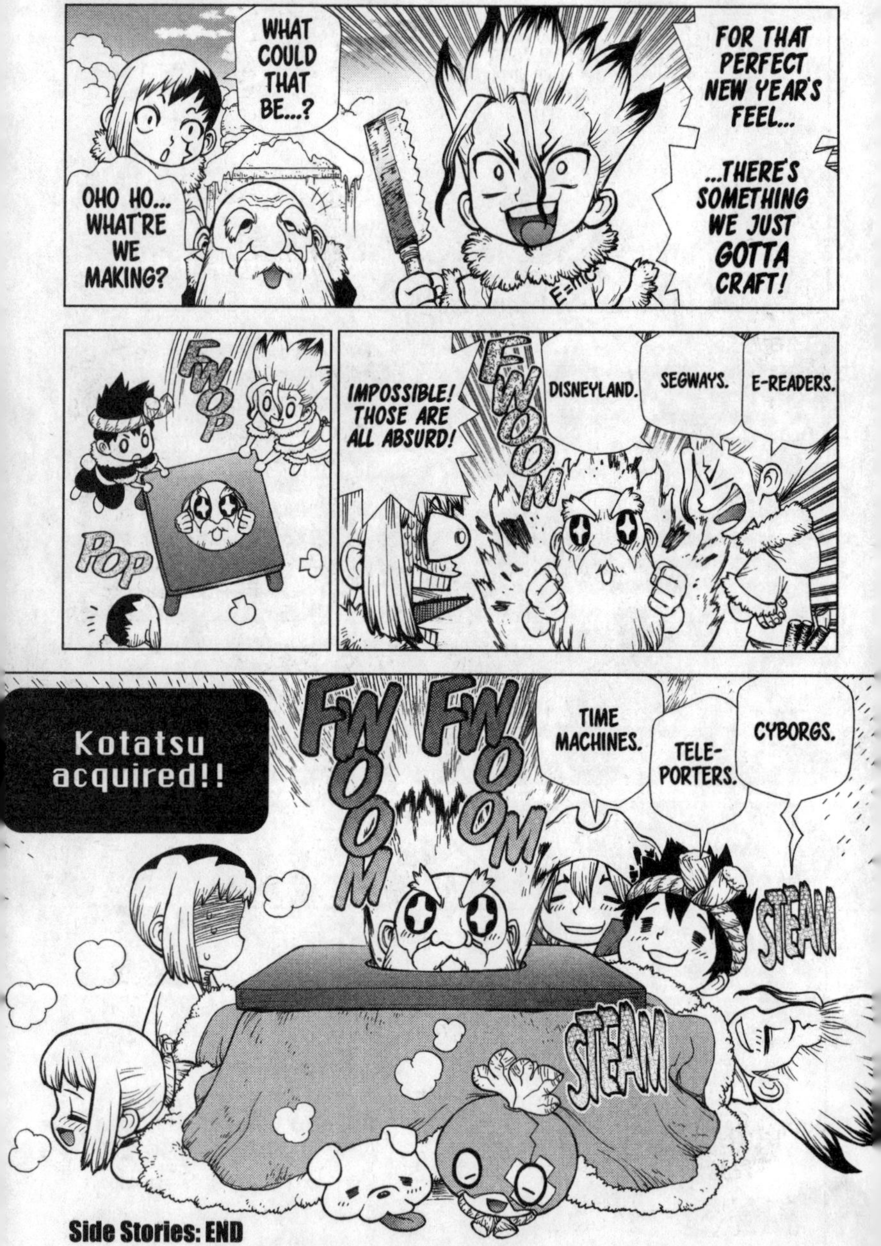
FOR THAT PERFECT NEW YEAR'S FEEL...
...THERE'S SOMETHING WE JUST GOTTA CRAFT!
E=mc
WHAT COULD THAT BE...?
OHO HO... WHAT'RE WE MAKING?
E-READERS.
SEGWAYS.
DISNEYLAND.
FWOOM
IMPOSSIBLE! THOSE ARE ALL ABSURD!
FWOP
POP
CYBORGS.
TELE-PORTERS.
TIME MACHINES.
FWOOM FWOOM
Kotatsu acquired!!
STEAM
STEAM

Side Stories: END

BOICHI

As the artist behind *Dr. Stone*, my original goal was to draw a fascinating, science-based story while sticking to the core principles of manga creation. However, I recently realized that in an era of human crises when we must believe in the power of science and human intellect, *Dr. Stone* is an allegory about people saving humanity. Senku never submits despite facing countless desperate situations. He's a character who keeps hoping and smiling, staying true to himself while striving to use science and reason to protect humanity.

Dr. Stone feels like the only series that keeps the whole world in mind.

Therefore, I'm grateful to Inagaki Sensei for entrusting me with this series. I'll continue to work hard to portray the noble human spirit embodied by this story.

No matter how long and difficult the scientific road map is, I know that humanity, like Senku, is going to triumph. No matter what obstacles lie ahead, failure is not an option.

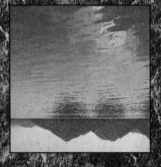

RIICHIRO INAGAKI

Most manga is in black and white, and I don't believe that's a flaw of the medium. One of manga's key aspects is how information is abbreviated, exaggerated and managed. That said, while black and white is all well and good, there are times when I wish I could show you all something in color! The drinks pictured above are real-life samples of the ones that Senku and crew have on their global voyage in the upcoming volume 17. Please pick up the next book to find out what those drinks are!

Boichi is a Korean-born artist currently living and working in Japan. His previous works include *Sun-Ken Rock* and *Terra Formars Asimov*.

Riichiro Inagaki is a Japanese manga writer from Tokyo. He is the writer for the sports manga series *Eyeshield 21*, which was serialized in *Weekly Shonen Jump*.

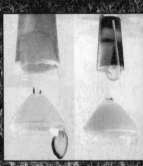

Dr.STONE

16

SHONEN JUMP Manga Edition

Story **RIICHIRO INAGAKI**
Art **BOICHI**

Science Consultant/**KURARE** with Yakuri Classroom of Doc Aruma Zirou, Cyrano, POKA
Translation/**CALEB COOK**
Touch-Up Art & Lettering/**STEPHEN DUTRO**
Design/**JULIAN [JR] ROBINSON**
Editor/**JOHN BAE**

Consulted Works:

- Asari, Yoshito, *Uchu e Ikitakute Ekitainenryo Rocket wo DIY Shite Mita (Gakken Rigaku Sensho)*, Gakken Plus, 2013
- Dartnell, Lewis, *The Knowledge: How to Rebuild Civilization in the Aftermath of a Cataclysm*, translated by Erika Togo, Kawade Shobo Shinsha, 2015
- Davies, Barry, *The Complete SAS Survival Manual*, translated by Yoshito Takigawa, Toyo Shorin, 2001
- Harari, Yuval Noah, *Sapiens: A Brief History of Humankind*, translated by Hiroyuki Shibata, Kawade Shobo Shinsha, 2016
- Jackson, Donald Dale, *The Aeronauts: The Epic of Flight*, translated by Asajiro Nishiyama and Kazuo Oyauchi, Time-Life Books, 1981
- Kazama, Rinpei, *Shinboken Techo (Definitive Edition)*, Shufu to Seikatsusha, 2016
- *Mechanism Encyclopedia*, Edited by Shigeru Ito, Ohmsha, 2013
- McNab, Chris, *Special Forces Survival Guide*, translated by Atsuko Sumi, Hara Shobo, 2016
- Olsen, Larry Dean, *Outdoor Survival Skills*, translated by Katsuji Tani, A&F, 2014
- *Sagara Oil Field: History and Mysterious Origin*, Haibara Public High School Hometown History Research Club, 2018
- Weisman, Alan, *The World Without Us*, Translated by Shinobu Onizawa, Hayakawa Publishing, 2009
- Wiseman, John, *SAS Survival Handbook, Revised Edition*, Translated by Kazuhiro Takahashi and Hitoshi Tomokiyo, Namiki Shobo, 2009

Printed in Canada

Published by VIZ Media, LLC
P.O. Box 77010
San Francisco, CA 94107

10 9 8 7 6 5 4 3 2 1
First printing, April 2021

VIZ MEDIA
viz.com

SHONEN JUMP

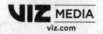

YOU'RE READING THE WRONG WAY

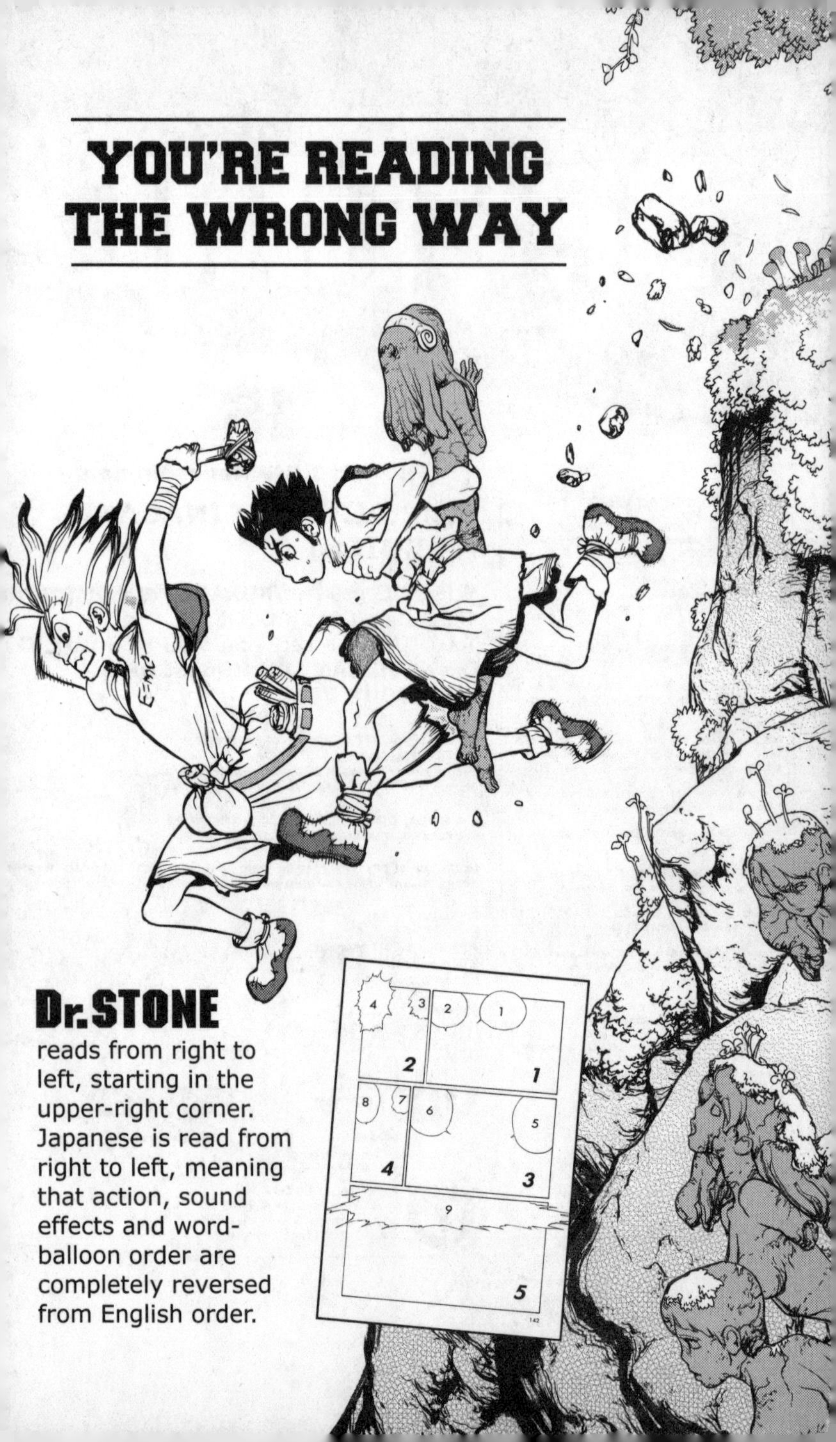

Dr.STONE

reads from right to left, starting in the upper-right corner. Japanese is read from right to left, meaning that action, sound effects and word-balloon order are completely reversed from English order.